American Anxieties

American Anxieties

A Collective Portrait of the 1930s

Edited by
Louis Filler

With a New Introduction by the Editor

Transaction Publishers
New Brunswick (U.S.A.) and London (U.K.)

New material this edition copyright © 1993 by Transaction Publishers, New Brunswick, New Jersey 08903. Originally published in 1963 by G. P. Putnam's Sons.

All rights reserved under International and Pan-American Copyright Conventions. No part of this book may be reproduced or transmitted in any form or by any means, electronic or mechanical, including photocopy, recording, or any information storage and retrieval system, without prior permission in writing from the publisher. All inquiries should be addressed to Transaction Publishers, Rutgers—The State University, New Brunswick, New Jersey 08903.

Library of Congress Catalog Number: 92-35736
ISBN: 1-56000-672-2
Printed in the United States of America

Library of Congress Cataloging-in-Publication Data

American anxieties: a collective portrait of the 1930s/edited by Louis Filler; with a new introduction by the editor.
   p.   cm.
   Originally published: The anxious years. New York: Putnam, 1963.
   ISBN 1-56000-672-2
   1. United States—History—1933-1945—Sources. 2. United States—History—1933-1945—Literary collections. 3. Depressions—1929—United States—Sources. 4. Depressions—1929—United States—Literary collections. 5. American literature—20th century. I. Filler, Louis, 1912-　. II. Filler, Louis, 1912- Anxious years.
E806.A617   1993
973.91'6—dc20   92-35736
                                                                  CIP

To Vic and Stella Filler's

Rina, Sara, Elie, Dina

with high hopes for a world

we can love and find precious

ACKNOWLEDGMENTS

"Revolt in South Dakota" is reprinted with the permission of Charles Scribner's Sons, from *Puzzled America* by Sherwood Anderson. Copyright 1935, by Charles Scribner's Sons.

"Waiting for Nothing" is reprinted from *Waiting for Nothing* by Tom Kromer, by permission of Alfred A. Knopf, Inc. Copyright 1935, by Alfred A. Knopf, Inc.

"Journal of Forgotten Days" by Albert J. Nock is reprinted with the permission of the Henry Regnery Company. Copyright 1948, by the Henry Regnery Company.

"Union Square" is reprinted from *The Strangest Places,* by permission of Leo Rosten. Copyright 1939 by Leo Rosten.

"No Comrade" is reprinted from *I Went to Pit College* by Lauren Gilfillan. Copyright 1934, 1961 by Lauren Gilfillan. Reprinted by permission of The Viking Press, Inc.

"Why I Am Not a Communist" by John Dewey is reprinted from *The Modern Monthly,* Volume 8, April 1934 by permission of Nina Melville. Copyright 1934, 1962 by *The Modern Monthly* (editor, V. F. Calverton).

"Seventy Thousand Assyrians" is reprinted from *The Daring Young Man on the Flying Trapeze* by permission of William Saroyan. Copyright 1934, 1962 by William Saroyan.

"The Vigilante" is reprinted from *The Long Valley* by John Steinbeck. Copyright 1936 by John Steinbeck. Reprinted by permission of The Viking Press, Inc.

"Daughter" is reprinted from *Kneel to the Rising Sun* by Erskine Caldwell, by permission of Little, Brown and Company. Copyright 1935, 1951 by Erskine Caldwell.

"The Happiest Man on Earth" is reprinted from *Best Short Stories of 1939* by permission of Albert Maltz. Copyright 1938, by Albert Maltz.

"Paper Work" is reprinted by permission of Heywood Broun and Constance M. Broun. Copyright 1934, 1941 by Heywood Hale Broun.

"Meditations of a Progressive" is reprinted from *The American Earthquake* by permission of Edmund Wilson. Copyright © 1958, by Edmund Wilson.

"The New Deal Mentality" by H. L. Mencken is reprinted with permission from *The American Mercury* Spring 1936. Copyright 1936 by *The American Mercury*.

The Introduction by Hallie Flanagan and "Triple-A Plowed Under" is reprinted from *Federal Theater Plays* by permission of Random House, Inc. Copyright 1938 by Random House, Inc.

"Waiting for Santy" by S. J. Perelman is reprinted with permission from *The New Yorker*. Copyright 1936, 1937, 1947, 1958 by S. J. Perelman.

"Bruno and the Black Sheep" is reprinted from *The Unpossessed* by Tess Slesinger. Copyright 1934, 1962 by Tess Slesinger. Reprinted by permission of Simon and Schuster, Inc.

"The Movement Toward the Left" by John Alroy is reprinted with permission from *The American Mercury,* February 1933. Copyright 1933, 1961 by *The American Mercury*.

A selection from *Union Square* is reprinted by permission of Albert Halper. Copyright 1933, 1961 by Albert Halper.

A selection from *Citizens* is reprinted by permission of Meyer Levin. Copyright 1940 by Meyer Levin.

A selection from *Those Who Perish* by Edward Dahlberg is reprinted by permission of The John Day Company, Inc., publisher. Copyright © 1934, 1962 by Edward Dahlberg.

A selection from *They Shall Not Die* is reprinted by permission of John Wexley. Copyright 1934, 1962 by John Wexley.

"I Can't Sleep" is reprinted by permission of Clifford Odets. Copyright 1936 by Clifford Odets.

"Nightmare Number Three" is reprinted from *Selected Works of Stephen Vincent Benet,* Holt, Rinehart and Winston, Inc. Copyright, 1935, by Stephen Vincent Benet. Reprinted by permission of Brandt & Brandt.

"No Credit," "Dirge," and "Lullaby" by Kenneth Fearing are reprinted from *Proletarian Literature in the United States,* an anthology, by permission of International Publishers. Copyright 1935, by International Publishers.

A selection from *America Was Promises* by Archibald MacLeish is reprinted by permission of Houghton Mifflin Company. Copyright 1939 by Duell, Sloan and Pearce, Inc.

"Power" by Muriel Rukeyser is reprinted by permission of Monica McCall, Inc. Copyright 1938 by Muriel Rukeyser.

"Canto XXXVII" and "Canto XXXVIII" are reprinted from *The Cantos of Ezra Pound* by permission of New Directions, Publishers. Copyright 1934, 1937, 1940, 1948 by Ezra Pound.

A selection from *Eimi,* copyright, 1933, 1961, by E. E. Cummings, is reprinted by permission of Harcourt, Brace & World, Inc.

"Battle (May-June 1940)," copyright 1940 by Robinson Jeffers, is reprinted from *Be Angry at the Sun* And Other Poems, by Robinson Jeffers, by permission of Random House, Inc.

"Redder Than the Roosevelts," "Among Those Present," "Hoover Speaking," and "General Moseley" are reprinted by permission of Heywood Broun and Constance M. Broun. Copyright 1935, 1941; 1936, 1941; 1936, 1941; and 1939, 1941, respectively, by Heywood Hale Broun.

"Politics" by Milton Hindus is reprinted from *Twice a Year* by permission of Dorothy S. Norman. Copyright 1938 by Dorothy S. Norman.

A selection from *Adventures of a Young Man* by John Dos Passos is reprinted by permission of Houghton Mifflin Company. Copyright 1939 by John Dos Passos.

"An Open Letter to American Intellectuals" is reprinted from *The Modern Monthly,* Volume 8, March 1934 by permission of Nina Melville. Copyright 1934, 1962 by *The Modern Monthly* (editor, V. F. Calverton).

"The Fallacy of the Theory of Social Fascism" by Sidney Hook is reprinted from *The Modern Monthly,* Volume 8, July 1934, 1962 by permission of Nina Melville. Copyright 1934 by *The Modern Monthly* (editor, V. F. Calverton).

"Recent Problems of Revolutionary Literature" by William Phillips and Philip Rahv is reprinted from *Proletarian Literature in the United States,* an anthology, by permission of International Publishers. Copyright 1935, by International Publishers.

"T. S. Eliot: Leisure-Class Laureate" by Ernest Sutherland Bates is reprinted from *The Modern Monthly,* Volume 7, February 1933 by permission of Nina Melville. Copyright 1933, 1961 by *The Modern Monthly* (editor, V. F. Calverton).

Introduction to *I'll Take My Stand* by Twelve Southerners. Copyright 1930, 1958 by Harper & Brothers. Reprinted by permission.

The River, by Pare Lorentz, published 1938 by The Stackpole Co., Harrisburg, Pa. Reprinted by permission.

CONTENTS

Introduction to the Transaction Edition   xiii
Introduction to the Original Edition   1

THE WAY THINGS ARE

Sherwood Anderson
   REVOLT IN SOUTH DAKOTA   32

Tom Kromer
   WAITING FOR NOTHING   39

Albert Jay Nock
   JOURNAL OF FORGOTTEN DAYS (SEPTEMBER 1934)   49

Leonard Q. Ross
   UNION SQUARE   57

Lauren Gilfillan
   NO COMRADE   65

John Dewey
   WHY I AM NOT A COMMUNIST   80

DRAW THY BREATH IN PAIN

William Saroyan
   SEVENTY THOUSAND ASSYRIANS   86

John Steinbeck
   THE VIGILANTE   94

Erskine Caldwell
   DAUGHTER   100

Albert Maltz
   THE HAPPIEST MAN ON EARTH   106

THE GOVERNMENT TRIED TO HELP

Heywood Broun
    PAPER WORK   118

Edmund Wilson
    "STILL"—: MEDITATIONS OF A PROGRESSIVE   120

H. L. Mencken
    THE NEW DEAL MENTALITY   126

Hallie Flanagan
    FEDERAL THEATRE INTRODUCTION   140

TRIPLE A PLOWED UNDER   145

THEY TRIED TO LAUGH

S. J. Perelman
    WAITING FOR SANTY   162

Tess Slesinger
    BRUNO AND THE BLACK SHEEP   165

John Alroy
    THE MOVEMENT TOWARD THE LEFT   172

AS THROUGH A GLASS DARKLY

Albert Halper
    From UNION SQUARE   176

Meyer Levin
    From CITIZENS   185

Edward Dahlberg
    From THOSE WHO PERISH   193

John Wexley
    From THEY SHALL NOT DIE   201

SOMETIMES THEY SEEMED TO TRY TO SING

Clifford Odets
    "I CAN'T SLEEP"   214

Stephen Vincent Benet
    NIGHTMARE NUMBER THREE   217

Kenneth Fearing
    NO CREDIT: DIRGE: LULLABY   220

Howard Nutt
    THE INTELLECTUALS   223

Archibald Macleish
    From AMERICA WAS PROMISES   224

Muriel Rukeyser
    POWER   231

Ezra Pound
    CANTO XXXVII, CANTO XXXVIII   234

E. E. Cummings
    From EIMI   244

Robinson Jeffers
    BATTLE (MAY-JUNE, 1940)   256

" 'TIS THE FINAL CONFLICT"

Heywood Broun
    FOUR TOPICAL PIECES   260

Milton Hindus
    POLITICS   268

John Dos Passos
    From ADVENTURES OF A YOUNG MAN   288

An Open Letter To American Intellectuals   310

Sidney Hook
    THE FALLACY OF THE THEORY OF
        SOCIAL FASCISM   319

SCALES AND MEASURES

William Phillips and Philip Rahv
   RECENT PROBLEMS OF REVOLUTIONARY
      LITERATURE   338

Ernest Sutherland Bates
   T. S. ELIOT: LEISURE CLASS LAUREATE   344

Introduction From I'LL TAKE MY STAND   355

THE BODY OF THE NATION

Pare Lorentz
   THE RIVER   364

Index   377

Introduction to the Transaction Edition

THERE IS AN HISTORICAL PERSPECTIVE that will have to be recaptured if we are to gain the benefits of Thirties study; I am tempted to add: or those of any era, including our own.

I recall, for example, a state historical society meeting at which a member read a paper on military ideas during the American Revolution. It was during lunch, and he may have thought it appropriate to take a light tone. It seemed that one of the Patriot ideas for fighting the war had been to build a submarine that would slide under water to the British fleet and blow up its ships. A submarine was actually built, in Philadelphia harbor, and launched.

And then, said our speaker in stand-up comedian tones, it *sank*. And the American sailors *drowned*.

There was a wave of laughter among the historians. I later complained to a colleague that there was something wrong, when historians laughed at a tragedy. Well, he answered, I suppose it was because it happened so long ago that laughter was a sort of compliment to the speaker's presentation. This historian taught Medieval History.

The Thirties only took place some sixty years ago. Yet we have difficulties with it. There are many still alive from that era. Why are they—and we—so removed from its reality? This is not only because of the changed economic conditions, especially since we also have joblessness, not to say homelessness; and that despite numerous "cushions" against helpnessness unknown in the 1930s. It is because our imaginations can't yet catch the *continuity* between the Thirties and our own fast-fleeting Nineties. We are a long way from the Battle of the Overpass in Dearborn, Michigan, where Walter Reuther and his comrades were fighting for their union, the United Auto Workers (UAW) against strikebreakers and thugs. Organized labor has a big job now explaining why it is needed any more than any other part of the population. We can be ruined by thoughtless policies in the investment field, as we can by misfortunes in labor. The housewife and the woman professional both have their problems. They were different. some women

[xiii

could not marry in the Thirties because "their man" lacked work and prospects. Today, with sex somewhat less controlled by economics and family alone, some may not marry for reasons involving psychology as well as sex.

The blacks in the earlier decade were complex in different ways. They, too, struggled between old longings for dignity and social distinction, and urgent necessity. Some moved toward communist goals, others to a dependence on welfare that in some cases actually improved their conditions in the Thirties. There was a different propaganda. Communist party officials expressed regret, Richard Wright said bitterly, that he was not more black. This was because when working on the Federal Writers Project (see p. 24) he had published *Uncle Tom's Children*, and gained some visibility they were eager to exploit. This was before *Native Son* exploded him into fame and notoriety.

Times have changed much for Richard Wright and his cause, but the question of how fares it with our blacks as ethnics in our own time can gain by comparing it with what Richard Wright and his friends made of their own time. The same will prove true of other ethnics who contribute to our American spectrum of figures in the arts, education, and other fields.

The clue to finding connections between Thirties people and Nineties people is less in personal accounts and statistics than in their common humanity, as shown extensively in the arts.

If we understood this, we can understand the thrill that went through the stalled country when Clifford Odets released his play *Waiting for Lefty*, in 1935, when spotlights fixed on actors on stage who told of their sufferings as cab drivers in New York, and what was happening to their families and personal hopes. Actors planted in the audience responded aloud to what was being said and done on the stage, until a young agitator urged them not to wait for their leader, Lefty—Lefty wasn't there and he might never come.

A man rushes on stage: Lefty has just been found, dead in an alley, killed by anti-union thugs. "Hear that? Hear that, boys?" cries the agitator. And what do we do now? "STRIKE! STRIKE!" comes a voice from the audience. "Say it again!" he shouts back. "STRIKE! STRIKE!" "Again and again!" "STRIKE! STRIKE! STRIKE! STRIKE! STRIKE! STRIKE!" By this time most of the audience are on their feet and crying "STRIKE!"

"Lefty," the dead cab-driver leader was only half-way to revolution and differs in many respects from more recent equivalents like Abbie Hoffman, who urged us to trust no one over thirty, exceptions being made for more mature protesters like David Dellinger. But that is the way all revolutions and would-be revolutionaries began, if they were to appeal to more than the malcontents, the desperately poor, and the people who had no heart for fights to the finish, but who came to approve those who were ready. The Thirties brought out a wide range of poets, storytellers, dramatists, and artists who tried to express not only what was happening, but how people felt about themselves and others.

We have trouble understanding Thirties people, for our lives are different. We have laws signed by mayors, governors, and Franklin D. Roosevelt himself intended to insure that the Thirties could never happen again, at least not in the old way. And they can't.

But if the Thirties people had fewer "safety nets" than we do, they had other things: family, for instance—sometimes too much family, true—family grudging them sleeping space, let alone food and cigarettes. And they lacked our "dependent classes" who saw welfare as a right. The needy in the Thirties could be bereft of support, of faith in self, of hope. Some of them surely put more hope in the Soviet leadership than merited, and were blind to the depths of depravity in Germany. But it is on the domestic front that we must first construct an equation of good and evil. Artists as well as politicians worked at balancing the ugly and beautiful of this time and that.

Poets did not do so well in the Thirties. It was too tough a time to allow ready indulgence in feeling. The decade literally killed the poet Vachel Lindsay, or, at least drove him to suicide by turning its back on him. But Kenneth Fearing, for example, lived as a Thirties poet. He has deserved better for his verse could touch feelings now. Take for instance his invocation, ironic yet tender to one he calls "Baby." She is a young woman who has nothing to do, who combs her hair, and combs it again, and plays a record, and does her nails—and, asks Fearing, "Is this, Baby, what you were made to do and to be?"

With such lines Fearing can evoke non-Left and non-Right feelings in our Nineties as well as they did in the Thirties. There is more, and I have been tempted to set down more. But there are still other things to notice about the human side of the Thirties. It wanted so much to see and hear the truth. The documentary genre was a feature of the time. It produced masterpieces in prose, poetry, and photographs. James Agee's *Let Us Now Praise Famous Men*, with photographs by Walker Evans survives, with its searing pictures of poor whites in the South. It has probable been helped, too, by Agee's legendary talents as a novelist, poet, and film critic.

The genius of Thirties film documentary was undoubtedly Pare Lorentz, whose film work for the Farm Security Administration literally focused American eyes on the farmers's troubles. Yet Lorentz's reputation will have to be rewon, if it is to help prepare us for our own season of torrents and earthquakes. Our farmers' condition has become too complex, too muddled by economics, farm subsidies, and farm manufacturing for us to remember the Thirties farmer who suffered droughts, floods, and dust storms, with little money from government.

Twenty years ago when I showed Lorentz's *The River* to classes, they sat in a dream, watching his camera focus on the dripping water of springtime—water that turned into streams, then into rivers pounding against dikes and sandbag barriers and threatening lands and human lives. And students listened with awe as a voice intoned Lorentz's invocations of towns and cities, rivers and mountains:

> Down as far west as Idaho
> > Down from the Glacier Peaks of the Rockies—
> From as far East as New York,
> > Down from the turkey ridges of the Alleghennies
> Down from Minnesota, twenty-five hundred miles,
> > The Mississippi River runs to the Gulf . . .

This went on and on, as rivers grew mighty and mountainous:

> New Orleans to Baton Rouge,
> > Baton Rouge to Natchez . . .

And we made cotton king. . . .

We built a hundred cities and a thousand towns . . .

And moved on.

But at what a cost—the soundtrack intoned. It described the torn-up forests, each tree made vivid as it fell from its imperial height, its corpselike remains floating down river. Lorentz showed the worn land made ugly by rain and lost topsoil. But then, then, then . . .

Men interposed themselves against rain with tractors and seed, fighting to give new life to muddy water and land. A new birth. Dams and watersheds and waterfalls that generated electricity. The Tennessee Valley Authority, TVA.

The River, by Pare Lorentz. I recall the shock of surprise I felt when a top student at a famous college said he had never heard of it—had never heard of TVA. But now things must be even more complicated for those

Introduction to the Transaction Edition [xvii

of us who care. An instructor tells me that he gave *The River* to a Twentieth Century class, and the students laughed.

I would not want to leave commentaries without mention of two other phenomena of the Thirties. One was a book *Waiting for Nothing*—an on-the-spot memoir that I had rediscovered. It was a book by a young man, one of many who, for personal reasons, fell from respectability to the bottom of life, searching for food, and, in winter, for warmth. Tom Kromer wrote an account of his empty days on pieces of old newspaper and sent the bundle to Lincoln Steffens, once famous as a muckraker. He was sufficiently impressed to send it to a publisher, who put it in print. Dedicated to "Jolene, who turned off the gas," it made no great impression. It remains a stark memento of hopeless, dehumanized life.

The second document of the time worthy of notice is that by Harriet Woodbridge, a young woman of wealthy family. Lauren Gilfillan, as she called herself, after graduating from Smith College—do they remember her there?—packed her typewriter and visited a western Pennsylvania coal-mine town to see for herself how people were living and thinking. She found friends among the poor, lived with them, and felt for them. She fell out with the communists in the area and returned home where she wrote and published *I Went to Pit College*, a straightforward account of her experiences which helped lighten the gloom of the time.

It was the highpoint of her life, as the thirties were to others despite rigorous experiences. For they felt alive then and with what seemed to them good dreams—better dreams than those of World War II and the aimless years ahead. when we compare our Thirties and our Nineties, using artifacts from both, we conjure up a pattern which helps us judge social action and social relations in which we may have or may not have participated.

I can only mention that famous, yet not famous experiment in government sponsorship of the arts, the Federal Arts Projects of the Works Progress Administration (WPA). This is a subject in itself. It can only here be said that it engaged numerous, you might almost say innumerable writers, artists, theater people, and musicians whose work is yet to be put in useful perspective for us. A noble survivor of those projects, long politically effective afterwards was Congressman Claude Pepper of Florida—the same Pepper who, with another U.S. Representative, offered Congress the unforgettable Coffee-Pepper Bill. It tried in the Thirties to institutionalize art in government, to make the Arts Projects permanent, part of our living culture.

Would the bill, if it had been passed, have in practice institutionalized second-rate bureaucrats and forced cultural trash on us from Washington?

Who knows? We debate the question today, in terms of our working body, the National Endowment for the Arts.

What can be said of the Thirties experiment is that numerous culture-bearers of self-evident stature were part of those amazing projects, from Orson Welles in theater to Thomas Hart Benton in art. Federal Art murals are on major campuses. Best known are such murals as those on the walls outside the Catalogue Room of the New York Public Library, and of the St. Louis Main Post Office. Orson Welles's *Julius Caesar* gave Shakespeare in modern dress on the Federal Theater Project. It suggested Benito Mussolini and the fascist salute of his Italian followers. It was Welles's best-known work before his motion picture *Citizen Kane*.

Yes, the Arts Projects are a project in themselves, and bring up memories of related government efforts to give employment to women in crafts and home arts, and to men in manual employment. Especially worth noting, regrettably in passing, would be the Civil Works Administration (CWA) that deliberately sought young men with too little to do in the city streets. It sent them out in fields and forests. There they used, or were taught to use, skill and muscle to help give form to backward rural areas. They put together cabins and hostels for their own use and that of others who worked to build up neglected areas, and in the process preserved their strength and mental balance.

It was a failure of post-World War II society that it did not maintain offices that would continue such work in a vast country of rivers and forests needing care precisely because of increased technology and growth that had no time for humane controls.

Something should be said of Thirties efforts at translating its life and outlook into fiction. In dark days humor and self-expression were precious. The era was generous to William Saroyan's self-indulgent prose and appreciated his brave attempts to be himself, an individual, telling fellow-Americans how he felt from day to day.

For somewhat similar reasons, though from widely different perspectives, the public took to the novelist Thomas Wolfe. It saw him as a full-blown genius in a great tradition and gave him space for his big frame and sprawling novels. Even grim Leftists tolerated hm and hoped he would "grow" into their viewpoint, dropping his anti-Semitic and anti-black attitudes. As Michael Gold, then known as the "dean" of proletarian literature, said, "They belong to us." All the cultural titans of the day and in the past "belonged," whether they realized it or not, to the party of the future: the Communist Party.

Such was the temper of the times that the Chicagoan Albert Halper, whose career was aborted by World War II, was subsidized to write his novel, *Union Square*. It contained personalities of the time who could be

Introduction to the Transaction Edition [xix

recognized, including Kenneth Fearing as a down-and-out poet and alcoholic. The novel, which still captures the tensions and cultural flavor of the period, was hailed and read on its appearance. Its success encouraged Halper to write a follow-up fiction, *The Foundry*, featuring "workers" and "bosses" in now archaic terms.

But another work, an essay on New York's Union Square is also worth reading even now, in a volume, *The Strangest Places*, by Leo Rosten—still happily with us—under the pseudonym Leonard Q. Ross. Rosten merely went to the square early in the morning, before people with nothing better to do began straggling in. He stayed there the whole day taking notes while people came and went, listening to malcontents expressing their views and arguing with others about theirs, until night freed them for home and other places.

Erskine Caldwell, troubadour of poor whites, Nathanael West, cynic of Hollywood and the press, Ruth McKenney (made famous by her book-turned musicale, *My Sister Eileen*), Albert Maltz, S. J. Perelman, Tess Slesinger. There were many, many more literary and cultural aspirants who won solid or less than solid places in the writing of the time. John Dos Passos was a larger story than the Thirties, or the Sixties, for that matter, as was John Steinbeck.

James T. Farrell and Meyer Levin, ethnically complementary, stand for many writers involved in communities that were feeling the blows of the Great Depression culturally as well as in their pocket books. Farrell at the time seemed a literary master whose flat prose and narrow detail expressed the essence of contemporary life, easily interpreted as predicting the decay and coming death of capitalist civilization. His main character, Studs Lonigan, was actually as famous as his author, yet for qualities that were all negative: ignorance, stunted ambition, herd feelings which led nowhere.[1]

Was that what the Irish of Finley Peter Dunne's "Mr. Dooley," of an older Chicago had come down to, producing Studs Lonigans? Joseph Kennedy was about to become owner of Chicago's Merchandise Mart, and had already fathered a child who would become president of the United States. But the Thirties were too grim for Farrell's readers to look upward to such heights, or even to notice the irony and wit hidden in Farrell's fiction. Later, a public freed of the Depression by war and income would drop Farrell, leaving him as an item in the encyclopedias. But not completely dead, perhaps. We may hear from him again some day.

Meyer Levin's novel, *The Old Bunch*, traced the complex connections of Jews in that same Chicago, and in that same time. You left the book feeling you had lived there and could recognize some of its places and people. Levin's equally large volume *Citizens* broadened the picture to include others whose turbulent lives came to a climax in the mighty "Little Steel" strike and its tragic finale of workers left dead by police fire. Levin's later novel *Compulsion*, based on the Leopold and Loeb murder of little Bobby Franks, makes up with his other books a kind of trilogy that startlingly contrasts the affluent 1920s with what became a Thirties of economic and social despair.[2] It even compares with our affluent 1950s in advancing technology and moving out of older ways and mores.

Some day we may want to look more deeply into the Thirties in ways that will bring out their dimensions, their essence, above all their humanity. This can help our ongoing search—for meaning, for entity. It is an amazing fact that today "liberal" and "conservative" do not help to define social trends. There have been eras, such as the Progressive Era, when it appeared that leaders and programs were sufficiently distinguishable to give us reason to follow one or another.

But though every forceful leader in our history has been judged as from left to right, from black to white, some judgments hold over others, especially if we throw "radical" into the game. No one doubts that there was a depression, and that it affected voters and longed-for solutions. Presently we are in a recession; how else can we characterize a time of stagnation and widespread anxiety?

I would not like to leave this subject without giving some sense of the sincere effort many contributed to making the Great Depression less nightmarish, and more hopeful.

Heywood Broun was only a columnist of the 1920s and the 1930s. He does not appear in literary works, and today is largely forgotten. Yet he had dealt with public matters out of a memory rich with stirring words from American lore. Broun was big, gracious, famous for his sloppy clothes and absentminded ways—people said he looked like an unmade bed. He took generous sides in public affairs. He helped organize the American Newspaper Guild, and wrote often and eloquently on the seamy sides of the Thirties. He made errors, as even people with nothing to do but do research have done, but his good will was never in question. I give him the last word (p. 118) as evidence that, yes, there were cheats, liars, and opportunists in the 1930s, as in every era, little noted because there was so much less to steal. But there were also Heywood Brouns.

Louis Filler

Notes

1. I offer one approach to the problem in my retrospective "Poor Jim: Some Notes on the Decline of James T. Farrell" (*University Bookman*, Summer issue, 1984), 111ff.
2. For a section of *Citizens*, see page 185, for notes on Levin's technique and purposes, see my essay "Compulsion," in my collection of essays, *A Question of Quality: Popularity and Value in Modern Creative Writing* (1976).

Introduction to the Original Edition

I
Newsreel

IT WAS THE LAST YEAR of Herbert Hoover's Administration. In Philadelphia, Pennsylvania, a Communist Party unit announced it would lead a march on the City Hall, where it would demand that something be done for the needy and the unemployed. Marchers were to convene in a city park. There, communists mounted a rough platform which displayed no American flag. Some of them stood below, carrying cheaply-made signs with slogans which denounced and declared. A small crowd attended. On the side, smiling and at ease and talking to one another, stood a group of policemen with nightsticks.

The communist speaker, his speech thick with foreign intonations, made them the theme of his discourse. They were "Cossacks" doing the bidding of their capitalist masters who scorned the poor, who ignored their sufferings, who tried to terrorize them into submission. But they would be taught their lesson. Under the leadership of the Communist Party, the fearless vanguard of the working class, the masses would rise and hurl back their oppressors and their henchmen.... Today, the workers were weak; tomorrow, the capitalists and their tools would flee from them in panic.

"And now, on to the City Hall!"

The communists got down from their platform to organize marching units. The police went into action. First they smashed the banners, while a number of rudely dressed persons who had stood among the others turned out to be plain-clothesmen, and now struggled with the men and women who had intended to lead the demonstration. The crowd began to fly in all directions. Patrol cars (then still called patrol wagons) appeared from nowhere, and then more police. Here one of them was chasing a woman. There another led toward a wagon a tall, blond boy with glazed eyes and blood running from the side of his head.... A tall, awkward man with the hollow eyes and prominent cheek-bones of a Russian fled one plain-clothesman only to be

[1

stopped by another whose blow to his chest boomed like a drum. Somewhere the man found breath to cry: "But I didn't do nothin'!" ... Elsewhere, a detective crouched quickly behind a trapped fugitive, in caricature of a child's trick, while another detective bowled him over with a blow to the face. ... A blond, bristling motorcycle policeman, oddly similar in features to the wounded young agitator, a blackjack in either hand, his whipcorded legs apart, looked swiftly in all directions for further culprits. ... But the square was cleared; the demonstration was over.

This must have been one of the last of such demonstrations, at least in the great northern cities, in which communists for no other reason than that they had organized a protest demonstration exposed themselves and others to inevitable beatings and dispersions. No doubt, they often sought martyrdom, or inspired others to bare their breasts to bullets, or their heads to clubs. No doubt, they were not sorry when events gave them another "victim of capitalist oppression," who could be accorded a "red funeral," and opportunities to express hatred of "fascist bosses and their bloodhounds." But, increasingly, communists — and other radicals — sought results for their pains. The 1930's were in motion.

It was not that policemen could not be found who were able or willing to swing clubs or fire bullets. But the climate of public feeling had changed. Americans no longer believed that the affairs of the harassed people did not intrinsically concern them. A momentous fact of the 1930's was that most people *were* employed. There were, after all, "only" fifteen million unemployed workers in a population of over a hundred and twenty million. But all wage-earners were terrified and insecure. They knew that the bell of unemployment tolled as insistently for them and for their families as for the declassed and the hungry. Each year graduated from the high schools and colleges jobless boys and girls, young men and young women. The boys lounged at street corners. The girls sat on the steps of their houses. They constituted a formidable host of bystanders, sympathizers, ... voters. They joined partisan ranks. They purchased radical literature, listened at radical rallies, saw radical plays which were in vogue. They made the easy solution of police repression impractical, during an economic crisis which wore hopelessly on and on and on.

With the advent of the New Deal, new tactics and strategies promising to the dispossessed and the fearful could be developed. Some programs were actually originated by the Government, rather than as a result of "mighty calls for action raised by the embattled proletariat." This was certainly true of the famous Federal Arts Projects. Writers, artists, and theater people milled about in the first years of the Depression without direction or common purpose; plans for their welfare were hammered out by New Deal intellectuals, and consummated because the practical politicians were too busy with great pork-barrel projects — post offices, roads, government housing — to worry about the relatively few millions of dollars involved in creating work for white-collar personnel. But action in behalf of the masses of the unemployed and distraught was a product of joint agreement between Administration spokesmen and the people's tribunes, and this rapprochement gave status and strength to the latter. Marches of the unemployed were harder to discourage than under Hoover, concerned as he had been for what he had called "the challenge to liberty." Now there was a government committed to a regard for people's wants. Union leaders were less liable to be beaten by the police, following the passage of the famous section 7 (A) of the National Recovery Act. It accomplished nothing solid, true. It was a sop thrown to labor, by practical men who were forging in N.R.A. a legal instrument which would enable business (they hoped) to revitalize the industrial process. But Section 7 (A) was at least a gesture to labor on its right to close ranks. Labor agitators sold to the nation as well as to their fellows the slogan: "Franklin D. Roosevelt wants *YOU* to organize!" Whether he did or didn't, labor organized. There continued to be police brutality, at the Ford Plants in the Detroit area, during the notorious "Little Steel Massacre" in Chicago [SELECTION], and elsewhere. But the increasing organization of workers — for relief, for jobs, for tenure, for union-recognition, for better pay and benefits — and the refining of their methods of waging industrial war, as in the epochal sit-down strike tactics, curbed the police and diluted their strength. May Day in New York belonged to labor and the radicals; their giant parades marched proudly through the city. The police took second place to them.

II
The Thirties

were a particular time and involved special circumstances. As in other times and circumstances, there was a spectrum of people and pursuits to choose from. Monks continued to tell their beads in California missions. Lumberjacks sat by their radios in the Oregon woods. The Sioux Indians in the Dakotas entertained vacationers as they had before. Night-clubbers were their foolish selves in bad times as in good. And so it continued to be. Four years after Americans, during the 1932 elections, had distinctly asserted their intention of having something attempted which would start a stalled industrial economy, Alfred M. Landon, from the "Sunflower State," would ask them to respond again to the vision of the Great Bonanza, the lucky, individualist hope which since the first American trail had been blazed had tempted miners, pedlars, speculators, (and common workmen), retail merchants, farmers, and all their women. Henry Ford offered his old homilies on free enterprise. The *Saturday Evening Post* marched stolidly through the gray decade. But the dullest American who read his *Post* and sat through his perishable films, who dreamed of the Big Break and voted for Landon, had no real faith in his own faith. That dull American laid down his body at night in misery and anxiety, and rose at dawn with an oppressive sense of little awaiting him. He pitied those he knew who were more miserable than he was, or he feared them. They, in turn, hated him and plotted his ruin. Events forced them to attempt to think, to discover whom to blame for the evil times which weighed upon them all. The needy and humiliated had nothing to lose by agitation and protest; perhaps they had something to gain. If they were not activists, they had no heart for standing in the way of those who were. And if they were unsympathetic to activists, they were too enfeebled in conviction about the reality of the American Way to stand in the way of those who were determined to change the world. Never before was lip service toward "The Star-Spangled Banner" more perfunctory. The Boy Scouts dwindled to a corporal's guard. The clichés of Religion, Home, Opportunity, Neighborliness were kept burning by lackeys, fools, and stipendiaries, while their parishioners struggled to recover a sense of their real relationships to their fellows.

The Intellectuals

I forget who offered the immortal thought that: "A person who says he loves poetry, and doesn't buy any, is a son-of-a-bitch." No doubt the problem of judgment goes deeper than this. For if Americans do not, generally speaking, read poetry, how many poets read Americans? Perhaps the most fundamental thing that one can say of our Intellectuals is that they are, for better or worse, Americans. We have had our expatriates, but not notably during the Thirties. The French and Italians had smiled and bowed and curtseyed to the Americans during the 1920's; endured their drunkenness, bad manners, fornications. Once the Depression hit and the American money ran out, their hosts whisked in the welcome-mat and told the expatriates to go to hell; and they frantically telegraphed home for ship fare.

Writers struggled like everybody else, during the 1930's, to make their impress upon the period, or simply to survive. One former would-

Introduction to the Original Edition [5

be poet, early in the Depression era, announced exuberantly his emancipation from art, in the pages of *Esquire*. He depicted himself as previously having sullenly defied his elders. He glowingly described the vision of conventional living which had appeared before him, and the happy aftermath: a job, a haircut, a good suit. It was an eloquent testimonial to the reality of the American Way, or, at least, an enthusiastic one; but it inaugurated no movement. The gray days persisted, and writers burdened with message, with anger, with troublous memories resisted skeptics and the foul fiend of fatuous optimism in their attempts to tell their stories. Paul Engle, in *American Song* (1934), was one of the relatively few who sought to generate a Whitmanesque energy as his answer to apathy or lack of faith, but achieved little more than a professorship in English at the State University of Iowa.

As E. L. Bernays had once abandoned poetry to become an advertising tycoon, and Robert Minor had repudiated satiric art to become a Communist Party wheelhorse, so some writers of the Thirties retooled and revised old attitudes and techniques for the gray days. Harold Loeb, who had recently been one of Ernest Hemingway's crowd of drifters, became an enthusiast for Technocracy, and headed a New Deal-sponsored investigation into American resources and plant equipment. Floyd Dell, who had earlier thought it important for adults to remember that they had once been children, prepared reports of New Deal goals and accomplishments as a salaried employee in Washington. Others who had established reputations for individualistic flairs and attitudes shifted their interests or simply filled jobs for money. In addition, there were numerous writers who forged careers based solidly on escapist premises, some with vast success. Clifton Fadiman, James M. Cain, J. P. Marquand, Alexander Woollcott and the "Algonquin Crowd," among scores and hundreds of others who claimed touches of distinction, and more, appealed successfully to public desires for thrills, pretension, high-level sentimentality, and reassurances of more or less subtle texture. Ruth McKenney was a typical phenomenon of the time. It is perhaps not well recalled that she was powerfully militant throughout much of the Thirties. Yet her most famous writings were those on Her Sister Eileen. And justly so. Those sketches are all that survive of her public life and work. It would be almost heartless to reproduce any of her "radical" writings, except for the most academic purposes.

A curious fact about some of the authors and spirits of the Thirties was that many whose work seemed intimately engaged with the needs of the times did not, in fact, satisfy their own deepest needs. Van

6] AMERICAN ANXIETIES

Wyck Brooks was almost an oddity in this respect. He had made his reputation in the 1910's as a brilliant critic, impatient of easy, undiscriminating prose, determined to sweep away the rubbish of literary failure and preserve a "usable past" consisting of nothing but the very cream of our culture. He would teach us to distinguish between a weed and a rose, he had said. He now reversed himself to become the "historian" of anything that had seen print in a given period and which had crossed his vision, a kind of gossip-columnist of American literature. Many thousands read or wandered through his lengthy chronicles of domestic writing, but their reading left no residue.

The best proof that the 1930's knew exactly what they wanted, and why, was Lincoln Steffens's *Autobiography* (1931). It was also a bestseller by one of the famous American reformers of all time, and evidently relevant to the new time, if only because Steffens was a mordant critic of his own past, and freely receptive to the bold, radical tenets which circulated among the young intellectuals he and his young wife Ella Winter knew. But all the expressed appreciation of his "rich, full life," of his wisdom and keen insight was superficial. No one really cared about or credited, in his heart, the tales Steffens told of his Progressive Era, of democracy in action, of the power of the press, of the Golden Rule as a living principle. Steffens's *Autobiography* was probably read as attentively for its delightful chapters of his happy youth in California as for its discussions of American political institutions. Steffens called himself a "comedian" in his old age, but the sly social jokes he told were little fathomed by his bemused readers. His two-volume *Letters* (1939) were a publishing failure, though they were a mine of instructive detail, and, among other things, constituted a check upon his autobiographical writings. But the Thirties were not scholarly in bent; they were too much concerned for remaking the world as it was, according to dogmatic principles.

This was not true of William Saroyan, who, as he told in a piece that went the rounds, sat in a cold room south of Golden Gate Park in San Francisco, smoking cigarettes, exercising to keep himself warm, and plotting stories and self-expression; the line between his tales and his memoirs was very thin. He advocated generosity, indifference to worldly vanities, and the great simplicities of life. The problem was to determine when these resulted in good stories and when they resulted in bad ones. But literary critics had no time for Saroyan, once it was clear that he did not intend to concern himself with politics. He wandered off by himself, on a course which led him to brilliant Broadway successes.

There was a demand for relevant statements with which to master

Introduction to the Original Edition [7

a hard time. There was, for example, the hard fact of Harlan County, Kentucky, where tough and confident mine-company deputies carried rifles and wore bullet belts. It was no escape from art for Theodore Dreiser in 1931 to have headed a committee of writers which entered that feudal terrain in order to gather materials for a report to the nation. There, local authorities made an extraordinary effort to discredit the aging novelist by planting a woman in his room. Dreiser confounded them by declaring, in an item which no newspaper in the country could resist, that he was not only the victim of a plot, but that he was no longer sexually potent and could have found no use for a woman.

The times sought mediating figures like Dreiser, but the United States produced no Romain Rollands, no Maxim Gorkys, whose stature was universally admitted, and who could help modify inter-party bitterness and personal spite with their seminal comments and judgments. Dreiser himself made efforts to contribute his muddled, if earnest, views to the Depression, and some of them were distinctly antisemitic. The intellectuals rose in horror, and Mike Gold, then the "Dean of American proletarian writers," in the increasingly influential pages of the communist *New Masses* warned him: "The Gun Is Loaded, Dreiser!"

Other writers of established achievement revealed how hectic were the decades of the twentieth century. They had turned and twisted about so many social and political corners as to have left Americans almost no sense of continuity. William Dean Howells, though dead no longer ago than 1920, was forgotten by all but a few deadhead academics, dug into their jobs for any duration. Edwin Markham was in his eighties, amazingly active among women's clubs, lecturing, commenting on all affairs, and constantly being feted by the affluent and influential. But so far as lively critics and writers were concerned, Markham was all but non-existent. Upton Sinclair kept up his flow of fiction, letters to the press, and reminiscences; but the greatest shock he delivered in the 1930's was not literary. In 1934, his EPIC Plan (End Poverty in California) made him a threat to the major political parties, and put the governorship of the state almost within his grasp.

The writers of the previous decade were tossed catastrophically in all directions. Sinclair Lewis reorganized somewhat, and one of his titles gave the period a famous phrase: "It Can't Happen Here," though his other late fictions were ineffective. Ernest Hemingway mixed his personal odyssey with rude and mindless pushes into leftwing associations. But F. Scott Fitzgerald could not adjust to the new age, and, as his friend and true acolyte John O'Hara contemptuously observed, persons who would later froth at the mouth in praise of his genius preferred to cross the street to avoid meeting him while he was still alive. James Branch Cabell was a remarkable example of what happened to Twenties writing in the Thirties. As he wrote in an *American Mercury* article (December, 1951), "They Buried Me Alive," his reputation fell overnight, from the top of the heap to the bottom. His *Jurgen,* which had sold under the counter for twenty dollars and more, now interested nobody. Cabell's new novels were very shadows of the publishing seasons. He tried changing his name, from James Branch Cabell to Branch Cabell. Nothing availed. The Thirties had no use for him, or for Henry Miller, or T. S. Eliot, or Hart Crane, or. . . .

Dos Passos, Farrell, Wolfe

Americans, it seems, will always buy escape materials of one sort or another, and put down their investment to amusement, seeking ("Who knows? Maybe stuff like that can happen?"), and just plain satisfying their shabby curiosities with appropriately shabby materials. This last accounts for the long, almost classic status of such authors as Fannie Hurst, Kathleen Norris, Edgar Rice Burroughs, and Zane Grey. But those same Americans are subject to hunger pangs, spiritual qualms, taxes, and natural calamities, and when the storm comes close they look for real shelters and realistic advice. The same Americans who had once produced the grand designs of Henry George and Edward Bellamy had once also produced the fictionally frayed and absurd pattern of a reconstructed world which Charles Sheldon's *In His Steps* (1896) perpetrated: the best-selling book in America after the Bible, until recent mass-producing techniques changed all best-selling standards and criteria. The Thirties produced Lloyd C. Douglas's nonsense, among other vaguely "inspirational" screeds. They produced such "fantasies" as *On Borrowed Time,* by one Watkin, about Death being caught in an apple tree ("Just suppose that . . . "). They produced historical novels, some of them very good, and regional writings by such craftsmen as Conrad Richter. But they also demanded fare directly relevant to their troubles. And there were writers ready and determined to satisfy wants.

John Dos Passos bestrode the era. He seemed the natural successor to Theodore Dreiser, and to have built upon him. Dreiser had struggled through the thick underbrush of American prejudice and ignorance; Dos Passos had inherited his cause and carried on his inquiry into the truth about American civilization. It seemed to empathetic readers quite just that Dos Passos would be moving closer, more sensitively than Dreiser himself could, to ideas and expectations of socialist and revolutionary change. Dos Passos was no hothead. He seemed no pampered pet of a coterie. A world-traveler, a man of reading and languages, and of comfortable family, he had voluntarily given ear to American speech, on all levels, from one end of the country to the other. Dos Passos himself later recalled that he and his fellows had had no interest in, no regard for, American history; but this seemed no deficiency in the 1930's. What good was history? — the history of a pre-Freudian, a pre-Marxian, and (most urgently) a pre-Depression America seemed simply irrelevant to live Americans, a mere diversion for empty-headed antiquarians, foolish progressives, DAR reactionaries, and other rotters and escapists.

In retrospect it is appalling that Dos Passos and his admirers should somehow have imagined that the non-Left of Texas, of Iowa, of Utah, and, indeed, of all the states, would somehow bend to their vision of a socialist America, merely because they chose to believe that it was better than the reality of Babbitt and Middletown that they satirized and otherwise derogated. In the end, it was Dos Passos and his friends who broke and fled. Yet his vision of *U.S.A.* was not all bad, not all wrong. There were, patently, such scamps and weaklings in every American town. His problem was with his presumed strong characters. The *U.S.A.* trilogy, published between 1930 and 1936, was remarkable in that Dos Passos's view of his protagonists changed in the course of his own work and his experience with the new breed of men, the revolutionists, who had been precipitated by the Depression. In *Forty-Second Parallel,* the first volume, they appeared the hope of the nation; by the time of *The Big Money,* volume three, they were being revealed as dogma-ridden, small of soul and mind, inadequate in their own right. What did Dos Passos want? His aim, he was later to maintain, had been freedom all the time. He found communist cruelty and rationalizations intolerable, and, having bitterly recorded them in his indifferently-read novel, *Adventures of a Young Man* (1939) [SELECTION], retired into stances and attitudes which he had newly borrowed from conservatives and reactionaries whom he found less intolerable than he did communists. A significant moment in his art was one during which, in the course of a study of Thomas Jefferson, he defended that great man's slaveholding proclivities. Dos Passos later undertook another series of novels, published as the trilogy *District of Columbia,* a fierce attack on the New Deal. Though Americans had turned clearly "right" by this time, they did not especially honor this hard-working author. The sum of his labors remained unresolved.

James T. Farrell seemed a comrade to Dos Passos, to some degree, and like him involved in determining the truth of a seamy civilization. He admired Dos Passos's writings, though the latter may not have reciprocated his feelings. Farrell's 1930's writings were in narrower vein than Dos Passos's, though they seemed impressive to the Thirties generation. The first of Farrell's Studs Lonigan trilogy — *Young Lonigan: a Boyhood in Chicago* — was introduced by a sociologist, Frederic M. Thrasher, who had studied the gangs of Chicago. Farrell, an intellectual Irish boy who had pondered the deterioration of family life among his people in Chicago, offered the petty details of their existence as it revolved about the pin-brained Studs. Readers who felt that the naturalistic detail gave them peep-show dividends probably missed something of Farrell's real design. He aimed to demonstrate that it was false standards rather than merely shoddy living which steadily undermined Studs. Farrell himself moved away from his own people toward what seemed the one valid position of the new time: that of Marxism and revolutionary intellectualism. He wrote essays, as well as novels and short stories, and seemed to be creating a canon of writings which would make him the American Balzac.

Naturalism was the literary method of the Thirties, and was identified with it. Yet the touchstone of Thirties writing was not naturalism, but concern for the meaning of American life in the throes of depression. Thus, Meyer Levin was a Thirties writer, even when he wrote about the Twenties. And, indeed, many writers made their mark as Depression authors, whose work had only Platonic relations with naturalism in purpose and weave.

One of the greatest of these — many thought *the* greatest — was Thomas Wolfe. Recall the defensive tone of the late Russell Maloney, in a *New York Times* article, which began: "I am one of the cads who do not believe that Tom Wolfe was a genius...." It is only recently that anti-Wolfe partisans have attained some sort of parity with their opponents, having as many critical warheads stockpiled as do their literary rivals who adore Wolfe. The Third Force of American criticism can now have things pretty its own way in this area, simply because both embattled camps — the pro-Wolfeites and the anti-Wolfeites — need the neutrals and must woo their tolerance, if nothing else.

You can ponder Wolfe in New York and in Asheville, North Carolina, where you can learn as much from the gnarled caretaker of the old, ugly Wolfe homestead, as from looking at the family graves and visiting around town, among people who are like people everywhere — thinking not of "Tom" Wolfe at all, but of their very own compulsions and immediate wants....

And in sum... Wolfe was Twenties in spirit and interests, and

Introduction to the Original Edition [11]

nothing but Twenties. His appeal to Thirties readers — even to young radical Jews who insisted on vibrating with him, and refused to take note of his callow and persistent anti-semitism — was no more than a token of their essential dissatisfaction with the psychological and social conditions which prevailed, and which they theoretically approved. It was a token of how thin were their isms, mere products of material frustration, which would disappear just as soon as their money situation changed .... Poor dears of the 1930's: like their beloved Tom Wolfe, they yearned to Live, to dally with mistresses in cute New York studios, to travel, to eat gargantuan beefsteaks, to "write," and especially about that most important of all subjects, Themselves. They yearned for ego. They hungered for a sense of the cosmic, and for freedom from their liberal catechism. They wallowed in secret dreams that their most trivial peccadilloes might somehow not lose dignity while being inflated to giant size. All this, Tom Wolfe acted out for them, leaving many a hint that he might yet be saved, might yet grow up, become social and mature in his attitudes, and perhaps even begin to take seriously their own concern for New Deal measures, peace, anti-fascism, the Soviet Union, and the workers-and-peasants cliché which served them in place of knowledge to explain everything that was happening in the world, from China to the Argentine.

There is a great temptation to include excerpts here from Wolfe's writings, not because they are relevant to the Thirties, but because they were accorded distinction in that time. Wolfe was assumed to be of that time because he was thought to be legitimate Thirties news. I do not include him, in order to be fair to him. He belongs in some other assemblage of writings: of experimentalists, individualists, poets, memoir-writers. He would not seem odd among selected authors of the time: Saroyan, perhaps, Dos Passos, Benét, cummings, Ezra Pound, of course, and John Peale Bishop. Among these, he would be another individualist, struggling to make sense of his own psyche. But in the larger framework of Thirties writing, I fear he might seem ... absurd. And Wolfe was no more absurd than other people who struggle between heaven and earth for status and proportions.

III

Writing is not *this* writer, or *that* writer; it is a flow of writing which takes its form and features from the need and dreams of a given time. Or it is a kind of mosaic, where pieces serve different purposes. Sometimes, there are center pieces, but always there is a theme. We tire of the theme and want a change. So we read, perhaps, Desmond Holdridge's *Escape to the Tropics,* or James Thomas Flexner's *Doctors on*

Horseback, or James Thurber's *Let Your Mind Alone!* (and, indeed, any of the *New Yorker* crowd of the Thirties), or Jerome Weidman's *I Can Get It for You Wholesale.* And we see and hear Maxwell Anderson's pretentious "prose poems," and Kaufman and Hart's shallow and unmemorable gabble. Only a very few Americans can concentrate on poetry, so persons who for better or worse take it seriously will work at it, and can read Edna St. Vincent Millay's *Conversation at Midnight,* or Robert Hillyer's *A Letter to Robert Frost,* or Louise Bogan's *The Sleeping Fury.*

But the world is still with us, and will either push us around, or be dominated by us. So we return to the major theme of our times, and give renewed attention to the great stoppage of work and opportunity, the fear that clutches at our hearts that we may lose our place in human affairs, the erosion of hope and human relations which have deprived us of our old expectations and forced us to create new ones.

Twenties and Thirties

"All through the Twenties," wrote John K. Hutchens, " . . . ran an excitement and concern about writing for its own sake. . . . If the decade had a theme song, it was the gorgeous melancholy of Gershwin's *Rhapsody in Blue.* If it had a journal it was *The New Yorker.* . . . Old standards went out of the window; so did a good deal of hypocrisy and inhibition. . . . " Ford cars and chain-owned newspapers, Hutchens went on, may have been standardizing the United States, but the writers were extraordinary in their variety.[1] Hutchens pridefully calls the roll of Twenties talents, and they make a varied and creative pattern. Moreover, many of them have enjoyed revivals or augmented esteem as old masters, though it remains to be seen how precious such authors as Fitzgerald and Hemingway will seem to us in the years ahead, and how their vogue will compare with the extraordinary national regard which have been showering upon Robert Frost and Carl Sandburg. We have been seeking a cultural unity, and finding good materials for the purpose. How much of the Thirties is likely to enter into the building of a new cultural unity?

The whole story is yet to be told, but times are changing, attitudes are in flux. A few years ago, students in the darkened auditoriums sat stolidly or with traces of irony in their mien and watched Pare Lorentz's *The River* as though it were a casual newsreel. Now they view it with awe and reverence. Steinbeck's *Grapes of Wrath* is generally recognized to be a classic. Recently, several professors cudgeled

---

[1] *The American Twenties: a Literary Panorama* (1952), p. 12 ff.

their brains for a novel other than Dos Passos's *U.S.A.* which could be used for a course in Twentieth Century America, and which would do what it does. They could think of nothing that remotely filled the bill more than or as well as *U.S.A.* Farrell's stock has fallen catastrophically, but it is a curious fact that no reference work would think of demoting him as a significant entry, and we may yet see some revivals in this area. But, in addition, add up such literary personages of the Thirties as Saroyan, Edmund Wilson, Kenneth Fearing, Erskine Caldwell, and Archibald MacLeish, among others whose claims to regard will be submitted, and there may yet be visions of things they have accomplished which have not heretofore met the eye, and revisions of careless judgments which have been set down.

Said Robert Penn Warren's Willie Stark, in *All the King's Men:* "A man don't have to be governor." Stark's tragedy was his later conclusion that, after all, a man *did* have to be governor, at a sacrifice of his idealism, and faith in justice and virtue, and in the practicality of truth. There was a tragedy of expediency in the 1930's, which the frankly opportunistic Twenties did not have to face. The Thirties held that a man had to eat, no matter how, and fight for status, at whatever cost, and it condemned the tragic vision of life as decadent, bourgeois, contemptible, and as evidently intended to reconcile the poor to starvation and slavery. Thus, the Thirties were, whether intentionally or unintentionally, radical.

The Left, and Steinbeck

The Thirties were willing to entertain the notion that capitalism was on trial, and was being found wanting. All manner of writer and critic proliferated who took off from this premise and developed it without qualification. A "distinguished" volume of critical and social evaluation of this time, by none other than the *New York Times* daily book reviewer, John Chamberlain, was entitled *Farewell to Reform*. This jaundiced view of the American potential did not harm Chamberlain's status with *Time* and *Life* and *Fortune,* to say nothing of the *New Republic*. His book is still cited as "stimulating" in the bibliographies of sleepy academic freeloaders who recall vaguely having read it during the Thirties, and who are not at all troubled by the fact that this rousing iconoclast has since become the firmest of firm defenders of the *status quo*. There were many such literary weathercocks. In a time receptive to radical doctrine, it was not surprising that the radicals themselves should have been accorded respect, and more. The *New Masses* stood, as it were, at the crossroads of American culture, and hailed new adherents to the faith, warned non-adherents that they were losing their chance of being saved, and reprobated deviators for having succumbed to corruption. The story of the role of communism in America can probably not be wholly recaptured in this generation. There are too many people whose feelings and actions are tied in with its extraordinary shifts and policies, and who must pass from the scene, before disinterested and, alas, dead analyses can be freely developed by industrious researchers. For present purposes, it can suffice that leftist programs and compulsions gave birth to a literature, some of which was substantial, some less so.

John Dos Passos was, of course, a novelist before he became a hope of "proletarian culture," but some younger authors entered the Thirties as full-fledged radicals, and ready to contribute to the literature of the new time coming, as they saw it. Jack Conroy's first book, his best, *The Disinherited* (1933), was a sober account of his youth in a midwestern coal-mining community, and elsewhere: a faithful record of hard times and meager opportunities, if somewhat deficient in broad social understanding and imagination. Albert Halper, a Chicagoan, worked with his hands and dreamed of fictions which ultimately took shape not only in *Union Square* [SELECTION], but in the proletarian vision of *The Foundry* (1934). Grace Lumpkin was of old southern family; her *To Make My Bread* (1932) for half its length contributed sensitively to knowledge of the mountain folk. Yet she felt compelled to bring them into the factories and to muddy her understanding of them with communist dogmas. Indeed, great numbers of literary talents could not resist adherence to communism, either through such affiliated communist agencies as the John Reed Clubs, groups in the theater, or in the dance, "Defence of the Soviet Union," and other groups, or directly in terms of the Communist Party. In 1935, a group of such persons edited the volume *Proletarian Literature in the United States, an Anthology*. It printed the material of sixteen fiction-writers, the verse of almost thirty poets, including that of Kenneth Fearing, Michael Gold, Horace Gregory, Alfred Hayes, Kenneth Patchen, Muriel Rukeyser, Genevieve Taggard, and Richard Wright, the drama of Clifford Odets and John Wexley, and the literary criticism of Malcolm Cowley, Granville Hicks, Bernard Smith, and Philip Rahv. The book made a touching effort to recognize the "people," as in its explanations of the folksongs it reproduced: "Ella May Wiggin was a martyr of Gastonia. Aunt Molly Jackson wrote songs for the Harlan, Kentucky, coal miners. *A Southern Cotton Mill Rhyme* is an old ballad discovered by Grace Lumpkin. *Do Lak Alabamy Boys* and *Death House Blues* are from Lawrence Gellert's collection of *Negro Songs of Protest*." But, by and large, "proletarian literature" was an exotic flower on the American scene, and produced a skimpy array of writings of quality. It reached its lowest point in the awarding, that same year of 1935, of the *New Masses* prize of publication to one Clara Weatherwax, for her novel *Marching! Marching!* — one of the poorest novels of the decade: a caricature of a novel.

It is not possible to understand 1930's radicalism without also understanding 1930's fascism and reaction: a grim world of gloomy racism, hatred of democracy, fear of and contempt for the needs of hungry men and women, malice toward Jews, Negroes, and other minority groups, and, above all, a determination to subject labor to the plans of industrialists through the free use of stool pigeons, company strong-arm men, strike-breaking agencies, and the cooperation of municipal police and, when possible, state and federal troops. Such programs reached into management and into legislatures, including the United States Congress, as John Roy Carlson later dramatically demonstrated in his *Under Cover* (1943), a shocking record of right-wing subversion, the materials for which he gathered at considerable personal risk.[2] With such desperate and malevolent plans abroad for terrorizing Americans, it can be understood why some of those who were most alert to the need for resisting the growth of fascism might have been as comfortable as they were with communist solutions to depression and war. Yet, sensitive as they sounded to fascist threats, they proved

[2]For samples of fascist thinking, though of a more tidy and respectable type, consult the titles of such publications as the *American Review*, which commenced publication in 1933. It was a remarkable effort to sell fascist ideals to an American elite. It picked up the defunct literary monthly, The Bookman, and set out to give a forum to genteel elements who were unhappy with Thirties liberalism and radicalism. The southern agrarians loomed large in their pages. The so-called English "Distributists" offered what the magazine called "a carefully reasoned alternative to the Capitalist-Communist dilemma." The editors emphasized what they called ethical problems, which they found inseparable from philosophy and religion. These "radicals of the right," in succeeding issues, carried out their promise to give "sympathetic exposition" to fascist economics, in terms of the unemployed, questions of the role of the state, "the restoration of property," and other areas, as well as a battery of cultural problems. A remarkable number of writers — some not ordinarily identified with such causes and attitudes as the magazine officially espoused — appeared in its pages. It ended publication in 1937.

Fascists were as a rule too busy to be literate, however; but Lawrence Dennis was a notable exception; see his *The Coming American Fascism* (1936). Most remarkable among potential fascist leaders was Huey Long, whose background, abilities, and national perspective gave him the best chance to develop a national organization; his assassination in 1935 inspired major novelists to attempts to crystallize his life and purposes in fiction. His own posthumously-published *My First Days in the White House* (1935) is worth pondering. For rightist impulses among intellectuals, see my "The Making of a Fascist," *Southwest Review*, Autumn, 1948.

less than sensitive to ominous aspects of communist tactics and strategy. They were not disillusioned by the disgraceful Madison Square Riot of February, 1934, when units of the Communist Party deliberately sought to "capture" a mass meeting of socialists memorializing their comrades who had died in Vienna while defending their homes and organizations from the brutal assaults of the Dolfuss regime. So influential were the communists that Max Eastman's *Artists in Uniform* (1934), a negative view of the status of artists and art in the Soviet Union, though well-written and controversial and by a then-famous critic, was all but ignored by readers and the critics. And the Moscow Trials of 1936, though they provided the first shock of awareness that people could be twisted like things to foul their own humanity, by arts which Arthur Koestler later probed in *Darkness at Noon* (1941) — such horrors were absorbed by communist sympathizers, were denied and defended without anguish.

But the "working-class" point of view, with its attendant "proletarian literature," was an extreme of Thirties literature. It touched odd and flexible types. Some non-historical-minded *Esquire* and *Fortune* readers might be surprised to learn the color of the Thirties's opinions which had been held by their cultural attaché, Dwight Macdonald. Some readers of *Newsweek* might rub their eyes to read Thirties effusions by their Henry Hazlitt, who now stands at the western bridge defending free enterprise to the uttermost.

A more permanently interesting phenomenon would be John Steinbeck's evolution through the 1930's, an evolution which included his publication of *In Dubious Battle* — almost a test for a critic of Thirties fiction. *In Dubious Battle* is in print, and is still occasionally hailed by some critic as a fine or great novel, and a worthy precursor of *The Grapes of Wrath*. Some readers feel that they have a stake in this view of the earlier novel. One of my students fought over it with me for more than an hour, and left somber and resentful. For he had been happy, as it were, with it, had experienced the catharsis of a literary satisfaction. He furnished evidence that there is more to reading than just reading. Ideas have consequences. . . .

First of all, *In Dubious Battle* is a communist novel; there is no other way of identifying the "Party" to which its protagonist adheres. But, in addition, it is a failure of a novel, an obvious failure. Steinbeck says or knows nothing about the Party which his protagonist, Jim Nolan, has decided to join. The Party does not live, as it should in a live novel. Steinbeck sketches a working-class background for Nolan, but it, too, lacks vitality and connotation. The Party organizer, Mac, is professional in his revolutionary attitudes, but he is a machine rather

Introduction to the Original Edition [17]

than a human being: a manufactured thing. Steinbeck believed too much, too intimately, in his wastrels of *Tortilla Flat* to be able to commit real parts of himself to communists or communism. All that comes through as true and vibrant in Steinbeck's would-be revolutionary prose is his hatred of California vigilantes, a major theme in a writer of German stock who remembers the cruel and stupid treatment to which Germans or persons of German background were subjected by nativist vigilantes during World War I. But though vigilantes inspire some of his most evocative pages, in shorter pieces [SELECTION] as in *The Grapes of Wrath,* there is not enough in this solitary theme to put life and form into *In Dubious Battle.*

The key to Steinbeck's odyssey was his search for justice: for God or its equivalent. This was a search which took the novelist through religious byways and experience; it is generally not realized how significant religion was in Steinbeck's development. Yet such of his titles as *The Pastures of Heaven* (1932), *To a God Unknown* (1933), and *Saint Katy the Virgin* (1936) should have suggested to his admirers how much of his thought had gone into such speculations. By now, it is an old chestnut that communism is a religion, yet it is a provocative thought how many communists must have "enjoyed" *The Grapes of Wrath* (as well as *In Dubious Battle)* who did not realize that it was a story on two levels. *In Dubious Battle* (a title appropriately gleaned from *Paradise Lost)* awkwardly and unsuccessfully sought to juxtapose this-worldly and other-worldly viewpoints. *The Grapes of Wrath* can no more than *Moby Dick* be adequately grasped without some grasp of Biblical lore. It fulfilled Steinbeck's quest and conclusions. Heavy with implications, easily bearing its double-burden of meaning, it stepped out of depression economics and political dogma to preach its enduring message of freedom and humility.

Tours de Force

We do not enjoy "long, distinguished careers," in this century. The decades have ended too catastrophically. Our sages, singers, and storytellers establish their images, prepare for eternity, and find themselves explaining to fresh young editors who they are — or were — and why it would be nice to have a chance at writing about this or that. The process works in reverse. Who, today, can say how Robert Frost thought and felt in the 1910's? And, by the way, who ever thinks about Edwin Arlington Robinson, with whom Frost used to be paired? Who recalls the Twenties's Carl Sandburg of Chicago journalism, the buddy of Ben Hecht, Harry Hansen, Sherwood Anderson, and others of the Windy City's "Renaissance"? We need never be surprised to discover another case in which "the name died before the man." Sometimes we have the same man living two careers, as in the case of Fulton Oursler, who was the iconoclastic author of *Behold This Dreamer!* (1924), and also one of the outstanding Catholic laymen and author of *The Greatest Book Ever Written* (1951), which blossoms every Christmas in the newspapers.

The Thirties followed the pattern, producing cascades of scorn for the Twenties; Mike Gold averred that he wanted to spit whenever he thought of them. It produced the more deadly indifference which spelled an end to the significance not only of Cabell, but of Joseph Hergesheimer, George Sterling, Ellen Glasgow, Elinor Wylie, William Ellery Leonard, Lester Cohen, Wilbur Daniel Steele, Paul Elmer More, Ben Hecht, Ruth Suckow, and scores of other writers, many of them no doubt permanently. But it produced, in addition, as many scores of writers who were able to speak pointedly to the Thirties, in their own terms, and often with (to their contemporaries) sharp effect. Robert Cantwell became almost a legend to those interested in writers as well as writings for having written with exciting promise, in his *Laugh and Lie Down* (1931), but who was, it was later alleged, undermined by service with *Time* magazine. In retrospect, *Laugh and Lie Down* reveals sensibility rather than insight, and his subsequent *Land of Plenty* (1934), a contribution to "proletarian literature," is directed by dogma rather than a personal vision or even style. But there were many such aspirants to significance, not to say social significance, during the 1930's, who committed themselves to the premises deriving from depression and fear of war. Inevitably, no doubt, their minds were fixed by a peculiar view of the past and present. They despised America's epic of World War I, and wanted to avoid repeating it. There was no harm, it seemed to them, in maintaining a regard for the Red Army as the defender of "the workers' fatherland." They derogated advertising as a stupefying conspiracy against freedom of thought and choice, but saw little wrong, and much that was forceful, and even novel and charming, in communist slogans and "Party Lines." The Leninist slogan of "democratic centralism" made sense to them: we reason together, but once a party decision has been reached, we act as one. Free as the fingers, united as a fist. More intellectuals were thrilled by such comparisons than were repelled by them. One poet, later a successful novelist, declared that a perfect line of poetry was the *Daily Worker* headline: "Down Tools for May Day."

Numerous writers hoped to build careers upon their understanding of the world's needs and conditions, and, in fact, to no small degree, did so. What they had in common *was* their belief that their writing constituted a contribution to the world's work, rather than to "mere" personal expression. This raised one of the questions which excited attention when, in 1936, Clifford Odets, then ranking as Broadway's leading younger dramatist, elected to accept a Hollywood offer to join the film colony as a writer. His first movie assignment, *The General Died at Daw*n, was carefully scrutinized for left-wing lines, or lines which could be interpreted as left-wing. Fiction by William Rollins, Jr., Josephine Herbst, Richard Wright, more or less successfully presented itself as warranting the regard of serious readers. Was theirs a proper approach to their fellow Americans? One Robert Whitcomb thought he would help clarify the question with his novel *Talk United States!* (1935). It consciously sought American intonations, American turns of phrase. It portrayed a worker capable of skilled labor, but concerned for American labor. This was perhaps its fatal flaw. Americans were not interested in labor. They read Erskine Caldwell's *Tobacco Road* (1932) avidly, not because it was concerned with poor whites, but for reasons which seemed too obvious to mention. It was no accident that Caldwell's collaborator on the long-running Broadway version of *Tobacco Road* should have been Jack Kirkland, who had no status whatever in anything to the left of money-making. Richard Wright's masterpiece, too, *Native Son (*1940), with its motifs of rape and violence, was not read, perhaps it was not even written, as left-wing literature. As one advertiser put it, "It appeals to the worst in people." Presumably, he knew. Not a few Americans were willing to receive appeals of this nature, nor did they necessarily discriminate between naturalistic writings having social significance and such works as John O'Hara's *Appointment in Samarra* (1934) and Horace McCoy's *They Shoot Horses, Don't They?* (1935), which had no social significance of any kind.

There were many *tours de force,* but one perhaps will speak for the others: for Howard Fast, Isidor Schneider, Edwin Seaver, Joseph Freeman, Granville Hicks, even Sherwood Anderson, who essayed one proletarian fiction and called it quits. Dalton Trumbo was destined to appear in the news, eloquently, in 1943 as one of the participants at the Writers' Congress, held under the auspices of the Hollywood Writers' Mobilization and the University of California. It featured messages from President Roosevelt and other dignitaries, as well as contributions from such directors, writers, and other creative personnel as Chet Huntley, Robert Rossen, Darius Milhaud, Hanns Eisler, and Carey McWilliams. Later still, Trumbo became the most famous and resourceful of the "Hollywood Ten" who suffered

20] AMERICAN ANXIETIES

legal, not to say professional, entanglements for communist associations. And still later, he was boldly featured as the scenarist of *Spartacus,* a film which was apparently not deliberately intended to bore audiences into an antipathy toward democracy. The Trumbo triumph signalled the official end of the blacklist Hollywood had maintained against anyone publicly defaced with pleadings of the Fifth Amendment to the Constitution, and other blemishes.

Trumbo's *Johnny Got His Gun* (1939) was, in any event, his major effort. His protagonist was Joe Bonham, who had suffered amputations of both his arms and his legs, as well as his features, during World War I, but whose life has been saved by surgery, with all his wits intact. Chapters introduce us to his Colorado family, his Los Angeles friends, his loves. Realistic thoughts tell Joe that he never knew what he was fighting for, or why he left his Karen to go to war, that honor is nothing, that nothing is more important than just to be alive. Joe is one of the dead, saved by an accident from being wholly one with them. He alone has the right to speak for them, and, speaking for them, he asserts that nothing is bigger than life. He learns to use the few perceptions available to him, by means of his skin and small body and head movements, to recognize time differences and to distinguish the movements and qualities of his visitors. He seeks to communicate with them, by means of a tapping system which escapes them until a remarkable nurse establishes contact with him. "What do you want?" he is asked, momentously. He has identified himself with the slaves, the underprivileged. He wants to earn his way. He can gather crowds as a sideshow attraction — one with a message declaiming the desirability of peace. The answer he receives is that what he asks is against regulations.

And so he has his cause. His is for those who love peace, and, significantly enough, will fight for it, if need be. "He was the future he was a perfect picture of the future and they were afraid to let anyone see what the future was like." And again: "We are men of peace we are men who work and we want no quarrel. But if you destroy our peace if you take away our work if you try to range us one against the other we will know what to do." Thus Joe enters back into life, and into the further possibility of multiple amputations. His creator went to Hollywood where, as Ring Lardner, Jr. (who was more permanently excommunicated from its revelries) observed, he dedicated himself to a higher standard of living.

Writers, Represented and Otherwise

There is an embarrassment of riches, in providing a faithful sam-

Introduction to the Original Edition [21

pling of the writings of the Thirties. I was even tempted to reproduce journalism from the Thirties, for example from Drew Pearson and the Alsops, if only because they are still happily go-go-going, but also because some of their varied judgments and news would be evocative and striking in the Sixties. I concluded, however, that their lack of literary tone, of genuine finesse, would militate against appreciation of the remarkable details of their columns. The dilemma was even crueler so far as Westbrook Pegler was concerned. For this old curmudgeon *had* tone. He had relevance. Pegler-haters forget that his attacks on Thirties union racketeers aided the labor movement and put some most unamiable characters behind bars. His services to labor and to the reading public in the Thirties were such that when he concluded to oppose unionism on principle, the fact was reported as a news item. As late as 1948, when his attacks on followers of Franklin D. Roosevelt had moved habitually out of the category of decency, we were suddenly brought face to face with the fact that he often hit targets more respectable minds missed, as with such revelations as the intellectual peccadilloes of Henry A. Wallace in that warm election year. Well, call me Coward; I concluded to leave the gifted and erratic journalist to the good offices of the League to Preserve the Essential Qualities of Westbrook Pegler for Posterity. And so with others of his journalistic fraternity. I offer Heywood Broun, and would gladly offer more Heywood Broun, for he seems to me to merit not one toast, but two, and more. But this is an anthology, not a volume of anybody's Selected Works.

A major problem was, in fact, to make sure that I was reproducing the works of authors who could be appreciated in selections, and who did not require elaborate explanation. Obviously, a short-story writer, an essayist, a lyricist had to be able to make his own point expeditiously, if at all. A novelist was a more complicated problem, as a rule. Nelson Algren posed no problem; I think less of his work than, say, Simone de Beauvoir did. But Henry Roth's *Call It Sleep* (1934) is, I think — a number of people think — one of the great creative writings of our time. The problem was to discover a selection out of its stream of conscious, subconscious, dialect, childish prose— a selection from it which was relevant to the Thirties, and this fine work failed this test; it is not written about the Thirties. But, finally, it is doubtful that it can deliver its own message in snippets; I would have had to dedicate three or four pages of exegesis to introduce it, and, thereafter, would have been uncertain that readers would have found introduction and excerpt effective and of interest. It is now notorious among inner-circle critics that Henry Roth gave up writing following his great effort. This is not solely the result of his lack of rapport with the Thirties. The Forties and Fifties did not want him, and, although *Call It Sleep* was recently reissued, apparently neither do the Sixties. In short, he is out of step with Americans as a whole, who can endure his non-writing with great fortitude. It is for them to demand selections from his works and to fill them with living connotation.

The are a number of writers of the Thirties though not with them, who might profitably be included in an expanded or revised edition of this anthology. Humphrey Cobb's *Paths of Glory* contains fine prose and experience; but it is all about World War I. Nathanael West's prose is now securely in the hands of a coterie, and, to that extent belongs to no one else. I suppose West's work was a protest against Thirties dogmatism and overconcern with economic justice, and that it fights the good fight for the individual; but e.e. cummings did that, too, in the selection I reproduce, and confronted the Thirties while doing so. It must stand for Roth and for West, and for others who, in one way or another, adorned the literature of the period without impact or direct pertinency.

Nevertheless, a word on the phenomenon of Daniel Fuchs, then a young man from Williamsburg, a shabby, ghetto-like section of Brooklyn across the bridge from Manhattan. He published three novels in the Thirties about struggling and entranced people. They are composed of varied, resourceful materials about people who live close to the limits of their vision and opportunities: who want to get married or don't, to make money, to avoid the dirt and stench of the slum, people involved in lies and even gangsterism, in drink, in worship of movie stars, and in hopes of gains at the race track. Here in Fuchs's novels is a spectrum of existentialist living among frustrating circumstances, varied with fantastic efforts to escape. Fuchs's contact with New Deal, communist, fascist, or other solutions for contemporary woe was almost nil. His novels did not sell. Why? I take it that equally frustrated Americans in Iowa, Indiana, and New Mexico had their own troubles — similar to those endured by Williamsburg habitants. They were, in similar fashions, psychologically handcuffed, but expressed themselves in other language and gestures. They had never heard of any Williamsburg but Williamsburg, Virginia, and had no urge to find out about New York or any section thereof. And, of course, the Williamsburg denizens would as soon have bought Fuchs's books as the natives of the Congo would have bought (or had any money to buy) books about themselves by big-game hunters, or even by their own London School of Economics graduates.

In his interesting introduction to his three novels, which were as

Introduction to the Original Edition [23

recently dredged out of the Thirties and reprinted in 1961, Fuchs tells how he began to wonder who really wanted and read stories. "It suddenly occurred to me that great numbers of people read the *Saturday Evening Post* each week." He wrote a story for that publication, and shortly after received a check for six hundred dollars. "I decided to become rich. I was in the middle of a fourth novel but broke it up and swiftly turned it into three or four short stories." It would be interesting to have the original manuscript for comparisons with the stories he now proceeded to sell, expecially to *Collier's* magazine. He joined the movie colony in Holly wood, and has since been there employed. He believes screen writers are engaged in the same problems which challenge writers everywhere: "We grapple with the daily mystery. We struggle with form, with chimera...." His novels had in many pages satirized movie clichés, and described movie plots and characters at ironic length. Mr. Fuchs is aware of how prompt people are to denounce others for having sold out, knows, too, I gather, how worthless are their judgments of others; how they themselves grab for the pignuts, be they editorships, professorships, or undeserved and bonanza Fellowships.

Still, there is the puzzle of achievement. What it amounts to is this: that people (present company totally excepted) *do* want some trash, "fantasy," as Mr. Fuchs calls it. Of course, people hope that the stuff will turn out to have been written by somebody named Bill Shakespeare or Nat Hawthorne (as one of my most talented students once called him). But if they lay down their money and ask for a double-order of junk with a side-dish of knowledge and just a smidgen of genius, it does seem impertinent to roll up a double-order of genius, and tell the customer it's good for him. If the boss is embarrassed by a full stock of genius, purchased or homemade, he had best enjoy most of it himself before it loses its flavor for everybody but the future, and reconcile himself to modest orders here and there. One of the rare chaps will turn out to be named Hank Thoreau, who will suddenly decide that he is not interested in selling anything — isn't interested in business at all.

There would probably be no gain in reproducing here a selection from Mr. Fuchs's movie scripts (or even his six-hundred dollar *Saturday Evening Post* story). His tales of Williamsburg — a section which he himself avoids — can be passed by, here, at present, as an American phenomenon. The prose of William Saroyan, of Meyer Levin, of Albert Maltz, of Albert Halper, and others, involves phrases, perceptions, experiences, ideas, and milieus which touch upon many of Fuchs's, and transmutes them with meanings which attempt to go somewhere, and to a degree do. It will, indeed, be a great day when an anthology of American literature can legitimately include selections from the writings of motion-picture scenarists.

The Government

It subsidized a very considerable amount of writing. Some people thought it should have subsidized much more — that talents were withering for lack of food, let alone literary encouragement. Writers on the Federal Arts Projects fought to set up an Arts post in the President's Cabinet and to make their jobs permanent. The legislative measure with the unforgettable name, the Coffee-Pepper Bill (named for Representative John M. Coffee of Washington, and Senator Claude D. Pepper of Florida), aimed to maintain a permanent corps of artists and writers on the government payroll, and though the Bill was defeated, New Dealers fought seriously in its behalf. Writing in the Thirties became social as it had never been before — after all, the communists could only talk about the bad time here and the good time coming; Federal writers wrote about *their* country, *their* government: its present sorrows, weaknesses, and promise. But I do not want to talk about its journalese, though the Federal Guide was in its way a great achievement, and the libraries of pamphlets and explanations of New Deal activity no small one.

The Federal Writers Project maintained a small creative bureau; Richard Wright wrote his first stories on the Project and published them as *Uncle Tom's Children* (1938). *American Stuff* (1937) was a collection of writings by Project workers, and included stories, verses, journalism, collections of folksayings, and other human and American matter. Project workers went out into the field and collected folksongs and personal narratives of the people. Ben A. Botkin, folklore editor of Federal Writers, later collected some of the narratives of then still-living ex-slaves, in *Lay My Burden Down* (1945). But such collections were only splinters of the forest of materials which such Project personnel as Merle Colby, George F. Willison, Jerre Mangione, Vardis Fisher, Lyle Saxon, Maxwell Bodenheim, among many others, coped with. They were poets, novelists, short-story writers, and essayists, but they had little time in which to develop themselves as personalities as well as government stipendiaries. Their story is buried in the Project files, hidden in the National Archives in Washington. Some of their materials were at last report in the Library of Congress, still unprocessed, still unstudied.

I offer here a sample of Federal writing, not from Federal Writers, as it happens, but from the Federal Theatre Project. Its "Living

Newspaper" was created to employ as many actors as possible. Its plays in this genre must be the only plays ever written which sported footnotes. I do not offer them so much as "literature"; I see them as pages torn out of the 1930's. These pages from the scenes of the "Living Newspaper" seem to me interesting, partly because of what they say, partly because of their probing of techniques suitable to a mass-medium.

But here is a thought. We have been through a cultural era which turned wholly away the masses in order to probe its own psyche. Jackson Pollock, Samuel Beckett, the five- or ten- or twelve-tone musicologists, and the little magazine storytellers took in each others's washing, and left the masses to Bob Hope. In such circumstances, Federal Writers, Federal theater, and Federal art disappeared from view; it was commonplace, journalistic, "representational," and so forth. And this, even though Federal Art had included among its personnel Beniamino Bufano, Ben Shahn, Jack Levine, Dong Kingman, Michael Siporin, Joseph Hirsch, and numerous other masters in murals, etchings, paint, and sculpture. Those who derogated government in the arts, whether they wanted to or not, stood exactly in the same position as did the Hearst newspapers which had, year in year out, denounced the Projects as a waste of public money, the foolish fancy of an irresponsible Administration, a haven for communists and incompetents. I do not argue the point. People should get what they want, and if it pleases them to take on faith the idea that government art means trash, so be it.

Authors, Authors

My major premise in choosing material for this collection has been that prose has to be clearly relevant to the Thirties; I thought long and often about William Faulkner and how he might best be included in this collection, if only because it is so important for us to remember that the South is part of our Union, part of our problem, part of our Thirties. I concluded that he was both too big and too small for what we had to offer. Faulkner's *Sanctuary* (1931) fitted my bill entirely: it is Thirties, it depicts a prototypical fascist, it is literature. But it is so much a part of our literary affairs, so famous, that those who know it hardly need a selection from it, and those who don't would want elaborate explanation which could only loosen its tight prose and disturb its overtones. Faulkner is as deep and national as Hawthorne, and as sectional. He belongs no more to the 1930's than Hawthorne belonged to the 1830's. For present purposes, let us leave these great men alone.

Irwin Shaw might well have been represented. But *Bury the Dead* (1936) is simply too well-known to reproduce. His *The Gentle People* (1939) might well be better-known; but the reader will pardon me if I prefer to let someone else break ground for Shaw's less famous pieces, using some more appropriate forum than this anthology. William Carlos Williams wrote prose as well as verse, and his *In the Money* (1940) was interesting fiction. But Williams was not really interested in the Thirties; he was Twenties plus good will — an excellent commodity, but dry fare for hungry people. Dorothy Parker actually threw herself into a Thirties stance, weeping in her literary cups for the unhappy poor. Unhappily, her literary mascara ran and left unsightly stains on her prose. Dorothy Parker was a female intellectual dandy, a chip off the old Twenties. Her best tales told not of society, but of unfeeling male clods who kicked girls around. I read Langston Hughes's verse with care, hoping for a poem which would send a sympathetic but not weak-minded reader. . . . It just wasn't there, and, for the usual reasons. Hughes is simplistic. He merely *wants*, rather than wants to understand. His verses on "Park Bench," for example, viewed the difference between Park Avenue and himself, noted that he had to beg a dime for dinner while Park Avenue had a butler and maid, and announced that he was waking up: "Say, ain't you afraid/ That I might, just maybe,/ In a year or two,/ Move on over To Park Avenue?" This "song" was published in 1938 under the auspices of the International Workers Order, and presumably reflected its aspirations toward a Park Avenue Branch of the Workers Republic.

It is not always possible to imagine just what people would find memorable. There were famous Thirties authors who have been thoroughly forgotten. Who recalls the graceful, sensitive prose of *Now in November* (1934), by Josephine Johnson? It was a tale of deteriorating farms and families and, though emphasizing persons over forces and society, not wholly irrelevant to the Thirties. I fear Johnson might seem a kind of hand-me-down Willa Cather, too pallid to be memorable. The need for relevance sadly turned me against George Jean Nathan's defiantly individualistic essays in dramatic realism, though need for a respect for the individual was anything but irrelevant to the Thirties. I labored to save James Gould Cozzens. I am one of the cads who thinks he is very interesting. Where else can I find such ready entrée to the High Church set? But his best novels are post-Thirties. And since relatively few people interested themselves in Cozzens's ecclesiastical solutions to life and depression, as expressed in *Men and Brethren* (1936), I had to forego the pleasure of his anthological company. It is really not one of his stronger efforts.

George Santayana . . . Pearl Buck . . . Anne Morrow Lindbergh . . . Margaret Mitchell . . . Lin Yutang. They were all of the Thirties, though rarely concerned for such questions as how people lived without having work to do, or what the end would be in the world-wide duel being waged between communists and fascists. I fought down a strong temptation to include a section from Dale Carnegie's *How to Win Friends and Influence People* (1937), even though it scarcely needs advertising— if only to remind readers of the want he satisfies, no matter what is happening in the world. Many an understrapper have I seen — clerks, warehouse white-collar personnel, gas company bill-checkers, bank tellers — waiting for busses and reading Dale Carnegie's masterpiece. Pale, ineffectual, drab, they have yearned to look arresting, to be impressive, to attract attention, respect. In their silent, loveless rooms, they have dreamed of victories. What cared they how the American farmer was doing, to say nothing of the "workers and peasants abroad"? I think William Saroyan once hoped to tap some hidden well-spring of imagination in such persons: to persuade them that romance was in the mind, not in the movies, that there was no need for trying to impress anybody; and that if one had nothing to say, a good idea was to shut up and listen. But Saroyan lives abroad now, mostly, and who else cares anything about these little men, these potential fascists?

IV

So the literary decade wore on, largely concerned for its own dignity, rather than its philosophic rectitude, and only relatively concerned for the gathering storm abroad. Hitler's friends were relatively quiet in the United States; few were willing, like Col. E. Alexander Powell, in *The Long Roll on the Rhine* (1934), to commit themselves in favor of his "revolution." The communists kept a torch alight for Stalin, and attracted some attention and some dedicated feelings, but the great majority of Americans watched events abroad passively, when they watched them at all. They were much more impressed by the abdication of Edward VIII in behalf of the woman he loved than by Nazi Germany's investment of the Saar. Persuaded as they were that Americans had died in vain during World War I, they felt secure in their anti-militarism — secure enough to believe their indifference to the world shielded them from involvement in its affairs. They patronized Robert E. Sherwood's *Idiot's Delight* (1936), which merely exploited in dramatic form the findings of a congressional committee which had investigated the munitions business, and they adopted the modish attitude of despising the Merchants of Death. The great strike movement of the middle Thirties interested them: general strikes in San Francisco and Minneapolis, giant strikes in Akron, Detroit, Chicago, and elsewhere, duels on the picket line and sit-down strikes. Above all, they pondered the policies of the New Deal, and by and large found that it was trying to minister to their wants.

Hence, it is not surprising that Thirties writing should have been realistic, pragmatic, regardful of society, and serious. There was too little humor, too little good humor. It fostered a concern for people, but as economic integers, as people who were insecure. Moreover, it suggested that they had duties to society, and would suffer if they reneged on their obligations. Even those who declared bitterly that "social significance" inhibited writers dared not deprecate social responsibility in principle.

In our time, Thirties writing, more than Thirties leaders and other social figures, has been on the defensive. Murray Kempton, in *Part of Our Time* (1955), an appeal in behalf of the Thirties, argues that it could not have been all bad. He points to gains in labor organization, in Negro opportunity, in resistance to fascism. He points to social security and other accomplishments of the Roosevelt Administration. No one outside communist ranks any longer defends the communist record. Interestingly, there has been some defense of Government art in the Kennedy Administration, though its partisans are vague on details.

No decade has actually required defense. All of them contain good and bad art. All of them need to apologize for obnoxious partisans, and can take pride in pleasing and distinguished characters. American competitiveness between the decades has been one of the more grotesque manifestations of American belief that one can "get ahead" by derogating everybody else. We feel compelled to declare that Americans are better than any other people in the world, that our twentieth century is better than our nineteenth. And so, naturally, we must take our stand in favor of one decade over another. On which side are you: the Twenties or the Thirties? I am on the side of both, to the extent that they produced, in this case, worthy and generous thinkers and littérateurs. They contributed to our sense of the possibilities of life. They produced a vision of affairs which we can mull over for possible use or rejection today. They can be criticized or approved. At their best, they can divert us and stimulate us, often in surprising ways — ways we have forgotten. Here is part of their record.

They were a product of a particular set of circumstances. They were ushered in by a devastating economic collapse in 1929, which bemused and frightened the nation. They were ushered out in 1939

Introduction to the Original Edition [29]

by Great Britain's capitulation to Adolf Hitler at Munich. Suddenly, war was not a threat, but a fact. A peace-time draft of men for the armed forces went under way. The *New York Times,* in an editorial, apologized to the young men in the name of the older generation for having left them so dreary a world as they were now compelled to meet. The government had found a solid formula for continuous production, but none whatever for continuing peace. The Thirties were over.

— Louis Filler

THE WAY THINGS ARE

> Heap o' stir an' no biskits.
> Enjoyin' poor health.
> Life is short an' full of blisters.
> Money thinks I'm dead.
>
> from "Phrases of the People,"
Americana No. 5, recorded by
Harris Dickson, Vicksburg, Miss.,
for the Federal Writers Project

While the crash only took place six months ago, I'm convinced we have now passed the worst and with continued unity of effort we shall rapidly recover. . . .

President Herbert Hoover, May 1, 1930:
from Edward Angly, comp., *Oh Yeah?* (1931)

Jesse Isidor Strauss, president of R. H. Macy & Co., published the following credo in New York newspapers, in March 1933:

> I trust my government.
> I trust our banks.
> I do not expect the impossible.
> I shall do nothing hysterical.
> I know that if I try now to get all my cash
>   I shall certainly make matters worse.
> I will not stampede. I will not lose my nerve.
> I will keep my head.

Macy's at that time sold only for cash.

from Mark Sherwin and Charles Lam
Markmann, *One Week in March* (1961)

Sherwood Anderson

REVOLT IN SOUTH DAKOTA

The 1930's found Sherwood Anderson high and dry: his short stories behind him, his Twenties probings into sexual feelings and attitudes no longer of public concern. He drew upon his old Ohio heritage: he was, after all, a man of the people, had once lived their individualistic hopes of material success and social dignity. He could understand how stunned were the farmers, workers, and businessmen in the small towns, who suddenly found themselves with nothing to do, and with little hope of getting anything remunerative to do, no matter how early they got up in the morning to look for jobs, no matter how much they prayed or did without. Anderson took to the road, writing articles for Today, *for several years a kind of unofficial organ of the New Deal. It printed a great variety of articles, editorials, expressions of faith and discontent which are still to be reviewed. From Anderson's travels "on the road" — which compare strikingly with those of Kerouac — came Anderson's book,* Puzzled America. *He revised his* Today *articles to some degree, and they were the better for the revision.*

THE American woman, Gertrude Stein, who had been out of America for twenty-five or thirty years, living all of those years in Paris, had come back. She had been going about America — having a look — sometimes in a car, sometimes in a train, again by plane. She wanted to talk. She was excited.

"But you should have a year, two years, five years, just to begin to see it," I said. I didn't think she could get much of us, understand much, in a few weeks of flying about.

Right away, however, she said something. "Even when you are in a plane," she said, "you can tell when you pass out of one State and into another." She thought it was true, that there was always a sharp difference. "Now you are in Missouri. You pass on into Iowa or fly over Ohio.

"There is something in the way in which the farm buildings are grouped, in the way the towns are built, in something you feel in the people in the towns."

Miss Stein, by her talk, set me thinking of a kind of individuality I had myself seen and felt in the States.

For example, there is South Dakota. I had come down out of Minnesota, had taken a look at North Dakota. Was it true, as Miss Stein said, that I should be able to tell, even before I began talking with people, going to meetings, going into churches and stores, when I had come into a quite different State?

Almost at once I did feel a sharp difference. If North Dakota is the most radical of the States up in the Northwest section of the Middlewest, South Dakota is surely the most conservative.

And why? To be sure the State went for Roosevelt this year, but for many years States to the south of it, Nebraska and Kansas being, to say the least, sometimes politically experimental, North Dakota and Minnesota being pretty definitely and permanently radical, why did South Dakota begin by being conservative and remain so?

It is a self-conscious State, much more so I thought than Minnesota or North Dakota. At least in the other States people did not keep asking me the question, "What do they think of us back East? Are they interested? Are you going to write, boosting our State?" The country newspaper man, over the border in Minnesota — I won't put down the name of his town — some of the patriots of South Dakota might go over the border and get him — he told me — "It's a State that never should have been settled," he said.

It was his notion that the buffalo grass that used to grow out on the wide, wind-swept plains would have held the country down. "Now, it may all blow away," he said. "They have got this notion of dry farming in their heads. It's dry all right," he said. I walked with the country newspaperman about the streets of the frozen little town while he told me of the dust storms that came out of South Dakota, out of the plains beyond the Missouri, making the skies black at midday.

"Why," said the newspaperman, "I have an uncle who took up a farm out there.

"It was a farm until he plowed it," he said. "Then it blew away." By his story the uncle went about over his fields, picking up Indian arrow heads that had been buried a foot under ground. "The dry soil that had been plowed had drifted like drifting snow," he said. "He had planted trees and they were all killed. The fences were buried under the dust drifts.

"And if it isn't a dry season there are the grasshoppers to eat you up," he said. I got a blue-enough picture from him.

You go into South Dakota having some such picture in your mind and what you find is disconcerting. I went to a meeting of the men's club at a church in a South Dakota town. All day I had been driving. Although I had been for days in heavy snows there was little or no snow on the plains.

It is true I had been seeing the sand-and-dust drifts, against the fences, trees killed by the drought, great patches of the trees' bark dropped off — there are no native trees — about each white farmhouse, sitting out on the long rolling plains, some farmer had planted trees about his house to serve as a wind break ———

— Now, in great sections of the State, the trees are all killed — man's eternal and so often tragic war with nature — his struggle to command and control — out on the plains it is all there, to be seen, in the raw.

You see all this, noting the desolation brought by the drought, expecting to find a desolated and downtrodden people mourning in the streets, and then you go into one of the towns. There is a surprise for you. The people do all seem to be wearing last year's clothes and driving cars, plenty of them groaning, sputtering Model T Fords, but there is an air of cheerfulness. Right out in the heart of the drought country I saw towns, far from any pine trees, all festooned with green for the holidays. The men at the men's meeting at the church were cheerful fellows. They didn't seem too much discouraged. I could have seen many sadder-looking more beaten men in any industrial town of the East. At the men's meeting in the church there was an effort made to raise money. A number of boys and girls from the country had been invited to a young people's meeting to be held in the town. There would be a certain expense. They were to stay but one day. It would cost fifty cents to feed a boy or a girl. "Who is willing to do it?" asked a man who had got to his feet. A merchant got up. "It isn't the money," he said. He thought a scheme ought to be worked out. "They should be made to feel they have earned it," he said. He thought it would be better for them. "But what, in Heaven's name are they to do?" some one asked. "I don't know," said the merchant.

I found a man at the men's meeting who wanted to talk. You always find them.

And so we went from the church to his house.

He also had got it into his head that I might be writing something about South Dakota and was afraid I wouldn't be fair. The man had five or six big ears of corn lying on the mantel in the living room of his house. "I can't offer you anything to drink," he said apologetically. "We're a dry State yet.

Revolt in South Dakota [35

"I mean about liquor," he added quickly. He seemed afraid that if I did write I would over-emphasize the drought, its consequences to the State, etc. He had a cousin who owned a farm in the Sioux River Valley, over near the Iowa line. He took one of the big ears and broke it into two pieces, demanding that I note how closely and firmly the grains of corn were set together. "It's from my brother's farm, right here in South Dakota and was raised this year," he said proudly. I had found this feeling everywhere, a kind of touchiness, as though, to these people of South Dakota, the land on which they lived was like a child that misbehaved sometimes — as for example the drought that could not be concealed — but that was nevertheless their child. "Be careful how you speak of it," they all seemed to be saying.

The man in whose house I sat began telling me — his voice full of resentment — of a writer from one of the big Eastern magazines who had come out during the drought. "The dirty cuss," he said vehemently. "I hate such men," he added. The writer had come into the land in the terrifically hot, dry summer and had seen and written of cattle dying and lying in fence corners, had been in sections of the State to which water had to be hauled by train, had been in one of the dust storms, the sky black with dust, top soil of thousands of acres blowing away, no cars running in the roads, men and women huddled in their houses, the street lights in towns lighted at noonday. "Man, what do you expect?" I asked. I tried to explain to him about us writers. "That sort of thing is just meat and drink for one of us.

"If not to find in all of this something terrible or strange and then to play up the terrible and strange, why do you suppose an Eastern magazine would send one of us out here?" I tried to explain to him how I had myself come into the State with my mind already half made up. For one thing I had been reading a novel, written out of the dry country — and a very good one, too — the bitterness of men and women on farms, seeing the crops slowly shrivel up, the ponds and wells go dry, a kind of insanity coming over the people.

"Yes, I know," the man said. He made a queer twisted movement with his lips. "Do you know what we did? We went to church and knelt down. It seemed to me we were like fools there, on our knees, Sunday after Sunday, praying for rain, and no rain coming at all.

"I guess if God wants to send rain he doesn't have to ask us," the man added, and when I left his house, to step out into the biting cold of the night — his house was at the very edge of his town — it was a moonlit night — he had come after me, bare-headed out of the house, and as we stood in the yard we could see for miles out over the South Dakota plains — there were farmhouses with big red barns out there, the cribs and barns empty now, they stuck up out of the land like sore thumbs that night, the trees so carefully planted and tended about the houses all dead now. The man still had something on his mind. "On the whole," he said, "I think we'd rather you writers let us alone." He got bitter.

"If you are going to write, saying ours is a no-good country, why not write in the same way about parts of Iowa and North Dakota?

"And Nebraska, too?

"Or better than that, why not come here in a good year?"

The man turned and walked away from me, back into the house, slamming his door. He was like many others I saw, very determined about the real worth to man, as a place to live, of his State.

As for the long and persistent dryness of the drought I myself saw something. There was a little white church sitting beside a road out in a great flat place. There was not a tree in sight. "It would be here they came to pray for the rain," I thought. This was in a very dry section of the State. That day I had seen places where the sand and dust drifts had all but covered the fences, had seen the corn in cornfields, cut and shocked, the shocks far apart, standing up hardly higher than my knees. I stopped the car and getting out went to walk around the church, thinking, as I did so, of what the man in the house had told me.

Thinking also of what I had seen. As when I had driven down out of the hills of southwestern Virginia, Kentucky, and Tennessee into Ohio, Illinois, and Indiana I had been struck by the opulence and magnificence of the farmhouses and out-buildings, so again in South Dakota. "In these other States, that is to say in Ohio, Indiana, and Illinois, there would at least have been forests," I told myself. In South Dakota they would have had to bring in the timber for all of the buildings, hauling it for hundreds of miles. "It would have cost like the Old Harry," I thought. "These people are right to be proud of what their land can do in a good year."

I walked around the country church. It was a week day and the church was closed. It didn't matter. The long dry year just passed had done its work well. It had curled up the boards covering the sides of the building so that you could look through and see the daylight streaming in from the opposite side, that certainly making a picture in the mind to be remembered, of people coming there, to worship, in the midst of the drought the sun-burned people, men and women ———

You have to think of them as coming from distant farmhouses, past their own fields, where the corn is shrivelled away to nothingness, the fields their own hands have plowed, planted, and tended, only to see the crops all burn away to a dry ash of dust.

Revolt in South Dakota

Then kneeling down in the church to pray, the very boards of the church cracking and curling under the dry heat, the paint on the boards frying in the hot winds, perhaps a breeze blowing, and the dust of the fields sifting in through the cracks. Dust in the mouths of the people as they prayed for the rain.

It may all be a matter of the land . . . the land men all, or nearly all, naturally conservative. The South Dakota newspaperman with whom I talked late into a cold night thought it was so. There are practically no industries in the State. In the far West, in the Black Hills, there is a gold mine out of which millions have been taken. They are still taking it, and the farmers would like to grab the mine. They would like to make it lift the load of taxes off of the land. More than a third of the people of the State, the farmers and the town people, are now on relief.

I went up into a little interior town. It was still very cold. Deep snow in Iowa and in Minnesota but none here. In the town they had been praying for the snow. It would put moisture back into the baked-out ground, help with next year's crop. In an Eastern magazine I had read an article, written so I had heard by a man of the town, an article full of the promise of revolt, and in a little country print shop I found two old men.

The print shop was very small. There was a small stove, and an old man came to sit with me. He was a gentle-faced old man with snow-white hair. We spoke of automobiles, and he told me that he owned a Ford. "It is a Model T," he said. "I bought it for twenty-five dollars." He said he had driven the Ford some twenty-five thousand miles. The old man had a passion. "I go to some print shop, like this," he said. "I work there. In my spare time I print little books.

"I am going to organize a new party," he said. He laughed softly, telling me of a convention he had called. I gathered that he had some plan for a new handling of the monetary question. "I named a town where we would hold the convention and drove there in my Ford." I gathered that this was during the summer when the whole country was burned dry, when the corn in the fields was going dead in the dry winds. I imagined him going along the road, meeting on the way men and women who were hauling water, perhaps from the Missouri River, hauling it across the plains, the sky overhead gray with the floating dust. The little old man had already given me one of his booklets to read, the booklets half the size of an ordinary envelope and printed on cheap newsprint, some eight small pages in each booklet. He had written a number of little childlike stories, each story to illustrate some phase of what would happen to society if his plan were adopted. Afterwards I saw the old man at a big Farmers Union meeting, a meeting to which I went filled with hope. I wanted a real story and had been told, it had been intimated to me, that at the meeting some of the orators among the farmers would break forth. I was to hear things that would startle me but nothing of the sort happened at all. Although I saw many destitute-looking farmers at the meeting, heard stories enough of men who a few years before were prosperous men and were now on relief, the meeting was very quiet, very orderly. There was a young high school girl who got up and sang, rather badly I thought. The mayor of the town made a speech. He was a man of fifty and boasted that he had never been out of his State. "I was born here. I am still here," he declared proudly. Several country boys, a small-town orchestra, played a piece on guitars and banjos. A big farmer leaned over and whispered to me. "They've been on the radio," he said. The meeting was much like some of the meetings of Kiwanis I attended a few years ago, when I was active in running my country newspapers in Virginia.

But there was my gentle little old man of the pamphlets. He was going about. He was distributing his booklets. He came and whispered to me. "I am stirring up a lot of interest here," he said. On that day, when I was visiting the little print shop, where he was employed temporarily and where he had talked to me at length, trying to make me understand his plan for the new party based on a new handling of our monetary system, that would save the agricultural West, his battered but still serviceable Ford standing in a vacant lot back of the shop, on that occasion I had been very insistent on the article I had read in the magazine.

As I have suggested there were two old men in the shop. The second man was setting up an advertisement. He was tall and silent but was also a sweet-faced man. "So there was this article," I said. "I am looking for signs of revolt.

"After all I am also a writer. I have come out here. If there is revolt here I would like to know of it. Who are the leaders? What's going on?" I asked. I had it in my mind that the article in question had been written by a native of the little town out on the plains. It had been quite specific. "In a few months, at most in a year or two, revolt would come." That was about the tone of what I had read. The tall old man, who was setting up the advertisement of a January white sale for the town's general store, came to stand by the stove. Both of the old men laughed. The smaller of the two men rubbed his hands together.

"That was like the convention I called for my new party," he said.

"You see I went to the town where the convention was to be held in my Ford. I drove a long ways. There vas a dust storm and I had to stay overnight in a barn.

"I was the only one who came," he said giggling.

He and the tall old man seemed deeply amused. "As for that article you read in that magazine," the tall man said, the article about the revolt coming in South Dakota" — (the whole thing must have been a standing joke between the two). "These Eastern fellows, writers, who come out here — " he looked at the small man and winked. "No," he said, "it wasn't written by any one in this town.

"There was an Eastern fellow, like you," he said. "He came out here. He was here for a while. He went about speaking to people as you are now doing. He was a lucky one," he said.

"Do you know what," said the smaller of the two men, leaning over the stove. His eyes were shining. "Do you know what?

"He sold the article he had written for a hundred and seventy-five dollars. Think of the booklets I could print and distribute for all of that money," said the little old man. "I could get my new party started at last."

He had stopped smiling. I thought there was a hungry look in his eyes and in the eyes of the tall one as well.

Tom Kromer

WAITING FOR NOTHING

Tom Kromer was of poor West Virginia background, had gone three years to college, and had some experience as a teacher. He drifted from his moorings, descended into Skid Road, and, living from day to day, all but lost his language and sense of direction. Somehow, he held on to basic principles of intellectual survival, and began to scribble his feelings and experiences on pieces of paper. The book, when published, was dedicated: "To Jolene who turned off the gas."

Waiting for Nothing was not very successful, but it at least called

> *Kromer to human attention. The communists made an effort to exploit him as a victim of capitalism. He wrote a review for the* New Masses *about another book which dealt with social conditions. But apparently his experiences had exhausted him. He found a job and disappeared from view.*

It is night. I am walking along this dark street, when my foot hits a stick. I reach down and pick it up. I finger it. It is a good stick, a heavy stick. One sock from it would lay a man out. It wouldn't kill him, but it would lay him out. I plan. Hit him where the crease is in his hat, hard, I tell myself, but not too hard. I do not want his head to hit the concrete. It might kill him. I do not want to kill him. I will catch him as he falls. I can frisk him in a minute. I will pull him over in the shadows and walk off. I will not run. I will walk.

I turn down a side street. This is a better street. There are fewer houses along this street. There are large trees on both sides of it. I crouch behind one of these. It is dark here. The shadows hide me. I wait. Five, ten minutes, I wait. Then under an arc light a block away a man comes walking. He is a well-dressed man. I can tell even from that distance. I have good eyes. This guy will be in the dough. He walks with his head up and a jaunty step. A stiff does not walk like that. A stiff shuffles with tired feet, his head huddled in his coat collar. This guy is in the dough. I can tell that. I clutch my stick tighter. I notice that I am calm. I am not scared. I am calm. In the crease of his hat, I tell myself. Not too hard. Just hard enough. On he comes. I slink farther back in the shadows. I press closer against this tree. I hear his footsteps thud on the concrete walk. I raise my arm high. I must swing hard. I poise myself. He crosses in front of me. Now is my chance. Bring it down hard, I tell myself, but not too hard. He is under my arm. He is right under my arm, but my stick does not come down. Something has happened to me. I am sick in the stomach. I have lost my nerve. Christ, I have lost my nerve. I am shaking all over. Sweat stands out on my forehead. I can feel the clamminess of it in the cold, damp night. This will not do. This will not do. I've got to get me something to eat. I am starved.

I stagger from the shadows and follow behind this guy. He had a pretty good face. I could tell as he passed beneath my arm. This guy ought to be good for two bits. Maybe he will be good for four bits. I quicken my steps. I will wait until he is under an arc light before I give him my story. I do not have long to wait. He stops under an arc light and fumbles in his pocket for a cigarette. I catch up with him.

"Pardon me, mister, but could you help a hungry man get — "

"You goddam bums give me a pain in the neck. Get the hell away from me before I call a cop."

He jerks his hand into his overcoat pocket. He wants me to think he has a gun. He has not got a gun. He is bluffing.

I hurry down the street. The bastard. The dirty bastard. I could have laid him out cold with the stick, and he calls me a goddam bum. I had the stick over his head, and I could not bring it down. I am yellow. I can see that I am yellow. If I am not yellow, why am I shaking like a leaf? I am starved, too, and I ought to starve. A guy without enough guts to get himself a feed ought to starve.

I walk on up the street. I pass people, but I let them pass. I do not ding them. I have lost my nerve. I walk until I am on the main stem. Never have I been so hungry. I have got to get me something to eat. I pass a restaurant. In the window is a roast chicken. It is brown and fat. It squats in a silver platter. The platter is filled with gravy. The gravy is thick and brown. It drips over the side, slow. I stand there and watch it drip. Underneath it the sign says: "All you can eat for fifty cents." I lick my lips. My mouth waters. I sure would like to sit down with that before me. I look inside. It is a classy joint. I can see waitresses in blue and white uniforms. They hurry back and forth. They carry heavy trays. The dishes stick over the edge of the trays. There are good meals still left in these trays. They will throw them in the garbage cans. In the center of the floor a water fountain bubbles. It is made of pink marble. The chairs are red leather, bordered in black. The counter is full of men eating. They are eating, and I am hungry. There are long rows of tables. The cloths on them are whiter than white. The glassware sparkles like diamonds on its whiteness. The knives and forks on the table are silver. I can tell that they are pure silver from where I am standing on the street. They shine so bright. I cannot go in there. It is too classy, and besides there are too many people. They will laugh at my seedy clothes, and my shoes without soles.

I stare in at this couple that eat by the window. I pull my coat collar up around my neck. A man will look hungrier with his coat collar up around his neck. These people are in the dough. They are in evening clothes. This woman is sporting a satin dress. The blackness of it shimmers and glows in the light that comes from the chandelier that hangs from the dome. Her fingers are covered with diamonds. There are diamond bracelets on her wrists. She is beautiful. Never have I seen a more beautiful woman. Her lips are red. They are even redder against the whiteness of her teeth when she laughs. She laughs a lot.

I stare in at the window. Maybe they will know a hungry man when they see him. Maybe this guy will be willing to shell out a couple of nickels to a hungry stiff. It is chicken they are eating. A chicken like the one in the window. Brown and fat. They do not eat. They only nibble. They are nibbling at chicken, and they are not even hungry. I am starved. That chicken was meant for a hungry man. I watch them as they cut it into tiny bits. I watch their forks as they carry them to their mouths. The man is facing me. Twice he glances out of the window. I meet his eyes with mine. I wonder if he can tell the eyes of a hungry man. He has never been hungry himself. I can tell that. This one has always nibbled at chicken. I see him speak to the woman. She turns her head and looks at me through the window. I do not look at her. I look at the chicken on the plate. They can see that I am a hungry man. I will stand here until they come out. When they come out, they will maybe slip me a four-bit piece.

A hand slaps down on my shoulder. It is a heavy hand. It spins me around in my tracks.

"What the hell are you doin' here?" It is a cop.

"Me? Nothing," I say. "Nothing, only watching a guy eat chicken. Can't a guy watch another guy eat chicken?"

"Wise guy," he says. "Well, I know what to do with wise guys."

He slaps me across the face with his hand, hard. I fall back against the building. His hands are on the holster by his side. What can I do? Take it is all I can do. He will plug me if I do anything.

"Put up your hands," he says.

I put up my hands.

"Where's your gat?" he says.

"I have no gat," I say. "I never had a gat in my life."

"That's what they all say," he says.

He pats my pockets. He don't find anything. There is a crowd around here now. Everybody wants to see what is going on. They watch him go through my pockets. They think I am a stick-up guy. A hungry stiff stands and watches a guy eat chicken, and they think he is a stick-up guy. That is a hell of a note.

"All right," he says, "get down the street before I run you in. If I ever catch you stemming this beat, I will sap the living hell out of you. Beat it."

I hurry down the street. I know better than not to hurry. The lousy son of a bitch. I had a feed right in my lap, and he makes me beat it. That guy was all right in there. He was a good guy. That guy could see I was a hungry man. He would have fixed me up right when he came out.

Waiting For Nothing [43

I pass a small café. There are no customers in here. There is only a guy sitting by the cash register. This is my place. I go in and walk up to him. He is a fat guy with a double chin. I can see very well that he hadn't missed many meals in his life.

"Mister," I say. "have you got some kind of work like washing dishes I can do for something to eat? I am damn near starved. I'll do anything."

He looks hard at me. I can see right away that this guy is no good.

"Tell me," he says, "in God's name, why do you stiffs always come in here? You're the fourth guy in the last half-hour. I can't even pay my rent. There ain't been a customer in here for an hour. Go to some of the big joints where they do all the business."

"Could you maybe give me a cup of coffee?" I say. "That would hold me over. I've been turned down at about twenty places already."

"I can't give you nothing. Coffee costs money," he says. "Go to one of the chain stores and bum your coffee. When you've got any money, where do you go to spend it? You go to the chains. I can't do nothing for you."

I walk out. Wouldn't even give a hungry man a cup of coffee. Can you imagine a guy like that? The bastard. I'd like to catch him on a dark street. I'd give him a cup of coffee, and a sock on the snout he wouldn't soon forget. I walk. When I pass a place where there are no customers, I go in. They turn me down flat. No business, they say. Why don't I go to the big places? I am getting sick in the stomach. I feel like vomiting. I have to get me something to eat. What the hell? I will hit one of these classy joints. Pride! What do I care about pride? Who cares about me? Nobody. The bastards don't care if I live or die.

I pass a joint. A ritzy place. It is all white inside. The tables are full. The counters are full. They are eating, and I am hungry. These guys pay good dough for a feed, and they are not even hungry. When they are through, they will maybe tip the waitress four bits. It is going to be cold tonight. Four bits will buy me a flop that will be warm, and not cold.

I go into this joint and walk up to the middle of the counter. I flop down in a seat. These cash customers gape at me. I am clean, but my front is seedy. They know I don't belong in here. I know I don't belong in here, too. But I am hungry. A hungry man belongs where there is food. Let them gape.

This waiter sticks the menu out to me. I do not take it. What do I want with a menu?

"Buddy," I say, "I am broke and hungry. Could you maybe give me something to eat?"

He shakes his head no, he cannot give me anything to eat.

"Busy. Manager's not in. Sorry."

I can feel my face getting red. They are all gaping at me. They crane their necks to gape at me. I get up out of this seat and walk towards the door. I can't get anything to eat anywhere. God damn them, if I could get my fingers on a gat.

"Say, buddy."

I turn around. A guy in a gray suit is motioning to me. He sits at the middle of the counter. I go back.

"You hungry?"

"I am damn near starved. I have not eat in two days, and that is the God's truth."

"Down on your luck?" he says.

"Down so far I don't know how far," I say.

"Sit down. I've been down on my luck myself. I know how it is."

I sit down beside him.

"What'll it be?" he says.

"You order it," I say. "Anything you say."

"Order up anything you want. Fill up."

"A ham sandwich and a cup of coffee," I tell this waiter.

He is all smiles now, damn him. He sees where he can make a dime. I bet he owns this joint. He said the manager wasn't in, and I bet he's the manager himself.

"Give him a beef-steak dinner with everything that goes with it," says this guy in the gray suit. "This man is hungry."

This is a good guy. He orders my steak dinner in a loud voice so everyone can see how big-hearted he is, but he is a good guy anyway. Any guy is a good guy when he is going to buy me a steak dinner. Let him show off a little bit. He deserves to show off a little bit. I sit here at this counter, and I feel like pinching myself. This is a funny world. Five minutes ago I was down in the dumps. Here I am now waiting on a steak dinner in a classy joint. Let them gape. What do I care? Didn't they ever see a hungry man before?

This waiter shoves my dinner in front of me. Christ, I've never seen anything look so good. This steak with all the trimmings is a picture for sore eyes. Big and thick and brown, it sits there. Around it, all around it, are tomatoes, sliced. I start in. I do not look up from my plate. They are all gaping at me. Fill up and get out of here, I tell myself.

The guy three seats down gets up and calls for his check. He is a little guy with horn-rimmed glasses. The check is thirty cents. I see it before the waiter turns it upside down. Why do they always have to turn a man's check upside down? Afraid the price will turn his stomach? This guy pulls a dollar out of his pocket and walks over to the cashier. I wonder how it feel to have a buck in your jeans. Four bits will set me on top of the world right now. A good warm flop tonight and breakfast in the morning. That's the way to live. Pay for what you get, and look every copper you pass on the street straight in the eye, and say: "You bastard, I don't owe you a cent."

The cashier hands this guy his change. He walks back and lays it down by my plate.

"Flop for tonight," he says.

He speaks low. He is not trying to show off like this guy in the gray suit. Not that I don't think that this guy in the gray suit is not all right. He is a good guy. He bought me a steak dinner when I was damn near starved. No, he is a good guy, but he likes to show off a little bit. I look up at this guy. He is walking out of the door. I do not thank him. He is too far away, and besides, what can I say? I can't believe it. Thirty cents, the check said. Thirty cents from a dollar. That makes seventy cents. I got seventy cents. A good warm flop tonight, breakfast in the morning, and enough left over for cigarettes. No fishing around in the gutters for snipes for me. I will have me a package of tailor-made cigarettes. I pick up this change and stick it in my pocket. That guy is a mind-reader. I was sitting here wishing I had four bits, and before I know it, I got seventy cents. That guy is all right. I bet that guy has had troubles of his own some time. I bet he knows how it is to be hungry. I hurry up with my dinner. In here I am only a hungry stiff. Outside with seventy cents in my kick, I am as good as the next one. Say, I'd like to meet that guy, and I had a million dollars.

"Do you remember the time you give me seventy cents in a restaurant? You don't? Well, you give me seventy cents in a restaurant one time. I was damn near starved. I was just about ready to bump myself off, and you give me seventy cents."

I hand him a roll of bills. It is a big roll of bills. I walk off. That guy won't have to worry any more about dough. There was plenty in that roll to keep him in wheatcakes the rest of his life.

I finish my pie and get up.

"Thank you, Jack," I say to this guy in the gray suit. "I certainly appreciate what you done for me. I was damn near starved."

"That's all right, buddy," he says. "Glad to help a hungry man."

He speaks loud. They can hear him to the other end of the counter. He is a good guy, though. He bought me a steak dinner.

I walk outside. I put my hand in my pocket and jingle my money.

It feels good to have money to jingle. I am not broke or hungry now. I cannot imagine I was broke and hungry an hour ago. No park for me tonight. No lousy mission flop.

I go down the street and walk through the park. I look at these benches with their iron legs and their wooden slats.

"To hell with you," I say. "I have nothing to do with you. I do not know you. You will leave no grooves in my back tonight. Tonight I will have me a good warm flop. I will have me a flop that will be warm, and not cold."

I look at these stiffs sprawled out on the benches. I like to walk to the time of the jingle in my pocket and think how miserable I was last night.

It is getting late, and I am tired. I head down the skid road and stop in front of my four-bit flop. There is no marquee in front to keep the guests from getting wet. There is no doorman dressed like a major in the Imperial Guards. They do not need these things, because all the suites are on the fourth floor. I am puffing when I get to the top of the rickety stairs. At the landing a guy squats on a stool in a wire cage.

"I want a four-bit flop," I say, "a four-bit flop with a clean bed."

This guy is hunched over a desk with his belly sticking out of a dirty green sweater. He rubs his hands together and shows his yellow teeth in a grin. He winks one of his puffy eyes.

"For a little extra, just a little extra," he says, "I can give you a nice room, a very nice room. But it is too big a room for one. You will be lonely. A little company will not go bad, eh? Especially if the company is very young and very pretty?" He licks his puffy lips. "We have a girl, a new girl. Only tonight she came. Because it is you, and she must learn, only a dollar extra, yes?"

I look at him, and I think of the fish-eyed, pot-bellied frogs I used to gig when I was a kid. I imagine myself sticking a sharp gig into his belly and watching him kick and croak.

"A four-bit flop is what I want," I say. "I do not wish to play nursemaid to your virgins. I am broke, and besides, I am sleepy."

"But you should see her," he says, "so tiny, so beautiful. I will get her. You will change your mind when you see her."

"I do not want to see her," I say.

"So high," he says. "Only so high she is, and so beautiful. I will get her. You will see how beautiful she is."

He climbs off his stool.

"Do you get me a flop or do I have to bury my foot in your dirty belly?" I say.

"Some other time, then," he says, "some other time when you have more money. You will see how very beautiful."

He waddles through the dirty hall. I follow him. His legs are swollen with dropsy. His ankles overflow his ragged house-slippers and hang down in folds over the sides. I can imagine I hear the water gurgling as he walks. He opens the door and holds out his hand for the money.

"How many beds in this room?" I say.

"Forty," he says, "but they are good, clean beds."

I walk into this room. It is a big room. It is filled with these beds. They do not look so hot to me. They are only cots. They look lousy. I bet they are lousy, but a stiff has got to sleep, lousy or not. Most of these beds are already full. I can hear the snores of the stiffs as they sleep. I pick me out a flop at the other end of the room. There is no mattress. Only two dirty blankets. They are smelly. Plenty of stiffs have slept under these blankets.

Four or five stiffs are gathered in a bunch over next to the wall. I watch them. I know very well what they are going to do. They are gas hounds, and they are going to get soused on derail.

"Give me that handkerchief," says this red-headed guy with the wens on his face. "I will squeeze more alky out of a can of heat than any stiff I know."

This little guy with the dirty winged collar examines this can of heat.

"The bastards," he says. "You know what? They're makin' the cans smaller and smaller. This can right here is smaller than they was yestiddy. The dirty crooks. They'd take the bread right out of your mouths, the bastards would."

He jumps up and down as he talks. His red eyes flash. The sweat stands in beads on his forehead. How can a guy get so mad about the size of a can of heat? Well, it does not take much to make you mad when you have been swigging heat for a year.

This red-headed guy takes this can of heat and empties it out in a handkerchief. The handkerchief is filthy, but that don't worry them none. What's a little filth to a gas hound? Pretty soon they will be high and nothing will worry them. Pretty soon they won't have any more troubles. This derail will see to that. They squeeze this stuff out of the handkerchief and let it drip into the glass. They pour water into the glass. The smell of this stuff will turn your stomach, but it don't turn their stomach. They are going to drink it. They take turns about taking a swig. They elbow each other out of the way to get at the glass. When it is all gone, they squeeze out some more. They choke and gag when this stuff goes down, but they drink it. Pretty soon they have guzzled all the heat they have. In a little while they are singing. I do not blame these guys for getting soused on derail. A guy can't always be thinking. If a guy is thinking all the time, pretty soon he will go crazy. A man is bound to land up in the booby-hatch if he stays on the fritz. So these guys make derail and drink it.

This stiff in the bed next to mine turns up his nose at these guys who are soused up on derail.

"I got my opinion of a guy who will drink derail," he says. "A guy who will drink derail is lower down than a skunk."

He pulls a bottle out from under his pillow. It is marked: "Bay Rum." There are directions on the label. It says it will grow new hair. It says it will stop the old from falling out. But this guy does not need the stuff to keep his hair from falling out. This stiff has not had a haircut for a year.

"This is the stuff," he says. "I have been drinkin' this old stuff for a year, and I don't even get a headache afterwards."

He sticks this bottle up to his trap, and he does not take it down until he has emptied it.

"This is good stuff," he says. "It has got derail beat all to a frazzle."

I do not see how it can be such good stuff when he has to gag so much when he downs it. But that is his business. If a guy has been drinking this stuff for a year, he ought to know if it is good stuff or not. Pretty soon this guy is dead to the world. He sprawls out on his bunk and sleeps. He sleeps with his eyes wide open. Christ, he gives me the willies with his eyes wide open like that. He looks like a dead man, but I never see a dead man with his face covered with sweat like his is. It is plenty chilly in this room, but his face is covered with sweat. That is the bay rum coming out of him. A guy that has been drinking this stuff for a year must have plenty inside him. I bet the inside of his gut is covered with hair. That would be a good way to find out if this bay rum is a fake or not. When this stiff croaks from swigging too much bay rum, just cut him open. If his gut is not covered with hair, then this bay rum is a fake.

I watch him. I cannot keep my eyes off him. His legs twitch. He quivers and jerks. He is having a spasm. He almost jumps off the bed. All the time his eyes are wide open, and the sweat pours out of him. But he does not know what it is all about. He is dead to the world. If this is the good stuff, I will take the bad stuff. I will not even put this stuff on my hair. I would be afraid it would sink down into my gut and give me the spasms like this guy has got. The rest of these stiffs do not pay any attention to him. These bay horse fiends are old stuff to them. But they are not old stuff to me. It gets on my nerves. If this guy is going to act like this all night, I am going to walk the streets. It will be cold as hell walking the streets all night, but it will not be as bad as watching this guy jump up and down with his eyes wide open, and him dead to the world.

I cover up my head with this dirty blanket and try not to think about him.

Albert Jay Nock

JOURNAL OF FORGOTTEN DAYS
(September 1934)

Albert Jay Nock died in 1945; so firm was he in resisting infringement upon his personal life that Who's Who *could not obtain the date of his birth. He was a curious combination of extreme conservative and radical attitudes. Nock admired Thomas Jefferson, believed in the rule of the best, and considered himself one of the elect. He favored an education based on history and the classics. Henry George's Single Tax seemed to him a proper solution to economic troubles. Capitalism impressed him as a vulgar permutation of democracy. Nock despised naturalism in literature, but heartily enjoyed Rabelais and Finley Peter Dunne's "Mr. Dooley" essays. The New Deal was, to him, another uprising of the rabble, Franklin D. Roosevelt another Woodrow Wilson: both traitors to the educated and responsible classes. Nock's* Myth of a Guilty Nation *(1922) was a powerful indictment of war-makers. He edited the distinguished* Freeman, *and published his challenging* Theory of Education in the United States *(1932). His* Memoirs of a Superfluous Man *(1934) can stand beside Henry Adams'* Education. *With all his self-conscious objectivity, he was not immune to some forms of genteel anti-semitism.*

1 SEPTEMBER — The letters that people write to newspapers, calling on Roosevelt to give them an "assurance" about this-or-that, show such invincible ignorance that they almost make a Calvinist of me. "Assurance" about the currency, the tariff, the government's progress towards collectivism, and so on. Now, just what would an as-

surance from Roosevelt amount to, if he gave one? He gave assurances enough during his campaign, and what were they worth? Exactly what any jobseeker's assurances are ever worth. Mr. Roosevelt has never been known to the public in any capacity but that of a jobholder or jobhunter, and the American public has had a century-and-a-half's experience to prove that a jobholder or jobhunter is invariably, first and foremost, a common liar. One wonders how the proverb about the burnt child dreading the fire ever got into currency, for there is very little truth in it.

2 SEPTEMBER — I am beginning to be a little worried over the question whether Roosevelt's subsidized voters are going to stay bought. The Republicans will certainly offer to outbid him, and I am afraid they will win some of them away. The reports I hear from the West are none too encouraging; still, as things stand now, he could hardly lose. But I don't like these strikes, for however they turn out, they set up an atmosphere of restlessness and distraction that is bound to be unfavorable to the Administration. I would like to see things go to pot in an orderly way, so that the Administration's case would be clear. If the threatened textile strike comes off, it will make a bad mess, especially if the Relief Administration surreptitiously underwrites it, which I am half afraid they will do.

4 SEPTEMBER — Mussolini surely spiked Hitler's guns. As long as things apparently must go the way they are going, I am not so sorry to see the Italian once more rehabilitated to the point where he can cut a figure in international affairs. The erstwhile humble Wop has been laying up a good deal of character during all these years when he was out of everybody's reckoning, and now it seems to be making him something to be taken into account. A century ago, whenever any treaty brought a European monarch out the small end of the horn, he was compensated with a slice out of Italy. The English came into Naples with a supercilious air, and told the inhabitants that they ought to clean things up and treat their horses better. The biddable Dago took himself at other peoples' valuation. He accepted himself as ignoble, lazy, dirty, Mafia-ridden and dishonest, and that was that. Maybe something like Fascism was necessary to transform him — who knows? — or, I should say, to put his transformation into action and make it effective. One hates to think so, yet one has the chastening reflection that God moves in a mysterious way, etc.

6 SEPTEMBER — Huey Long's incredible doings in Louisiana raise

the question why one should pick on Hitler, and the further question whether self-righteousness is ever anything but a sawdust asset. One thinks, too, that when Al Capone takes a look at Long, Hitler, *et id genus omne*,[1] he must feel like a wretched piker. What might he now have been if he had only gone about things the right way!

7 SEPTEMBER — If I am any dab at a guess, the American vocabulary is going to be strained until its seams bust, some three years from now, when people really wake up and express themselves about Mr. Roosevelt. By comparison, the name of Woodrow Wilson will be a sweet and beautiful memory, in respect of actual damage done. It will take about that long, I fancy, for us to find out what a capital levy of forty-one cents in the dollar really means, and above all, what we have got in return for it. But resentment will evaporate in bad language, and perhaps a vote to bring on another "change of impostors," as John Adams said, such being the American way. How interesting it is, that in this most pretentious and swaggering country, a man can get himself elected to any kind of office on the strength of any kind of promises, then disregard them at his utter pleasure, with no action taken, or even any notice taken!

8 SEPTEMBER — An interesting experience. After a few words on public affairs, X remarked, "The real trouble is that the average American is a congenital crook." It startled me a little, because X never impressed me as a very perspicacious person. I was struck, too, the other day, when Y, who likewise never appeared the sort to set the river afire, casually called Roosevelt's misfeasances with the currency by their right name of capital tax. The point is that when men like X and Y talk that way, the cat may be wriggling out of the bag. It does not do to be too hopeful, and say that when it is out, something may begin to be done; but one is safe in saying that nothing can be done until it *is* out — which is of course a very different story.

10 SEPTEMBER — Something put me in mind today of Cassandre's interesting observation that there seems to be some sort of relationship between the indifference to squalor and the love of beauty. Traditionally, the artist is taken for granted as living in filth and disorder, and never washing. Also it seems that the parts of the world where the highest regard for beauty prevails are usually very dirty and squalid. Cassandre pretends that this correspondence of the two tend-

---

[1] And all that sort. [*Ed.*]

encies is probably natural, cleanliness being a newly acquired trait, apparently quite foreign to man in his natural state; and the artistic temperament is the one that is especially predisposed to revert to nature. This is plausible, and there may be something in it.

11 SEPTEMBER — Every day I am impressed anew by the lack of intellectual integrity in people who, one would think, should have it. There is a certain softness about it that I find disagreeable. If we had a modern Celsus, he might write a very brilliant chapter on the *kouphotes ton Amerikanon*.[1] K. and L. in conversation this evening agreed fully that Roosevelt's whole pre-Presidential record marked him as nothing in the world but an unscrupulous and self-seeking fellow, but they said they believed that when he became President he put all that behind him like another Henry V, and was out disinterestedly for the public good — and this in the face of the unconscionable Farley, and Roosevelt's own intervention in the Maine campaign, which was as flagrant and flagitious a piece of vote-buying as was ever seen anywhere in the world! What can any one think of that sort of pulpy self-deception? Back in the seventeenth century Bishop Butler laid down the greatest lesson in intellectual integrity ever put before people of our race and speech: "Things and actions are what they are, and the consequences of them will be what they will be; why then should we desire to be deceived?" It seems impossible, however, for Americans even to learn from Emerson that cause-and-effect is the chancellor of God; but as an Iron Chancellor its works and ways make those of Prince de Bismarck look like cheap failures.

13 SEPTEMBER — *Iolanthe* last night, in the cycle of Gilbert and Sullivan that D'Oyly Carte's troupe from the Savoy is giving here. I am presumptuous to say so, no doubt, but I am sure I have heard the thing better done. The reviewers are touting the troupe in what seems to me an uncritical way, almost servile, so if it be true that they are infallible, my judgment must be wrong. However, Gilbert and Sullivan, even indifferently done, are more than worth an evening. Besides, I remember Cassandre's saying, after a wretched performance at the Opéra-Comique, that it is a good thing to sit through a poor rendering once in a while, just to help one realize how good the best is.

14 SEPTEMBER — The hideous wreck of the *Morro Castle* shows how thoroughly corrupt the ethics of business are. Rea Irvin asked me to-

---

[1] The frivolity of the Americans.

day whether a thing like that could happen on a Dutch ship. I doubt it. The *Morro Castle* was built on American specifications, which allow a great deal of wood in the interior and superstructure; and its whole personnel seems to have been incompetent, disorganized and untrustworthy. Apparently the acting captain did as well as any one could, considering the owners' attitude towards salvage and the unreliability of his crew. It would be as easy to build an unburnable ship as an unsinkable ship; both are perfectly practicable, but an unsinkable ship would be inconvenient for passengers to get about in, and a fireproof ship would not be so pretty and would have fewer gadgets for passengers to play with. It would be an interesting experiment if some line put one fireproof and unsinkable ship into commission, to see what patronage it would get.

15 SEPTEMBER — With all deference to dissenting opinion, I say that the Communists are the most useful citizens we have. How could we have a strike or a food riot, or an incident like that of the *Morro Castle*, if we had no Communists? Governor Green, of Rhode Island, I see, was prompt to the minute with the right kind of talk about Communists in the textile strike up there, and he was hot after calling in Federal troops, but his legislature would not back him up, and he was left looking pretty cheap. There is amusement in this for any one who knows Rhode Island at all. It is the one State whose governor has no power or authority — practically none — but is in all essential respects a purely ornamental figure; and it is *vox populi* almost unanimously that Mr. Green fills the bill very well as a decorative person and also as a prize ass. I heard this on all sides when he took office; he got into a mess at once over some appointments. I did not pay much attention at the time, but his carryings-on over this textile strike seem to show that part of his reputation, at least, is honestly come by.

16 SEPTEMBER — A fine sprightly performance of *Pinafore* last night. I think this is the best of Gilbert and Sullivan's operettas. This troupe leaves something to be desired in the way of singing, the women especially, as I thought when I heard *Iolanthe* the other night. Still, the music of *Pinafore* makes pretty heavy demands on the average musical-comedy voice. It is odd that I should know the music of *Pinafore* throughout, with not the faintest idea of when or how I learned it; I never saw a performance until last night. I think, however, that my musical memories may be a little unusual. My earliest recollection is of a melody in the finale of the third act of *La Traviata*. I was then about three years old. Between three and ten a number of airs from

operas and operettas fixed themselves in my memory from hearing them hummed about the house — airs of Offenbach, Halévy, Lecocq. My father was one of eight children, my mother one of ten; all but two on each side had superb voices and excellent musical taste, my parents perhaps the best of the lot. They gave me everything in music except a voice; I have, one might say, no voice at all, to my great regret. The love of music ran especially deep in my mother's family, however, and I am thankful that I inherited it in full. Another thing that ran very deep in her family was the ability to write; not one of them but who could write admirably. Since then I noticed that the name of Jay seems to be a mark of good writing. Mr. Jefferson said that John Jay wielded "the best pen in America," and apparently he did. Among contemporaries, John Jay Chapman wrote admirably, and so did William Jay Gaynor. I am said to write well, and I see that Ellery Sedgwick has just now dug up another member of the tribe to appear in the *Atlantic,* Elizabeth Jay Etnier, who writes extremely well and gracefully.

17 SEPTEMBER — Two hours last evening with a young man just back from a couple of years in Germany. He has been in a position to know the new régime unusually well, and his accounts of it are hard to listen to. He spoke very objectively; according to him, Hitler really has the support of the great body of the nation, which is almost incredible. What he says of men whom I know, and who are enthusiastically behind Hitler, is especially hard to believe; yet I have no doubt it is all true enough. I saw so many lunatic Americans during the war that I ought to be ready to believe anybody capable of any kind of lunacy, but I did think better of these Germans whom I know. This young man was glad to leave Germany, and though he has lived there for years, he has no desire ever to go back. He said, "It is bad enough to have your friends killed, but when your friends are out killing people all night, that is too much." He spoke of this quite dispassionately, with no rancour; one could see that his experiences had put him above that. Curiously, he says that while Hitler's lieutenants are mostly a hard lot, Hitler himself is really a very good fellow, as good a type of pure zealot, probably, as exists. Well, one could say something in that way for Robespierre, no doubt. I went away thoroughly out of heart and depressed, and have not recovered my spirits all day.

18 SEPTEMBER — In talking with F. about the evidence in the case of the *Morro Castle,* he said, "I know it is a perfectly horrible thing

to say, but the whole affair leaves me cold. I have no feeling whatever about it. I got all that sort of thing out of my system during the war." I reminded him of the blanket of gloom that settled over the whole country when the *Titanic* sank, and he recalled it at once as one of the most interesting phenomena in our history, showing by comparison how insensitive to mass disaster we have become. "But," he said, "you must remember that then we had one foot on top of the world, and the other all but. The perfection of human nature in a perfected human society was only a matter of the next few months. We were all like Mark Twain on top of the Rigi watching the sunrise and worshipfully thinking how grand it was, only to discover in a minute or so that he had slept all day, and that what he was looking at was the sunset."

20 SEPTEMBER — The Jewish holiday Yom Kippur yesterday closed New York up as tight as a white-oak knot. One would say there was not a hundred dollars' worth of business done in all the town. It sets one's mind back on Hitler's policy. The question is not what one thinks of it as an American, but what one would think of it if one were a German in Germany, where the control of cultural agencies is so largely in the hands of Jews — the press, drama, music, education, etc. — and where there is, or was, a superb native culture essentially antithetical. Is one's own culture worth fighting for? I think so. I think I would fight for it. I would not fight for territory, trade expansion or the greed of profiteers, but I think I would fight for culture. That seems to be what peoples like the Catalans and Irish have always done, and there is a fine irony in the fact that materialized and brutalized peoples like the British and ourselves have never been able to get through their heads why the Irish should fight, in any given instance, or what they had to fight about. Give them redress of their material grievances and offer them advantageous trade terms — what more can any people want? The Irish wanted something more than that, and wholly different; and so, possibly, do the Germans.

22 SEPTEMBER — One good result of Prohibition is that women now go into saloons on equal terms with men, and with no more self-consciousness about it than they have about going into a dry-goods store. This apparently tends to civilize our drinking practices somewhat. Women got used to mixing with men in the speak-easies, and now they do it openly. This is what I notice in New York, at least; I do not know what they do in other parts of the country.

23 September — The Senate's investigation of the traffic in munitions has given publicity to a great deal of useful knowledge, but I do not think it will affect the prospects of disarmament in the least. All the talk about disarmament is thoroughly dishonest, and has proved so, again and again. As long as you have nations, you will have armaments; and as long as you have nationalism, you will have nations; and you will have nationalism as long as the existing theory of the State predominates. Therefore any talk about disarmament, even if sincere, is superficial and puerile.

24 September — There is a curious irony in the fact that the mystery of the Lindbergh extortion case is being unravelled through the suspect's possession of gold certificates. Roosevelt forcibly robbed the American people of nearly half their gold values, and thereby this minor swindle comes to light; it is a new version of the old adage that it takes a thief to catch a thief. I am against robbery, wherever found, but I confess that as long as Roosevelt and Co. are at large, my sumpathy is with Hauptmann, as it was with Capone while Hoover, Mellon and Co. were at large.

25 September — The revenue from liquor taxes has not come up to expectations, and bootlegging still goes on. The businesslike way to deal with this would be to reduce the taxation. The political way is to keep the taxes ridiculously high, and increase the force of officials to run down bootleggers. It is needless to observe that the Treasury has chosen to follow the political way, because it enlarges the range of patronage, enhances corruption, and strengthens the party machine. In a private organization, a policy like this would be suicidal; the contrast is significant. One would think people might sometime be led to fathom out the underlying reason why, in general, political organization thrives on policies that would be fatal to non-political organization; and whether *ipso facto* political organization is not inimical to society.

26 September — A sweet-mannered German girl stopped me today to ask a direction. Her English was rather broken, so I replied in German, and walked a block with her to put her on her way. She asked me presently if I were German, and seemed astonished when I told her I was not. I have several times had this experience of being casually taken for a German by Germans, on the strength of my speech, and I think it is because I began to learn German quite young — about eleven, as I remember, and got it from cultivated Hanoverians. I know the French language rather better than German, I think, but

speak it barbarously, managing the Italian intonation much better, though I do not know Italian nearly so well. But I could never think it worth while to make much effort after what the schools call "a good pronunciation," for one uses foreign languages chiefly for literary purposes; for conversation it is enough if one can get oneself easily understood.

27 SEPTEMBER — Our regular spell of "Labour Day weather" has come late this year. We are in the midst of it now, and it is most enervating and depressing.

28 SEPTEMBER — I wonder sometimes — though knowing our public as I do, I should not — why so few people seem aware that the principle of absolutism was introduced into the Constitution by the income-tax amendment. I notice today that some Senator is fathering an antiwar bill, which proposes to double the tax on all incomes below $10,000, and take 98 per cent of all that are above that figure; this raise to become effective on the day the United States declares war. This would be constitutional; it would be constitutional for Congress to take 100 per cent of all income, at any time. Then the only thing needful to make Louis XIV look cheap would be for Congress to vote the disbursing power into the President's hands, as an indirectly subsidized Congress, like the present one, could be counted on to do.

29 SEPTEMBER — A very fine performance of *Princess Ida* last night. If there were any power of self-criticism in England, every girls' school in the country would have closed the day after that opera was first put on. In fact, I can see how the Empire could have stood up under any strain of war without and knavery within, but I can't see for the life of me how it ever stood up against Gilbert and Sullivan.

Leonard Q. Ross

UNION SQUARE

> *Leonard Q. Ross (pseudonym for Leo C. Rosten) is best known for* The Education of H*Y*M*A*N K*A*P*L*A*N, *but his* The Strangest Places *(1939) has distinctions of its own. It is one*

of the few efforts in essay-journalism of the 1930's which copes with the times, while avoiding left-wing agitation on the one hand, and the escapist "charm" of the Atlantic Monthly *on the other. Mr. Rosten sought people rather than causes, though they sometimes stumbled across his path, as when die-hard Washington socialites made a fantastic effort to present an opera in spite of uncooperative unionists. Ross took trips to Chinatown, watched strip-tease shows in Chicago, suffered with other expectant fathers in the maternity ward, and otherwise found light and life which should have found more and closer appreciation than a grim time was willing to grant.*

I GOT to Union Square about ten o'clock one morning and looked around. I wanted to spend a day there and see what it was like — not the Union Square of the enormous political demonstrations, but its daily life. The park itself, an oval set within the square, is like an elongated wheel with six spokes. The spokes are wide walks, each leading to the tall flagpole in the center, which was put up in 1926 by the Tammany Society in honor of that celebrated statesman, Boss Murphy. Habitués of Union Square call it "Moiphy's Flagpole," with contempt. Small trees line the six walks and an iron rail fence keeps you off the grass. There are long wooden benches all along, where men sit, loaf, read newspapers, or sleep. Some men perch on the top rail of the fence, their feet on the lower rail, like boys on the dunce's seat.

It was bright and sunny that day, with a cool touch of autumn in the air. The thin trees, spaced far apart, cast little shadow. Many of the men on the benches read with a serious frown, with a great effort, their lips moving slowly as they spelled the words off the pages of their newspapers. I saw papers in many languages — English, Russian, Yiddish, Italian, Greek, Polish — and many copies of the *Daily Worker*.

Five of the walks that lead to "Moiphy's Flagpole" are no different from those in any city park: they are quiet except for the low, steady rumble of traffic from the streets around. But the sixth walk, the walk leading to the flagpole directly north from Fourteenth Street, is different. Here there were little crowds of men standing and the air hummed with talk. Whenever two men stopped to talk, a group formed around them and soon there were raised voices and an excited buzz as an argument broke out. There was nothing formal about it and nothing oratorical: no speakers' stands, soapboxes, or rostra. Someone began to talk to someone else, from a bench or the fence or standing in the middle of the walk itself; then a few men stopped to listen, and soon a crowd was pressing in. This went on all day, crowds forming and dissolving, men moving on, new arguments beginning.

"I don't notice the Communists attacking Roosevelt and the Democrats," said a man in a soft, New England voice. "Watch their speeches! They lambaste Landon, Hoover, the Republicans, J. P. Morgan. But never Roosevelt and the New Deal. Deep in their hearts, Browder and the rest of them are praying for Roosevelt and the Democrats."

A man with beetling red eyebrows, who had been standing on the outskirts of the group, pushed his way to the center and said, "Just a minute. Let's get this straight. Sure, we'd rather have the Democrats. Roosevelt is a kind of liberal. Confused, but a kind of liberal. But we can't *support* him. We've got to build a strong workers' opposition. We can't let Roosevelt think he's got the workers behind him or he'll make even more compromises with the right."

"You *know* it's between the Democrats and the Republicans," said the man from New England. "Why throw away your vote?"

The man with the beetling eyebrows retorted: "If you've got to vote for one of the *bourgeois* parties, vote for the Democrats. Sure. But the workers will vote the Communist ticket."

I noticed that this man kept going from group to group, not talking much, but interrupting occasionally to repeat, "Just a minute. Let's admit it. Sure, Roosevelt's a liberal. But that doesn't mean we should *support* him...." He made a deep impression on those who listened. I noticed he carried a book under his arm, and after following him around for a while I got a look at the title. It was "Duruy's General History of the World," and stuck into it, as if to mark a place, was a folded copy of the *New Masses*.

As I wandered from group to group, it was like seeing a series of jumbled newsreel shots, different in content and tempo. A man in a white Palm Beach suit argued with a teamster about unemployment and relief. A young man with a waxed mustache told an elderly gentleman all about 1776: "Did the French say, like you say, 'Let us go over *there,* where there is a democracy'? Hell, no! What did they say? They said, 'Goddamit, if America can do it, so can we!' And they made their own revolution — in 1789! So what would have happened if everyone said, like you do, 'If you do not like it here, go to Russia'? Why *should* we go over to Russia? We belong right here. I was born right here! This is our country, ain't it?"

A young man, very thin and intense, ranted against "Hearst's lies." His opponent kept saying, "Well, read another paper! We've got a free press."

The young man cried, "What paper? The capitalistic *Times?* The

Fascist *Herald Trib?* The *Post,* I suppose? That's a hot one. The *Post* puts up a fake labor attitude because they're tryin' to get circulation from the masses, that's all. It's like a young girl actin' like a virgin when she's on the town!" A few men laughed appreciatively at that.

There was one group crowded around a strange pair. A young fellow, no more than nineteen, wearing a polo shirt, was saying, "What about marriage? I suppose that's swell, huh? I suppose you'd like to see *your* daughter living with a man she ain't gonna marry!"

"*Mein Gott!*" screamed his opponent. "Gottamit! *Mein Gott!*" I had to crane my neck to see him over the heads of the crowd. He was no more than five feet three, an old man wearing a yellowed straw hat which was crumbling at the edges. He had on a high celluloid collar and a striped blue shirt. He clutched an umbrella stiffly in one hand and waved a chewed-up stub of a cigar in the other. He was practically toothless. His face was white with fury, and his voice was high and squeaky. "Vhere you *hoid* is in Soviet Union no marritch? Vhere you rad soch dem, rotten lies? How you tink is in Soviet Union pipple hevink families, you fool? How you tink is *growink* Soviet Union?"

"You can't change people!" cried the young man, his eyes blazing. "What if everyone has a job? O.K. Next they wanna play golf five times a week, that's what. So then everyone wants a yacht! That's what they want next — *a yacht!*"

The little old man jumped up and down, screaming with rage. "Podden me, you fool! You plain crazy! Vy you vorryink awreddy abot yachts? Golf five times a veek ain't good enough awreddy? Concitrate! Concitrate mit de *had,* you fool!" His voice gave out and became a thin cry as he wailed: "Concitrate on *golf five times a veek!*"

"How do *you* know what's happening in Russia?" cried the young man in the polo shirt. "I read the papers and see — "

"Gottamit, you crazy!" screamed the old man, clutching his straw hat with the hand that held the umbrella. "Plain crazy! You talkink lies! I ken't stend it! Go vay, please, you fool. Go vay!"

He pushed his way out of the crowd. Other voices took up the argument with the young man in the polo shirt. The old man stopped near me, stamping his feet in rage. "I ken't *stend* it," he kept saying. "I ken't stend it! If is old man talkink foolishments, I no care. He old. He fool. He got noddink in de had. But vhen is young, fine American boy mit aducation talkink craziness it's hoitink me in de hot, like you stickink in a knife! Yachts! *Mein Gott!* Yachts he vants it awreddy! *Isn't enough golf five times a veek!*" He sighed and shook his head. "Vhere dey gattink soch tarrible ideas! Mus' be *poison* dey loinink in de school — tarrible *poison!* Capitalist *poison!*"

The old man walked away, waving his umbrella. I saw him go to another group and listen for a while. Then he made a wry face and walked on.

One of the largest groups was clustered around a man who sat on the fence, a brown paper portfolio under his arm. I was told that this man was named "Leech," and was in Union Square every day, usually at the same place. He would argue with anyone and answer any questions. "He's smart. He knows history. He's got awful deep ideas," someone near me said.

I listened to the man on the fence for quite a long time. He was arguing with a well-dressed man, and was drawing parallels between Chamberlain and the Fascists, the Spanish civil war and the Russian civil war, between Russia and America. He analyzed the problems of the government in France and insisted that the policy of compromise would lead to a "real Leftist government." He quoted Gladstone, Jefferson, Karl Marx, Justice Holmes, and Lenin. He often said, "We Communists have shown . . ." He spoke with a wealth of historical references. When he answered the question of someone who spoke with an accent, he did it gently and in simple words; but those who spoke like native Americans he answered with heat, irony, and a kind of condescension, as if they should have known better.

Around one o'clock someone on a bench nearby called out, mockingly, "Time to knock off for your coffee, Leech!" and someone went "Haw! Haw! What shift are you working on today?"

Most of the men in Union Square were dressed simply and not too well. Many of them were bareheaded. A few wore no coats. I saw none who looked like the usual caricature of the "radical" — no wild hair or flowing ties. They looked like the sort of men you would find in a working-class neighborhood any night after the day's work. I heard half a dozen strange dialects and accents, a testimony to the labor with which many of these men spoke English. There was also good, strong, colorful New Yorkese, occasionally a Southern drawl, several Midwestern twangs. There was the accent of Germans, Russians, Italians, Jews, Poles, Scandinavians. One Irishman, a magnificent fellow with a shock of blond hair and a barrel chest, was in the thick of an argument with a man who had said something about "the brotherhood of man." The Irishman's brogue was rich and musical as he cried, "Ay'm tellin' ye, min arre livin' lake cattle in America! Good min. Better min than th' likes o' ye will iver be. Ye're nawthin' but a Chrrister! A damn, confusin' Chrrister!"

The men in the crowds listened gravely, like people trying to learn something or understand something, like men who found it difficult to concentrate and to whom politics was a fascinating but difficult thing. They didn't laugh much. They didn't heckle. They listened quietly, with respect. They respected men who could argue and express themselves. They looked like men in search of some truth, some compelling and universal symbol in which they could believe.

There was a giant of a Negro in overalls, his teeth glistening as he listened. Occasionally he would shake his head and laugh. "Man, dat boy sho' talks a pow'ful English. Better'n I kin talk, an' I was bo'n right yere in dis country!" He seemed to be enchanted by words, and listened to the wildest torrent of ideas with delight. A messenger boy in a Postal Telegraph cap hovered on the edge of one crowd and then another, as if he had to tear himself away at any minute, but couldn't. A man sat on the fence reading the *Morning Telegraph*. Every once in a while he would cry out to the crowd near him, "Jesus Christ! Pipe down! Can't a guy even read in peace?" He was very disgusted.

As the men broke away from one group and went to another, slowly, aimlessly, like men with a great deal of time, I talked to several of them. I wanted to find out how they happened to be in Union Square and how often they came. Only one or two had merely stopped off to listen while passing through. The rest came regularly. One man said, "I come here because there's always something doing. What else have I got to do?" Another, "I like to leesen to man talking good — abot politics." A young chap told me, "It drives you nuts sticking around the house all day. That's why I stick around here." A husky fellow in a blue sweater said, "This is a damn good place to wise up to yourself. I've learned a lot since I began coming around."

Most of them were men out of work: a housepainter, a tailor, a man from Illinois who had once had his own farm, a shipping clerk, a teamster, a boy out of high school. One man said he worked nights. Two or three were hoping for WPA jobs; one complained about politics and "the cut you gotta give some damn politician." All of them spoke with earnestness of how long they had been trying to get a decent job.

Right through the afternoon the arguments went on, and groups kept forming and re-forming without a consistent pattern. I noticed that the sympathies of the crowd were generally with the more militant speakers. I noticed, too, that after listening for a while to a speaker with whom they disagreed, those who listened would begin talking among themselves and label him. They always labeled the speaker whose arguments they didn't like. It was as if they had to classify men and arguments into sharp, simple categories, so they could understand them better. "He's a Trotskyist," someone would say, and many heads would nod. Or, "He's a Socialist!" "He's a scab." One man said, of any speaker he didn't like, "He's the baloney." This elicited several knowing nods. An Italian with a long black mustache kept saying, "Joosta *Fascista*. Man who talk lak dat — joosta *Fascista*."

I heard men referred to as "counter-revolutionists," "White Russians," "deviationists," "opportunists." A serious young man in glasses called someone "a confusionist." All these labels were uttered with contempt.

Hawkers circulated through the crowds ceaselessly. One of them, wise in the ways of trade, carried a large can and called, "Soviet candies. Genuine Soviet candies. Two for a penny." A haggard-looking man tried to get contributions for the Browder Radio Campaign Fund; for ten cents you got a pink ticket out of a little book, and he took your name and address. A wild-eyed fellow was circulating a cheap, mimeographed leaflet announcing a meeting of the One Big Union Club. He would start a hot argument with someone, yelling at the top of his voice until a crowd gathered. Then he would ignore his opponent completely and begin passing out the leaflets. He did this several times during the afternoon. It infuriated his opponents, but the crowds didn't mind. They seemed to know him. I heard him referred to as a "wobbly," an "I.W.W."

Around five o'clock, people began pouring into Union Square from Broadway and Fifth Avenue. There were many pretty girls and well-dressed men. No one paid any attention to them and none of them stopped in the sixth walk. They just cut across the square to get to the subway at Fourteenth Street.

I went to get a bite to eat around six. On my way back to the park I stopped to talk to a policeman, a handsome young Italian who was walking along the Fourth Avenue side of the park. Had I listened to "the nuts inside," he asked. I told him I had and asked, "How long do these arguments go on?"

"Jeeze," he said. "They start in the morning around ten, and they don't even begin to break up until eleven at night. The last ones aren't over until one or two in the morning. That's when there's an occasional cuttin'-up match. You know — arguments, fights, razors. Then we gotta run 'em in. Otherwise we don't bother 'em."

I asked him if it was a tough beat to be on.

"Naw," he said, swinging his club. "They behave pretty good most of the time. You get used to the nuts."

More people had come into the park, and for the first time I noticed women and a few children sitting on benches. These people were dressed a little better than those I had seen all through the day. They were people who had jobs. More groups had formed, bigger groups, and the arguments were more excited. The air was thick with talk about shops, unions, Fascism, war, strikes, WPA, Spain, China.

The evening crowds introduced a wider variety of topics for discussion. I saw one group roaring with laughter at the conversation of a Negro who wore bright yellow suspenders and a battered felt hat. There was no brim to the hat. He was telling them how to eat rattlesnakes.

"Skin 'em an' boil 'em an' mmmmhhh! You got somet'in'!"

"Is maybe soch sneks a tousand yiss old?" asked a meek little man.

"Man, yo' sho' confused!" laughed the Negro. "Lookayere. One rattle is one year, see? Now, how in 'ell kin one po' snake lug aroun' a tousand rattles? Man, dat po' snake be paralyzed!"

The crowd roared.

"But I seen a toitle in Bronx Pahk is eight hundred yiss old, dey said," said the man.

"Man, whatchoo confusin' now?" snickered the Negro. "Why, a turtle ain't no mo' relation a rattler den a snail to Jesse Owens!" The crowd howled again.

I wandered over to "Murphy's Flagpole" and read the inscription which runs around the base: "HOW LITTLE DO MY COUNTRYMEN KNOW WHAT PRECIOUS BLESSINGS THEY ARE IN POSSESSION OF AND WHICH NO OTHER PEOPLE ON EARTH ENJOY — THOMAS JEFFERSON." It was hard to make out the words, it was getting so dark.

But soon the lights went on and high overhead the big illuminated clock in the tower of the Edison Building at Fourteenth Street and Irving Place looked down on Union Square and gave testimony to the passing of time. On Fourteenth Street the blue and red neon signs shone: "Kitty Kelly Shoes," "Jacob Ruppert Beer," "Ohrbach's." Facing them, at the south end of the square, was the statue of Washington, seated on his huge bronze horse.

In the shadow of the statue I found two Italians talking quietly. They were dressed in what seemed to be their Sunday clothes: dark suits, white wash ties, velour hats. The white wash ties made their faces look even darker and more swarthy.

One man was saying, "How you wan die? Lak a man, no?"

"I no care how die," said the other.

"No, fran'. Is two kinds die. Is gooda die, is bada die. Gooda die is: man go lay downa bed — leetle beet seeck, mebbe. He closa da eye, nize, quiet. He sleep. He die. Datsa *gooda* die."

The other man was staring at the ground. "Die is alla same," he said.

"Is *no* alla same, fran'," protested the other. "In war is bada die.

Bambino keel. Gasa choke. Mucha blood. How you lak I com op, I geeva you lak thees — oomp!" He imitated the sudden thrust of a bayonet. *"Datsa* kind die you lak?"

The other man didn't look up. He just stared at the ground. There was dull weariness in his voice as he said, "Die is die."

Lauren Gilfillan

NO COMRADE

> *Lauren (Harriet Woodbridge) Gilfillan was simply a girl who had graduated from Smith College, who wanted to know more about life, and who hoped to write about it. She took her typewriter to a mining region in western Pennsylvania to see for herself how people were weathering the depression there. Though alone, and of manifestly different social origins than her Pennsylvanians, she gained the regard of the people among whom she lived. She fought a battle for personal cleanliness, begged funds in Pittsburgh for the Strike Committee, went down into the mines, and was part of the daily life of her friends and associates. However, the radicals began to hover over the scene. In the last days of her stay, before she was forced to retreat — and ultimately write* I Went to Pit College *(1934)* *— her relations with the communists reached a crisis.*

I HAD gone down to the relief kitchen one night, and the men were there, sitting in the darkness. The tiny tongue of the one miner's lamp threw abysmal shadows into the corners. That little room grew so big in the night — an endless mysterious cavern. The light made orange triangles of the men's European noses. We looked like bandits plotting in a cave.

For the sixteenth time I had been trying to relight my "cutty pipe." Johnny was holding the lamp for me. Suddenly out of the shadows a new voice spoke.

"Why the hell don't somebody introdooce us? That's the way they do in sassiety, ain't it?"

I held up the light and let it shine down upon his face. Jewish. An ironic mouth. I smiled.

"You tell me who you are."

"Oh, I'm just another miner." I should have been warned by his voice. "Who are you?"

I laughed. "Oh, I'm just another bum."

But he wanted to *know*. He wanted to know everything — where I came from, how I got here, where I was living, what I thought of the place, when I was going to leave. Nobody had been so curious before. He dug into my past life. Nobody had asked me that. I didn't want to talk about my background. I wanted to be as nearly as possible in keeping with my present environment. I made gay evasions in the bantering idiom I heard every day. Could he see what I was writing? What did he want to see my writing for? Oh, sure, I'd show it to him some day.

Everybody had stopped talking. They sat back and listened. We were the center of the stage. We plunged into a long argument on idealism and materialism. He said I was an idealist. He hated idealists. They never did anything but talk about it. They never made the world any better. College! What the hell was I doing down here if I went to college? To write about it? What was there so unusual to write about?

"It's dramatic — this!" I flung out an arm.

"Dramatic! You're going to write dramatic little stories, huh? How do you like the communists? *They're* dramatic, ain't they?"

"Oh, yes!" I began to sing:

Arise, ye prisoners of starvation,
Arise, ye wretched of the earth.

I raised my right fist in the communist salute.

'Tis the final conflict,
Let each stand in his place.
The International Soviet
Shall be the human race.

"Oh, so you know the songs, too. You've got a pretty little voice. She's a pretty little thing, ain't she?" He glanced significantly at Johnny.

When I got up to go, Johnny said he'd take me home. I turned to look at my new friend. He was looking at me.

"Good night," I said.

"Good night — Comrade."

Johnny and I were still on the road from Seldom Seen to Avelonia.

"Y'remember that night, Laurie."

I nodded.

No Comrade [67

"Well, y'see, that there fella was Jim Snyder, state organizer for communism. I guess you got him perty suspicious."

"I'm afraid so, Johnny."

That had been a week ago. During the week that followed, things did not go so well with me. I tried not to notice a certain coolness in my acquaintances. Massingale would not allow me to go to the strike committee meeting. Julie and Helen Koller looked at me askance. Stanley turned gruff and taciturn. Some instinct told me not to take food from the relief, though I still went on the picket.

Now Jim Snyder was back again. Last night while I was away at Seldom Seen, he and a committee of comrades had gone to Johnny's house demanding to search my papers. Johnny had vigorously protested, but Mr. Cersil, torn between loyalty and a miner's hospitality, had yielded at last. Jim Snyder had opened my traveling bag and searched the pockets of my clothes. He had found a typewritten story of the crusade to Pittsburgh with accompanying communist songs, notes on the trial at Washington, and jottings of remarks various people had made to me. Besides that they had viewed with rage my city clothes, monogrammed ivory mirror, powder and lipstick, camera and typewriter, and, what was most damning of all, they had found a letter from my mother, illegible to them, enclosing five checks for five dollars each.

"And, bozha moi, are they sore at me," Johnny groaned, kicking at a stone in the road and sending it spinning over the embankment, "for tryin' to keep 'em from messin' in your things. I'm in it as deep as you."

"Oh, poor Johnny," I said. "And you hold a high position in the Y.C.L.;* too. You're a unit organizer and unit treasurer and everything."

"Oh, to hell with communism! They're a lot of stupid lummoxes. Real miners ain't communists. The communists've allus been in Avelonia and they allus will be. They just make a lotta noise. But I sorta hate to have 'em treatin' me as if I was a pansy. You should 'a' seen Jim Snyder look at me last night!"

"My goodness, I wish I'd been there. It would have been exciting."

"Too damn excitin'. I'm glad you wasn't." Johnny doubled up his youthful fist. "You'd 'a' seen the fur fly all right."

We reached the outskirts of Avelonia.

"Now you go home or somewhere," I said to Johnny. "Don't stay

---

*Young Communist League.

with me. I'm just going to walk around and see what's what. I'll see you at the mass meeting."

"Aw, please, Laurie, don't go bumming around by yourself. It's dangerous."

"Nobody's going to hurt me," I said.

With more trepidation than I had let Johnny see, I began to saunter through the patch. It was the beginning of a very hot day. Avelonia lay stark and hideous under the blistering sun. I walked over soot and cinders between the rows of shacks. Already people were sitting on the porches — silent, motionless. They watched my progress narrowly, as usual. More than ever before I wondered what they were thinking.

I trudged on, over the railroad tracks, past the Roman Catholic church that looked like a schoolhouse, past the schoolhouse that looked like a barn. Silence and the hot sun. My feet scuffled loudly in the cinders. Past the Economy Store where men sat without speaking. They would sit there until hot afternoon cooled into evening, until evening blackened into night. And how black the nights were in Avelonia. As I passed, they all stared at me with that unsurprised curiosity peculiar to a miner's eyes. I could never diagnose that look. They had accepted me, and yet . . . they thought their own thoughts — in a foreign language. I was a foreigner, and so they all knew me, these men who were looking at me now. They knew whence I came, where I lived, what I did, and what I said — from morning to night. Each had his own theory about me. I said I was a writer. Writing for whom? I might be a communist, I might be a socialist, a capitalist, a stoolpigeon. Some said I was Pinchot's spy. Some knew I was in the Secret Service. But first and last I was a foreigner, to be treated with hospitality, to be offered food and lodging, to smile with, to laugh at, to fall in love with — but never to be trusted.

I was keenly aware of all this as I walked in silence past those silent faces. One of the men was trying to roll the remainder of his tobacco in a filthy scrap of newspaper.

"Little girl, you got a cigarette?"

I produced my pack and he reached out a rootlike fist. He fumbled for matches. He had none. I lit his cigarette. I looked at the other miners. Not one of them was smoking. I passed the pack around and each took one without speaking.

They handed around the flaming match, and pulled hard. I smiled at them and their eyes lighted in answer.

"Where you goin'?" one of them said.

"Oh, nowhere. Just bummin' around."

No Comrade [69

They exchanged significant glances. One of them said something in Slovak, and then he remarked politely, "Well, there ain't nottin' much else to do around here."

I sat down on the unpainted steps, and they moved over to give me room. I lit a cigarette, and we smoked in silence. A hearse passed.

"Who die?" one said.

"How I know? People die every day."

"That guy Weiniger, he got plenty business." He made a half sound of laughter in his throat. "He get paid plenty too."

"Well, he need it. He got to eat."

I got up to go. " 'By."

They nodded in farewell. As I moved away I heard one of them recounting:

"Nex' morning, day find him dere, sittin' straight up in bed, stark dead. Nobody never knew — "

The first person I met whom I knew was Alec Sporka. Alec and I had often joked together at the relief.

"Hello, Alec," I said.

Alec hesitated. His hands hung straight and stiff at his sides, and he opened his mouth like a fish. Then he stumbled on without speaking.

I felt a strange little pang beneath my breastbone. I had lived with these people, slept with them, shared their food, gone hungry with them. I felt a bond between us. I didn't want them to dislike me.

It was sweltering hot. The perspiration rolled from my forehead. When I came to a slag heap, smoking endlessly, I saw a figure sprawled in the ashes at the base. It was Flaherty. He was drunk as usual.

Flaherty had been a miner all his life until one fatal day in the mine when a sliver of coal had flown into his eye and blinded it forever. He had received a compensation on which he existed — but the accident had ruined his life. Now he wandered about Avelonia by day, hating all mankind, and slept in bachelors' quarters by night with one woman after another. There was nothing left for him but drink.

I stopped and stood looking down at the prostrate figure.

"Hello, Flaherty."

Flaherty wobbled to his feet.

"Hello, yourself. Wanna drink?"

"No, thanks."

Flaherty shook an ash-smeared finger in my face.

"Listen, you! You're goin' to git tarred and feathered and thrown outa this place, do you know that!" He staggered along beside me. "You're writin' a book, hain't yuh? And before they throw yuh out,

I'm gonna tell you a few things yuh ought to know. They're a lot of damned dirty crooks around here and you put *that* in your book! The way they run this place" — a loud hiccup popped through his lips — "I'm goin' to tip you off. At that there Christ-bitten relief, they feed the starvin' miners. Yeah! Those God damned sons of bitches trade off the food for liquor, that's what they do. They sell the fatback for booze. They bought it offa me. That scalawag Stanley, he's gonna git pinched for flagrant graft, and that big-shot bastard, Fritz, him that gits the relief from Pittsburgh, he'd better resign before this place gits too hot fer 'im. He's in cahoots with the United Miners, he's workin' fer the capitalists. You put that in your book!" Flaherty fell flat on the cinders and I waited for him to get up again. "Them as runs the relief, they hain't miners and never was. They been crooks and criminals all their lives. Livin' off the people's starvation! They're allus yellin' they're patriotic strikers. Yeah! They hain't never worked a lick in their lives. And them others what are on the blacklist. They go to shoutin' how they hain't scabbed yet. They couldn't scab if they begged the operators on their knees. There's them as takes relief from the socialists when they perfess to be red-hot communists. Some is socialists one day and communists the day after, 'cordin' to who gives 'em grub. Liars and crooks all of 'em."

"And you! You're puttin' your head in a noose and you put *that* in your book? It's women what gits us into trouble. In 1913 when the unions begun, the women weren't in it. The men was doin' it all. Now the women and children choke up the picket, and we have riots and git killed. If a man can't fight fer himself, the women ain't any help neither. It was the women who got Russia into this. Them young girl organizers. Now the miner's got to fight the operators *and* Russia. It was probably on account of the women that the unions had a split.

"Them National Miners, they're all ferriners. They don't pay no taxes. If we all paid taxes we wouldn't have no high taxes. A fella was in the company thirty years, and he ain't got no citizen papers. They shipped him back to Russia, and good for him, too. Let them fight their *own* government!

"If people'd mind their own business, if the men'd fight the women at home and not on the picket, they'd be a lot better off. The world was never so bad off as it is now, and you put *that* in your book!"

Flaherty leaned against an outhouse, exhausted by his long tirade.

"I gotta have a drink. Watta hell, drink yourself to death and forgit it all. Come on, and git a drink. Watta hell!"

What the hell, indeed, I thought. "All right," I said.

I followed Flaherty up to one of the shacks. We crawled under the steps and fell down into sort of a dirt cellar. It contained a table and two chairs, the legs planted in the soft earth. Flaherty collapsed into one of the chairs and I sat down in the other.

"Service," Flaherty yelled, slapping the table with the palm of his withered hand. A woman in bare feet, her unkempt black hair hanging about her shoulders, came down the steps. Her eyes popped at the sight of me, but she said to Flaherty:

"Got the money?"

"Money! I'm the richest God damned son of a bitch in this God damned stink-hole."

He fumbled into his pocket and to my amazement pulled out a roll of filthy bills. He threw one on the table and the woman snatched it greedily.

"Two drinks!" Flaherty shouted. "One for me and one for my woman."

The woman brought us two thick dirty cups and a dark bottle. Flaherty poured my cup with a shaking hand. Some of the liquor slopped over on the table. Immediately the little cellar was filled with an overpowering reek.

"Drink that," Flaherty said, "and you'll be drunk fer five days straight. You'll git up in the mornin' dyin' o' thirst, and you'll drink a quart o' water and git drunk all over agin."

So this was the famous "corn" the miners drank. Flaherty tipped the bottle to his mouth and drank steadily, gulp, gulp, gulp. I took a sip. Phew! I spat the horrible stuff out of my mouth.

Flaherty leaned in his chair, his eyes closed. I got up, climbed the steps and out into the sun, in my mind's eye the picture of Flaherty, sprawling there, dead to the world.

I was nearing the relief kitchen. Men sat on the steps as usual. In a sudden spasm of fear, I kept to the far side of the road. Stanley came to the door and stood watching me as I passed.

A scrap of white in the black road caught my eye. I picked it up. It was a printed leaflet. I read:

Workers! White and Negro! Native and Foreign Born!

United in PROTEST against the boss terror and persecution of militant workers, etc.

Come to the MASS MEETING at Carnival grounds, Avelonia, Pa.

Hear ———, National Negro Organizer of the I.L.D., fighting for the rights of the workers. Sacco and Vanzetti were burned to death in the electric chair by the bosses.

All out to the MASS PROTEST DEMONSTRATION.

Demand the release of the prisoners arrested for working class activity.

Demand the removal of all armed forces from the mining section.

Down with lynching, Jim Crow, and oppression of the Negro workers.

Demand the release of Mooney and Billings and the nine Scottsboro boys.

I knew that there was to be a soccer game before the mass meeting. I walked on to the field where they were playing. A crowd of young people and children sat around a straw stack under the blazing sun and a team of young men kicked a ball about the field. As I approached the straw stack, everybody stopped talking and looked at me.

"Hello," I said. Damning silence.

I sat down next to Shirley, surrounded by a crowd of ragged little girls. They edged away from me, pulling back their skirts as if from the plague. Anna was there in the black evening dress. She came and sat on the other side of me.

"Hello, honey," she said. Anna was the only person who would speak to me.

"Let's sing, 'Forward, Ye Workers,'" Shirley said to the little girls. She struck up the tune.

> Whirlwinds of danger are raging around us,
> O'erwhelming forces of darkness assail,
> Still in the fight see advancing before us
> Red Flag of liberty that yet shall prevail.
>
> *Then,* forward, ye workers, freedom awaits you,
>   O'er all the world on the land and the sea.
>   On with the fight for the cause of humanity,
>   March, march, ye toilers, and the world shall be free.

It was a wild Russian melody. The children's voices were like a scream in the night. I thought,

> An infant crying in the night,
> An infant crying for the light
> And with no language but a cry.

"Let's sing 'The Class That Lives in Luxury,'" Shirley said, turning more of her back toward me.

Conditions, they are bad,
And some of you are sad.
You cannot see your enemy,
The class that lives in luxury.

You working men are poor,
Will be forever more,
As long as you permit the few
To guide your destiny.

Shall we be slaves and work for wages?
It is outrageous, has been for ages.
This earth by right belongs to toilers,
And not to spoilers of liberty.

Working men, unite;
You must put up a fight
To make us free from slavery
And capitalistic tyranny.

This fight is not in vain
We've got a world to gain.
Will you be a fool, a capitalist's tool,
And serve your enemy?

The first time I had heard the children sing, I had sung with them. Now they flung words at me as if they were a hymn of hate. I looked the crowd over. Stunted, half-naked, white-faced children; immature young men with mature, grave faces; Anna, grotesque in her evening dress and red pimpled arms; Shirley, with her red chiseled mouth and inscrutable gray eyes.

Whenever I encountered a pair of eyes, they shot me a glance of aversion, and then looked away.

"Now this is silly of you," I said to myself. "To feel hurt because they treat you like this. They don't hate you. They hate what they think you stand for — and you do stand for it, and you can't get away from it, no matter what your material condition. You had no business trying to masquerade as one of these people. They have a right to be angry. And you aren't going to stay here forever. You'll go back to civilization and a bath every day. Think of having a nice warm soapy bath!" But still I felt heartsick, lonely, and miserable. I felt very tired, and also — I smiled wryly to myself — hungry.

The soccer game came to an end. All got up and trooped over the scorching field to the road. I sat where I was, the target of many a backward glance.

When all were gone, I lay down in the straw, faint with fatigue. My cheeks felt hot.

"I've been going on nerves," I said to myself. "Can't stand this much longer."

A sudden voice startled me.

"Sit up. I want to talk to you."

I sat up and looked into the smoldering gray eyes of Shirley. She *was* beautiful.

"Well, Shirley," I said. "You sit down." I patted the straw. "You haven't been very talkative lately. What is it you want to say?"

Shirley did not sit down. She remained standing before me. She wore the dress I had first seen her in — the sleezy tan crêpe with the sleeves cut out. The perspiration glistened on her olive forehead. She looked worn and tired, too, but — militant.

"I want you," Shirley said in her low biting voice, "to leave Avelonia today. Go back to college. You need more education."

"Shirley," I said, "I have no intention of leaving today. I do indeed need education, but not in a college classroom. Did you ever hear this story:

"Mary Smith knocked at the door of the world.

" 'Who's there?' the world said.

" 'I'm Mary Smith, A.B.'

" 'Oh, come in, Mary,' the world said. 'I'll teach you the rest of the alphabet!' "

"It's a good joke," Shirley said. "But I haven't much time to waste on you. I want to warn you that if you don't leave Avelonia of your own accord, you will be made to go."

"And who will force me to go? The law?"

"The law of the working class. You don't belong here, representing capitalism."

"And do you belong here — representing communism?"

"What do you think!"

"I don't know," I said.

"Listen," Shirley said, "you're not the only one who's had an education. I went to college for two years and I was expelled for being a communist. And so I belong here. But I understand you. I know your type. You say you are poor. All the world is divided into two classes — capitalist and labor. You belong to the upper middle class which has been pushed into the working class by the depression, but you still retain your old attitude."

"I never had an attitude."

"You make me mad. You're just an adventuress who wants excitement. You don't feel sorry for these people. Their misery is just so much grist for your mill. You're going to write a book. Well," with a trace of bitterness, "you have a baby face and pert manners which get on with the capitalist firms. You think you're an artist. Art is divided into three classes: the kind which presents a system toward truth and reform. That is the kind that lasts. Shelley, Shaw, Ibsen, Sinclair, Dreiser, they all did that. There is the kind of art which shows conditions and offers no remedy. Burns, Sinclair Lewis. Then there is the class you belong to, the Ivory Tower — art for art's sake!" Shirley snorted indignantly. "You'll write a melodramatic story and it won't be worth that!" She snapped her fingers smartly. "You're the kind of person I want to see killed!"

Shirley stood before me there in the dried-up field, the sun beating down on her glistening blue-black hair. Her shoulders in their poverty-stricken clothing were thrown regally back, her arm was unconsciously raised at right angles in the Young Communist salute, her thumb and forefinger still touching as if caressing a ring, and her gray eyes flashed sparks of accusing fire. She was an avenging Semiramis, a Jewish Joan of Arc bearing a red flag.

"Shirley," I said with awe in my voice, "you're gorgeous."

Shirley dropped her arm and turned on her heel.

"Well, I've warned you. I'm going to the mass meeting now."

"I'm coming too."

"All right, come on. I'll be glad to see you get what's coming to you."

We walked in silence in the direction of the Carnival Grounds. We went down the main street and passed the drug store. I turned and went in, and Shirley walked on without me.

"Listen," I said to the drug store clerk. "You know me." He nodded. "Well, I want pencil and paper. I haven't money with me now, but I'll write you an I.O.U. and pay you tonight."

He gave me a pencil and a small tablet.

"I might as well take notes," I thought. "It doesn't matter now."

I met Cecil. He stopped.

"Say, listen, kid, where'd you think you're goin' so fast?"

"That's the first thing you ever said to me," I smiled.

"Yeah? And it may be the last. You headin' toward the mass meetin'?"

I saw a look of trouble in his blue eyes, and his round Dutch features were drawn into a worried frown. "Listen, kid. I like you and I hate to see you git in trouble. 'Cause I ain't gonna be the one to protect you when they start to murder you. If I was you, I'd pack up and catch the next train out of here. You're lookin' peaked."

"I don't seem to feel so good," I said.

"Well, take my advice and keep away from Jim Snyder and them miners. You're such a little half-pint."

"Yes, I'm small," I said. "That's the reason why they can't touch me."

Johnny came running up.

"For the love of God, where have you been? The I.L.D. has been huntin' all over the place for you, Laurie."

"I went to the soccer game. I'm sorry I missed them."

"Sorry! Are you crazy? What they wouldn't do to you is nobody's business." Johnny turned pale under his tan. "I hate to think of it."

"Jesus, Cersil," Cecil grinned. "You're a glutton for punishment. Remember who you're talkin' to. This here's your home town, yuh know." Cecil sauntered off.

Johnny looked after him and then at me.

"Are you goin' to the mass meetin'?"

"Uh-huh."

Johnny gave me a despairing look and for the first time left my side and walked away.

With my heart beating a little quickly, I approached the Carnival Grounds. It was a solid mass of people. All Avelonia was there, looking more European than ever. Shaggy heads, miners' caps, shawls, bare-footed children. The subdued buzzing rise and fall of foreign voices dwindled almost into silence as I drew near. I skirted the grounds followed by many pairs of eyes — familiar faces now became estranged, inimical. There were Alec Sporka, Stanley, Julie and Helen Koller and Mr. and Mrs. Koller, Fritz, Big Mike, Black Joe, Red Pete, Rosie Cepres, Shorty, Andy, Steve — all of them stared at me without greeting and I offered none. I arrived safely at a corner of the field and sat down under a tree. The meeting was about to begin.

Jim Snyder got up on a soap box, in the center of the crowd.

"Comrades! — and others. We meet today to commemorate the murder of two defenders of the working class, Sacco and Vanzetti.

"Der may be among us today some people who are not members of the working class. Dey may be a spy, a capitalists' tool, a wolf in ship's clothing." Jim looked directly over at me and paused. A murmur arose in the audience. All eyes turned toward me. I felt a little dizzy. I waited. Everybody waited. It was so still that you could hear the roar of a mine tipple in the distance. No one moved. Jim went on.

"We must ostracize dees people. We must have nottin' to do with dem and tell dem nottin'. We must treat dees people as our enemies.

"Well, den de first announcements dis afternoon is about de school kids. We have went to de school board for food, shoes, and clothes. De miners' children ain't got much on in front and nottin' behind." (Quick relieved laughter on the part of the audience.) "De school board say —— "

I heard no more of Jim's speech for a man had come sauntering through the crowd and had sat down beside me. He was a Negro with a very intelligent face. He regarded me keenly.

"What are you writing, Comrade? Do you mind if I call you Comrade? You look like one."

"I'm not a communist," I said, "but you may call me Comrade. I was just writing down what Jim was saying about the school strike."

"And what he was saying about you?"

"Yes."

"For whom are you writing, Comrade?"

"Just for myself. I'm free-lance writer — or at least I hope to be."

"You cannot expect me to believe that."

"Well, it's the truth."

The man shook his dark head sadly. "I represent the I.L.D. The I.L.D. is not an organization to be trifled with. I ask you not to write anything to harm the struggling miners."

"Don't worry," I said. "I'm in sympathy with the miners."

"Yes, I think you must be," he said, "or you would not come to live with them. I will trust you to present a sympathetic story of the life of these poor people."

"I'll write what I have seen and what I have felt about it."

"Ah, but there are two ways of saying everything."

Jim was announcing the next speaker. "I'll leave you with this little warning," the man said, and walked up to the box.

"There are writers who make fun of the poor people," he began. "One writer said of the miners' homes, 'They can study the stars through their roofs, the trees through the walls, and the ground through the floor' —— "

A little dark man stood looking down at me. "Com-er-att, what is that you write?"

I explained again.

Now a colored woman was speaking. "I have been organizing in Kentucky. There is a price on my head. What did the Red Cross say when we went for milk for the children? They said: 'We have to keep supplies for national catastrophes!' It is perfectly natural for the miners to starve." She went on telling of conditions in Kentucky. They were the same all over the United States and in England. "There is a disease in Kentucky called 'flux' which is merely another name for starvation, a wasting away of the flesh. You say, 'We are all reds and fighting for ourselves.' The Kentucky miners say, 'We are all reds and *proud* of fighting for ourselves.' " (Short applause from the crowd.) "You don't know what starvation means yet. The fight is just begun."

The little foreign man got up.

"To those who do not understan', I speak in Italian. Compagni! Sacco e Vanzetti!" The little man spoke with passion and fiery gestures.

The colored woman was holding my arm.

"What are you writing, Comrade?"

Just then there was a commotion in the crowd. A boy came running down the road, shouldered his way to Jim Snyder, and said something. Jim rushed up to the platform.

"Cops comin'!" Like a shot the colored woman left my side. I scrambled to my feet. The crowd surged and swirled. Before you could say Jack Robinson all the speakers were in an automobile and whizzing down the road at breakneck speed.

Just as they disappeared, the Buick full of state police drove up. A cop jumped out of the car.

"Which way did they go?" he shouted at the miners.

No one answered.

"God damn the lot of you!" The cop hesitated. I was standing on the road now. The cop's eyes fell on me. He whirled toward me.

"And who do you think you are, you think you're so God damn smart! Well, we know who you are. You're the girl that keeps the kids from going to school! You watch your step or you'll find yourself where you don't want to be."

He started for the car.

"Come back," I called after him. "I want to talk to you."

But the cop jumped into the car and they raced away in the direction in which the speakers had vanished.

The arrival of the police had caused a general dispersal of the crowd. Miners and their families were trailing off in all directions. Many of the men headed for the relief.

"It might as well be now," I thought, and started walking slowly after them. Again I ran the gantlet of eyes, eyes, eyes. I neared the relief. It was crowded with men. When they saw me, they all stood still, waiting. I reached the steps and faced a solid block of miners.

"Let me by, please," I said. "I want to talk to Stanley."

A pause. Then they fell back and let me pass between them, and I was acutely conscious of strong arms and hands on both sides of me, behind me. I stood in the door of the relief. Stanley sat on the far end of the counter talking to Jim Snyder. He looked very big and brawny. I walked toward Stanley. Jim Snyder sat behind him, looking at me with an ironic inscrutable face. When Stanley saw me, he leaped to his feet.

"Stanley," I said. "What's the matter?"

Stanley stood for a second, unmoving, speechless with rage. Then words burst from his lips.

"You get the hell outa here, you! You spy!"

He came toward me, hunching his big shoulders, doubling his fist. My knees wobbled. I retreated toward the door.

"Don't touch me!"

Stanley stood still. The men stood about, muttering and murmuring.

"What the hell you wanta tell the cops?" Jim Snyder said. "Get us all arrested, huh?" I had only wanted to get the point of view of the police.

Jim's speech was the signal for a tumult of guttural voices which broke out into outraged shouts.

"Spy! Capitalist! No good! Stool-pigeon! Mussolini!" The miners surged around me, shaking their fists. I remember a blurred impression of faces — Big Mike, Black Joe . . . I turned to go and the men again fell back, muttering, making way for me. I walked out of the door.

"You git the hell outa here," Stanley's voice. "And don't you never come back!"

The door slammed shut in my face.

I stood there looking at the shut door. At the words, "National Miners Relief. No picketing, no relief." "Mass meeting today at two o'clock."

I walked slowly down the steps — and ran bang into Johnny.

"Laurie!"

"Well, Johnny," I said. "I've been evicted."

I did not go to the relief again. I couldn't have anyway, for it was closed the next morning.

The sheriff was closing the relief kitchens one after the other. Avelonia, closed, had reopened immediately. The sheriff had sent out injunctions forbidding picketing. Avelonia had continued to picket. Now the sheriff had dispatched a special injunction to Avelonia to the effect that, if there was another picket, legal action would be taken. Avelonia was going to picket.

It was a cold rainy morning. At five-thirty promptly, the old standbys arrived at the relief. They huddled on the steps, an apprehensive handful of men, waiting for re-enforcements. One man came up, two, three. By a quarter of six, twenty men had collected. That was not enough. They waited five minutes. Four police cars drove up, and ranged themselves along the road in front of the group of men standing on the porch of the relief. A straggling miner came hurrying up the road. When he saw the police cars, he turned and retraced his steps.

One by one the men on the porch edged down the steps, and walked away with hanging head. There was no one left.

A policeman got out of a car and hung upon the door of the relief the sign: CLOSED.

John Dewey

WHY I AM NOT A COMMUNIST

A number of persons had the status of social consciences during the Depression, and were esteemed for their proven sincerity and disinterestedness. They were exploited, when possible, by "actionalists" who desired their endorsement. Franz Boas, Lincoln Steffens, Theodore Dreiser, John Dos Passos, Sinclair Lewis were several among many more whose utterances were assayed for their usefulness to leftists, communists, and others. John Dewey disappointed many impatient doers. Later in the decade he headed the Dewey Commission that cross-examined Leon Trotsky in Mexico City and concluded that Soviet charges were false which held that he had headed a counter-revolutionary center united with fascists to overthrow the Russian regime. At that point, communists turned against Dewey completely, and maintained, as they still maintain, that his was the philosophy of imperialism. It was perhaps a sign of the times that Dewey, who held respectable positions in respectable institutions, should have thought it relevant to explain why he was not *a communist, rather than why he was anything else.*

Why I am Not a Communist

HAVING HAD the opportunity to see the contribution of Mr. Bertrand Russell, I have doubts as to whether I can say much that he has not already said. But I begin by emphasizing the fact that I write with reference to being a Communist in the Western world, especially here and now in the United States, and a Communist after the pattern set in the U.S.S.R.

1. *Such* Communism rests upon an almost entire neglect of the specific historical backgrounds and traditions which have operated to shape the patterns of thought and action in America. The autocratic background of the Russian Church and State, the fact that every progressive movement in Russia had its origin in some foreign source and has been imposed from above upon the Russian people, explain much about the form Communism has taken in that country. It is therefore nothing short of fantastic to transfer the ideology of Russian Communism to a country which is so profoundly different in its economic, political, and cultural history. Were this fact acknowledged by Communists and reflected in their daily activities and general program, were it admitted that many of the practical and theoretical features of Russian Communism (like belief in the plenary and verbal inspiration of Marx, the implicit or explicit domination of the Communist party in every field of culture, the ruthless extermination of minority opinion in its own ranks, the verbal glorification of the mass and the actual cult of the infallibility of leadership) are due to local causes, the character of Communism in other countries might undergo a radical change. But it is extremely unlikely that this will take place. For official Communism has made the practical traits of the dictatorship *of* the proletariat and *over* the proletariat, the suppression of the civil liberties of all non-proletarian elements as well as of dissenting proletarian minorities, integral parts of the standard Communist faith and dogma. It has imposed and not argued the theory of dialectic materialism (which in the U.S.S.R. itself has to undergo frequent restatement in accordance with the exigencies of party factional controversy) upon all its followers. Its cultural philosophy, which has many commendable features, is vitiated by the absurd attempt to make a single and uniform entity out of the "proletariat."

2. Particularly unacceptable to me in the ideology of official Communism is its monistic and one-way philosophy of history. This is akin to the point made above. The thesis that all societies must exhibit a uniform, even if uneven, social development from primitive communism to slavery, from slavery to feudalism, from feudalism to capitalism, and from capitalism to socialism, and that the transition from capitalism to socialism must be achieved by the same way in all coun-

tries, can be accepted only by those who are either ignorant of history or who are so steeped in dogma that they cannot look at a fact without changing it to suit their special purposes. From this monistic philosophy of history, there follows a uniform political practice and a uniform theory of revolutionary strategy and tactics. But where differences in historic background, national psychology, religious profession and practice are taken into account — and they must be considered in every scientific theory — there will be corresponding differences in political methods, differences that may extend to general policies as well as to the strategy of their execution. For example, as far as the historic experience of America is concerned, two things among many others are overlooked by official Communists whose philosophy has been projected on the basis of special European conditions. We in the United States have no background of a dominant and overshadowing feudalism. Our troubles flow from the oppressive exercise of power by financial over-lords and from the failure to introduce new forms of *democratic* control in industry and government consonant with the shift from individual to corporate economy. It is a possibility overlooked by official Communists that important social changes in the direction of democratization of industry may be accomplished by groups working *with* the working-class although, strictly speaking, not *of* them. The other point ignored by the Communists is our deeply-rooted belief in the importance of individuality, a belief that is almost absent in the Oriental world from which Russia has drawn so much. Not to see that this attitude, so engrained in our habitual ways of thought and action, demands a very different set of policies and methods from those embodied in official Communism, verges to my mind on political insanity.

3. While I recognize the existence of class-conflicts as one of the fundamental facts of social life to-day, I am profoundly skeptical of class war as *the* means by which such conflicts can be eliminated and genuine social advance made. And yet this is a basic point in Communist theory and is more and more identified with the meaning of dialectic materialism as applied to the social process. Historically speaking, it may have been necessary for Russia in order to achieve peace for her war-weary soldiers, and land for her hungry peasants, to convert incipient class-war into open civil war culminating in the so-called dictatorship of the proletariat. But nonetheless Fascism in Germany and Italy cannot be understood except with reference to the lesson those countries learned from the U.S.S.R. How Communism can continue to advocate the kind of economic change it desires by means of civil war, armed insurrection and iron dictatorship in face of what

has happened in Italy and Germany I cannot at all understand. Reliable observers have contended that the communist ideology of dictatorship and violence together with the belief that the communist party was the foreign arm of a foreign power constituted one of the factors which aided the growth of Fascism in Germany. I am firmly convinced that imminent civil war, or even the overt threat of such a war, in any western nation, will bring Fascism with its terrible engines of repression to power. Communism, then, with its doctrine of the necessity of the forcible overthrow of the state by armed insurrection, with its doctrine of the dictatorship of the proletariat, with its threats to exclude all other classes from civil rights, to smash their political parties, and to deprive them of the rights of freedom of speech, press and assembly — which Communists *now* claim for themselves under capitalism — Communism is itself, an unwitting, but nonetheless, powerful factor in bringing about Fascism. As an unalterable opponent of Fascism in every form, I cannot be a Communist.

4. It is not irrelevant to add that one of the reasons I am not a Communist is that the emotional tone and methods of discussion and dispute which seem to accompany Communism at present are extremely repugnant to me. Fair-play, elementary honesty in the representation of facts and especially of the opinions of others, are something more than "bourgeois virtues." They are traits that have been won only after long struggle. They are not deep-seated in human nature even now — witness the methods that brought Hitlerism to power. The systematic, persistent and seemingly intentional disregard of these things by Communist spokesmen in speech and press, the hysteria of their denunciations, their attempts at character assassination of their opponents, their misrepresentation of the views of the "liberals" to whom they also appeal for aid in their defense campaigns, their policy of "rule or ruin" in their so-called united front activities, their apparent conviction that what they take to be the end justifies the use of *any* means if only those means promise to be successful — all these, in my judgment, are fatal to the very end which official Communists profess to have at heart. And if I read the temper of the American people aright, especially so in this country.

5. A revolution effected solely or chiefly by violence can in a modernized society like our own result only in chaos. Not only would civilization be destroyed but the things necessary for bare life. There are some, I am sure, now holding and preaching Communism who would be the first to react against it, if in this country Communism were much more than a weak protest or an avocation of literary men. Few communists are really aware of the far-reaching implications of the

doctrine that civil war is the *only* method by which revolutionary economic and political changes can be brought about. A comparatively simple social structure, such as that which Russia had, may be able to recover from the effects of violent, internal disturbance. And Russia, it must be remembered, had the weakest middle class of any major nation. Were a large scale revolution to break out in highly industrialized America, where the middle class is stronger, more militant and better prepared than anywhere else in the world, it would either be abortive, drowned in a blood bath, or if it were victorious, would win only a Pyrrhic victory. The two sides would destroy the country and each other. For this reason, too, I am not a Communist.

I have been considering the position, as I understand it, of the orthodox and official Communism. I cannot blind myself, however, to the perceptible difference between communism with a small *c,* and Communism, official Communism, spelt with a capital letter.

DRAW THY BREATH IN PAIN

> They lounge at corners of the street
> And greet friends with a shrug of shoulder
> And turn their empty pockets out,
> The cynical gestures of the poor.
>
> Stephen Spender, Poems (1934)

> One: When do we eat?
> The other: What is worth looking at?
>   What is worth listening to?
>
> Carl Sandburg, The People, Yes (1936)

William Saroyan

SEVENTY THOUSAND ASSYRIANS

William Saroyan was one of the geniuses of the 1930's, bursting suddenly out of nowhere to express a message of brotherhood and individualism. It doubtless helped him that a misprint in Story, *which published his "The Daring Young Man on the Flying Trapeze" in 1934, described him as seventeen years old, rather than twenty-seven; but his career did not depend on this accident. His flood of tales, manifestos, reminiscences touched readers who had almost forgotten that people had names and separate destinies. Ernest Hemingway lectured Saroyan on the duties of an artist, in one of Hemingway's interesting* Esquire *articles of the time which he was to repudiate in 1958. (Hemingway enjoined publishers from reprinting his pieces on the ground that such publication would hurt his money-making potential.)*

Saroyan suffered from a lack of intelligent criticism. He wrote some absurd pieces, and also some of the finest stories of the time, and spent his energies impartially on both.

I HADN'T had a haircut in forty days and forty nights, and I was beginning to look like several violinists out of work. You know the look: genius gone to pot, and ready to join the Communist Party. We barbarians from Asia Minor are hairy people: when we need a haircut, we *need* a haircut. It was so bad, I had outgrown my only hat. (I am writing a very serious story, pehaps one of the most serious I shall ever write. That is why I am being flippant. Readers of Sherwood Anderson will begin to understand what I am saying after a while; they will know that my laughter is rather sad.) I was a young man in need of a haircut, so I went down to Third Street (San Francisco), to the Barber College, for a fifteen-cent haircut.

Third Street, below Howard, is a district; think of the Bowery in New York, Main Street in Los Angeles: think of old men and boys, out of work, hanging around, smoking Bull Durham, talking about the government, waiting for something to turn up, simply waiting. It was a Monday morning in August and a lot of the tramps had come to the shop to brighten up a bit. The Japanese boy who was working over the free chair had a waiting list of eleven; all the other chairs were occupied. I sat down and began to wait. Outside, as Hemingway *(The Sun Also Rises; Farewell to Arms; Death in the Afternoon; Winner Take Nothing)* would say, haircuts were four bits. I had twenty cents and a half-pack of Bull Durham. I rolled a cigarette, handed the pack to one of my contemporaries who looked in need of nicotine, and inhaled the dry smoke, thinking of America, what was going on politically, economically, spiritually. My contemporary was a boy of sixteen. He looked Iowa; splendid potentially, a solid American, but down, greatly down in the mouth. Little sleep, no change of clothes for several days, a little fear, etc. I wanted very much to know his name. A writer is always wanting to get the reality of faces and figures. Iowa said, "I just got in from Salinas. No work in the lettuce fields. Going north now, to Portland; try to ship out." I wanted to tell him how it was with me: rejected story from *Scribner's,* rejected essay from *The Yale Review,* no money for decent cigarettes, worn shoes, old shirts, but I was afraid to make something of my own troubles. A writer's troubles are always boring, a bit unreal. People are apt to feel, *Well, who asked you to write in the first place?* A man must pretend not to be a writer. I said, "Good luck, north." Iowa shook his head. "I know better. Give it a try, anyway. Nothing to lose." Fine boy, hope he isn't dead, hope he hasn't frozen, mighty cold these days (December, 1933), hope he hasn't gone down; he deserved to live. Iowa, I hope you got work in Portland; I hope you are earning money; I hope you have rented a clean room with a warm bed in it; I hope you are sleeping nights, eating regularly, walking along like a human being, being happy. Iowa, my good wishes are with you. I have said a number of prayers for you. (All the same, I think he is dead by this time. It was in him the day I saw him, the low malicious face of the beast, and at the same time all the theatres in America were showing, over and over again, an animated film-cartoon in which there was a song called "Who's Afraid of the Big Bad Wolf?", and that's what it amounts to: people with money laughing at the death that is crawling slyly into boys like young Iowa, pretending that it isn't there, laughing in warm theatres. I have prayed for Iowa, and I consider myself a coward. By this time he must be dead, and I am sitting in a small room, talking about him, only talking.)

I began to watch the Japanese boy who was learning to become a barber. He was shaving an old tramp who had a horrible face, one of those faces that emerge from years and years of evasive living, years of being unsettled, of not belonging anywhere, of owning nothing, and the Japanese boy was holding his nose back (his own nose) so that he would not smell the old tramp. A trivial point in a story, a bit of data with no place in a work of art, nevertheless, I put it down. A young writer is always afraid some significant fact may escape him. He is always wanting to put in everything he sees. I wanted to know the name of the Japanese boy. I am profoundly interested in names. I have found that those that are unknown are the most genuine. Take a big name like Andrew Mellon. I was watching the Japanese boy very closely. I wanted to understand from the way he was keeping his sense of smell away from the mouth and nostrils of the old man what he was thinking, how he was feeling. Years ago, when I was seventeen, I pruned vines in my uncle's vineyard, north of Sanger, in the San Joaquin Valley, and there were several Japanese working with me, Yoshio Enomoto, Hideo Suzuki, Katsumi Sujimoto, and one or two others. These Japanese taught me a few simple phrases, *hello, how are you, fine day, isn't it, good-bye,* and so on. I said in Japanese to the barber student, "How are you?" He said in Japanese, "Very well, thank you." Then, in impeccable English, "Do you speak Japanese? Have you lived in Japan?" I said, "Unfortunately, no. I am able to speak only one or two words. I used to work with Yoshio Enomoto, Hideo Suzuki, Katsumi Sujimoto; do you know them?" He went on with his work, thinking of the names. He seemed to be whispering, "Enomoto, Suzuki, Sujimoto." He said, "Suzuki. Small man?" I said, "Yes." He said, "I know him. He lives in San Jose now. He is married now."

 I want you to know that I am deeply interested in what people remember. A young writer goes out to places and talks to people. He tries to find out what they remember. I am not using great material for a short story. Nothing is going to happen in this work. I am not fabricating a fancy plot. I am not creating memorable characters. I am not using a slick style of writing. I am not building up a fine atmosphere. I have no desire to sell this story or any story to *The Saturday Evening Post* or to *Cosmopolitan* or to *Harper's.* I am not trying to compete with the great writers of short stories, men like Sinclair Lewis and Joseph Hergesheimer and Zane Grey, men who really know how to write, how to make up stories that will sell. Rich men, men who understand all the rules about plot and character and style and atmosphere and all that stuff. I have no desire for fame. I am not out to win the Pulitzer Prize or the Nobel Prize or any other prize. I am out here in the far West, in San Francisco, in a small room on Carl Street, writing a letter to common people, telling them in simple language things they already know. I am merely making a record, so if I wander around a little, it is because I am in no hurry and because I do not know the rules. If I have any desire at all, it is to show the brotherhood of man. This is a big statement and it sounds a little precious. Generally a man is ashamed to make such a statement. He is afraid sophisticated people will laugh at him. But I don't mind. I'm asking sophisticated people to laugh. That is what sophistication is for. I do not believe in races. I do not believe in governments. I see life as one life at one time, so many millions simultaneously, all over the earth. Babies who have not yet been taught to speak any language are the only race of the earth, the race of man: all the rest is pretense, what we call civilization, hatred, fear, desire for strength. . . . But a baby is a baby. And the way they cry, there you have the brotherhood of man, babies crying. We grow up and we learn the words of a language and we see the universe through the language we know, we do not see it through all languages or through no language at all, through silence, for example, and we isolate ourselves in the language we know. Over here we isolate ourselves in English, or American as Mencken calls it. All the eternal things, in our words. If I want to do anything, I want to speak a more universal language. The heart of man, the unwritten part of man, that which is eternal and common to all races.

Now I am beginning to feel guilty and incompetent. I have used all this language and I am beginning to feel that I have said nothing. This is what drives a young writer out of his head, this feeling that nothing is being said. Any ordinary journalist would have been able to put the whole business into a three-word caption. Man is man, he would have said. Something clever, with any number of implications. But I want to use language that will create a single implication. I want the meaning to be precise, and perhaps that is why the language is so imprecise. I am walking around my subject, the impression I want to make, and I am trying to see it from all angles, so that I will have a whole picture, a picture of wholeness. It is the heart of man that I am trying to imply in this work.

Let me try again: I hadn't had a haircut in a long time and I was beginning to look seedy, so I went down to the Barber College on Third Street, and I sat in a chair. I said, "Leave it full in the back. I have a narrow head and if you do not leave it full in the back, I will go out of this place looking like a horse. Take as much as you like off the top. No lotion, no water, comb it dry." Reading makes a full man, writing a precise one, as you see. This is what happened. It doesn't make much of a story, and the reason it that I have left out the barber, the young man who gave me the haircut.

He was tall, he had a dark serious face, thick lips, on the verge of smiling but melancholy, thick lashes, sad eyes, a large nose. I saw his name on the card that was pasted on the mirror, Theodore Badal. A good name, genuine, a good young man, genuine. Theodore Badal began to work on my head. A good barber never speaks until he has been spoken to, no matter how full his heart may be.

"That name," I said, "Badal. Are you an Armenian?" I am an Armenian. I have mentioned this before. People look at me and begin to wonder, so I come right out and tell them. "I am an Armenian," I say. Or they read something I have written and begin to wonder, so I let them know. "I am an Armenian," I say. It is a meaningless remark, but they expect me to say it, so I do. I have no idea what it is like to be an Armenian or what it is like to be an Englishman or a Japanese or anything else. I have a faint idea what it is like to be alive. This is the only thing that interests me greatly. This and tennis. I hope some day to write a great philosophical work on tennis, something on the order of *Death in the Afternoon,* but I am aware that I am not yet ready to undertake such a work. I feel that the cultivation of tennis on a large scale among the peoples of the earth will do much to annihilate racial differences, prejudices, hatred, etc. Just as soon as I have perfected my drive and my lob, I hope to begin my outline of this great work. (It may seem to some sophisticated people that I am trying to make fun of Hemingway. I am not. *Death in the Afternoon* is a pretty sound piece of prose. I could never object to it as prose. I cannot even object to it as philosophy. I think it is finer philosophy than that of Will Durant and Walter Pitkin. Even when Hemingway is a fool, he is at least an accurate fool. He tells you what actually takes place and he doesn't allow the speed of an occurrence to make his exposition of it hasty. This is a lot. It is some sort of advancement for literature. To relate leisurely the nature and meaning of that which is very brief in duration.)

"Are you an Armenian?" I asked.

We are a small people and whenever one of us meets another, it is an event. We are always looking around for someone to talk to in our language. Our most ambitious political party estimates that there are nearly two million of us living on the earth, but most of us don't think so. Most of us sit down and take a pencil and a piece of paper and we take one section of the world at a time and imagine how many Armenians at the most are likely to be living in that section and we put the highest number on the paper, and then we go on to another section, India, Russia, Soviet Armenia, Egypt, Italy, Germany, France, America, South America, Australia, and so on, and after we add up our most hopeful figures the total comes to something a little less than a million. Then we start to think how big our families are, how high our birth-rate and how low our death-rate (except in times of war when massacres increase the death-rate), and we begin to imagine how rapidly we will increase if we are left alone a quarter of a century, and we feel pretty happy. We always leave out earthquakes, wars, massacres, famines, etc., and it is a mistake. I remember the Near East Relief drives in my home town. My uncle used to be our orator and he used to make a whole auditorium full of Armenians weep. He was an attorney and he was a great orator. Well, at first the trouble was war. Our people were being destroyed by the enemy. Those who hadn't been killed were homeless and they were starving *our own flesh and blood,* my uncle said, and we all wept. And we gathered money and sent it to our people in the old country. Then after the war, when I was a bigger boy, we had another Near East Relief drive and my uncle stood on the stage of the Civic Auditorium of my home town and he said, "Thank God this time it is not the enemy, but an earthquake. God has made us suffer. We have worshipped him through trial and tribulation, through suffering and disease and torture and horror and (my uncle began to weep, began to sob) through the madness of despair, and now he has done this thing, and still we praise Him, still we worship Him. We do not understand the ways of God." And after the drive I went to my uncle and I said, "Did you mean what you said about God?" And he said, "That was oratory. We've got to raise money. What God? It is nonsense." "And when you cried?" I asked, and my uncle said, "That was real. I could not help it. I had to cry. Why, for God's sake, why must we go through all this God damn hell? What have we done to deserve all this torture? Man won't let us alone. God won't let us alone. Have we done something? Aren't we supposed to be pious people? What is our sin? I am disgusted with God. I am sick of man. The only reason I am willing to get up and talk is that I don't dare keep my mouth shut. I can't bear the thought of more of our people dying. Jesus Christ, have we done something?"

I asked Theodore Badal if he was an Armenian.

He said, "I am an Assyrian."

Well, it was something. They, the Assyrians, came from our part of the world, they had noses like our noses, eyes like our eyes, hearts like our hearts. They had a different language. When they spoke we couldn't understand them, but they were a lot like us. It wasn't quite as pleasing as it would have been if Badal had been an Armenian, but it was something.

"I am an Armenian," I said. "I used to know some Assyrian boys in my home town, Joseph Sargis, Nito Elia, Tony Saleh. Do you know any of them?"

"Joseph Sargis, I know him," said Badal. "The others I do not know. We lived in New York until five years ago, then we came out west to Turlock. Then we moved up to San Francisco."

"Nito Elia," I said, "is a Captain in the Salvation Army." (I don't want anyone to imagine that I am making anything up, or that I am trying to be funny.) "Tony Saleh," I said, "was killed eight years ago. He was riding a horse and he was thrown and the horse began to run. Tony couldn't get himself free, he was caught by a leg, and the horse ran around and around for a half hour and then stopped, and when they went up to Tony he was dead. He was fourteen at the time. I used to go to school with him. Tony was a very clever boy, very good at arithmetic."

We began to talk about the Assyrian language and the Armenian language, about the old world, conditions over there, and so on. I was getting a fifteen-cent hair cut and I was doing my best to learn something at the same time, to acquire some new truth, some new appreciation of the wonder of life, the dignity of man. (Man has great dignity, do not imagine that he has not.)

Badal said, "I cannot read Assyrian. I was born in the old country, but I want to get over it."

He sounded tired, not physically but spiritually.

"Why?" I said. "Why do you want to get over it?"

"Well," he laughed, "simply because everything is washed up over there." I am repeating his words precisely, putting in nothing of my own. "We were a great people once," he went on. "But that was yesterday, the day before yesterday. Now we are a topic in ancient history. We had a great civilization. They're still admiring it. Now I am in America learning how to cut hair. We're washed up as a race, we're through, it's all over, why should I learn to read the language? We have no writers, we have no news — well, there is a little news: once in a while the English encourage the Arabs to massacre us, that is all. It's an old story, we know all about it. The news comes over to us through the Associated Press, anyway."

These remarks were very painful to me, an Armenian. I had always felt badly about my own people being destroyed. I had never heard an Assyrian speaking in English about such things. I felt great love for this young fellow. Don't get me wrong. There is a tendency these days to think in terms of pansies whenever a man says that he has affection for man. I think now that I have affection for all people, even for the enemies of Armenia, whom I have so tactfully not named. Everyone knows who they are. I have nothing against any of them because I think of them as one man living one life at a time, and I know, I am positive, that one man at a time is incapable of the monstrosities performed by mobs. My objection is to mobs only.

"Well," I said, "it is much the same with us. We, too, are old. We still have our church. We still have a few writers, Aharonian, Isahakian, a few others, but it is much the same."

"Yes," said the barber, "I know. We went in for the wrong things. We went in for the simple things, peace and quiet and families. We didn't go in for machinery and conquest and militarism. We didn't go in for diplomacy and deceit and the invention of machine-guns and poison gases. Well, there is no use in being disappointed. We had our day, I suppose."

"We are hopeful," I said. "There is no Armenian living who does not still dream of an independent Armenia."

"Dream?" said Badal. "Well, that is something. Assyrians cannot even dream any more. Why, do you know how many of us are left on earth?"

"Two or three million," I suggested.

"Seventy thousand," said Badal. "That is all. Seventy thousand Assyrians in the world, and the Arabs are still killing us. They killed seventy of us in a little uprising last month. There was a small paragraph in the paper. Seventy more of us destroyed. We'll be wiped out before long. My brother is married to an American girl and he has a son. There is no more hope. We are trying to forget Assyria. My father still reads a paper that comes from New York, but he is an old man. He will be dead soon."

Then his voice changed, he ceased speaking as an Assyrian and began to speak as a barber: "Have I taken enough off the top?" he asked.

The rest of the story is pointless. I said *so long* to the young Assyrian and left the shop. I walked across town, four miles, to my room on Carl Street. I thought about the whole business: Assyria and this Assyrian, Theodore Badal, learning to be a barber, the sadness of his voice, the hopelessness of his attitude. This was months ago, in August, but ever since I have been thinking about Assyria, and I have been wanting to say something about Theodore Badal, a son of an ancient race, himself youthful and alert, yet hopeless. Seventy thousand Assyrians, a mere seventy thousand of that great people, and all the others quiet in death and all the greatness crumbled and ignored, and a young man in America learning to be a barber, and a young man lamenting bitterly the course of history.

Why don't I make up plots and write beautiful love stories that can be made into motion pictures? Why don't I let these unimportant and boring matters go hang? Why don't I try to please the American reading public?

Well, I am an Armenian. Michael Arlen is an Armenian, too. He is pleasing the public. I have great admiration for him, and I think he has perfected a very fine style of writing and all that, but I don't want to write about the people he likes to write about. Those people were dead to begin with. You take Iowa and the Japanese boy and Theodore Badal, the Assyrian; well, they may go down physically, like Iowa, to death, or spiritually, like Badal, to death, but they are of the stuff that is eternal in man and it is this stuff that interests me. You don't find them in bright places, making witty remarks about sex and trivial remarks about art. You find them where I found them, and they will be there forever, the race of man, the part of man, of Assyria as much as of England, that cannot be destroyed, the part that massacre does not destroy, the part that earthquake and war and famine and madness and everything else cannot destroy.

This work is in tribute to Iowa, to Japan, to Assyria, to Armenia, to the race of man everywhere, to the dignity of that race, the brotherhood of things alive. I am not expecting Paramount Pictures to film this work. I am thinking of seventy thousand Assyrians, one at a time, alive, a great race. I am thinking of Theodore Badal, himself seventy thousand Assyrians and seventy million Assyrians, himself Assyria, and man, standing in a barber shop, in San Francisco, in 1933, and being, still, himself, the whole race.

John Steinbeck

THE VIGILANTE

The Grapes of Wrath towers over all the writing of the 1930's: the one novel of its time which can stand easily beside Moby Dick, The Scarlet Letter, Huckleberry Finn, *and* An American

The Vigilante

Tragedy. *It raises to the first importance the question of why John Steinbeck did not and has not written another great American epic. Several of his finer tales in* The Long Valley *(1938), of which the following is one, help give a sense of what interested and disturbed this master.*

His winning of the Nobel Prize in 1962 was a bitter pill for some literary elements who had felt that they had moved triumphantly with the times by rejecting the naturalism of the thirties.

THE great surge of emotion, the milling and shouting of the people fell gradually to silence in the town park. A crowd of people still stood under the elm trees, vaguely lighted by a blue street light two blocks away. A tired quiet settled on the people; some members of the mob began to sneak away into the darkness. The park lawn was cut to pieces by the feet of the crowd.

Mike knew it was all over. He could feel the let-down in himself. He was as heavily weary as though he had gone without sleep for several nights, but it was a dreamlike weariness, a grey comfortable weariness. He pulled his cap down over his eyes and moved away, but before leaving the park he turned for one last look.

In the center of the mob someone had lighted a twisted newspaper and was holding it up. Mike could see how the flame curled about the feet of the grey naked body hanging from the elm tree. It seemed curious to him that negroes turn a bluish grey when they are dead. The burning newspaper lighted the heads of the uplooking men, silent men and fixed; they didn't move their eyes from the hanged man.

Mike felt a little irritation at whoever it was who was trying to burn the body. He turned to a man who stood behind him in the near-darkness. "That don't do no good," he said.

The man moved away without replying.

The newspaper torch went out, leaving the park almost black by contrast. But immediately another twisted paper was lighted and held up against the feet. Mike moved to another watching man. "That don't do no good," he repeated. "He's dead now. They can't hurt him none."

The second man grunted but did not look away from the flaming paper. "It's a good job," he said. "This'll save the county a lot of money and no sneaky lawyers getting in."

"That's what I say," Mike agreed. "No sneaky lawyers. But it don't do no good to try to burn him."

The man continued staring toward the flame. "Well, it can't do much harm, either."

Mike filled his eyes with the scene. He felt that he was dull. He wasn't seeing enough of it. Here was a thing he would want to remember later so he could tell about it, but the dull tiredness seemed to cut the sharpness off the picture. His brain told him this was a terrible and important affair, but his eyes and his feelings didn't agree. It was just ordinary. Half an hour before, when he had been howling with the mob and fighting for a chance to help pull on the rope, then his chest had been so full that he had found he was crying. But now everything was dead, everything unreal; the dark mob was made up of stiff lay-figures. In the flamelight the faces were as expressionless as wood. Mike felt the stiffness, the unreality in himself, too. He turned away at last and walked out of the park.

The moment he left the outskirts of the mob a cold loneliness fell upon him. He walked quickly along the street wishing that some other man might be walking beside him. The wide street was deserted, empty, as unreal as the park had been. The two steel lines of the car tracks stretched glimmering away down the street under the electroliers, and the dark store windows reflected the midnight globes.

A gentle pain began to make itself felt in Mike's chest. He felt with his fingers; the muscles were sore. Then he remembered. He was in the front line of the mob when it rushed the closed jail door. A driving line forty men deep had crashed Mike against the door like the head of a ram. He had hardly felt it then, and even now the pain seemed to have the dull quality of loneliness.

Two blocks ahead the burning neon word BEER hung over the sidewalk. Mike hurried toward it. He hoped there would be people there, and talk, to remove this silence; and he hoped the men wouldn't have been to the lynching.

The bartender was alone in his little bar, a small, middle-aged man with a melancholy moustache and an expression like an aged mouse, wise and unkempt and fearful.

He nodded quickly as Mike came in. "You look like you been walking in your sleep," he said.

Mike regarded him with wonder. "That's just how I feel, too, like I been walking in my sleep."

"Well, I can give you a shot if you want."

Mike hesitated. "No — I'm kind of thirsty. I'll take a beer. . . . Was you there?"

The little man nodded his mouse-like head again. "Right at the last, after he was all up and it was all over. I figured a lot of the fellas would be thirsty, so I came back and opened up. Nobody but you so far. Maybe I was wrong."

"They might be along later," said Mike. "There's a lot of them

The Vigilante

still in the park. They cooled off, though. Some of them trying to burn him with newspapers. That don't do no good."

"Not a bit of good," said the little bartender. He twitched his thin moustache.

Mike knocked a few grains of celery salt into his beer and took a long drink. "That's good," he said. "I'm kind of dragged out."

The bartender leaned close to him over the bar, his eyes were bright. "Was you there all the time — to the jail and everything?"

Mike drank again and then looked through his beer and watched the beads of bubbles rising from the grains of salt in the bottom of the glass. "Everything," he said. "I was one of the first in the jail, and I helped pull on the rope. There's times when citizens got to take the law in their own hands. Sneaky lawyer comes along and gets some fiend out of it."

The mousy head jerked up and down. "You God-dam' right," he said. "Lawyers can get them out of anything. I guess the nigger was guilty all right."

"Oh, sure! Somebody said he even confessed."

The head came close over the bar again. "How did it start, mister? I was only there after it was all over, and then I only stayed a minute and then came back to open up in case any of the fellas might want a glass of beer."

Mike drained his glass and pushed it out to be filled. "Well, of course everybody knew it was going to happen. I was in a bar across from the jail. Been there all afternoon. A guy came in and says, 'What are we waiting for?' So we went across the street, and a lot more guys was there and a lot more come. We all stood there and yelled. Then the sheriff come out and made a speech, but we yelled him down. A guy with a twenty-two rifle went along the street and shot out the street lights. Well, then we rushed the jail doors and bust them. The sheriff wasn't going to do nothing. It wouldn't do him no good to shoot a lot of honest men to save a nigger fiend."

"And election coming on, too," the bartender put in.

"Well, the sheriff started yelling, 'Get the right man, boys, for Christ's sake get the right man. He's in the fourth cell down.'

"It was kind of pitiful," Mike said slowly. "The other prisoners was so scared. We could see them through the bars. I never seen such faces."

The bartender excitedly poured himself a small glass of whiskey and poured it down. "Can't blame 'em much. Suppose you was in for thirty days and a lynch mob came through. You'd be scared they'd get the wrong man."

"That's what I say. It was kind of pitiful. Well, we got to the nigger's cell. He just stood stiff with his eyes closed like he was dead drunk. One of the guys slugged him down and he got up, and then somebody else socked him and he went over and hit his head on the cement floor." Mike leaned over the bar and tapped the polished wood with his forefinger. " 'Course this is only my idea, but I think that killed him. Because I helped get his clothes off, and he never made a wiggle, and when we strung him up he didn't jerk around none. No, sir. I think he was dead all the time, after that second guy smacked him."

"Well, it's all the same in the end."

"No, it ain't. You like to do the thing right. He had it coming to him, and he should have got it." Mike reached into his trousers pocket and brought out a piece of torn blue denim. "That's a piece of the pants he had on."

The bartender bent close and inspected the cloth. He jerked his head up at Mike. "I'll give you a buck for it."

"Oh no, you won't!"

"All right. I'll give you two bucks for half of it."

Mike looked suspiciously at him. "What you want it for?"

"Here! Give me your glass! Have a beer on me. I'll pin it up on the wall with a little card under it. The fellas that come in will like to look at it."

Mike haggled the piece of cloth in two with his pocket knife and accepted two silver dollars from the bartender.

"I know a show card writer," the little man said. "Comes in every day. He'll print me up a nice little card to go under it." He looked wary. "Think the sheriff will arrest anybody?"

" 'Course not. What's he want to start any trouble for? There was a lot of votes in that crowd tonight. Soon as they all go away, the sheriff will come and cut the nigger down and clean up some."

The bartender looked toward the door. "I guess I was wrong about the fellas wanting a drink. It's getting late."

"I guess I'll get along home. I feel tired."

"If you go south, I'll close up and walk a ways with you. I live on south Eighth."

"Why, that's only two blocks from my house. I live on south Sixth. You must go right past my house. Funny I never saw you around."

The bartender washed Mike's glass and took off the long apron. He put on his hat and coat, walked to the door and switched off the red neon sign and the house lights. For a moment the two men stood on the sidewalk looking back toward the park. The city was silent.

There was no sound from the park. A policeman walked along a block away, turning his flash into the store windows.

"You see?" said Mike. "Just like nothing happened."

"Well, if the fellas wanted a glass of beer they must have gone someplace else."

"That's what I told you," said Mike.

They swung along the empty street and turned south, out of the business district. "My name's Welch," the bartender said. "I only been in this town about two years.

The loneliness had fallen on Mike again. "It's funny — " he said, and then, "I was born right in this town, right in the house I live in now. I got a wife but no kids. Both of us born right in this town. Everybody knows us."

They walked on for a few blocks. The stores dropped behind and the nice houses with bushy gardens and cut lawns lined the street. The tall shade trees were shadowed on the sidewalk by the street lights. Two night dogs went slowly by, smelling at each other.

Welch said softly — "I wonder what kind of a fella he was — the nigger, I mean."

Mike answered out of his loneliness. "The papers all said he was a fiend. I read all the papers. That's what they all said."

"Yes, I read them, too. But it makes you wonder about him. I've known some pretty nice niggers."

Mike turned his head and spoke protestingly. "Well, I've knew some dam' fine niggers myself. I've worked right 'longside some niggers and they was as nice as any white man you could want to meet. — But not no fiends."

His vehemence silenced little Welch for a moment. Then he said, "You couldn't tell, I guess, what kind of a fella he was?"

"No — he just stood there stiff, with his mouth shut and his eyes tight closed and his hands right down at his sides. And then one of the guys smacked him. It's my idea he was dead when we took him out."

Welch sidled close on the walk. "Nice gardens along here. Must take a lot of money to keep them up." He walked even closer, so that his shoulder touched Mike's arm. "I never been to a lynching. How's it make you feel — afterwards?"

Mike shied away from the contact. "It don't make you feel nothing." He put down his head and increased his pace. The little bartender had nearly to trot to keep up. The street lights were fewer. It was darker and safer. Mike burst out, "Makes you feel kind of cut off and tired, but kind of satisfied, too. Like you done a good job — but tired and kind of sleepy." He slowed his steps. "Look, there's a light in the kitchen. That's where I live. My old lady's waiting up for me." He stopped in front of his little house.

Welch stood nervously beside him. "Come into my place when you want a glass of beer — or a shot. Open till midnight. I treat my friends right." He scampered away like an aged mouse.

Mike called, "Good night."

He walked around the side of his house and went in the back door. His thin, petulant wife was sitting by the open gas oven warming herself. She turned complaining eyes on Mike where he stood in the doorway.

Then her eyes widened and hung on his face. "You been with a woman," she said hoarsely. "What woman you been with?"

Mike laughed. "You think you're pretty slick, don't you? You're a slick one, ain't you? What makes you think I been with a woman?"

She said fiercely, "You think I can't tell by the look on your face that you been with a woman?"

"All right," said Mike. "If you're so slick and know-it-all, I won't tell you nothing. You can just wait for the morning paper."

He saw doubt come into the dissatisfied eyes. "Was it the nigger?" she asked. "Did they get the nigger? Everybody said they was going to."

"Find out for yourself if you're so slick. I ain't going to tell you nothing."

He walked through the kitchen and went into the bathroom. A little mirror hung on the wall. Mike took off his cap and looked at his face. "By God, she was right," he thought. "That's just exactly how I do feel."

Erskine Caldwell

DAUGHTER

> *Erskine Caldwell made a massive assault on the poor white of the South from a position of intimate knowledge and an unshakable faith in human equality. He enticed his readers with earthy humor and elemental sexual and social attitudes. He persuaded them — in the North. Droves of theater-goers enjoyed* Tobacco Road.

Millions of readers thumbed his tales; they were not all good. Like William Saroyan, Caldwell gained and lost as a result of having innumerable readers and no critics. He gained the freedom to do as he pleased artistically. He lost the opportunity to influence his own people: the southern whites. Those who read Caldwell in the North had a pleasant sense of being morally superior to those whom they casually called "white trash," apparently under the impression that this was a technical and universally-accepted term, in the South as well as in the North. They paid Caldwell generously to entertain them with stories of easy virtue and non-directed living. But a volume entitled The Best of Erskine Caldwell, *if carefully made up, would have been lean and hard, and would have displayed the sober challenge which the poor whites in truth represented.*

Daughter is actually much more than a masterfully articulated account of an impulsive crime; it probes at much that was basic in the feelings of those who lived through the thirties, much of whose faith in the American Promise had turned to despair. (See also the Archibald MacLeish selection.)

AT SUNRISE a Negro on his way to the big house to feed the mules had taken the word to Colonel Henry Maxwell, and Colonel Henry 'phoned the sheriff. The sheriff had hustled Jim into town and locked him up in the jail, and then he went home and ate breakfast.

Jim walked around the empty cell-room while he was buttoning his shirt, and after that he sat down on the bunk and tied his shoe laces. Everything that morning had taken place so quickly that he even had not had time to get a drink of water. He got up and went to the water bucket near the door, but the sheriff had forgotten to put water in it.

By that time there were several men standing in the jail yard. Jim went to the window and looked out when he heard them talking. Just then another automobile drove up, and six or seven men got out. Other men were coming towards the jail from both directions of the street.

"What was the trouble out at your place this morning, Jim?" somebody said.

Jim stuck his chin between the bars and looked at the faces in the crowd. He knew everyone there.

While he was trying to figure out how everybody in town had heard about his being there, somebody else spoke to him.

"It must have been an accident, wasn't it, Jim?"

A colored boy hauling a load of cotton to the gin drove up the street. When the wagon got in front of the jail, the boy whipped up the mules with the ends of the reins and made them trot.

"I hate to see the State have a grudge against you, Jim," somebody said.

The sheriff came down the street swinging a tin dinner pail in his hand. He pushed through the crowd, unlocked the door, and set the pail inside.

Several men came up behind the sheriff and looked over his shoulder into the jail.

"Here's your breakfast my wife fixed for you, Jim. You'd better eat a little, Jim boy."

Jim looked at the pail, at the sheriff, at the open jail door, and Jim shook his head.

"I don't feel hungry," he said. "Daughter's been hungry, though — awfully hungry."

The sheriff backed out the door, his hand going to the handle of his pistol. He backed out so quickly that he stepped on the toes of the men behind him.

"Now, don't get careless, Jim boy," he said. "Just sit and calm yourself."

He shut the door and locked it. After going a few steps towards the street he stopped and looked into the chamber of his pistol to make sure that it had been loaded.

The crowd outside the window pressed in closer. Some of the men rapped on the bars until Jim came and looked out. When he saw them, he stuck his chin between the iron and gripped his hands around it.

"How come it to happen, Jim?" somebody asked. "It must have been an accident, wasn't it?"

Jim's long thin face looked as if it would come through the bars. The sheriff came up to the window to see if everything was all right.

"Now, just take it easy, Jim boy," he said.

The man who had asked Jim to tell what had happened, elbowed the sheriff out of the way. The other men crowded closer.

"How come, Jim?" he said. "Was it an accident?"

"No," Jim said, his fingers twisting about the bars. "I picked up the shotgun and done it."

The sheriff pushed towards the window again.

"Go on, Jim, and tell us what it's all about."

Jim's face squeezed between the bars until it looked as though only his ears kept his head from coming through.

"Daughter said she was hungry, and I just couldn't stand it no longer. I just couldn't stand to hear her say it."

"Don't get all excited now, Jim boy," the sheriff said, pushing forward one moment and being elbowed away the next.

"She waked up in the middle of the night again and said she was hungry. I just couldn't stand to hear her say it."

Somebody pushed all the way through the crowd until he got to the window.

"Why, Jim, you could have come and asked me for something for her to eat, and you know I'd have given you all I got in the world."

The sheriff pushed forward once more.

"That wasn't the right thing to do," Jim said. "I've been working all year and I made enough for all of us to eat."

He stopped and looked down into the faces on the other side of the bars.

"I made enough working on shares, but they came and took it all away from me. I couldn't go around begging after I'd made enough to keep us. They just came and took it all off. Then daughter woke up again this morning saying she was hungry, and I just couldn't stand it no longer."

"You'd better go and get on the bunk now, Jim boy," the sheriff said.

"It don't seem right that the little girl ought to be shot like that, Jim," somebody said.

"Daughter said she was hungry," Jim said. "She'd been saying that for all of the past month. Daughter'd wake up in the middle of the night and say it. I just couldn't stand it no longer."

"You ought to have sent her over to my house, Jim. Me and my wife could have fed her somehow. It don't look right to kill a little girl like her."

"I'd made enough for all of us," Jim said. "I just couldn't stand it no longer. Daughter'd been hungry all the past month."

"Take it easy, Jim boy," the sheriff said, trying to push forward.

The crowd swayed from one side to the other.

"And so you just picked up the gun this morning and shot her?" somebody said.

"When she woke up again this morning saying she was hungry, I just couldn't stand it."

The crowd pushed closer. Men were coming towards the jail from all directions, and those who were then arriving pushed forward to hear what Jim had to say.

"The State has got a grudge against you now, Jim," somebody said; "but somehow it don't seem right."

"I can't help it," Jim said. "Daughter woke up again this morning that way."

The jail yard, the street, and the vacant lot on the other side was filled with men and boys. All of them were pushing forward to hear Jim. Word had spread all over town by that time that Jim Carlisle had shot and killed his eight-year-old daughter, Clara.

"Who does Jim share-crop for?" somebody asked.

"Colonel Henry Maxwell," a man in the crowd said. "Colonel Henry has had Jim out there about nine or ten years."

"Henry Maxwell didn't have no business coming and taking all the shares. He's got plenty of his own. It ain't right for Henry Maxwell to come and take Jim's, too."

The sheriff was pushing forward once more.

"The State's got a grudge against Jim now," somebody said. "Somehow it don't seem right, though."

The sheriff pushed his shoulder between the crowd of men and worked his way in closer.

A man shoved the sheriff away.

"Why did Henry Maxwell come and take your share of the crop, Jim?"

"He said I owed it to him because one of his mules died a month ago."

The sheriff got in front of the barred window.

"You ought to go to the bunk now and rest some, Jim boy," he said. "Take off your shoes and stretch out, Jim boy."

He was elbowed out of the way.

"You didn't kill the mule, did you, Jim?"

"The mule dropped dead in the barn," Jim said. "I wasn't nowhere around. It just dropped dead."

The crowd was pushing harder. The men in front were jammed against the jail, and the men behind were trying to get within earshot. Those in the middle were squeezed against each other so tightly they could not move in any direction. Everyone was talking louder.

Jim's face pressed between the bars and his fingers gripped the iron until the knuckles were white.

The milling crowd was moving across the street to the vacant lot. Somebody was shouting. He climbed up on an automobile and began swearing at the top of his lungs.

A man in the middle of the crowd pushed his way out and went to his automobile. He got in and drove off alone.

Jim stood holding to the bars and looking through the window. The sheriff had his back to the crowd, and he said something to Jim. Jim did not hear what he said.

A man on his way to the gin with a load of cotton stopped to find out what the trouble was. He looked at the crowd in the vacant lot for a moment, and then he turned and looked at Jim behind the bars. The shouting across the street was growing louder.

"What's the trouble, Jim?"

Somebody on the other side of the street came to the wagon. He put his foot on a spoke in the wagon wheel and looked up at the man on the cotton while he talked.

"Daughter woke up this morning again saying she was hungry," Jim said.

The sheriff was the only person who heard him.

The man on the load of cotton jumped to the ground, tied the reins to the wagon wheel, and pushed through the crowd to the car where all the swearing was being done. After listening for a while, he came back to the street, called a Negro who was standing with the other men on the corner, and handed him the reins. The Negro drove off with the cotton towards the gin, and the man went back into the crowd.

Just then the man who had driven off alone in his car came back. He sat for a moment under the steering wheel, and then he opened the door and jumped to the ground. He opened the rear door and took out a crowbar as long as he was tall.

"Pry that jail door open and let Jim out," somebody said. "It ain't right for him to be in there."

The crowd in the vacant lot was moving again. The man who had been standing on top of the automobile jumped to the ground, and the men moved towards the street in the direction of the jail.

The first man to reach it jerked the six-foot crowbar out of the soft earth where it had been jabbed.

The sheriff backed off.

"Now, take it easy, Jim boy," he said.

He turned and started walking rapidly up the street towards his house.

Albert Maltz

THE HAPPIEST MAN ON EARTH

Albert Maltz was one of the communist successes of the 1930's. His plays, bluntly anti-capitalistic, pro-radical labor, pro-peace, were standard fare to those who sympathized with or accepted their point of view. Maltz's collection of short stories was titled simply The Way Things Are. *As the Depression wore on, it seemed to millions of Americans that life had become stabilized, meager, uneventful, unpromising: this was the way things were, the way they would be. In 1940, Maltz produced a novel,* The Underground Stream, *which intended to expose "fascist" organizations in the Detroit area. It was a hopelessly poor novel — far below John Steinbeck's* In Dubious Battle, *inadequate as this was — yet it was given regard by persons sympathetic to its general outlook, and its name still appears here and there, among scribes who have concerned themselves less for standards of fiction than they have for the memories of the New Deal. Maltz's strength was his understanding of the frustration of persons endowed with human gifts, willing and eager to work, to be useful, whom a clogged social and economic system rendered useless.*

JESSE felt ready to weep. He had been sitting in the shanty waiting for Tom to appear, grateful for the chance to rest his injured foot, quietly, joyously anticipating the moment when Tom would say, 'Why of course, Jesse, you can start whenever you're ready!'

For two weeks he had been pushing himself, from Kansas City, Missouri, to Tulsa, Oklahoma, through nights of rain and a week of scorching sun, without sleep or a decent meal, sustained by the vision of that one moment. And then Tom had come into the office. He had come in quickly, holding a sheaf of papers in his hand; he had glanced at Jesse only casually, it was true — but long enough. He had not known him. He had turned away..... And Tom Brackett was his brother-in-law.

Was it his clothes? Jesse knew he looked terrible. He had tried to spruce up at a drinking fountain in the park, but even that had gone badly; in his excitement he had cut himself shaving, an ugly gash down the side of his cheek. And nothing could get the red gumbo dust out of his suit even though he had slapped himself till both arms were worn out.... Or was it just that he *had* changed so much?

True, they hadn't seen each other for five years; but Tom looked five years older, that was all. He was still Tom. God! was *he* so different?

Brackett finished his telephone call. He learned back in his swivel chair and glanced over at Jesse with small, clear blue eyes that were suspicious and unfriendly. He was a heavy, paunchy man of forty-five, auburn-haired, rather dour-looking; his face was meaty, his features pronounced and forceful, his nose somewhat bulbous and reddish-hued at the tip. He looked like a solid, decent, capable business man who was commander of his local branch of the American Legon — which he was. He surveyed Jesse with cold indifference, manifestly unwilling to spend time on him. Even the way he chewed his toothpick seemed contemptuous to Jesse.

'Yes?' Brackett said suddenly. 'What do you want?'

His voice was decent enough, Jesse admitted. He had expected it to be worse. He moved up to the wooden counter that partioned the shanty. He thrust a hand nervously through his tangled hair.

'I guess you don't recognize me, Tom,' he said falteringly, 'I'm Jesse Fulton.'

'Huh?' Brackett said. That was all.

'Yes, I am, and Ella sends you her love.'

Brackett rose and walked over to the counter until they were face to face. He surveyed Fulton incredulously, trying to measure the resemblance to his brother-in-law as he remembered him. This man was tall, about thirty. That fitted! He had straight good features and a lank erect body. That was right too. But the face was too gaunt, the body too spiny under the baggy clothes for him to be sure. His brother-in-law had been a solid, strong young man with muscle and beef to him. It was like looking at a faded, badly taken photograph and trying to recognize the subject: the resemblance was there but the difference was tremendous. He searched the eyes. They at least seemed definitely familiar, gray, with a curiously shy but decent look in them. He had liked that about Fulton.

Jesse stood quiet. Inside he was seething. Brackett was like a man examining a piece of broken-down horseflesh; there was a look of pure pity in his eyes. It made Jesse furious. He knew he wasn't as far gone as all that.

108] ALBERT MALTZ

'Yes, I believe you are,' Brackett said finally, 'but you sure have changed.'

'By God, it's five years, ain't it?' Jesse said resentfully. 'You only saw me a couple of times anyway.' Then, to himself, with his lips locked together, in mingled vehemence and shame, What if I have changed? Don't everybody? I ain't no corpse.

'You was solid-looking,' Brackett continued softly, in the same tone of incredulous wonder. 'You lost weight, I guess?'

Jesse kept silent. He needed Brackett too much to risk antagonizing him. But it was only by deliberate effort that he could keep from boiling over. The pause lengthened, became painful. Brackett flushed. 'Jiminy Christmas, excuse me,' he burst out in apology. He jerked the counter up. 'Come in. Take a seat. Good God, boy' — he grasped Jesse's hand and shook it — 'I *am* glad to see you; don't think anything else! You just looked so peaked.'

'It's all right,' Jesse murmured. He sat down, thrusting his hand through his curly, tangled hair.

'Why are you limping?'

'I stepped on a stone; it jagged a hole through my shoe.' Jesse pulled his feet back under the chair. He was ashamed of his shoes. They had come from the Relief originally, and two weeks on the road had about finished them. All morning, with a kind of delicious, foolish solemnity, he had been vowing to himself that before anything else, before even a suit of clothes, he was going to buy himself a brand-new strong pair of shoes.

Brackett kept his eyes off Jesse's feet. He knew what was bothering the boy and it filled his heart with pity. The whole thing was appalling. He had never seen anyone who looked more down and out. His sister had been writing to him every week, but she hadn't told him they were as badly off as this.

'Well, now, listen,' Brackett began, 'tell me things. How's Ella?'

'Oh, she's pretty good,' Jesse replied absently. He had a soft, pleasing, rather shy voice that went with his soft gray eyes. He was worrying over how to get started.

'And the kids?'

'Oh, they're fine.... Well, you know,' Jesse added, becoming more attentive, 'the young one has to wear a brace. He can't run around, you know. But he's smart. He draws pictures and he does things, you know.'

'Yes,' Brackett said. 'That's good.' He hesitated. There was a moment's silence. Jesse fidgeted in his chair. Now that the time had arrived, he felt awkward. Brackett leaned forward and put his hand

The Happiest Man on Earth

on Jesse's knee. 'Ella didn't tell me things were so bad for you, Jesse. I might have helped.'

'Well, goodness,' Jesse returned softly, 'you been having your own troubles, ain't you?'

'Yes,' Brackett leaned back. His ruddy face became mournful and darkly bitter. 'You know I lost my hardware shop?'

'Well, sure, of course,' Jesse answered, surprised. 'You wrote us. That's what I mean.'

'I forgot,' Brackett said. 'I keep on being surprised over it myself. Not that it was worth much,' he added bitterly. 'It was running downhill for three years. I guess I just wanted it because it was mine.' He laughed pointlessly, without mirth. 'Well, tell me about yourself,' he asked. 'What happened to the job you had?'

Jesse burst out abruptly, with agitation, 'Let it wait, Tom, I got something on my mind.'

'It ain't you and Ella?' Brackett interrupted anxiously.

'Why, no!' Jesse sat back. 'Why, however did you come to think that? Why, Ella and me' — he stopped, laughing. 'Why, Tom, I'm just crazy about Ella. Why she's just wonderful. She's just my whole life, Tom.'

'Excuse me. Forget it.' Brackett chuckled uncomfortably, turned away. The naked intensity of the youth's burst of love had upset him. It made him wish savagely that he could do something for them. They were both too decent to have had it so hard. Ella was like this boy too, shy and a little soft.

'Tom, listen,' Jesse said, 'I come here on purpose.' He thrust his hand through his hair. 'I want you to help me.'

'Damn it, boy,' Brackett groaned. He had been expecting this. 'I can't much. I only get thirty-five a week and I'm damn grateful for it.'

'Sure, I know,' Jesse emphasized excitedly. He was feeling once again the wild, delicious agitation that had possessed him in the early hours of the morning. 'I know you can't help us with money! But we met a man who works for you! He was in our city! He said you could give me a job!'

'Who said?'

'Oh, why didn't you tell me?' Jesse burst out reproachfully. 'Why, as soon as I heard it I started out. For two weeks now I been pushing ahead like crazy.'

Brackett groaned aloud. 'You come walking from Kansas City in two weeks so I could give you a job?'

'Sure, Tom, of course. What else could I do?'

'God Almighty, there ain't no jobs, Jesse! It's a slack season. And you don't know this oil business. It's special. I got my Legion friends here but they couldn't do nothing now. Don't you think I'd ask for you as soon as there was a chance?'

Jesse felt stunned. The hope of the last two weeks seemed rolling up into a ball of agony in his stomach. Then, frantically, he cried, 'But listen, this man said *you* could hire! He *told* me! He drives trucks for you! He said you *always* need men!'

'Oh! ... You mean *my* department?' Brackett said in a low voice.

'*Yes,* Tom. That's it!'

'Oh, no, you don't want to work in my department,' Brackett told him in the same low voice. 'You don't know what it is.'

'Yes, I do,' Jesse insisted. 'He told me all about it, Tom. You're a dispatcher, ain't you? You send the dynamite trucks out?'

'Who was the man, Jesse?'

'Everett, Everett, I think.'

'Egbert? Man about my size?' Brackett asked slowly.

'Yes, Egbert. He wasn't a phony, was he?'

Brackett laughed. For the second time his laughter was curiously without mirth. 'No, he wasn't a phony.' Then, in a changed voice: 'Jiminy, boy, you should have asked me before you trekked all the way down here.'

'Oh, I didn't want to,' Jesse explained with naïve cunning. 'I knew you'd say "no." He told me it was risky work, Tom. But I don't care.'

Brackett locked his fingers together. His solid, meaty face became very hard. 'I'm going to say "no" anyway, Jesse.'

Jesse cried out. It had not occurred to him that Brackett would not agree. It had seemed as though reaching Tulsa were the only problem he had to face. 'Oh, no,' he begged, 'you can't. Ain't there any jobs, Tom?'

'Sure there's jobs. There's even Egbert's job if you want it.'

'He's quit?'

'He's dead!'

'Oh!'

'On the job, Jesse. Last night, if you want to know.'

'Oh!' ... Then, 'I don't care!'

'Now you listen to me,' Brackett said. "I'll tell you a few things that you should have asked before you started out. It ain't dynamite you drive. They don't use anything as safe as dynamite in drilling oil wells. They wish they could, but they can't. It's nitroglycerin! Soup!"

'But I know,' Jesse told him reassuringly. 'He advised me, Tom. You don't have to think I don't know.'

'Shut up a minute,' Brackett ordered angrily. 'Listen! You just have to *look* at this soup, see? You just *cough* loud and it blows! You know how they transport it? In a can that's shaped like this, see, like a fan? That's to give room for compartments, because each compartment has to be lined with rubber. That's the only way you can even *think* of handling it.'

'Listen, Tom —— '

'Now wait a minute, Jesse. For God's sake just put your mind to this. I know you had your heart set on a job, but you've got to understand. This stuff goes only in special trucks! At night! They got to follow a special route! They can't go through any city! If they lay over, it's got to be in a special garage! Don't you see what that means? Don't that tell you how dangerous it is?'

'I'll drive careful,' Jesse said. 'I know how to handle a truck. I'll drive slow.'

Brackett groaned. 'Do you think Egbert didn't drive careful or know how to handle a truck?'

'Tom,' Jesse said earnestly, 'you can't scare me. I got my mind fixed on only one thing: Egbert said he was getting a dollar a mile. He was making five to six hundred dollars a month for half a month's work, he said. Can I get the same?'

'Sure, you can get the same,' Brackett told him savagely. 'A dollar a mile. It's easy. But why do you think the company has to pay so much? It's easy — until you run over a stone that your headlights didn't pick out, like Egbert did. Or get a blowout! Or get something in your eye, so the wheel twists and you jar the truck! Or any other God damn thing that nobody ever knows! We can't ask Egbert what happened to him. There's no truck to give any evidence. There's no corpse. There's nothing! Maybe tomorrow somebody'll find a piece of twisted steel way off in a cornfield. But we never find the driver. Not even a finger nail. All we know is that he don't come in on schedule. Then we wait for the police to call us. You know what happened last night? Something went wrong on a bridge. Maybe Egbert was nervous. Maybe he brushed the side with his fender. Only there's no bridge any more. No truck. No Egbert. Do you understand now? That's what you get for your God damn dollar a mile!'

There was a moment of silence. Jesse sat twisting his long thin hands. His mouth was sagging open, his face was agonized. Then he shut his eyes and spoke softly. 'I don't care about that, Tom. You told me. Now you got to be good to me and give me the job.'

Brackett slapped the palm of his hand down on his desk. 'No!'

'Listen, Tom,' Jesse said softly, 'you just don't understand.' He opened his eyes. They were filled with tears. They made Brackett turn away. 'Just look at me, Tom. Don't that tell you enough? What did you think of me when you first saw me? You thought: "Why don't that bum go away and stop panhandling?" Didn't you, Tom? Tom, I just can't live like this any more. I got to be able to walk down the street with my head up.'

'You're crazy,' Brackett muttered. 'Every year there's one out of five drivers gets killed. That's the average. What's worth that?"

'Is my life worth anything now? We're just starving at home, Tom. They ain't put us back on relief yet.'

'Then you should have told me,' Brackett exclaimed harshly. 'It's your own damn fault. A man has no right to have false pride when his family ain't eating. I'll borrow some money and we'll telegraph it to Ella. Then you go home and get back on relief.'

'And then what?'

'And then wait, God damn it! You're no old man. You got no right to throw your life away. Sometime you'll get a job.'

'No!' Jesse jumped up. 'No. I believed that too. But I don't now,' he cried passionately. 'I ain't getting a job no more than you're getting your hardware store back. I lost my skill, Tom. Linotyping is skilled work. I'm rusty now. I've been six years on relief. The only work I've had is pick and shovel. When I got that job this spring I was supposed to be an A-1 man. But I wasn't. And they got new machines now. As soon as the slack started they let me out.'

'So what?' Brackett said harshly. 'Ain't there other jobs?'

'How do I know?' Jesse replied. 'There ain't been one for six years. I'd even be afraid to take one now. It's been too hard waiting so many weeks to get back on relief.'

'Well, you got to have some courage,' Brackett shouted. 'You've got to keep up hope.'

'I got all the courage you want,' Jesse retorted vehemently, 'but no, I ain't got no hope. The hope has dried up in me in six years' waiting. You're the only hope I got.'

'You're crazy,' Brackett muttered. 'I won't do it. For God's sake think of Ella for a minute.'

'Don't you *know* I'm thinking about her?' Jesse asked softly. He plucked at Brackett's sleeve. 'That's what decided me, Tom.' His voice became muted into a hushed, pained whisper. 'The night Egbert was at our house I looked at Ella like I'd seen her for the first time. *She ain't pretty any more, Tom!*' Brackett jerked his head and moved away. Jesse followed him, taking a deep, sobbing breath. 'Don't that tell you, Tom? Ella was like a little doll or something, you remember. I couldn't walk down the street without somebody turning to look at

The Happiest Man on Earth [113

her. She ain't twenty-nine yet, Tom, and she ain't pretty no more.'

Brackett sat down with his shoulders hunched up wearily. He gripped his hands together and sat leaning forward, staring at the floor.

Jesse stood over him, his gaunt face flushed with emotion, almost unpleasant in its look of pleading and bitter humility. 'I ain't done right for Ella, Tom. Ella deserved better. This is the only chance I see in my whole life to do something for her. I've just been a failure.'

'Don't talk nonsense,' Brackett commented, without rancor. 'You ain't a failure. No more than me. There's millions of men in the identical situation. It's just the depression, or the recession, or the God damn New Deal, or . . . !' He swore and lapsed into silence.

'Oh, no,' Jesse corrected him, in a knowing, sorrowful tone, 'those things maybe excuse other men. But not me. It was up to me to do better. This is my own fault!'

'Oh, beans!' Brackett said. 'It's more sun spots than it's you!'

Jesse's face turned an unhealthy mottled red. It looked swollen. 'Well, I don't care!' he cried wildly. 'I don't care! You got to give me this! I got to lift my head up. I went through one stretch of hell, but I can't go through another. You want me to keep looking at my little boy's legs and tell myself if I had a job he wouldn't be like that? Every time he walks he says to me, "I got soft bones from the rickets and you give it to me because you didn't feed me right." Jesus Christ, Tom, you think I'm going to sit there and watch him like that another six years?'

Brackett leaped to his feet. 'So what if you do?' he shouted. 'You say you're thinking about Ella. How's she going to like it when you get killed?'

'Maybe I won't,' Jesse pleaded. 'I've got to have some luck sometime.'

'That's what they all think,' Brackett replied scornfully. 'When you take this job your luck is a question mark. The only thing certain is that sooner or later you get killed.'

'Okay, then,' Jesse shouted back. 'Then I do! But meanwhile I got something, don't I? I can buy a pair of shoes. Look at me! I can buy a suit that don't say "Relief" by the way it fits. I can smoke cigarettes. I can buy some candy for the kids. I can eat some myself. Yes, by God, I want to eat some candy. I want a glass of beer once a day. I want Ella dressed up. I want her to eat meat three times a week, four times maybe. I want to take my family to the movies.'

Brackett sat down. 'Oh, shut up,' he said wearily.

'No,' Jesse told him softly, passionately, 'you can't get rid of me. Listen, Tom,' he pleaded, 'I got it all figured out. On six hundred a month look how much I can save! If I last only three months, look how much it is — a thousand dollars — more! And maybe I'll last longer. Maybe a couple years. I can fix Ella up for life!'

'You said it,' Brackett interposed. 'I suppose you think she'll enjoy living when you're on a job like that?'

'I got it all figured out,' Jesse answered excitedly. 'She don't know, see? I tell her I make only forty. You put the rest in a bank account for her, Tom.'

'Oh, shut up,' Brackett said. 'You think you'll be happy? Every minute, waking and sleeping, you'll be wondering if tomorrow you'll be dead. And the worst days will be your days off, when you're not driving. They have to give you every other day free to get your nerve back. And you lay around the house eating your heart out. That's how happy you'll be.'

Jesse laughed. 'I'll be happy! Don't you worry, I'll be so happy, I'll be singing. Lord God, Tom, I'm going to feel *proud* of myself for the first time in seven years!'

'Oh, shut up, shut up,' Brackett said.

The little shanty became silent. After a moment Jesse whispered: 'You got to, Tom. You got to. You got to.'

Again there was silence. Brackett raised both hands to his head, pressing the palms against his temples.

'Tom, Tom ——' Jesse said.

Brackett sighed. 'Oh, God damn it,' he said finally, 'all right, I'll take you on, God help me.' His voice was low, hoarse, infinitely weary. 'If you're ready to drive tonight, you can drive tonight.'

Jesse didn't answer. He couldn't. Brackett looked up. The tears were running down Jesse's face. He was swallowing and trying to speak, but only making an absurd, gasping noise.

"I'll send a wire to Ella,' Brackett said in the same hoarse, weary voice. 'I'll tell her you got a job, and you'll send her fare in a couple of days. You'll have some money then — that is, if you last the week out, you jackass!'

Jesse only nodded. His heart felt so close to bursting that he pressed both hands against it, as though to hold it locked within his breast.

'Come back here at six o'clock,' Brackett said. 'Here's some money. Eat a good meal.'

'Thanks,' Jesse whispered.

'Wait a minute,' Brackett said. 'Here's my address.' He wrote it on a piece of paper. 'Take any car going that way. Ask the conductor where to get off. Take a bath and get some sleep.'

'Thanks,' Jesse said. 'Thanks, Tom.'

'Oh, get out of here,' Brackett said.
'Tom.'
'What?'
'I just —— ' Jesse stopped. Brackett saw his face. The eyes were still glistening with tears, but the gaunt face was shining now, with a kind of fierce radiance.

Brackett turned away. 'I'm busy,' he said.

Jesse went out. The wet film blinded him, but the whole world seemed to have turned golden. He limped slowly, with the blood pounding his temples and a wild, incommunicable joy in his heart. 'I'm the happiest man in the world,' he whispered to himself. 'I'm the happiest man on the whole earth.'

Brackett sat watching till finally Jesse turned the corner of the alley and disappeared. Then he hunched himself over, with his head in his hands. His heart was beating painfully, like something old and clogged. He listened to it as it beat. He sat in desperate tranquillity, gripping his head in his hands.

THE GOVERNMENT TRIED TO HELP

I am not willing that the vitality of our people be further sapped by the giving of cash, of market baskets, of a few hours of weekly work cutting grass, raking leaves or picking up papers in the public parks. We must preserve not only the bodies of the unemployed from destitution but also their self-respect, their self-reliance and courage and determination.

Franklin D. Roosevelt, *Annual Message to Congress,* January 4, 1935.

There is nothing the New Deal has so far done that could not have been done better by an earthquake. A first-rate earthquake, from coast to coast, could have reestablished scarcity much more effectively. . . .

Benjamin Stolberg and Warren Jay Vinton, *The Economic Consequences of the New Deal* (1935)

People are still interested in the six million pigs that were killed in September of 1933. . . . I suppose it is a marvelous tribute to the humanitarian instincts of the American people that they sympathize more with little pigs which are killed than with full-grown hogs. . . . But we must think about farmers as well as hogs. And we must think about consumers and try to get a uniform supply of pork from year to year at a price which is fair to farmer and consumer alike.

Henry A. Wallace, in 1935, quoted in *Democracy Reborn* (1944)

God damn it! Here are a lot of people broke and we are putting them to work making researches of one kind or another. . . . As soon as you begin doing anything for white collar people, there is a certain group of people who begin to throw bricks. I have no apologies to make. . . . One hundred and fifty projects up there deal with pure science. What of it? I think those things are good in life. They are important in life. . . .

Harry Hopkins at press conference, in Robert E. Sherwood, *Roosevelt and Hopkins: an Intimate History* (1948)

Heywood Broun

PAPER WORK

> *Heywood Broun's journalism was one of the delights of the 1920's and the 1930's. He became a warm advocate of New Deal measures; some insisted he was, whether consciously or unconsciously, a front for conniving radicals. His sudden turn, in 1939, to Catholicism was considered to be an event of the time. A few months later, he was dead. Monsignor Fulton Sheen, who had aided in his conversion, and who officiated at his funeral, declared he had never seen a more manifest example of grace. But Broun's journalist friend George Britt, passing his coffin in St. Patrick's Cathedral in New York, remarked sadly, "They got you, pal."*

WILLIAM JAMES said that mankind must find a moral equivalent for war. Blow, bugles, blow, and let us put a ribbon with palms upon the breast of Travis Harvard Whitney. No soldier could have been more gallant than the man who crumpled at his desk in the Civil Works Administration. Before he would submit to being taken to the hospital where he died, Whitney insisted on giving directions to his assistants as to how the work should go on. He was torn with agony but it was his commitment to put two hundred thousand men and women back to work. This was just something which had to be done.

I saw him once, and in the light of his death I am not likely to forget. He called up to say that if the Newspaper Guild would furnish him a list of unemployed reporters he thought he could place some under the CWA.

"When do you want to see us?" I asked.

"Come down now," he answered.

We expected to find an office and an office boy and probably a couple of secretaries, but Whitney had a desk thrust right in the middle of a large and bustling room. He sat there and rode the tumult like a city editor. There were no preliminaries of any kind. The tall, gaunt man with deep-sunken eyes began by asking: "Now when do I get that list?"

I've heard so much about red tape and bureaucracy that I didn't suppose he meant immediately. "It will take a little time," I told him. "We haven't got a very big clerical force or much office space, and of course John Eddy will have to check up on the names for you. Let me see — this is Thursday — suppose we get you that list a week from Saturday and then on Monday we can really begin to get to work on it."

He indicated impatience. "That won't do at all," he said. "You don't understand. This is a rush job. Every day counts. Can't you let me have part of the list the day after tomorrow? This ought to be done right away. Can't you call me on the phone tonight?"

"Where can I get you after dinner?" I asked.

"Right here."

"How late?"

"I can't tell. I'll be here until I finish."

Travis Whitney made good that promise. He worked all day and he worked all night. He knew he was critically ill when he took the appointment. Doctors had told him of the necessity of rest and probably of an operation. "I think I can last," was his rejoinder.

And he set himself to win that race. Two hundred thousand jobs before the end came. I think it was Lord Nelson who had an ensign lash him to a mast at the battle of Trafalgar. Whitney's courage was better than that. He chained himself to his desk by a sheer act of will.

The people around could see him grow dead gray in the late hours. Almost you could hear the step of his adversary advancing. But all he said was, "We must hurry." He felt not only the pangs of his own physical torture but the bite of the wind upon the bodies of men who walked the streets without shelter.

I don't know what the economic philosophy of Travis Whitney may have been. He didn't have time to talk about it. "Some day" just couldn't fit into his scheme of things. His thought was of two hundred thousand jobs which must be made and handed out without delay. He had the harassed look of a flapjack cook in a lumber camp. "Right away" rang in his ears like a trumpet call. Maybe somebody came and said to him, "But don't you realize that you're not solving anything? This is just a temporary expedient. When the revolution comes — "

And I imagine Travis Whitney turned a deaf ear and only said, "Two hundred thousand jobs and this has got to be now."

He couldn't make the life force last until he had surged across the line. They put him on his shield and carried him away, and I hope that on his tomb will be written "Killed in action."

Unquestionably this shambling, thin man peering a little dubiously through glasses had a concern. It was a passion. I suppose it is a little difficult to make paper work seem as exciting or romantic as cavalry charges. But you see he had found his moral equivalent for war. And I rather think that when next I hear the word "heroism" my immediate mental association will not be that of any brass hat on a hill but of Travis Whitney bent over his desk. And maybe I will see him as a man against the sky. And I will hear him as he says, "More gently, death, come slower. Don't touch me till my job is done."

Edmund Wilson

'STILL"-: MEDITATIONS OF A PROGRESSIVE

In 1946, the ex-communist critic Granville Hicks, reconsidering Edmund Wilson, reported a young acquaintance as having commented upon a then-recent photograph of the critic. It reflected "a heavy-faced, middle-aged man with a stubborn mouth and arrogant, resentful eyes." Said Hicks's acquaintance: "What a mean son of a bitch Edmund Wilson must be!"

Nevertheless, Wilson's "Marxist period" of the 1930's contained the same traits which characterized his later and earlier periods: he was first and foremost an individualist, who pursued lines of thought as he preferred. This was his strength and his limitation. Where others sought group attitudes and communicable phrases, he pondered what he himself wished to know and how he himself preferred to say it. In general, his values were those of the Twenties, rather than of the Thirties; but whereas his friend F. Scott Fitzgerald was unable to adjust himself to Thirties needs, Wilson boldly undertook to define them. In effect, he demanded government action, couched in Marxian terms without modifying to any degree his personal attitudes and behavior. In his criticism, he worked intensively to assay literary results, and sometimes revealed himself as unwilling to be disturbed by facts. Thus, he assumed that Henry Adams, who had

"Still" - : Meditations of a Progressive

written a biography of the poet George Cabot Lodge, must, like himself, have held Lodge in disesteem, and so written ironically. The fact that Adams believed Lodge to have been a genius never seemed to have come to Wilson's attention. But Wilson's stubborn individualism made a first-rate observer of him during the Thirties; he reported what he saw, rather than what the communists, or the New Dealers, or his colleagues on the New Republic or the New Yorker would have preferred he see.

THE BRIGHT DRAB glare of the airport grounds. As you get into the red-painted plane, they hand you a small oil-paper packet: two close little rows of seats in a narrow moth's body. Well, well, there's cotton and chiclets in the package—the cotton is to stick in your ears and the gum to steady your nerves. "Air-Sickness Containers Located under Each Seat" — that sounds ominous. I might as well use the gum and the cotton. The porter shuts the door—now we're off: faster, faster, faster, higher roaring pressure of speed of starting — great fun: now we've dropped the ground. The muddy flat Potomac; Washington a litter of brickyard fragments; the grayish Capitol, the white government buildings — like what? — like nothing but government buildings even from way up above, and not very handsome ones; the little aligned suburban houses. I don't like these elevator drops, when you feel your seat falling away. The March fields below; worn-out patches on an old nap-bare carpet that shows the warp and woof. The long straight roads with little black cars that travel straight and fast along them. The passengers are very quick, seem under a certain strain.

Still, all those people at the progressive Conference* did get to the point of getting together — and what a mixed assortment they were — curious to think about what being progressive meant to the different ones! The senators at least had in common that they represented the agricultural West. Norris is an old-fashioned Western type who hates the industrial people — preoccupied with the power question. Bob La Follette has inherited the family radical tradition. Cutting is so much of New Yorker that one forgets he's Senator from New Mexico. He's rather like an English liberal — like some of the men in the Labor government — we've never, so far as I know, had that type in the Senate before. He sounds as if he were aiming at something like the English system, the President and the Cabinet responsible to Con-

---

*At that time the word "progressive" had not yet been taken over by the Communists. [*E. W.'s note* (1958).]

gress, a congressional majority controlling policy. Would this really help very much? All right no doubt for a Congress made up of Cuttings and La Follettes, but there are only a few such men — the rest are professional politicians. — Phelps Putnam, the poet, with his black clothes and his monocle, hanging around the conference — a little too much like Wyndham Lewis in his menacing fascist make-up. Still, it shows that the literary guys are taking public matters more seriously — God knows that our belated bleeding-heart romanticism has run out even for a writer like Phelps who is able to do something first-rate with it. — I wonder what Hergesheimer was doing at a back table in the Carlton dining room. Could he conceivably have been interested in the conference or does he simply get a kick out of a place like the Carlton? Those dreadful flavorless expressionless mannequins that paraded back and forth in Chanel and Patou gowns all the time we were having lunch — dreadful flavorless lunch — the only time they looked at all human was when they smiled at each other across the room. — Costigan's quite a fine old type,† with his Spanish hatchet-face and his dry yellow skin — his speech a little dry, too, but it's clear he knows his stuff — I can never get the hang of the tariff, but it is plain that, when these questions come up nobody sees very far beyond his own little racket — the man who held up the Sears, Roebuck catalogue and said that there were 30,000 articles listed in it and how was anybody ever going to know enough about them to work out the tariff properly — he pointed out that paint-brush handles were protected. — The Colorado beet-grower and the Filipino: the Filipino, very tense and formal, in gold glasses and a dapper cutaway, announced that if the United States would give the Philippines their freedom, they would willingly forego the free trade for their cocoanut oil and sugar. The beet-grower, a hearty loquacious fellow, rose to his feet to state that he was proud to be one of what people called the "wild jackasses of the West," that the wild jackasses never brayed unless there was some reason for it, that just now they were being ruined by free sugar imports from the Philippines, and that he hoped to God the Senate of the United States would have the decency and the brains to give the Filipinos their freedom! Another Filipino got up and declared that he sympathized with the American sugar interests, but that, after all, the United States had taken over the Philippines against their will and . . . "But honest, ain't ye glad now we did it?" the beet-grower interrupted. "Would ye want to be back with your swamps an' your bad roads an' no schools an' " . . . The Filipino said no, they were not glad. Those

†Edward P. Costigan, Senator from Colorado, 1930 — 36. [*E. W.*]

were the respective extents to which those two believed in progressivism.

The flat thick muddy branches of Chesapeake Bay like lung lobules on an anatomical chart — a few barges like beetles on the water, their noses turned toward Baltimore. Dull end of a March day — pale coldish sun now setting among faintly rusty clouds — on the horizon, dimness. — Hoover didn't look so unhealthy or so unattractive as one expected — grayish hair, pink face, smoke-blue eyes — the thing is that, since the depression, he's been becoming in people's minds a kind of great pulpy empty ectoplasm, and embodiment, hardly human, of the administration's stupidity and impotence. One hardly expected to find him a man. He muttered something about restriction in the oil industry. I wonder whether his rather sly smile, when he dismissed the reporters with "That's all for today," implied that they'd submitted to him questions about the Progressive Conference. He makes them write out all their questions beforehand and then refuses to answer most of them. Everybody at the conference was either denouncing Hoover or wondering why he behaved as he did — he does seem to be a case of political ambition completely devoid of ideals or ideas — I suppose he has the exaggerated respect for the rich which comes from having started poor — that's no doubt the real hole in the skimmer of the American poor-boy-to-President idea — people who've had a hard time to make money are likely to end by taking it too seriously. — That plane in the airport below is fluttering around like a moth that's just been burned in a lamp. — They wouldn't let in old John Dewey on account of what they regard as his merely loose talk about the need for a third party. Still, I suppose that was the kind of thing that had to be pretty rigorously limited — they were certainly quite right in keeping out Prohibition. Ben Marsh of the People's Lobby, Dewey's political manager, announced that he was going to come in order to heckle the speakers. He claimed that the independent senators might have been able to force an extra session and get some of these matters attended to, that Hoover would have been glad of the excuse to call one. But he never made good his threat. — Still, one would like to see them come out and say, "Capitalism has got to go. It's just a question of time, so we're trying to make the transition easy." If they're going in for scaring the manufacturers, they might as well scare them good and proper. I imagine that what they're afraid of is scaring their constituents, too. But why are these American progressives so tongue-tied with inhibitions? — they're shy of the whole language of real political thought. The surest way to shake and embarrass an American political reformer, the surest way to make him back down, has always been to accuse him of socialism — that's what they did with Bryan, and we ought to be beyond that stage. I suppose that we still have a feeling that God is going to strike us dead if we admit that our old-fashioned republic isn't the last word in political science.

Big red bee-body of the motor always outside the window, with its barb-armed behind and blunt head — springs quivering in the fierce jingle and continual beat of the rhythm — what if that thick hoop that keeps them in place flew off. — Leo Wolman's brother Sam met a man in the lavatory at the Carlton who asked him what he thought of the conference — Sam said that he hadn't been to it. Well, the man said, he had come all the way from Boston for it. What did he think about it? asked Sam. "Well," said the man, "I don't see what's the use of their planning what to do with industry when industry's controlled by capital." — Leo Wolman's story about Lincoln Steffens — he met Steffens and found him beaming for the first time in history. "What's the matter? You look so cheerful," said Wolman. "I've been waiting for this moment for years — to see all you fellows together, up against a blank wall and not knowing what to do about it!"

Neutral brown land underneath, tree-bristling or mud-spongy — the water a dullish mirror. Those long roads that look like pipes, bent at moderate angles or curving only a little, with black cars traveling eternally along them. Well: this is a little dull — the time has come to read the *New Yorker*.

Long gray buildings — is this the Du Pont works? — gray colony of company houses. There's something solemn and grim about a great industry like that — it seems to weigh upon the executives as oppressively as it does on the workers — it's something like the weight of the army — but why the hell should it be? — I suppose that anything effective must come from the labor end. What can the progressives do but whip up a certain publicity and try to create a favorable atmosphere? — perhaps put through a little legislation. — Suppose Hillman got to be president of the AF of L — they had to ask William Green* to speak — he was hissed when he opposed the recognition of Russia. One of the labor experts was hopeful to a sensational degree — he thought that the AF of L would eventually throw out its leaders and would then, under enlightened leadership from one of the independent unions, embark on a whirlwind campaign — it would be easy to pick up the auto workers — if the Communists could go down South and get the textile workers, what couldn't a legitimate movement do? — Is this utopian? Somebody was telling me that he was talking to a

*President of the American Federation of Labor. [*E. W.*]

"Still" - : Meditations of a Progressive

representative of the Socialist Labor Party and asked him what he thought was going to happen. It was obvious, said the Socialist Laborite: capitalism was soon going to break down, and the Socialist Labor Party would step in and take over the government.

Philadelphia still seen by daylight, but with little yellow lamps on the bridges and along the notched streets — 6:15, exactly as scheduled. — I wonder whether Cutting has ever read Marx — he evidently reads a good deal — and has been to the Soviet Union, as few other Senators have. Still, those men in the British Labor government have unquestionably read Marx. I suppose that it is never possible for people to get to the point of taking any very drastic action till their interests are pretty seriously affected. A man who is badly off may take steps to better himself — but how can people with property go to the length of dispossessing themselves? — it seems to be true that a high standard of living, unless you're a saint or an eccentric, is something that you can't get away from — you can't help feeling more solidarity with other people with the same standard of living than with anybody else whatever, no matter how worthy or how badly off. It is only when people are far-sighted enough to see their standard of living threatened that they do anything more than talk. Borah denounced "the capitalists" for inflating General Motors and so forth, reminded us that 80 per cent of the money was owned by 4 per cent of the people, but then hastened to assure his audience — the big radio audience arranged for him rather than the one in the room — that he didn't propose to confiscate their money: "Let them keep it!" he thundered, with a blend of magnanimity and scorn. Somebody else had a plan for raising the standard of the poor without lowering the standard of the rich. The real trouble, no doubt, is that neither the politicians nor the intellectuals — the people who ought to supply the ideas — have been seriously hit by the depression — I've done unusually well this winter myself — I suppose that nobody at that conference was in anything but very comfortable circumstances — well-paid journalists, distinguished professors, grange and labor officials, idealistic manufacturers, political people with sound positions. — Well, there, with its gun-barrel chimneys, is a big public service plant, declaring itself in block electric letters, all alone on the Jersey mudbanks, somewhere in the neighborhood of Trenton — a few small boats resting on the river at evening — roaring red flames flaring from inside some factory — Trenton in the gathered darkness, a thickish ringworm rash of lights that twinkle in the haze, irregularly, as if in areas that grow successively sensitive but with a sort of steady rhythm — a red and dark sooty west, the looping streams. — It's probably unfortunate that Washington is detached from the rest of the country — a special city for political life, no wonder American politics has a way of not seeming serious — and literary New York's just as much cut off from the general life of the country — though it's the biggest industrial city, if you count Newark in — which we'll presently be coming to now. — The black countryside, a last glint of cold streams, roads in the dead black with the same little cars traveling, but now with their little lights on — unidentifiable lights of towns, embedded in the dark of distance — I can't even tell where Princeton is.

Another bigger rash of lights — that's Newark — an electric sign: a thick red arrow jerking back and forth, first points one way, then the other — thick wormwinding ribbons of water cut out on the black in clear gray. We're going into the big twinkling limitless light-bed, ruled strongly across with lines of light. — Up against a thing like that, there's not much that anybody can do, I suppose. — Still, you don't want to let it buffalo you. — Is there any real political consciousness coming to life down there? — that new independent union that Frank Vogel was trying to start in Detroit — that $8 that those Arkansas farmers sent in to the *Daily Worker,* vastly to the staff's surprise. — Could there be another farmer-labor movement? Could the white-collar workers be induced to support it? Could those progressive senators lead it?

A great criss-cross web of lights — signaling in the dark — field pricked out with green, yellow and red. This turning and milling in the air makes you a little sick — lists very far over to the left, encounters a pointer of light — down — gliding just above the ground — takes the opening neatly and cleanly in the enclosure picked out with green lights — a bump, taxiing in — the pilot gives her her head in a last snorting triumphing charge, tilted tail-down, to the port.

H. L. Mencken

THE NEW DEAL MENTALITY*

> *A few persons were astounded to discover, in the 1930's, that Mencken was conservative (at least) in his social thinking. V. F. Calverton, editor of the* Modern Monthly, *an eclectic left-wing in-*

*Reprinted by permission of *The American Mercury,* Inc. Copyright 1936, by The American Mercury.

tellectual journal, and a fellow Baltimorean, exposed him as a royalist in his thought. Most liberals and radicals found it more convenient and comfortable to distinguish between the firmly anti-radical, anti-New Deal Mencken of the 1930's, and the iconoclastic Mencken of the 1920's and the American Mercury, *who had derided the "booboisie" of the time, the George F. Babbitts, and thus presumably helped blaze the trail for 1930's radicalism. What they failed to appreciate was that Mencken's method and goals were the same in both eras. He had not favored progress or humanitarianism, and he had been no friend of socialism. His cause had been the individual, his foe Puritanism and conformity. He was as atheistic as the radicals, but as opposed to authority as a Kentucky hillbilly. He read incessantly, but with the energy of a journalist and polemicist, rather than of a scholar. The inability of the right wing of American social politics to utilize his brilliance during the 1930's was one sign of its essential incapacity to mount an intellectual assault against reigning liberal ideologists.*

AT EVERY time of stress and storm in history one notes the appearance of wizards with sure cures for all the sorrows of humanity. They flourished, you may be certain, in Sumer and Akkad, in the Egypt of all the long dynasties, and in the lands of the Hittites and Scythians. They swarmed in Greece, and in Rome some of them actually became Emperors. For always the great majority of human beings sweat and fume under the social system prevailing in the world they live in — always they are convinced that they are carrying an undue share of its burdens, and getting too little of its milk and honey. And always it is easy to convince them that by some facile device, invented by its vendor and offered freely out of the bigness of his heart, all these injustices may be forced to cease and desist, and a Golden Age brought in that will give every man whatever he wants, and charge him nothing for it.

There is thus no actual newness in the so-called New Deal. Its fundamental pretension goes back to the dark abysm of time, and even its most lunatic details are not novel to students of world-saving. If it differs from the other current panaceas — for instance, Communism, Fascism, and Nazi-ism — it is only in its greater looseness and catholicity, its more reckless hospitality to miscellaneous nonsense. It is a grand and gaudy synthesis of all the political, economic, social, socio-political, and politico-economic quackeries recorded in the books, from the days of Wat Tyler to those of Bryan, the La Follettes, Lloyd George, Borah, Norris, and Debs. Indeed, it goes far beyond Wat to the *Republic* of Plato, and on the way down the ages it sucks in the discordant perunas of Augustine, Martin Luther, J. J. Rousseau, Robert Owen, Claude Henri Saint-Simon, Karl Marx, Sockless

Jerry Simpson, Thorstein Veblen, and Henry George. This mess, boiling violently in a red-hot pot, is now ladled out to the confiding in horse-doctor's doses, to the music of a jazz band. Let them swallow enough of it, so they are assured, and all their sorrows will vanish. Let them trust the wizards manning the spoons, and they will presently enter upon fields of asphodel, where every yen that is native to the human breast will be realized automatically, and all the immemorial pains of doing-without will be no more, and what goes up need never come down again, and two and two will make five, five and a half, six, ten, a hundred, a million,

It is hardly necessary to rehearse the constituent imbecilities of this grandiose evangel — its proposal to ease the privations of the poor by destroying food and raising the cost of living, its proposal to dispose of the burden of debt by laying on more and more debt, its proposal to restore the impaired common capital by outlawing and demolishing what is left, and so on and so on. The details are of no more significance than they were when an oldtime doctor sat down to write a shotgun prescription. It is, in fact, only by accident that this or that crazy device gets out in front. Each wizard roots with undeviating devotion for his own, and a large part of the money wasted so far has gone into helping Wallace to prevail against Hopkins, and Hopkins to upset and flabbergast Ickes. Whenever one of the brethren gets a new hunch, there is a sharpening of activity, and the taxpayer goes on the block for another squeeze. And whenever one of them comes to grief, which is almost every day, the others rush into the gap with something worse.

That under all this furious medication there lies a sub-stratum of veritable pathology may be accepted without argument. Even the dumbest yokel does not succumb to even the most eloquent hawker of snake-oil on days when his liver and lights are ideally quiescent. It takes a flicker of pain along the midrifff to bring him up to the booth, and something more than a flicker to make him buy. In the present case there are qualms and tremors all over the communal carcass, for the whole world was lately mauled by a long, wasteful, and fruitless war, and the end of that war saw many millions of people reduced to poverty, terror, and despair. Immeasurable values had been destroyed, and the standard of living had declined everywhere. There was, of course, only one way to restore what had been lost, and that was for all hands to return to work, and earn it over again by patient industry. But in the post-war years any such scheme seemed too slow and painful, especially to romantic Americans, so resort was had to what appeared to be quicker contrivances. One of them, as everybody knows, was the anticipation of income by credit buying, and another was the accumulation of bogus values by gambling. These contrivances appeared to work for a while, and we were assured by high academic authority that a New Economy had come in; but suddenly they ceased to work, and there ensued a grand bust, with the losses of the war multiplied two or three times, and every participant in the joy-ride rubbing his pocket, his occiput, and his shins. Nor did the spectators fare much better. Indeed, some of them were hurt even worse than the joy-riders.

What to do? The old prescription was still indicated — patience, industry, frugality. A few austere souls began to preach it, albeit somewhat timorously, and some even ventured to take it, but for the majority it was far too unpalatable to be endured. They craved a master elixir that would cure them instantly and without burning their gullets, a single magical dose whose essences would run up and down their legs like electricity, and purge them of all their malaises at one lick, and waft them whole and happy to the topmost towers of Utopia. In brief, what they craved was quackery, and that is precisely what they got. From all points of the compass "the astrologers, the Chaldeans, and the soothsayers" came galloping — some from near and some from far, some from college classrooms and some from chicken-farms, some from the voluptuous dens of Rotary and Kiwanis and some from the chill crypts of the Y.M.C.A., some in glittering military uniforms and some in the flapping chemises of prophets and martyrs — but all busting with enlightened self-interest, all eager to grab favorable spots and loose their spiels.

For a while it was very confusing, but gradually something resembling order began to emerge from chaos. Upon the troubled face of the waters there appeared the shine of a serene and benignant Smile, the calming influence of a Master Mind. Why should inspired men fight like cats and dogs? Why should the Uplift be pulled to pieces on the very day of Armageddon, with an unparalleled chance for Service in front of it? Why not gang the suckers, and take them *en masse*? Why not, in Hopkins' immortal words to his stooge Williams, "give *everyone* a job"? To see the way was to consummate the dizzy deed. There and then the New Deal was born.

II

The resemblance of all such arcana to the theological revelation must be plain to every connoisseur of buncombe. There is something transcendental about their very absurdity, and their agents quickly take on a truly sacerdotal cockiness. They always deny the fact heatedly, and the communist apostles, in particular, are sensitive about it, but, as I shall show presently, its truth is always evident.

The New Deal, it must be allowed in fairness, is measurably less celestial than some of its rival quackeries. It lacks, at least so far, the formal theologies of fascism and Nazi-ism, and it has not produced a hagiology comparable to that of communism. But maybe that is only because it is American, and the sacred sciences, in this country, fall short of the polish and refinement they show in Europe. If you are willing to call the Methodist-Baptist brand of spiritual bush-whacking a kind of theology, then undoubtedly the More Abundant Life comes under the definition too, for it had its Billy Sunday in General Hugh Johnson, J. D., it has borrowed dogmas as well as dervishes from the Y.W.C.A., and in its ardor to set up new moral values it is almost as evangelical as the Anti-Saloon League.

On technical grounds, of course, any professional theologian would reject it as bogus and against God, just as any professional pathologist would reject chiropractic; but such trade vanity, with its sour overtones of jealousy, is hardly to be accepted as evidence. The fact remains glaringly plain that Hopkins, Ickes, Tugwell, Wallace, and the rest carry on their complicated and otiose hocus-pocus, not on the level of the earthly, like medical men excavating tonsils, but on the level of the spiritual, like medicine men casting out devils. The ordinary business of the country, though they seem to be in charge of it, interests them very little. They do not bother to keep its windows washed, to catch the rats in its cellar, or to audit and pay its bills. Such lowly offices, though they may be necessary, are below the threshold of attention of the Habakkuks who now govern and ruin us. They concentrate their wizardry upon Larger and Deeper Things — the redistribution of wealth, the scotching of the Nine Old Villains of Capitol Hill, the extermination of the Constitution, and the repeal of all the ordinary laws of arithmetic. Their aim is to make over the Republic completely, so that its one function will be the Uplift, and there will be no more challenge to their own hegemony. In brief, they are priests undertaking an essentially supernatural enterprise — a general overhauling and redesigning of human society and human nature, impossible on its face but well within the bounds of orthodox miracle.

To dismiss them as mere frauds would probably be a far too facile disposition. Such sorcerers, indeed, always end by convincing themselves. It happened to Munyon, it happened to Lydia Pinkham, and now it is happening all over again. Moreover, the process is helped

The New Deal Mentality [131

along in the present case by the heady effects of power. A few years ago all the New Deal Isaiahs were obscure and impotent fellows who flushed with pride when they got a nod from the cop at the corner; today they have the secular rank of princes of the blood, and the ghostly faculties of cardinal archbishops. Each is the hero of a Cinderella story more marvelous than any ever recorded at Hollywood, where five-and-ten-cent-store girls become great ladies overnight, and the pants-presser of yesterday needs forty valets to press his pants today. What would *you* do, friend, if you were hauled suddenly out of a bare, smelly schoolroom, wherein the razzberries of sophomores had been your only music, and thrown into a place of power and glory almost befitting Caligula, Napoleon I, or J. Pierpont Morgan, with whole herds of Washington correspondents crowding up to take down your every wheeze, and the first pages of their newspapers thrown open to your complete metaphysic? You would conclude at once, I fancy, that you were a very smart fellow, and it would be pretty hard for you to keep your head. Well, all the Brain Trust pedagogues have been through that dreadful test, and if it is a fact that they have sometimes lost theirs, then certainly it is not a fact to surprise philosophers.

My belief is that, taking one day with another, they have kept a reasonably tight grip upon their expanding egos, and so conducted themselves quite as well as could have been expected. Does Hopkins bask and wallow in the high privilege of making Governors of great American Commonwealths wait in his ante-chamber? Perhaps; but so far he has certainly not got to the point of making Their Excellencies kiss his hand. And does Ickes, when he rises to denounce the crimes of entrenched widows and money-mad orphans, thunder with the accents of Moses on Sinai? It may be so, but let us remember that he has not yet proposed to boil them in oil. What these boys would do to the Bill of Rights if they could get it up a dark alley, I do not profess to say. As things now stand, the Bill gives solace if not protection to communist fellow-travelers mauled by the constabulary, and is thus tolerated; but it is obviously almost as obnoxious to the New Deal theology as the Fourteenth Amendment, and if it could be got rid of I suppose it would be duly thrown out. But that is only speculation, for the New Deal is now on the defensive, and its evangelists must proceed somewhat cautiously. So those who venture to doubt their magic are consigned to infamy only, and not to concentration camps.

My belief is that there are other jitney messiahs among us who, if they had the same power, would use it much more imperiously — for example, the sunkist Utopian, Upton Sinclair, and that greasy old evangelist, Heywood Broun. Sinclair is essentially an early Christian demonologist, and sees the Republic as a den swarming with devils. It is his honest belief that they are depraved beyond redemption. Their souls, in his view, are black all through. I do not name any of these devils, for they change from time to time as Sinclair proceeds from one revelation to another. But you may be sure that if he is ever thrust into the eminence he dreams of beneath his California upas tree, and finds himself with the power of a Hopkins or a Genghis Khan in his hands, he will fall upon his current abominations with a kind of ferocity that will make that of Hitler and Mussolini look puerile. Indeed, I believe seriously that if he had his way he would make a capital offense, or at least a crime carrying penal servitude, to doubt a single jot or tittle of the great truths of thought-transference, vegetarianism, and spondylotherapy, let alone the More Abundant Life. When you get among apostles, you get among carnivora with sharp teeth.

Broun is also an ornament of the celestial faculty, though it may be that he doesn't know it. He has been a boloney-addict for years, and the New Deal was thus as easy for him as a carpet-tack to a sword-swallower. There was a time, as I recall, when he ran for Congress as a Socialist, and dreamed of having *Das Kapital* printed serially in the *Congressional Record*. Of late he has turned labor leader, with the Hon. John Llewellyn Lewis, the blood-sweating boss of the miners, as his apparent model. His special devil is the Hon. William Randolph Hearst, LL.D., to the laying of whom he devotes many columns of space in the pious Scripps-Howard papers. The chief crime of Hearst, it appears, is that he refuses to yield his neck to the Newspaper Guild, of which Broun is the commander-in-chief and ranking ecclesiastic. Inasmuch as the Scripps-Howard papers also refuse to yield their necks, there would seem to be something odd here, but it is not well to inquire too particularly into the jurisprudence of world-savers. Broun is by nature a portly, amiable, and somewhat frumpy fellow, and if the messianic delusion had not fetched him he would have spent his old age going to baseball games, mooning over his fan mail, and quietly scratching himself. But now that he has been seized by the thirst to serve and alarm humanity, there is no telling where he will fetch up. It wouldn't surprise me to hear that he had hitch-hiked out to San Simeon, broken through Hearst's cordon of lions and hyenas, slit his weasand, and stolen his girl.

How far Hopkins and Ickes, Tugwell and Wallace would be willing to go on the road to Moscow, if only the going were safer for salaried men, I do not know. All of them, like Sinclair and Broun, are apparently members of the "I Am Not a Communist, But — " Club. The idea of this club seems to be to enjoy all the solaces of the Marxian communion without actually submitting to baptism. There is undoubtedly some sense in the device, and if not some sense then at least some prudence, but I must confess that my own preference is for the open and unashamed followers of the Moscow Holy Ghosts. Most of them, to be sure, are indubitably jackasses, and the fact is made sharply apparent every time they venture to expound their childlike faith; but there is something refreshing about their willingness, and even eagerness, to exhibit their jackassery. I give you, in point, their current dogma that Mike Gold, who has a sentimental weakness for unclean and miserable people, is in consequence superior as a thinker and an artist to Mark Twain, who preferred clean and saucy ones. There is something truly magnificent and even monumental about this idea. It passes far beyond the bulk and beam of ordinary imbecilities. Indeed, it deserves to be ranked with the great inventions of theology, and the comrade who swallows it, though he may shout *"Religia opium dlia naroda"* with Lenin, is plainly thinking *"Credo quia absurdum"* with Tertullian.

He is likewise with Tertullian in many another situation, for the whole communist rumble-bumble is shot through with concepts borrowed from the sacerdotal art and mystery. If you will take a hortatory article from any religious paper of the more naïve sort, you may, by changing a few words here and there, convert it into an excellent editorial for the *New Masses*. There is the same innocent acceptance of the obviously not true, the same touching confidence in an often postponed Day of Judgment, and the same shrill impatience with dissenters. The Comrades have restored heresy to its old high place among the crimes and misdemeanors. And they have borrowed a principle cherished by every state church, whether Christian or heathen, since the memory of man runneth not to the contrary — the principle, to wit, that tolerance is a good wherever the church itself is in a minority and under pressure from rivals, but an evil wherever it is dominant. Thus we come upon the dogma preached frankly by Comrade Roger W. Baldwin — that it is a grievous wrong to deprive communists of free speech in New York, but an act of merit to take it from non-communists within the bounds of the Red Zion.

The Comrades, as I have said, sweat under every such imputation that they have borrowed their whole bag of tricks from the theologians, but the facts are too bald and glittering to be gainsaid. What they whoop and howl for is intrinsically an evangel, not a philosophy. The effort to read metaphysical subtleties into the muddy writings of

Marx always leads to absurdity, and the effort to build him up as an economist and so give him scientific standing is just as vain. There is, indeed, nothing more idiotic than the current lucubrations of the Marxian dialecticians; even when what they have to say comes closest to rational exposition, it is hard to distinguish from the hooey of the spectral ex-judges and pseudo-professors who go about the country lecturing on Christian Science. Marx, of course, was not actually a scientist, nor even a metaphysician: he was a prophet, and one of the worst since Biblical times. Not one of his major prognostications, so far as I am aware, has ever come off. But you have but a small understanding of the believing mind if you conclude that the fact disturbs his followers.

What attracts such moon-calves to him most forcibly is precisely what pulls in customers for the New Deal; his habitual departures from objective reality, his rejection of all the known varieties of commonsense. They go to him, not for information, but for consolation, and he has it on tap in endless quantity. In him they find surcease of that vague but poignant unhappiness which goes with their congenital inferiority, their incurable incapacity to get on in the world according to the immemorial rules, their carking and uncomfortable envy of their betters. He promises to return from Gehenna in a pink cloud, and strike off their chains, and blast their enemies, real and imaginary, and put more hope and ease into their quaking hearts than Yahweh thought to give them. Here, manifestly, we are up to our ears in theology. The Comrades are exact reincarnations, down to the last wart, of the poor folk who went into the mountains during the first thrilling days of the Christian era, and there poked out defiant tongues at a world that had used them so evilly, and sat down in full confidence to await the bursting of the Heavens, the glorious descent of the Son of Man, the relief of all sorrow, and the righting of all wrong.

The New Deal offers a less potent medicine, but what it offers belongs indubitably to the same category. It, too, is a kind of religion, though somewhat cheaper and less sophisticated than the variety propagated from Moscow. It is to the latter, roughly speaking, as the bucolic abracadabra of the Holy Rollers, the Foot-Wash Baptists, and the Hookworm-Belt Methodists is to the elegant arcana of Holy Church. Its chief exponents are natural evangelists who, but for the grace of God, would have had to work off their divine frenzy by teaching Bible classes. Ickes, though he may flirt with antinomianism today, was plainly cast in the mold of a Methodist bishop, and Hopkins, if he had not taken to the Uplift, would have made a formidable rival to the Rev.

Gypsy Smith. Even Tugwell, though he is the intellectual of the outfit, has an unmistakable flavor of the Salvation Army about him. The theology merchanted by these gentlemen is a theology diluted with Rotarianism, cow-state Progressivism, and the heresies of the Harvard Yard, but nevertheless it remains a theology.

What has it to offer the poor fish who fall for it? What it has to offer, I greatly fear, is only a long series of splitting headaches. It may sooth them transiently, but it leaves all their chronic agonies unrelieved, all their pathetic questions unanswered. When they throw it off in the end they will be precisely where they were when they embraced it — helpless, disconsolate, forlorn. Yet they go on cherishing it with innocent and unflagging devotion, as little children cherish the concept of Santa Claus. They believe in it as firmly as they believe that they have immortal souls and will be transformed into gaseous vertebrates when they die, and that a horse-hair put into a bottle of water will turn into a snake. They were born to be hornswoggled as the sparks fly upward, and they will serve as suckers for the quacks until the last trump.

III

The average Americano (like the average Englishman, or German, or Frenchman, or Ethiopian) does not really prefer the true to the false; he prefers the false to the true, for the false is always more comforting. Years ago, with the pessimism of youth, I defined truth as something somehow discreditable to someone. The definition may stand even today, but if I were making it over I'd probably substitute *uncomfortable* for *discreditable*. The stark black facts always cause a wave of shivers to run through the human race; what it craves, now and always, is solace, relief, assurance. That is why it turns so eagerly to theology, with its promise of pie in the sky; and to poetry, with its sonorous declaration that all's well with the world and that every poor simpleton is the captain of his soul; and to alcoholic drink, with its cheap admission to confidence, optimism, and a pervasive sense of well-being, its benign generation of warm flashes up and down the spine. And that is why, in days of universal woe, it turns to such quackeries as communism, fascism, Nazi-ism, and the New Deal.

They are foolish on their faces and they never work, but nevertheless there is a powerful soothing in them, and so, at least transiently, they help their converts to bear the unbearable. Hawked on a cold market they would go unregarded, but when the common will to believe and be fooled is whipped up by a preliminary sounding of fire-alarms and bursting of star shells, and every evil is magnified to cosmic dimensions, and every fear pushed on to paranoia — when such a preparatory shelling of the human woods is carried on by adroit men, then the great masses of confiding anthropoids are willing to believe anything, and to be led anywhere. The present becomes completely intolerable to them, and the future looks as sinister as the entrance to a coal-mine. Show them the gates of Utopia, and though the turnstile be built like a rat-trap and the gilt be shabby and the plaster breaking through, they will swarm in with loud hosannahs, seeing glories that are not there and hoping hopes that are hollow and vain.

For to most human beings, life on this earth is not only an insoluble riddle, but also a painful affliction, so they have to take something to deaden its pangs. The elixirs traditionally in use for that purpose are those I have just named, to wit, religion, poetry, and alcohol. Each, of course, is marketed under many labels and flavored with various essences, some heady and some mild. The poor idiot who finds surcease from a ruffianly boss and a shrewish wife in the he-man exultations of a Robert W. Service is plainly not using the same bottle as the Harvard *elegante* who pulsates to the soft, unearthly vespers of a T. S. Eliot. Nor does it take any great acumen to detect that the consolation which our Holy Christian Faith provides for a Trappist groveling in his cell is not precisely the consolation provided for a Holy Roller in the throes of tetany, or that a Wall Street banker guzzling champagne in a room full of naked show-girls is not on all fours with an honest farmer sneaking a shot of radiator alcohol behind the barn-door. Human ingenuity has played upon these ancient hooches through many centuries, and as a result they take protean forms. But fundamentally they are all alike, for their one purpose is to tone down the apparently unavoidable unpleasantness of human existence, and thereby make it bearable to forlorn, bewildered, and unhappy men and women.

I have never heard of a person who did not resort to one or another of them at some time or other. Try to find such a prodigy in history, and you will be baffled. We all suffer a great deal in this lugubrious vale, and there come days when even the most resolute of us falters before the impenetrable enigmas of life and death. We may not need medication regularly, but we undoubtedly need it now and then. My own device, on such disagreeable occasions, is to swallow a dilute solution of ethyl alcohol, choosing the most palatable form available and the best society that will endure me. But there are other men, equally made in God's image, who prefer either religion or poetry, or, better still, some combination of the two, and I am surely not one to cavil at their choice. Protestantism, at least as we know it in the United States, tends to be theology undiluted and unadorned, and is thus brought down to the unappetizing level of a dose of castor-oil, but Catholicism contains a considerable admixture of poetry, and I suspect that this poetry fetches quite as many customers as the underlying theories of being and becoming. Similarly, there are kinds of poetry which borrow a good deal from religion — for example, the strophes of the Mr. Eliot aforesaid, those of the makers of Negro spirituals, and those of John Milton. Sometimes even alcohol enters into the symbiosis, as witness the Christian sects, now happily extinct, whose members caught the mood for devotion by getting tight, and the obvious fact that all poetry seems lovelier and more reassuring after a few beers.

The demand for these invaluable anodynes tends to diminish, of course, with the progress of knowledge. In the dark reaches of exploded time, before even poetry and alcohol were invented, the only hope for a man with a toothache lay in propitiating the gods, but now even a New Dealer goes to a dentist, and after first making it a great deal worse the dentist eventually makes it better. A revolutionary change has come over the world in this respect during the past century or two. Down to the days of our great-great-grandfathers most of the everyday phenomena of nature remained as completely unfathomable as they had been in the days of Cro-Magnon Man, and in consequence poets were important public functionaries, almost everyone went to church, and there was far too much boozing. But now many of the more common mysteries have been penetrated, and men are no longer upset by them, and do not have to use drugs, whether material or spiritual, to escape from worry about them. To argue today, as Martin Luther did in 1525 or thereabout, that thunder-storms are caused by demons, would make even a Mississippi New Dealer laugh, though I should add in fairness that he still believes with Dr. Luther that demons produce asthma and carbuncles. But this last is only because the recent discoveries about the true nature of asthma and carbuncles are not yet bruited in the Bible country. In the course of another century or two they will be heard of and accepted there, as many another fact of science is already accepted, though perhaps not unanimously.

As good a classification of men as any I have ever heard may be made along the lines of their need for and use of these pain-killers. As I have said, there are few if any who never use them at all, but certainly there are some who use them very little, at least compared to the common run of *Homo sapiens*. It is the habit of such men, when they confront a disquieting phenomenon, to try to penetrate to its hidden causes. They neither deny that it is before them nor seek to get rid of its challenge by anesthetizing their wits, but tackle it boldly and frankly and with as much shrewdness as they can summon up. We owe everything we are today to such enterprising and iconoclastic fellows. They are the true fathers of what passes among us as civilization. Their labors have cleared off whole herds of the archipelagoes of one-time mysteries, and so gradually narrowed the fields of religion, poetry, and alcohol. There are areas — for example, those of astronomy and meteorology — in which they have displaced religion altogether, and reduced poetry to the estate of incidental music, and even made alcohol useless, save perhaps as a means of keeping up the connubial ardor of astronomers and meteorologists, and so assuring the continuance of their valuable species. And there are other areas — for example, that of medicine — in which they have made such great progress during the past century that they promise to achieve a really revolutionary triumph on some not too remote tomorrow.

Such men are anything but popular. The crowd never cheers them, and they are often under attack by persons with a vested interest in the remedies they displace. I can recall no time when scientists and theologians ever really laid down together like lion and lamb, or scientists and poets, or even scientists and saloon-keepers. If you will subscribe to any religious paper and read it attentively you will find that it never admits the tremendous achievements of modern science save grudgingly, and never praises a concrete scientist save when he happens to be a narrow specialist and is willing to let priests do his thinking for him outside the bounds of his specialty. And if you will read the poetry magazines, now so numerous, you will find that they never print anything in celebration of the merits of such men as Max Planck, Frederick Banting, Karl Landsteiner, and George Minot, though they have plenty to say about Lenin, Big Bill Haywood, and the Scottsboro colored boys. Nor do you hear these scientists hymned by bartenders, who all appear to prefer Al Smith.

This unpopularity, as I have hinted, is mainly due to the fact that whenever the scientists unveil another mystery they invade and injure the business of their predecessors and rivals. But there is something deeper, and that is the difference between the wide and easy confidence merchanted by the latter and the skepticism that seems to be an inevitable outgrowth of scientific inquiry. Religion, poetry, and alcohol do not presume merely to solve a few problems, lying within narrow bounds; they offer a general solution of *all* problems, or, at all events, a general cure for the fatigues and distresses that go with attempts to solve them. And so, exactly, do communism, fascism,

The New Deal Mentality

Nazi-ism, and the New Deal. Science is much less grandiose. When it succeeds in its enterprises, it commonly succeeds in a very complete manner, leaving no room for doubt and no ground for dubiety, but too often it manages only to prove that the problem before it cannot be solved by the means at hand, and sometimes it provides strong evidence that what is unsolved is probably eternally insoluble.

This concept of the insoluble is intolerably obnoxious to the vast majority of human beings. Their will to believe urges them to refuse flatly to embrace it, and in that refusal they are supported vigorously by the quacks who prey upon them. Along with it, and as a natural corollary, they reject the concept of the irremediable. The idea of progress, distorted in its passage through their coagulated minds, is converted into an idea of *infinite* progress, invariably benign. For every pain, they hold, there is a predestined cure; for every evil, an infallible means of putting it down.

IV

It is among such innocents that the recurrent New Deals of the world find their customers. In every such New Deal, as I have shown, there is a strong flavor of dogmatic theology, and in every one, I should add, there is also some show of poetry, and even a touch of booziness. The wizards now rampant at Washington, in some of their aspects, are far more poets than theologians. At every excuse, they turn from the harsh prose of exegesis to the lascivious measures of hymnody, and sing down the groans of doubt. Moreover, there is about their giddy gladness something that clearly transcends the spiritual; if it were not notorious that they are all extremely abstemious men, one might almost call it spirituous. Such radiant confidence in the triumph of the true, the good, and the beautiful is familiar in places where good fellows get together, and the woes of life are conveniently forgotten, and happy voices are raised in close harmony. As I have hinted, I am myself a votary of this ancient device for dulling the sharp edge of despair. Politics, the most protean of impostures, borrows it gladly, using it to ameliorate alike the brutality of theology and the insipidity of poetry.

I am surely not one to cry it down, or to cry theology down, or even poetry. They have all made life more bearable on this meanest of planets to hosts of miserable men and women. But let us be realistic for a moment. Can prayer really raise the wind? Is there actually any poetry capable of balancing a budget? Can even 100-proof hooch dissolve the redness of red ink? The answer, I regret to say, must be nay in every case. The laws of nature stand against all such miracles, however lovely it would be to see them achieved; and if those laws are ever to be repealed it will have to be by far more potent magicians than Hopkins and Morgenthau, Tugwell and Ickes. They have done their level damnedest, and angels could do no more, but it is not enough. They have entertained the patient superbly, but he continues to be racked by aches and pains. Not one of his malaises, whether actually inflicted on him by Yahweh or only put into his whirling head by artful suggestion, has been cured, or even relieved. He goes on swallowing the philters prescribed so copiously and submitting to endless pummellings, scratchings, and gougings, but he remains sick.

Pretty soon, I suspect, he will grow tired of his illness, and begin longing to be up and about again. He will begin by trying to move a toe. If it revolves in its socket he will proceed to a knee, and then to a hip, and then to all the other hinges of his corporeal frame. And what of the Munyons grouped about him? What will he have to say to them when he sits up at last, and takes a good look at them? Alas, I am in great fear that his remarks will be of an extremely bellicose, objurgatory, and even obscene character. It wouldn't surprise me at all to see him rise up from his bed, have at them with the missionary frenzy of a Broun flaying a Hearst, and chase them back headlong to their forlorn classrooms and chicken-farms, their empty law-offices and dismal Y.M.C.A.'s. In brief, it wouldn't surprise me to see the New Deal terminate in what, on less exalted levels, would be described graphically as the bum's rush.

Hallie Flanagan

FEDERAL THEATRE

The story of the Federal Theatre Project of the W.P.A. is yet to be recaptured, as is that of the Federal Arts Projects as a whole. Those who vaguely imagine that Federal Theatre no more than employed incompetents in commonplace capacities have forgotten that it sired Orson Welles, among others of manifest talent and resources. Though the New York Times *did not answer it, it did*

Federal Theatre [141

ask a crucial question: "They must not starve, but need they act?" Congress voted "No" in 1939; Federal Theatre was the first of the Projects to feel the government axe. Its director, Hallie Flanagan, here defends its principles and achievements. Triple A Plowed Under *exemplifies the "living newspaper": one of the Federal Theatre innovations.*

IN THE summer of 1935, after Mr. Harry Hopkins, in accordance with the spirit of the Relief Act passed by Congress, had taken the position that unemployed theatre workers should be given a chance to work again, I asked Elmer Rice to take the directorship of the Federal Theatre for New York City. Although he was interested in the plan for a Government-sponsored theatre, and although he was undismayed by the fears deterring a number of other theatrical people, namely, that the relief rolls would afford little theatrical talent, and that the one dollar out of every ten allowed for a other-than-labor costs would be too small for adequate productions, he hesitated.

"What could we do with all the actors?" he kept saying. "Even if we had twenty plays in rehearsal at once, with thirty in a cast, that would keep only a fraction of them busy." Not wanting to lose Elmer Rice, I snatched at a straw. "We wouldn't use them all in plays — we could do Living Newspapers. We could dramatize the news with living actors, light, music, movement." Elmer Rice caught the idea in the air. "I can get the Newspaper Guild to back it." Acting with his usual velocity once his mind was made up, he accepted the directorship for New York, secured the sponsorship of the Guild, and appointed Morris Watson to head the Living Newspaper company.

The staff of the Living Newspaper was set up like a large city daily, with editor-in-chief, managing editor, city editor, reporters and copyreaders, and they began, as Brooks Atkinson later remarked, "to shake the living daylights out of a thousand books, reports, newspaper and magazine articles," in order to evolve an authoritative dramatic treatment, at once historic and contemporary, of current problems. With Arthur Arent as editor and later as playwright, the Living Newspaper from the first was not concerned with surface news, scandal, human interest stories, but rather with the conditions back of conditions.

For the first Living Newspaper we decided on *Ethiopia,* partly because it was the big news of the moment, and partly because we had a large group of Negro dancers and actors on our project. By November the research was complete, the script ready, rehearsals under way, and the Biltmore Theatre the rendezvous for directors, actors and writers interested in the new form.

Then something happened which was to have a profound bearing not only on the Living Newspaper, but on the entire history of the Federal Theatre. The State Department heard of the play, became concerned, and there was transmitted through my administrative superior, Mr. Jacob Baker, an order that no dramatic representation could be made upon any Federal Theatre stage of any living foreign ruler. We explained that the scenes showing Mussolini and Haile Selassie were factual and not caricatured in any way. We were assured that on any American subject we would have freedom of expression, but that the actual portrayal of foreign rulers might involve our diplomatic relations. Elmer Rice, because he believed that this action prophesied that we could never do any socially valuable play, resigned under dramatic circumstances, making his reasons known in a speech given before an invited audience of newspaper men at a private showing of the banned play on January 24, 1936.

Great as was the loss of Elmer Rice to the Federal Theatre, his protest against censorship has been a potent factor in keeping that theatre, in spite of various local fights, some of which we have lost, close to the line laid down by Harry Hopkins when at its inception he said that it was to be "a free, adult, uncensored theatre."

The best proof of that fact may be found in the plays in this volume.

Every Living Newspaper has been different in history and technique, and every one has been exciting to produce. During the rehearsals of *Triple-A Plowed Under* we had one night a rebellion of some of the actors who sent word by the stage manager that they did not want to appear in this kind of performance. Philip Barber, director for New York, Morris Watson, Arthur Arent, Joe Losey and Gordon Graham, the directors, and I met with them after the rehearsal and listened to impassioned speeches explaining why this swift, pantomimic, monosyllabic, factural document was not drama and why no New York audience would sit through it. They complained that there was no plot, no story, no chance to build up a character, no public interest in the subject matter. "Who in New York cares about the farmer, about wheat, about the price of bread and milk?"

After they spoke from the floor, those of us who believed in the Living Newspaper — and this included some members of the company — had a chance to tell them that we realized that we were taking a long shot, but that we thought we must take long shots if the Federal Theatre was to succeed. In addition to the production of classics, modern plays, vaudeville and variety, children's plays and dance plays, we felt we should experiment with new forms, particularly because we wished to supplement and stimulate, rather than to compete with commercial Broadway productions. We argued that people today are interested in facts, as proved by the enormous increase in circulation of newspapers and news sheets and by the *March of Time*. We urged the actors to withhold judgment as to the effectiveness of the play until we added two powerful elements which were an intrinsic part of the plan, the musical score and the light score. We ended with a mutual agreement: the actors were to give us all they had through the first performance; if the play failed we promised to drop all plans for future Living Newspapers. We then proceeded to screw our courage to the sticking point, and we had need of it, for the last days of rehearsal were hectic. It was reported that an organization calling itself the World War Veterans threatened to close the show on the ground that it was unpatriotic. Rumor ran through the project that the curtain would never be allowed to rise, that the performers would be hauled off the stage and into patrol wagons. Opening night found the actors full of misgivings, the audience full of tension, and the lobby full of police.

The danger point was a line by Earl Browder — not, as Heywood Broun later carefully explained, really Earl Browder, but merely an actor representing Earl Browder. At this juncture an irate gentleman arose in the back of the house, and in stentorian tones started singing the *Star-Spangled Banner,* demanding that the audience join him. The police who had been warned by the Veterans' Association to be on guard against Communist activities evidently misunderstood the nature of the song and promptly ejected the gentleman. The play went on; not only on that night but through many succeeding months, not only in New York, but later in Chicago, San Francisco, Cleveland and Los Angeles.

In *Power,* the struggle inherent in all Living Newspapers becomes, through the character of the Consumer, more explicit. It is the struggle of the average citizen to understand the natural, social and economic forces around him, and to achieve through these forces, a better life for more people. If you think such a struggle is undramatic, reserve judgment until, through the roaring waterfalls and vast machines of *Power,* you see the torchlight procession of workers and hear them sing:

> "Oh, see them boys a-comin'
> Their Government they trust,
> Just hear their hammers ringin',
> They'll build that dam or bust!"

Critics, who had hitherto accused us of biting the hand that fed us, now accused us of licking that hand. As a matter of fact, we were doing neither. We were producing a play which seemed to us dramatic. The public apparently shared that belief. Sixty thousand people considered the theme dramatic enough to buy seats for *Power* before it opened its sensational New York run.

Melodrama? Of course. Like all so-called new forms the Living Newspaper borrows with fine impartiality from many sources: from Aristophanes, from the *Commedia del' Arte,* from Shakespearean soliloquy, from the pantomime of Mei Lan Fang. Being a flexible technique and only in its beginning, it still has much to learn from the chorus, the camera, the cartoon. Although it has occasional reference to the *Volksbühne* and the Blue Blouses, to Bragaglia and Meierhold and Eisenstein, it is as American as Walt Disney, the *March of Time* and the *Congressional Record,* to all of which American institutions it is indebted. Any technical discussion of its diverse elements — factual and formal, musical and acrobatic, abstract and concrete, visual and audible, psychological, economic, and social — forms the subject, not for an introduction, but for a later volume.

In the meantime it is not to be imagined that New York has a monopoly on the Living Newspaper, or that *Ethiopia, 1935, Triple-A Plowed Under, Power* and *One-Third of a Nation* tell the story. Not only are these New York editions re-enacted in many other cities, but Oregon has its own Living Newspaper on *Flex,* Iowa on *Dirt,* Newark on the history of the Negro. Denver is writing one on the sugar-beet industry, and Cincinnati on *Flood Control.*

In *Spirochete,* Arnold Sundgaard, a writer of the Chicago Federal Theatre, tells in Living Newspaper form the story of the fight against syphilis, tells it with such effect that the daily press, *Variety,* and *BillBoard,* report it as sensational entertainment, while Paul de Kruif and the Assistant Surgeon General of the United States enlist its service in the nationwide struggle against the disease, even the nameless mention of which once put Ibsen in the pillory.

All of which seems to indicate that the truth is not only stranger but often more entertaining and more dramatically effective than fiction. In fact, this conclusion might be said to apply to the entire history of the Federal Theatre.

HALLIE FLANAGAN
Director, Federal Theatre

Washington, D.C.
May 11, 1938

TRIPLE A PLOWED UNDER

A Living Newspaper
SPONSORED BY
THE NEWSPAPER GUILD OF AMERICA
*Written by the Editorial Staff of the Living Newspaper
Under the Supervision of Arthur Arent*

SCENE ONE
(War and Inflation)*

CHARACTERS
VOICE OF LIVING NEWSPAPER
LINE OF SOLDIERS
TABLEAU OF FARMERS
FIRST MAN
SECOND MAN
WOMAN, middle-aged, prosperous

(As overture ends, voice over the LOUDSPEAKER *speaks.)*

VOICE OF LIVING NEWSPAPER (*over* LOUDSPEAKER): Triple-A Plowed Under. (*Curtain rises*) 1917 — Inflation.
(*At rise red spotlight is on* SOLDIERS *marching in continuous columns up ramp placed upstage left. After a brief interval there is an increasing volume of marching feet. The entire scene is played behind scrim. Spotlight on three* SPEAKERS *and crowd of* FARMERS, SPEAKERS *stand on highest level, right. Some of the* FARMERS *stand on lowest level, right, and some at stage level, right.*)
FIRST SPEAKER: Your country is at war.
SECOND SPEAKER: Your country needs you.
FIRST AND SECOND SPEAKERS (*together*) If you can't fight — farm.
FIRST SPEAKER: The fate of our country rests upon the farmers.
SECOND SPEAKER: Do you want our land invaded?
FIRST SPEAKER: Do you want your daughters ravaged by Huns?
WOMAN: Farmer, save the nation! (*Trumpet.*)
FIRST SPEAKER: The boys in the trenches need the men in the fields.
WOMAN: Farmer, save our boys. (*Trumpet.*)
SECOND SPEAKER: Every bushel of barley is a barrel of bullets.

*Based on communications between Hallie Flanagan, Director, Federal Theatre Project, and Paul H. Appleby, Dept. of Agriculture, Washington, D.C., February 12 and 13, 1936.

WOMAN: Farmer, save democracy. (*Trumpet.*)
FIRST SPEAKER: Every hand with a spade is a hand-grenade.
WOMAN: Farmer, save our honor. (*Trumpet.*)
SECOND SPEAKER: Every man behind a plow is a man behind a gun.
WOMAN: Farmer, save civilization. (*Trumpet.*)
FIRST SPEAKER: Every head of cattle can win a battle.
WOMAN: Farmer, save our flag. (*Trumpet.*)
FIRST SPEAKER: Plant more wheat.
SECOND SPEAKER: Plant more potatoes.
FIRST SPEAKER: More corn!
SECOND SPEAFER: More cotton!
FIRST SPEAKER: More food, more seed, more acres!
SECOND AND FIRST SPEAKER (*together*): More! More! More!
WOMAN: Farmer, save the world!

Portals close

SCENE TWO – A
(*Deflation*)*

CHARACTERS
VOICE OF LIVING NEWSPAPER
SUB-SCENE A
    AN EXPORTER
    A JOBBER
SUB-SCENE B
    CITY BANKER
    COUNTRY BANKER
SUB-SCENE C
    COUNTRY BANKER
    FARMER

VOICE OF LIVING NEWSPAPER (*over* LOUDSPEAKER): The 1920's. Deflation.
(*This scene is played in a series of three sub-scenes, on three levels. The highest level is stage right, the intermediate level, center, and the lowest level, left. First scene on highest level is lighted from directly overhead. Only the scene actually playing is lighted. Blackout at the end of each scene, as the spotlight comes up on the next*

---

*Based on communications, February 12 and 13, 1936, between Hallie Flanagan, Director, Federal Theatre Project, and Paul H. Appleby, Dept. of Agriculture, Washington, D.C.

scene. Chart indicating deflation is projected on scrim throughout this series.)

EXPORTER: Bad news, Frank. I can't ship any more of your wheat.

JOBBER: What will I do with my stocks?

EXPORTER: I don't know! I can't ship any more to Europe – the war's over.

JOBBER: It's been over a long time, but they still need to eat, don't they?

EXPORTER: Yes, but they're raising their own. I'm afraid we won't ship much more wheat to Europe unless they have another war.

JOBBER: That's a short explanation of a serious problem.

EXPORTER: Well, anyway, you see why I can't take your shipment.

JOBBER: I don't see a damn thing.

Blackout

SCENE TWO – B

(*Spotlight comes up on middle level,* CITY BANKER *seated at desk,* COUNTRY BANKER *standing at his side, left.*)

CITY BANKER (*as if there had been a previous conversation*): It's just good banking, that's the only answer I can give you.

COUNTRY BANKER: It may be good banking for you fellows here in the city, but I tell you that if I pay up all my paper now I've got to bankrupt every farmer in my district.

CITY BANKER: I'm sorry. I'm not permitted to be concerned over that. I wouldn't be true to my trust if I didn't keep this bank's money in lucrative channels. It just happens that at the moment stock and bond collateral is the safest investment. Besides, we get considerably more returns there.

COUNTRY BANKER: What's going to happen when we bankrupt the farmers? Are you going to eat your stocks and bonds?

CITY BANKER: I have no time for levity, Mr. Brown. The fact is, agriculture is no longer a lucrative investment; stocks and bonds are. Now do you see that I must call in your paper?

COUNTRY BANKER: I don't see a damn thing.

Blackout

SCENE TWO – C

(*Spotlight comes up on lowest level, left,* COUNTRY BANKER *seated at desk, and* FARMER *seated at his side, right.*)

BANKER (*as if there had been previous conversation*): I've got to have the money.

FARMER: I can't understand it. Only a little while ago they were preaching and haranguing for us to raise more crops and more crops. Damn it, I bought more land and cleared all the woods on my place, and planted it to wheat, and now it's rotting in the fields.

BANKER: That was war, Fred.

FARMER: Well, hell, people still need to eat, don't they? And they can't tell me there aren't people who couldn't eat what's lying out in my fields now. My son, Jim, in New York says he can't walk down the street without having hungry men beg him for money.

BANKER: Well, I don't see what I can do, unless they ease up on me, and they aren't going to do that.

FARMER: Well, if you foreclose on me I'll be in the breadline myself. Then how are any of us going to eat?

BANKER: When that happens the big boys will begin to feel it, and maybe they'll get up another war.

FARMER (*grimly*): Can't have another war. Every day I get veterans asking for a handout, and not a one of them would go back to war, and by God, I wouldn't raise wheat for another war.

BANKER: At any rate, you see my situation, Fred.

FARMER: I don't see a damn thing.

Blackout

SCENE THREE

(Farmer, Dealer, Manufacturer, Worker — Vicious Circle)**

CHARACTERS

VOICE OF LIVING NEWSPAPER

A FARMER

A DEALER

A MANUFACTURER

A WORKER

VOICE OF LIVING NEWSPAPER (*over* LOUDSPEAKER): In the troubled fifteen years, 1920 to 1935, farm incomes fall five and one-half billion dollars;* unemployment rises seven million, five hundred and seventy-eight thousand.† (*Four spotlights come up on the four protagonists of this scene.* FARMER, *stage right, turns head sharply left, speaks to* DEALER.)

**Digest of article "A.A.A. Philosophy" by Rexford G. Tugwell, *Fortune Magazine*, January 1934.

*a. "The Agricultural Situation" — Bureau of Agricultural Economics. b. Yearbook of Agriculture — 1935.

†a. National Bureau of Economic Research. b. National Industrial Conference Board, November 1935.

Federal Theatre [149

FARMER (to DEALER): I can't buy that auto. *(Light goes out.* DEALER *turns head sharply left, speaks to* MANUFACTURER.*)*
DEALER *(to* MANUFACTURER*)*: I can't take that shipment. *Count of one, light out.* MANUFACTURER *turns head sharply left, speaks to* WORKER.*)*
MANUFACTURER *(to* WORKER*)*: I can't use you any more. *(Light goes out.* WORKER *speaks directly front.)*
WORKER: I can't eat. *(Light goes out.)*

SCENE FOUR
(Farmers' Holiday)

CHARACTERS
VOICE OF LIVING NEWSPAPER
A. MILO RENO
B. MILO RENO
PRESIDENT OF COMMISSION MERCHANTS
THREE COMMISSION MERCHANTS

SCENE FOUR – A

VOICE OF LIVING NEWSPAPER: Des Moines, Iowa. Farmers pin hopes on farm holiday leader, Milo Reno.*
(Lights on MILO RENO *on proscenium on right.)*
MILO RENO: As President of the Farmers' Holiday Association, representing five thousand farmers, I wish to announce the five points of our program during the coming strike.

1. We will pay no taxes or interest until we have fully cared for our families.
2. We will pay no interest-bearing debts until we receive the cost of production.
3. We will buy only that which complete necessity demands.
4. We will stay in the homes we now occupy.
5. We will not sell our products until we receive the cost of production, but will exchange our products with labor and the unemployed for the things we need on the farm on the basis of cost of production for both parties.†

You can no more stop this movement than you could stop the Revo-

---
*ature:*New York Times,* August 16th and 26th, 1932.
†"Bryan! Bryan! Bryan! Bryan!", *Fortune Magazine,* January 1934, p. 68.

lution of 1776. I couldn't stop it if I tried.‡ (*Off stage voices shout "Strike! Strike!" Follow* RENO *with spot to stage left, where light comes up on* COMMISSION MERCHANTS *behind desk. Lights shift to left.*)

SCENE FOUR – B

PRESIDENT OF COMMISSION MERCHANTS (*holding out contract and pen to* MILO RENO): Mr. Reno, I have here the terms drawn up by the committee of Commission Merchants.... We want you to call off that strike.... Will you sign? (*Pause,* MILO RENO *turns to where off stage voices are still rumbling "Strike! Strike!" He turns back, and signs.*)

Blackout

SCENE FIVE
(*Milk Prices*)

CHARACTERS
VOICE OF LIVING NEWSPAPER
MIDDLEMAN
FARMER
CONSUMER, A WOMAN

VOICE OF LIVING NEWSPAPER (*over* LOUDSPEAKER): Milk flows to market.
(*Light directly over the* MIDDLEMAN *seated at table.* FARMER *and* CONSUMER *on truck, right and left of* MIDDLEMAN. *Scene is played on metronome count through entirety, a speech and a beat, etc.*)
FARMER (*holding up quart can of milk*): How much do I get?
MIDDLEMAN: Three cents.*
FARMER: Three cents?
MIDDLEMAN: Take it or leave it.
FARMER: I'll take it. (*Hands over milk and pockets coins.*)
WOMAN CONSUMER: I want a quart of milk.
MIDDLEMAN (*who has been pouring milk from can into bottle*): Fifteen cents.
WOMAN CONSUMER: Fifteen cents?
MIDDLEMAN: Take it or leave it.
WOMAN CONSUMER: I'll take it. (MIDDLEMAN *holds out his hand, takes money, and slaps pocket.*)
Blackout ....

‡*Seeds of Revolt* by Mauritz A. Hallgren – (Alfred Knopf, 1933).
**New York Herald Tribune,* July 5, 1934.

SCENE TWENTY-THREE
(Supreme Court ... AAA killed)

CHARACTERS

VOICE OF LIVING NEWSPAPER
VOICE OVER LOUDSPEAKER
SUPREME COURT JUSTICE ROBERTS — figure in silhouette
SUPREME COURT JUSTICE STONE — figure in silhouette
SEVEN OTHER SUPREME COURT JUSTICES — figures in silhouette
DANIEL O. HASTINGS, SENATOR FROM DELAWARE — in silhouette
ALFRED E. SMITH — in silhouette
EARL BROWDER — in silhouette
THOMAS JEFFERSON — in silhouette
FIRST MAN
SECOND MAN
THIRD MAN
A WOMAN
FOURTH MAN
FIFTH MAN

VOICE OF LIVING NEWSPAPER (*over* LOUDSPEAKER): January 6, 1936. ... Supreme Court invalidates AAA in Hoosac Mills case.*

VOICE (*also over* LOUDSPEAKER): The majority opinion — Justice Roberts.

(*As travelers open from rear, projection of Constitution is thrown on glass curtain. Discovered in shadow against projection are* JUSTICE STONE, THREE OTHER JUSTICES, *then* JUSTICE ROBERTS, *and the* FOUR REMAINING JUSTICES, *right.* ROBERTS *rises to one-foot platform directly in front of him.* FIVE JUSTICES *who concurred in his opinion, turn in profile as he begins to speak.*)

JUSTICE ROBERTS: ... Beyond cavil the sole objective of the legislation is to restore the purchasing price of agricultural products to a parity with that prevailing in an earlier day; to take money from the processor and bestow it on the farmers. The Constitution is the supreme law of the land, ordained and established by the people. All legislation must conform to the principles it lays down. The power to confer or withhold unlimited benefits is the power to coerce or destroy. This is coercion by economic pressure. The judgment is affirmed.*

(*He steps down;* JUSTICE STONE *steps up.*)

*New York Times, January 7, 1936.
*New York Times, January 7, 1936.

152] HALLIE FLANAGAN

VOICE OVER LOUDSPEAKER: The minority opinion — Justice Stone.
(*The* FIVE JUSTICES *concurring with* JUSTICE ROBERTS *turn to full front. The* TWO *concurring with* STONE, *turn in silhouette.*)

JUSTICE STONE: Courts are concerned with the power to enact statues, not with their wisdom. The only check upon their own exercise of power is our own sense of self-restraint. For the removal of unwise laws from the statute books, appeal lies not to the courts, but to the ballot, and to the processes of democratic government.

So may the judicial power be abused. "The power to tax is the power to destroy," but we do not for that reason doubt its existence. Courts are not the only agents of government which must be assumed to have the capacity to govern.†

(*As* JUSTICE STONE *steps down,* SENATOR HASTINGS *enters, right, steps on higher platform at back, throwing his shadow into a much larger projection than that of the* JUSTICES.)

SENATOR HASTINGS: This re-establishes Constitutional government. It gives back to the States the power they intended to reserve when they adopted the Constitution. The chances are it will improve the condition of the country, as did the decision of the NRA.*

(HASTINGS *steps down and exits left.* ALFRED E. SMITH *enters right, steps on platform vacated by* HASTINGS.)

ALFRED E. SMITH: We don't want the Congress of the United States singly or severally to tell the Supreme Court what to do. We don't want any administration that takes a shot at the Constitution in the dark, and tries to put something over in contradiction of it, upon any theory that there is going to be a great public power in favor of it, and it is possible that the United States Supreme Court may be intimidated into a friendly opinion with respect to it. But I found, all during my public life, that Almighty God built this country, and he did not give us that kind of a Supreme Court.†

(SMITH *steps down, and exits left.* BROWDER *enters right; steps on platform vacated by* SMITH.)

EARL BROWDER: The reactionaries seek to turn both "Americanism" and the Constitution into instruments of reaction, but neither of these things belongs to them. Nowhere does the Constitution grant the Supreme Court power over Congress, but it does make Congress the potential master of the Supreme Court.‡ I repeat, the Con-

---
†*Ibid.*
**New York Times,* January 7, 1936.
†*Ibid.,* January 26, 1936.
‡*Daily Worker,* February 13, 1936.

stitution of the United States does not give the Supreme Court the right to declare laws passed by Congress unconstitutional.§

(BROWDER *steps down and exits left.* THOMAS JEFFERSON *enters right, steps on platform vacated by* BROWDER.)

THOMAS JEFFERSON: There must be an arbiter somewhere. True, there must. But does that prove it is either the Congress or the Supreme Court? The ultimate arbiter is the people of the Union, assembled by their deputies in convention at the call of Congress or two-thirds of the States.*

(*Travelers slowly close, with* JEFFERSON *remaining standing on platform, center.*)

VOICE OVER LOUDSPEAKER: Farmers voted, by more than 6 to 1, for continuance of Triple-A.† (MEN *start crossing stage in front of travelers, from right to left.*)

FIRST MAN: The AAA is dead.... (*Exits left.*)

SECOND MAN: No more allotment checks.... (*Exits left.*)

THIRD MAN: What the hell're we agoin' to do this winter? (*Exits left.*)

A WOMAN: How're we goin' t' get coal? (*Exits left.*)

FOURTH MAN: They say the people wrote the Constitution.... (*Exits left.*)

FIFTH MAN: Them people have been dead a long time.... (*Also exits.*)

Blackout

SCENE TWENTY-FOUR
(*The Big "Steal"*)

CHARACTERS
VOICE OF LIVING NEWSPAPER
HENRY A. WALLACE, SECRETARY OF AGRICULTURE

VOICE OF LIVING NEWSPAPER (*over* LOUDSPEAKER): January 21st, Buffalo, New York, Court refunds processing tax on order of Supreme tribunal.‡ (*Pause*) Secretary Wallace.

(*Lights on* WALLACE *speaking into microphone.*)

SECRETARY WALLACE: ... It doesn't make sense. In the Hoosac Mills case the Supreme Court disapproved the idea that the Government

§*Ibid.*, January 11, 1936.
*Jefferson's letter to Mr. Johnson, June 12, 1823 — in *Congressional Digest*, December, 1935.
†*World Almanac*, 1936, p. 167.
‡*New York Times*, January 21, 1936.

could take money from one group for the benefit of another. Yet in turning over to the processors this $200,000,000 which came from all the people, we are seeing the most flagrant example of expropriation for the benefit of one small group. You will get some idea of its size when you contrast these refunds with the profits of the processors in their most prosperous years. Cotton mills reported profits of $30,000,000 in 1920. Their processing tax refunds amount to $51,000,000 in cotton. Flour mills reported profits of about $20,000,000 on their wheat flour business in 1929. Their processing tax refunds amount to $67,000,000. Packers' profits on their hog business in 1929 were in the neighborhood of $20,000,000. Their tax refunds were $51,000,000.

This return of the processing tax under order of the Supreme Court is probably the greatest legalized steal in American history!*

Blackout

SCENE TWENTY-FIVE
(*Soil Conservation*)

CHARACTERS
VOICE OF LIVING NEWSPAPER
CHESTER A. DAVIS — Administrator of AAA
FIRST REPORTER
SECOND REPORTER
MESSENGER
CLERKS, STENOGRAPHERS, ETC.

VOICE OF LIVING NEWSPAPER (*over* LOUDSPEAKER): Washington, January 1936. Administrator Chester A. Davis.*
(*Light upon* CHESTER A. DAVIS; *this scene is played around his desk.*)
CHESTER A. DAVIS: . . . and we've got to find something to take the place of AAA . . . something that is constitutional, and that the various farm blocs will approve. . . .
FIRST REPORTER (*slowly after a slight pause*): Why don't you use the Soil Conservation Act passed last year? Sure, that's the one.
SECOND REPORTER: It's as broad as Barnum and Bailey's tent and it covers all the ground the AAA did.
CHESTER A. DAVIS (*scornfully*): Impossible. That Act was just a tem-

*New York Times, January 29, 1936.
*Scene based on article in Time Magazine, January 27, 1936.

porary stop-gap dealing with the WPA or something. It has no bearing on this case.

FIRST REPORTER: I tell you it has. I was looking it over this morning and ...

SECOND REPORTER (*excitedly*): I was with him. It authorized conservation, acquisition of land, compensation for farmers who ...

CHESTER A. DAVIS (*holding up his hand*): Wait a minute. (*He presses a button on his desk and speaks into the telephone*) Send in some copies of the Soil Conservation Act. (*There is an expectant silence as they regard each other. The* REPORTERS *are excited,* DAVIS *smiles skeptically. A* MESSENGER *enters and deposits some sheaves of paper on his desk.* DAVIS *takes one, and the* REPORTERS *make a dash for the others. As* DAVIS *reads, the* OTHERS *read along with him. When they break into speech, it is in tones of intense excitement.* CHESTER DAVIS *speaks up, reading*) The Soil Conservation Act passed on mmm (*mumbling*) ... and authorized the creation of mm-mm-mm-mm-mm-mm-mm. *One*: — Conservation measures including methods of cultivation, the growing of vegetation and changes in the use of land.... *Two*: — Co-operation of agreements with any agency or any person.... *Three*: — Acquisition of lands or rights or interest therein....

SECOND REPORTER (*excitedly*): *Four*: United States Government contributions to those who conserve the soil, *in form of money, services, materials, or otherwise.*

FIRST REPORTER: *Five*: The hiring of employees.

SECOND REPORTER (*more excited than he was before*): *Six*: The expenditure of money for *anything,* from the purchasing of law books right down to passenger-carrying vehicles. (*The words rushing out*) And most important of all ...

Seven: the transfer to this work authorized of such functions, moneys, personnel, and the property of other agencies in the Department of Agriculture as the Secretary may see fit!

CHESTER DAVIS (*who has become progressively more excited though inarticulate to this point — jumping up*): My God, there's the farm program for 1936. (*Tremendous excitement, elation, his fingers begin to punch the various buttons on his desk, sending out a general alarm. Simultaneously,* SECRETARIES, ASSISTANTS, STENOGRAPHERS, CLERKS *rush in. He continues, shouting*): Get my Planning Board together. Get my assistant, get me Wallace. Get me Wilson, get me Stedman, get me ... (SECRETARIES, CLERKS, MESSENGER *cross and crisscross from right to left as* DAVIS *gives orders.*)

Blackout

156] HALLIE FLANAGAN

SCENE TWENTY-SIX
(Finale)

CHARACTERS

VOICE OF LIVING NEWSPAPER
DELEGATION OF FARMERS CARRYING PLACARDS, REPRESENTING:
South Dakota
Minnesota
North Dakota
Wisconsin
Nebraska
Iowa
Kansas
Idaho
Indiana

SECRETARY WALLACE
MAN IN EVENING CLOTHES
WOMAN IN EVENING CLOTHES
                                      from Scene Fifteen
WOMAN STRIKE LEADER
OTHER WOMAN
FARMER
DEALER
MANUFACTURER
WORKER
A GROUP OF UNEMPLOYED WORKERS
A GROUP OF UNEMPLOYED FARMERS
                                    From Scene Twenty

                    from Scene Three

VOICE OF LIVING NEWSPAPER: Huron, South Dakota, February 20th, 1936. . . . Farmers meet in Convention to draft program.*
(*Portals part just sufficiently to admit line of* FARMERS *carrying banners of the States — South Dakota, Minnesota, North Dakota, Wisconsin, Nebraska, Iowa, Kansas, Idaho and Indiana. Half of the* FARMERS *enter from the left, and go right in front of portals, the other half enter from right and go left in front of portals. As last* FARMER *enters, portals close and straight line evenly spaced is formed in front of portals.*)

Farmers' National Weekly, February 14, 1936.

VOICE (*over* LOUDSPEAKER): Now, while the Soil Conservation Act is being written, is the time to make Congress and the Administration feel the pressure of the organized good sense of the American farmers. We believe that the following main points represent what the farmers must have in order to live decently, and at the same time time protect the interests of the other sections of the working population.†

FARMER FROM SOUTH DAKOTA: Past commitments for the benefit payments under the old AAA must be paid in full.

FARMER FROM MINNESOTA: Whatever legislation may be passed should include cash payments to working farmers *at least equal* to the benefit payments under the AAA.

FARMER FROM NORTH DAKOTA (*one step forward*): Additional cash relief if the benefit payments are inadequate for a farm family to maintain a decent American standard of living.

FARMER FROM WISCONSIN: A decent American standard of living means cost of production prices.

FARMER FROM NEBRASKA: Cost of production prices mean far higher prices than today, whereby the farmer can at least pay his bills, operating costs and living expenses.

FARMER FROM IOWA: Increased production is needed by the nation today, the United States Department of Agriculture reports.

VOICE (*over* LOUDSPEAKER): To feed one hundred and twenty-five million people according to the best standards, forty million acres would have to be added to production.

FARMER FROM KANSAS: Therefore we oppose the policy of reduction . . .

FARMER FROM IDAHO: . . . but we do not oppose soil conservation except when used as a means of giving the Secretary of Agriculture power to force farmers to reduce production of good land.

FARMER FROM INDIANA: There are adequate resources available to meet the financial obligation incurred in this program. We suggest diversion to farm relief of a large part of the immense war appropriations, and increasing taxation on the wealth and income of the great financial and industrial interests of this country. *With special emphasis on the giant corporations which handle food productions!*

FARMER FROM SOUTH DAKOTA: The farmer has been sold down the river.

(*Curtains part revealing full stage set.* MAN *and* WOMAN *in evening clothes are on highest level upstage left.* SECRETARY WALLACE *is on*

---

†*Farmers' National Weekly*, February 7, 1936.

intermediate level upstage, WOMEN *from the Meat Strike scene are left center in front of* WALLACE, *and* MAN *and* WOMAN *in evening clothes and* UNEMPLOYED *are on ramp, right, while* FARMERS *are on ramp, left.*

FARMERS *previously in line across footlights move toward ramp left, a few to prosecenium, down right.* FARMERS, UNEMPLOYED, *etc., when speaking, step a little forward so that they may be marked apart from crowd. All on stage turn heads toward speaker to indicate source of voice. The reaction is particularly marked in case of* LOUDSPEAKER, *with all heads turned toward voice and holding that position until* LOUDSPEAKER *is finished. Other definite and marked reactions in this scene are gestures on the "up, up" of the* FARMERS, *and the "down, down" of the* WOMEN; *the movement of* FARMERS *and* UNEMPLOYED *as the* FARMER *steps forward between the two groups, and the gestures drawing them together on the line, "then our problem is the same," gestures toward and against* MAN *and* WOMAN *in evening clothes and* SECRETARY WALLACE *on lines such as "no charity," "jobs," "jobs." "We need help, not words." There should be a balanced reaction away from crowd in fear, disgust, etc., on the part of the* MAN *and* WOMAN *in evening clothes.*)

SECRETARY WALLACE: In 1935 the AAA paid benefits of five hundred and eight million dollars.[*]

A FARMER: [†] Soil Conservation benefits must at least be equal to the benefits of the Triple-A.

MAN IN EVENING CLOTHES: We must carry on with soil conservation.

VOICE (*over* LOUDSPEAKER): A dollar one, a dollar two . . .

ANOTHER FARMER (*taking step forward*): Soil Conservation is the Triple-A in false whiskers.

STILL ANOTHER FARMER: Farm prices must stay up.

WOMAN (*strike leader*): Food prices must go down.

ALL FARMERS (*in chorus*): UP! UP!

ALL WOMEN: DOWN! DOWN!

FARMER [‡] (*from Scene Three*): I can't buy that auto.

DEALER (*from Scene Three*): I can't take that shipment.

WORKER (*from Scene Three*): I can't eat. (*Jumps to intermediate level.*)

VOICE (*over* LOUDSPEAKER): There is now piled up in the banks a

---

[*]*New York Times,* March 4, 1936.
[†]Creative and digest of news.
[‡]Digest of article "A.A.A. Philosophy" by Rexford G. Tugwell, *Fortune Magazine,* January 1934.

Federal Theatre [159

huge savings reserve, and it lays a basis for a new speculative boom
— (*All look toward* LOUDSPEAKER.)
MANUFACTURER (*from Scene Three*): I can't use you any more. (*Jumps to intermediate level.*)
MAN IN EVENING CLOTHES:* Back to normalcy.
VOICE (*over* LOUDSPEAKER): ... which may result in a far more disastrous collapse than any heretofore experienced.
MAN IN EVENING CLOTHES (*to woman with him*): The rugged individualism of our forefathers will solve our problem.
A FARMER: Our problems are of the soil.
AN UNEMPLOYED WORKER: Ours of the belly.
MAN IN EVENING CLOTHES: Of course we need the farmer.
VOICE (*over* LOUDSPEAKER): A dollar three, a dollar four . . .
SECRETARY WALLACE: We have come to the time when we have to learn to live one with another. We have no more cheap land, no great foreign markets, no one to impose upon.
A FARMER: We need help, not words!
SECRETARY WALLACE: We, down in Washington, do not believe we have the final answer to the problem—but we believe that, no matter who is in power a year hence, the kind of thing exemplified in the Soil Conservation Act will be going forward.
ONE FARMER: We need help!
ALL FARMERS: We need help!
ONE UNEMPLOYED: We need food!
ALL UNEMPLOYED: We need food!
ALL FARMERS: We need food!
ONE WOMEN: We need a decent standard of living.
ALL WOMEN: We need a decent standard of living.
ALL UNEMPLOYED: So do we. We need a decent standard of living.
ALL FARMERS: So do we.
A FARMER: Then all our problems are the same!
ALL UNEMPLOYED: Then all our problems are the same.
WOMAN IN EVENING CLOTHES: All must be helped, John.
FARMER, UNEMPLOYED AND WOMAN: No charity!
AN UNEMPLOYED: Jobs!
ALL UNEMPLOYED: Jobs!
A FARMER: Help.
AN UNEMPLOYED: We need a State that permits no man to go hungry.
MAN IN EVENING CLOTHES: Rugged individualism.
A WOMAN: No profiteering.

*Remainder of scene is creative.

160] HALLIE FLANAGAN

ALL UNEMPLOYED: Jobs.
ONE FARMER: We can't harvest.
ALL FARMERS: We can't harvest.
ONE WOMAN: We can't buy.
ALL WOMEN: We can't buy.
ONE UNEMPLOYED: We can't eat!
ALL UNEMPLOYED: We can't eat!
VOICE (*over* LOUDSPEAKER. *News flashes of events that have occurred that day — especially with reference to a Farmer-Labor Party. Below are three flashes that were used*):*

Local Farmer-Labor Party conventions in Connecticut, Massachusetts, Pennsylvania and South Dakota declared for a national Farmer-Labor Party. Two county conventions at Minneapolis passed a resolution demanding that the State Farmer-Labor Party meeting in convention at Minneapolis March 17th, take the lead in a national Farmer-Labor Party.

Washington: Before a cheering audience at the St. Nicholas Arena last night, Congressman Ernest Lundeen, of Minnesota, said: "Labor unions and farmer organizations will soon become irresistible political powers."

Great Falls, Montana: The semi-annual conference of the Farmers' Holiday Association held here today had as its major decision the endorsement of a resolution for the formation of a Farmer-Labor Party. This resolution was proposed by Reid Robinson of the Butte Miners' Union.

FARMER: We *need* you.
CHORUS OF FARMERS: We *need* you.
LEADER OF UNEMPLOYED: We need *you*.
CHORUS OF UNEMPLOYED: We need *you*. (FARMERS *and* UNEMPLOYED *jump close together, arms extended. Light on them is intensified. Lights on* WALLACE *and* WOMAN *and* MAN *in evening clothes fade. Tableau of* FARMERS, WOMEN *and* UNEMPLOYED *hold.*)

Curtain

---

*Daily spot newspaper quotes used, quotes changing with the news.

THEY TRIED TO LAUGH

Wasn't the Depression Terrible?

title of book by O. Soglow and David G. Plotkin (1934)

S. J. Perelman

WAITING FOR SANTY

The New Yorker, *then as now, was weak on social criticism, but it resisted the clichés of the radicals. One of its cartoons showed a stereotyped malcontent outside a police-station, sneering directly into the face of a policeman's horse. S. J. Perelman, one of the magazine's brightest stars, parodies the title and spirit of the once-famous* Waiting for Lefty, *by Clifford Odets, incorporating scarcely burlesqued samples of Odetsian folk-poetry (cf.* Awake and Sing!)

A CHRISTMAS PLAYLET
(*With a Bow to Mr. Clifford Odets*)

SCENE: *The sweatshop of S. Claus, a manufacturer of children's toys, on North Pole Street. Time: The night before Christmas.*

At rise, seven gnomes, Rankin, Panken, Rivkin, Riskin, Ruskin, Briskin, and Praskin, are discovered working furiously to fill orders piling up at stage right. The whir of lathes, the hum of motors, and the hiss of drying lacquer are so deafening that at times the dialogue cannot be heard, which is very vexing if you vex easily. Note: The parts of Rankin, Panken, Rivkin, Riskin, Ruskin, Briskin, and Praskin are interchangeable, and may be secured directly from your dealer or the factory.

RISKIN (*filing a Meccano girder, bitterly*): A parasite, a leech, a bloodsucker -- altogether a five-star nogoodnick! Starvation wages we get so he can ride around in a red team with reindeers!
RUSKIN (*jeering*): Hey, Karl Marx, whyn'tcha hire a hall?
RISKIN (*sneering*): Scab! Stool pigeon! Company spy! (*They tangle and rain blows on each other. While waiting for these to dry, each returns to his respective task.*)
BRISKIN (*sadly, to Panken*): All day long I'm painting "Snow Queen"

on these Flexible Flyers and my little Irving lays in a cold tenement with the gout.
PANKEN: You said before it was the mumps.
BRISKIN (*with a fatalistic shrug*): The mumps — the gout — go argue with City Hall.
PANKEN (*kindly, passing him a bowl*): Here, take a piece fruit.
BRISKIN (*chewing*): It ain't bad, for wax fruit.
PANKEN (*with pride*): I painted it myself.
BRISKIN (*rejecting the fruit*): Ptoo! Slave psychology!
RIVKIN (*suddenly, half to himself, half to the Party*): I got a belly full of stars, baby. You make me feel like I swallowed a Roman candle.
PRASKIN (*curiously*): What's wrong with the kid?
RISKIN: What's wrong with all of us? The system! Two years he and Claus's daughter's been making googoo eyes behind the old man's back.
PRASKIN: So what?
RISKIN (*scornfully*): So what? Economic determinism! What do you think the kid's name is — J. Pierpont Rivkin? He ain't even got for a bottle Dr. Brown's Celery Tonic. I tell you, it's like gall in my mouth two young people shouldn't have a room where they could make great music.
RANKIN (*warningly*): Shhh! Here she comes now! (*Stella Claus enters, carrying a portable phonograph. She and Rivkin embrace, place a record on the turntable, and begin a very slow waltz, unmindful that the phonograph is playing "Cohen on the Telephone."*)
STELLA (*dreamily*): Love me, sugar?
RIVKIN: I can't sleep, I can't eat, that's how I love you. You're a double malted with two scoops of whipped cream; you're the moon rising over Mosholu Parkway; you're a two weeks' vacation at Camp Nitgedaiget! I'd pull down the Chrysler Building to make a bobbie pin for your hair!
STELLA: I've got a stomach full of anguish. Oh, Rivvy, what'll we do?
PANKEN (*sympathetically*): Here, try a piece fruit.
RIVKIN (*fiercely*): Wax fruit — that's been my whole life! Imitations! Substitutes! Well, I'm through! Stella, tonight I'm telling your old man. He can't play mumblety-peg with two human beings! (*The tinkle of sleigh bells is heard offstage, followed by a voice shouting, "Whoa, Dasher! Whoa, Dancer!" A moment later S. Claus enters in a gust of mock snow. He is a pompous bourgeois of sixty-five who affects a white beard and a false air of benevo-*

lence. But tonight the ruddy color is missing from his cheeks, his step falters, and he moves heavily. The gnomes hastily replace the marzipan they have been filching.)

STELLA (*anxiously*): Papa! What did the specialist say to you?

CLAUS (*brokenly*): The biggest professor in the country . . . the best cardiac man that money could buy. . . . I tell you I was like a wild man.

STELLA: Pull yourself together, Sam!

CLAUS: It's no use. Adhesions, diabetes, sleeping sickness, decalcomania — oh, my God! I got to cut out climbing in chimneys, he says — me, Sanford Claus, the biggest toy concern in the world!

STELLA (*soothingly*): After all, it's only one man's opinion.

CLAUS: No, no, he cooked my goose. I'm like a broken uke after a Yosian picnic. Rivkin!

RIVKIN: Yes, Sam.

CLAUS: My boy, I had my eye on you for a long time. You and Stella thought you were too foxy for an old man, didn't you? Well, let bygones be bygones. Stella, do you love this gnome?

STELLA (*simply*): He's the whole stage show at the Music Hall, Papa; he's Toscanini conducting Beethoven's Fifth; he's —

CLAUS (*curtly*): Enough already. Take him. From now on he's a partner in the firm. (*As all exclaim, Claus holds up his hand for silence.*) And tonight he can take my route and make the deliveries. It's the least I could do for my own flesh and blood. (*As the happy couple kiss, Claus wipes away a suspicious moisture and turns to the other gnomes.*) Boys, do you know what day tomorrow is?

GNOMES (*crowding around expectantly*): Christmas!

CLAUS: Correct. When you look in your envelopes tonight, you'll find a little present from me — a forty per cent pay cut. And the first one who opens his trap — gets this. (*As he holds up a tear-gas bomb and beams at them, the gnomes utter cries of joy, join hands, and dance around him shouting exultantly. All except Riskin and Briskin, that is, who exchange a quick glance and go underground.*)

CURTAIN

Tess Slesinger

BRUNO AND THE BLACK SHEEP

Tess Slesinger (1905-1945) contributed tone and satirical prose to a decade which dearly needed both. In addition to her novel, The Unpossessed *(1934), the title of which parodies Dostoevski's* The Possessed, *she also published a collection of short stories:* Time: the Present *(1935). She later contributed her talents to Hollywood.*

"TELL HIM from me," Bruno shouted to Emmett through the door of his living-room which had turned overnight into Filing Cabinet headquarters, "that his stuff is sure-fire sale and sure-fire manure and we're not having any in our stable. Tell him to shovel it under someone else's door and get to hell out of our way — we're busy; we're a man of action, a man of Magazine. Besides we've got to meet a boat next Saturday." (He drew a deep and happy breath of memory.) He turned complacently to the Six Black Sheep squatting on window-sills and tables, like a young army too restless to take to chairs, their bright undergraduate sweaters like scattered parts of a flag at rest; and met the ultra-critical eye of their lean and undernourished Chairman as he sat swinging his feet against Bruno's grand piano. "Nothing," Bruno added, chiefly to irritate young Firman, "stinks quite like a bad writer. Unless it's the slightly foetid odor of a bad writer gone phoney propagandist. . . . Tell him we're not running a dirty propaganda sheet, Emmett," he roared, "we keep open house and open forum and if he can't take it slam the receiver in his propaganda face. . . . But what's the matter, Comrade Chairman? what have I said that isn't kosher?"

For Firman, perched like a young Jewish owl on the music stool, had kicked the piano disgustedly, while his eyes behind his glasses gleamed with intelligent dislike. "Oh nothing," said young Firman coldly (did that lad exist, thought Bruno, returning the look and the sentiment irresistibly, only to remind him that he must have been

[165

just such a conscientious bore himself fifteen years ago?). "Nothing, only that the open forum policy is untenable from the ground up. Every written word," said Firman, hitching the glasses higher on his nose, "is propaganda." Six Sheep bowed in a haughty phalanx of assent; their sudden sway putting the flag together for a moment.

"I see you know your catechism," Bruno said. "We will proceed to the next step. How about poetry? One at a time now, children."

"An opiate," said Little Dixon briskly.

"Propaganda for spending your life sitting on your ass reading it," said Cornelia Carson promptly. Bruno failed to place her counterpart in any of the girls of his own day; she seemed an exclusive twentieth century product, half-boy, half-girl, born yesterday, of movies, radio and matter-of-fact class-consciousness.

"For forgetting what's wrong with the world and getting all tangled up being lyrical about the birds," said one of the Maxwell brothers.

"I'd have all the lyric poets jailed for counter-revolutionaries," said Firman, gathering the comments of his committee and fitting them precisely into his dialectic nutshell. He spoke with jagged edges to his speech but when he came to revolution he slipped it out with the U sound round and slippery as a peeled banana.

"And intentions?" Bruno began, thinking how the pleasant sophistries of his own day had changed to dogma in the mouths of this younger generation; when Emmett Middleton came sidling through the door like an uncertain deer; paused and looked about him for a place to sit as though he weren't sure whether to cast his lot with his contemporaries or with Bruno. "Has our maiden contributor bit the dust, Emmett?" The boy smiled gratefully, as though Bruno's notice decided him; he chose for his seat at last the corner of Bruno's desk where he sat enthroned on Bruno's right and above his fellow-classmen. "I thought propaganda was intentional, deliberate?" Bruno quirked an eye on Firman, aware sheepishly that he had bought Emmett for an ally.

"In Russia," said Cornelia Carson in her dry two-tone, boy-and-woman voice, "intentions don't count." "Only results matter," said Kate Corrigan, commonly known as "Irish," laying the next step. "This is the age for objectivity, the subjective went out with individualism." "Everything in the world," Firman mounted the ladder and intoned from the top rung, "is propaganda. A tree is propaganda. Propaganda for cutting it down and making it into guns. For reforestation. For pulp magazines...."

"And just for lolling under counter-revolutionarily, I suppose, to the fat professors like myself," said Bruno; perceiving that a superior form of Blake's disease had taken the youngsters by storm. "Oh who will come and lie with me, under the propaganda-tree. . . . Pardon me, Firman, I have a touch of horse-blood." He met Firman's eye ironically; saw in them a reflection of his own look and drew back startled by the felt resemblance. "But you asked for an interview, Firman. Let's get on with it, I'm a man of action this week, ask my secretary. . . ."

"Yes, Doctor Leonard hasn't got all night," said Emmett in the tone of class monitor; "make it s-snappy, Firman."

"Nor yet all week," said Bruno happily. Five days to Elizabeth's boat; five days to seeing his earliest friend, to tearing down the walls of fog that they had let be built between them; to reaching out, touch hands at last, beg for forgiveness, beg for love. . . . "Now what's on the Black Sheep's mind?"

The Sheep scrambled out of their silence and clattered eagerly for his attention. Only Emmett, diffident, kept still, dissociating himself from his colleagues (Bruno wondered what weakness in himself had made him choose the weakest of their number to befriend) till he saw which way the land lay.

"The point is, Doctor Leonard" "and they won't give us a column in the Campus Pilgrim" "open forum is all very nice" "but like all open forums" "it's only open to one side" "try to slip in one intelligent thought, one protest" "I wish you'd all shut up," said Arnold Firman vigorously; "how can he hear if we all yell at once like a damned cheering-squad."

Their enthusiasm for whatever it was that was eating them touched him but it made him feel a hundred years old or more. It had been so long, so many years, since his own contemporaries had gathered like an army behind him. "I gather that the Black Sheep are even hotter under the collar than usual," he said dryly; "but my senile brains, you know . . . Firman, the ancient mariner looks to you."

The boy approached his desk with an air of timid impertinence, as though to show he dared be at home in the enemy's territory, as though despite embarrassment to himself he claimed his rights. "Doctor Leonard. Before we go any further . . . excuse me for getting personal — " the lids fell half-way over his eyes — "but we've been hearing about your Magazine for so long now; rumor whispers — and yet . . . *is* there a Magazine, Doctor Leonard?" He raised profoundly sceptical brows.

From behind their glasses the two Jews in the room glared at one another with what (Bruno was certain) must be the identical look. "Your scepticism, Firman," he spoke coldly; but he could never avoid a faint intimacy when he spoke to Firman, "does you credit. But the Magzine," and he felt stronger at once, as though he had needed his own words for re-conviction, "the Magazine, to my own surprise, is rapidly becoming a fact. Great trees from little shoe-strings grow; but our Magazine was founded on a Filing Cabinet. Behold, children! The first installment's paid — and Emmett's mother's going to meet the next. Although, I think, she doesn't know it yet." Emmett blushed with pride.

"Well then," young Firman said; and stood as though he planted his thin chest against invisible but omnipresent enemies impersonated momently in Bruno. "The Pilgrim is supposed to be the mouthpiece of the whole student body. 'Open forum' it says on the title-page; and some drivel about inviting all opinions. But it turns out that it's only open to the opinions of the conservatives, the foot-ball heroes, the stinking-fascists."

Football! Was that the worm that gnawed that hollow intellectual chest? Bruno felt a wave of nostalgia, the strange and nauseating kinship, binding and repugnant, which a cripple feels when meeting a fellow-cripple on the street. Jew on a window-sill! When did not a smart young Jew turn his back with hate upon the football heroes of his world — and pinch his heart at night with longing to be one of them? One batters on closed gates begging for admission; and when the gate stays fast, the battering turns imperceptibly from pleading to attack.

"Why?" said Arnold Firman rhetorically. He spoke with the relentless persistence of one climbing endless ladders toward an unwavering and unforgettable goal. "Because of football politics. Because of fraternity politics. Because the same stinking-fascism that rules the board of directors runs the student-body too. Because, as I said before, the open forum principle is untenable, because propaganda is inherent in every written word. Now — when the Black Sheep resigned from the Campus Club last year in protest against the fraternities. . . ."

"Can the Roberts rules of order, Firman, and get to the point," said Cornelia Carson briefly. She was a small girl, taut and tightly drawn on strong dry wires; it occurred to Bruno that she might not have enough to eat.

Firman pulled himself up short. "Objection sustained, sister. I thought for a minute I was on the soap-box. The point is, Doctor Leonard, that the Pilgrim's pages are so filled with football drivel that the Black Sheep can't get a word in edgewise. Last month we sent in an article on the Scottsboro case — from the youth angle, you know. They sent it back. 'We haven't room,' they said, 'for anything but collegiate topics.' And it's the same with everything we write."

The Black Sheep nodded like one man. They all reached boiling point, catching heat from their leader, at once.

"We think the student body has a right to know the facts" "whether they want to or not, the dumb yeggs" "if we have to ram it down their throat" "what's education *for*" "we're sick and tired of being told to shut up like a bunch of God damn kids," cried Cornelia, summing up, "when the Scottsboro boys are younger than we — and they're going to hang them like sure-enough adults."

The telephone cut like a barbed wire through their unity. They dwindled angrily into silence; drew together whispering and gesturing in their bright wool sweaters, the parts of the flag almost fitting together. Emmett jumped up — "I'll take it here," said Bruno grimly; he wanted respite from the mounting fire. Jeffrey's voice came like a thin thread sounding the note of his own contemporaries. Behind his back the army of the future milled. He heard Jeffrey through. "I don't give a damn," he shouted back, "Fisher or no Fisher, Comrade or no Comrade, I won't print lies. And badly written ones at that. Stop acting like a God damn procurer. Alienate, hooey. If literary conscience alienates them we'll start a lefter wing. Tell your Comrade Fisher that a truth in the hand is worth twenty propagandist lies in the bushes, from the early Esquimaux. . . . And don't buy any more pen-holders. All we need now is an umbrella stand and a spittoon. Goodbye, you God damned fool. See you on the barricades. Yes, I'll speak to Emmett. Yes, sometime this week if his mother can make it. Goodbye, goodbye." He slapped down the receiver with vigor. He would have to wait for Elizabeth; his friends were mad. "See, Firman? Man of action. Brusque. Determined. Editorial sense combined with courage. . . . But I think you were saying something. All of you at once, if I'm not mistaken."

The flag broke up as Firman rose again; behind him the woolly parts waved as though the same wind blew them all. The pose of angry unconcern fell from Firman's face; the very lines that made it ugly made it, for a moment, fine. The eagerness in those lidded eyes, unaccustomed as they were to holding light, was singular and moving; Bruno warmed despite himself. An ugly Shelley, the boy stood, raised by some inward urge, forgetful at last of a world forever hostile; and behind him his small army stood solid.

"Doctor Leonard. The Black Sheep need a mouthpiece of their own. We want a chance to speak. Not on such little issues as football — that's just a symbol, so far as we're concerned." (Take that, Leonard, Bruno told himself; these kids are smart; maybe they *apply* their lingo.) "And not just to the students of this campus. We feel that college students don't live in glass houses, the campus is a miniature fascist state, run by the same lousy factors that the outside world is run by. We want to open students' eyes. We want to talk to all the students in the country...."

Excitement mounted among the Sheep. They leaned forward, their eyes alight on Bruno. Firman at their head looked like a tough little Jewish Napoleon — Bruno felt himself drawing back from their concerted onslaught. Young Emmett squirmed, his eyes swinging like a nervous pendulum from Firman's face to Bruno's.

"We'd like to strike a bargain with you, Doctor Leonard. We'd like to volunteer to work for you, free, do all the dirty work, the grubby odds and ends, on your Magazine. If you'd let us, in turn," here Firman's passion made him shy; "if you'd let us — I suppose you think we have a hell of a lot of nerve — if you'd let us have one department in it. A student forum, run by students, you see, run for them. If you'd let us run it," he concluded bravely. He fell back and became a private in his own army again.

The Sheep leaned forward, their eyes big with their daring and their hope, and shouted.

"relate collegiate topics" "apply Marxism" "correlate" "emphasize" "denounce" "teach" "explain"

Twelve years had passed since Bruno and *his* friends had grown so heated. Twelve years since Bruno the valedictorian had remained behind to be instructor, then professor, in their hated Alma Mater; since Elizabeth had said (she was fifteen then; precocious but sentimental; impelled trustfully to always speak her mind): I hope you won't get glued behind that desk, I hope you won't grow fat and jowly and sad like our fathers. No, he had not got glued; this he told himself sternly now; and all this week he had been feeling in himself (since his cable to Elizabeth, since her quick response) the strength stored up in all these dozen years.

He suddenly resented Firman and his devoted army as though they threatened the twelve-year dead triumvirate of Bruno, Jeffrey, Miles; as though they eagerly dug graves for the generation fifteen years their senior. Into their smug united strength he felt impelled to hurl a knife.

"Spare my aged ear-drums," he dropped his words heavily on the gold and budding flower of their zeal. "Sheep in wolves' clothing I call it — you want to get in on the ground floor, do you? and buy the old man out?" But his irony was heavy, without meaning even to himself. In young Firman's fierce pale eyes was coldly marked acceptance of the fifteen years which separated them. The army of the younger generation, led against him by his counterpart, the bitter Jew. He longed for autonomy of contemporaries; for Elizabeth, so close a reflection of himself. He resented Emmett, the boy's imagination fired, hanging between two armies, between two generations.

"But I don't know, you see — " He found himself hesitating; but he discovered that he knew he would accept them; to include them was peculiarly fitting, ironically just; but also he felt vaguely apprehensive. "You might all get kicked out of school," he threatened them lightly.

"We don't give a damn," the younger generation cried. He could see Emmett barely suppressing a smile of pride for his colleagues.

"I'll have to think it over," he said; he knew he sounded like an irritating and unreasonable parent; but his mind was made up. "I'll have to put it to the others too. There's plenty of time anyway," he said uneasily.

"There isn't plenty of time," they shouted back. "We want to do something — NOW." They stood, a half-dozen lean and half-grown children; but Bruno saw their banner waving; their numbers multiply.

"All I can do," he said firmly, "is put your suggestion before Flinders and Blake;" but he knew the Black Sheep must be voted in; they would lend a life and a fury and off-set the tired-radical element.

"Thanks, Doctor Leonard." "Three cheers!" "Hurray!" they cried, accepting it as a matter settled in their favor; and rose like a triumphant army moving on to conquer further fields. The parts of the flag sprang together; moved in a swirling many-colored block toward the door. "We'll work like hell, Doctor Leonard," said Cornelia Carson in her boy-and-woman voice.

Emmett had leaped off his perch to the floor; stood hesitantly beside the desk; for a moment Bruno thought he made an odd gesture forwards, incomprehensibly, perhaps from habit, as a child automatically rises and follows its class out of assembly, to join his generation. Bruno touched his arm; he fell back quickly. "If you can put up with my company, Emmett — we might go over the manifesto again; we might even play chess." Emmett brightened; smiled ostentatiously at the backs of the departing Sheep.

The little bastard Firman, Bruno thought; the smart wise-cracking little Jew; *is there a Magazine?* the nerve of the little devil. But *was there?* It was up to Elizabeth. The door closed on Firman's army; the room was ten shades darker. "Get out the masterpiece, Emmett," he said; "it's filed under something or other. We'll go over it with Jeffrey's red pencil."

John Alroy

THE MOVEMENT TOWARD THE LEFT

> *This portrait of an intellectual appeared in the* American Mercury. *Numerous persons who considered themselves sophisticated saw nothing funny in it at all, and indeed the serious application of this boob's clichés played a significant and terrible part in the rise of Nazism. "Social Fascism" was one of Stalin's remarkable linguistic contributions to working-class unity. Social Democrats, he asserted, were not different from fascists but their complement, the other side of the same coin. Sincere "rank and file" socialists, therefore, ought to abandon their organizations and join the communists in a "united front from below." Stalin's slogan, in Germany, inspired another slogan which intended no humor: "Kick the little social fascists out of the kindergarten." It helped to drive a wedge between the two great mass organizations, the socialists and the communists, numbering some eleven million members, between whom the forces of Adolf Hitler, to the number of some seven million, marched triumphantly.*

IMAGINE HIM telling me it's no good as if a lousy Liberal bastard like him would know what was good or bad when he doesn't know any more about literary criticism than some of these fellows with the capitalist press that pull down big jack writing reviews about books they don't understand because how could they understand them not having the Marxian viewpoint and they have the guts to tell men like me that have studied and worked and examined every angle of the whole business and have read just about everything Marx and Lenin wrote about Literature yes and a lot that Trotzky wrote too because Trotzky was a damn good critic before he turned Social Fascist and the Soviet was perfectly right to liquidate him a damn counter-revolutionary like that even if he did know a lot about revolutionary tactics and maybe did some good work in the October Revolution but then he sells out and fellows like this Rivera that you'd suppose would have enough guts to stick go over with him and join the Left opposition but after all I guess that's about all you could expect from a fellow like Rivera because all he's interested in is just selling a lot of pictures to birds like Rockefeller and making himself plenty of jack and having shows in capitalist galleries which after all is just plain mugwumpism because the fellows who own capitalist galleries aren't interested in real proletarian art at all but just in making money just like the capitalist press that doesn't even know there is such a thing as class struggle and think a fellow that's writing really class-conscious stuff is all wet just think of a guy like that telling me that story's no good as if he knew what makes a story good or bad but of course I really shouldn't have shown it to him at all except that I thought he ought to know something about technique at least with all the writing he's done and getting published in all the high-priced bourgeoise magazines and everything and then come to find out he doesn't even know anything about technique and all he could say was why don't you join the Communist party if you feel that way not realizing of course that I'm of more value outside the party and he said having the hero join the Communist party at the finish was sentimental and just tacked on and didn't come logically with the character I'd built up not being a competent enough critic to understand the great conflict involved in making the decision to join no and he didn't realize that the one way of solving the problem is to become a militant member of the party but he'd have just let him walk out on it and leave the whole thing unsolved and if he thinks the hero in the story shouldn't have joined the party what makes him think I ought to when I have more important work to do and can really help the Revolution more by not joining but by being a free-lance writer putting out revolutionary stuff but I don't suppose a Social Fascist could get the point in a hundred years and another thing just to show what kind of a guy he is I'm almost positive he was ditching his drinks although he lied and said he was pouring them in as fast as they came around and that he could prove it by Elizabeth as if I'd take Elizabeth's word for anything with her typical bourgeoise attitude toward everything and pretending she's such a humanitarian and her poor heart just bleeds over all the suffering and so damn pleased with herself because she got a job for some bird that was down and out not realizing that it doesn't do any good to help out the individual victim of the system but it's the system itself you have to attack but that's the whole trouble with Liberals they get soft hearted over individual examples of the cruelty of the system and close their eyes to the big thing that's staring them in the face and think they're so noble when they help out one guy but won't turn their hand to help out all the oppressed mass of workers and they just seem not to see at all that a real class-conscious minority is growing in this country and about the first people to be liquidated after the Revolution will be the Liberals because they've always been obstructionists and counter-revolutionaries anyway and never have contributed any real help although I guess the party can use them now with the money they give different organizations and then besides their writing sort of wakes people up a little just like feeding milk to a baby before he's old enough to eat real food but of course the stuff they write is actually just manure and not worth a damn and not one of these Liberal writers can appreciate real proletarian literature because they haven't any grounds for criticism not having studied dialectics but getting all their ideas from schools and capitalist writers and people like them and it's apparent how much these editors of the capitalist press know about what's going on hell I'd feel disgraced to have my work appear in one of their publications like this fellow Carter who started out to be a radical and then sold out and runs things in magazines like *Scribner's* and *Pagany* and that poem in *Pagany* had a French title besides as if that isn't the height of Social Fascism running a poem with a French title and then trying to explain it away by saying it's a quotation from Baudelaire as if anyone gives a damn whether it's a quotation from Baudelaire or any other damn bourgeois when he was really just trying to put on the ritz and show how much he knows about French and why the hell shouldn't he be able to talk French when he had a father with enough money to send him to Paris and another thing they say you can judge a magazine by the stuff it rejects more than by the stuff it runs and it certainly holds true because I know some swell stuff they've turned down but what can you expect of them anyway only I can't understand a sheet like the *New Masses* missing the beauty of good work like they do unless they're too filled up with material or something like that but even so they've run some pretty crappy stuff lately themselves and oh boy did the I.U.R.W.* light into them serves them right too because they certainly had it coming although they're still the best magazine in this country which isn't saying much because there isn't a first class revolutionary sheet in America but some day there will be with all the good writers getting themselves posted on Marxism and these fellows aren't going to be able to just keep on selling out to the bourgeoisie forever because after all the movement's too strong to let a few yellow bastards whip it.

*International Union of Revolutionary Writers

AS THROUGH A GLASS DARKLY

    The poor creep about the streets in covering only less miserable than nakedness; their clothes have already lasted a long time; they are patched and cared for, for they must last a long time yet. The men's hair is shaggy; they do not look at you nor do their eyes avoid you; they are apparently looking at nothing. . . .

>John Peale Bishop, in Fall River, Mass., in 1936 or 1937; from his *Collected Essays* (1948)

We don't know . . . we aren't sure . . . we're wondering

>Archibald MacLeish, *Land of the Free* (1938)

We are lived by powers we pretend to understand:
They arrange our loves; it is they who direct at the end
The enemy bullet, the sickness, or even our hand.

>W. H. Auden, "In Memory of Ernst Toller (d. May 1939)"

Albert Halper

From UNION SQUARE

> *Albert Halper was one of the uncompromising naturalists of the time, a Chicago-born drifter and worker who identified himself with writers on the one hand, and workers on the other. In striving to tell the Truth he mixed his concern for flat statement with Marxist assumptions which directed his largely humorless observance of the "facts". Thus,* The Foundry *(1934) was about a foundry in which he had labored, and which was presumably the center and soul of a tangle of lives.* Union Square *(1933) better reflected the intellectual and real world Halper inhabited. The original for his poet Jason was said to have been Kenneth Fearing.*

IN THE AFTERNOON Leon paid a visit to his friend the ex-poet. Before climbing the flights he stuck his fingers into Jason's mail-box to see if the postman had brought anything on his second trip. He drew out a small pink letter bearing a Philadelphia postmark; there was no return address. Leon took it upstairs with him.

Jason was lying on the cot, staring at the ceiling when Leon entered after knocking three times. The ex-poet has just finished a tale called "Patricia Pets Her Way to Happiness." He was all fagged out. Leon placed the letter upon the table, and Jason, rolling his head to one side, saw the pinkness of it, but made no move to pick it up.

"I was just going by," said Leon, sitting down.

Jason did not answer; he looked to be a very sick young man and stared with slack eyes toward the ceiling.

After a long silence Leon said, "You ought to see a doctor."

"How was the meeting last night?" Jason asked, changing the subject.

Now it was Leon's turn to sit in silence. Jason, because he had once been a Party member, knew very well how the meetings went; they had not changed since he had dropped out. He prodded the little fellow until Leon, against his will, found himself answering the ex-poet.

"The meeting was a bit stormy," said Leon.

"Did Comrade Lukotas get up and shoot his gab off?"

"Comrade Lukotas spoke a few words," came the answer.

Jason cackled. In the end, because his chest pained, because he was tired out from writing hack and did not want to think about anything, he tore into his little friend and, as usual, did it very skillfully, using communism as his scalpel. Lately all their talks were ending this way.

Every time Leon came up to visit Jason he resolved beforehand not to be ensnared, not to talk communism with his friend, but little by little, goaded and prodded, he found himself sucked into the whirlpool. He was no match for Jason, and he knew it. Jason had the cool, calculating mind of a fiend when it came to forensics, he could make black look white, he had won prizes in economics in a large midwestern university and had once wanted to write a book on social science. At the Party meetings he had caused all sorts of rows, tangling up the chairmen and the speakers, shooting his bitter barbs from all angles of the floor, accusing the sub-committees of short-sightedness and mismanagement. Everybody felt relieved when he dropped out of the Party.

Right now he used the same old tactics on Leon. He agreed with everything the little fellow said at first, nodding his head as he lay there flat on his back. But as soon as Leon made one vague remark he started slashing. Both agreed on generalities, both were in favor of a social revolution; they agreed on a number of things.

Then Leon, branching out, let a few words fall concerning the Party here in America. Jason was ready for him. From then on, the little fellow was on the defensive.

The first thing Jason did was to inquire about the membership. How many comrades had the Party now?

"Ten thousand," answered Leon.

"All right. Let's make it twelve thousand. With this handful you're going to overthrow capitalism here. Fine. Now, comrade, a few questions. Is it true, or isn't it, that every year forty per cent of the comrades drop out? Is it true, or isn't it, that there is such a big turnover?"

No answer.

"Is it true, or isn't it, that most of the membership is among the foreign-born workers? Is it true, or isn't it, that these comrades are located in New York, most of them, in the most European city in America? Do you really think, Comrade Leon Fisher, that a movement appealing to the American masses can be successful as long as the agitators of the movement are not Americanized themselves and have not de-Russianized the propaganda they're trying to hammer into the heads of American labor?"

"You distort the facts," said Leon, savagely.

"Do I? All right. But don't forget that the Russian revolution was strictly a Russian movement, engineered by Russian revolutionaries and applicable only to the old imperial regime." A pause. "However, tovarish, if these prosperous times continue, I predict that the communist movement here will gain in strength in spite of the Communist Party."

No answer.

"And what about the solidarity they're always preaching about, Comrade Leon? Look at all the splits you've had in the past few years. You've got the left-wingers, right-wingers, left of the left, Trotzkyites and other factions. And each piece fights the others; they hate each other worse than they hate the capitalists. How about the solidarity they're always preaching about?"

But now Leon came to life, he had his back to the wall.

"It shows the Party at least is alive!"

"No," said Jason. "It shows that the Party has small men at the helm. There are no leaders big enough, strong enough to weld the factions. If the Party here didn't have Russia to look up to, the whole movement here would be laughed off the map."

Leon struck out as well as he was able. "Do you favor the Socialists then?" he demanded.

Jason gave a snort. Socialists? No.

"Well, what then?"

"I am in favor of being neither rich nor poor, just having a small circle of friends, that's all." The ex-poet was at it again.

"You're dodging now," said Leon. "We're gaining strength, look at the good work we've done at the strikes at Gastonia, Passaic, and Kentucky."

Jason waved these comments aside. "The Party had no competition there. It had the whole field to itself and naturally the strikers took whatever help was offered."

"And in the last few years most of the promising writers and artists have swung over to our side," Leon said.

Again Jason waved the words aside. "That's only natural. Any young artist, if he's any good at all, is a radical, and the most radical movement in the limelight now is communism. Anyway, in New York it's getting to be known as a Jewish movement. I come from the west and I know my people. I'd like to see a lot of brawny American workingmen following those Jewish agitators over the ramparts along Fourteenth Street. No, frankly I can't picture it."

Leon winced and turned his head aside. Through the windows which were covered with film, gray light filtered and lay across the ex-poet's tired face.

"You're too hard on the Party," Leon said, feeling sorry for his friend.

"I merely state the facts," answered Jason. "How much progress has the Party made among American unions? Take the great Railroad Brotherhoods for instance. Take the carpenters, plumbers, and bricklayers."

In the end, however, Leon remained unshaken. He was a visionary and felt that in time all obstacles would be swept aside before the march of communism. He felt also that Jason would re-enter the Party. He knew his friend.

They sat in silence a long time after that.

Later on, just before he got up to go, Leon spoke a few words about his plans concerning the future, how he was going to paint and do a lot of Party work now. He spoke about the meeting last night again and said a few new members were present. He dropped a few words about a new blond comrade who came from New Orleans.

Jason, rolling his head on the pillow, looked at the little fellow keenly. Leon, still talking, said a Mexican had come up with her.

"Did the girl wear a brown coat, did she have a brown coat with a black belt?" asked Jason.

Leon's heart began to pound. Was Jason making fun of him again? He didn't answer, didn't say a word.

"But I tell you I saw them," said Jason. "They walked by looking for rooms this morning."

Leon, his heart still hammering, said he'd have to go now. "I put a letter on the table for you."

"Thanks," said Jason and lay quiet on the cot. So much talking after hacking out the story had hollowed him out; his face seemed to have fallen inward.

At the door Leon hesitated and stared toward the bed. "Jason," he said slowly, "... Jason, you ought to see a doctor. I've got some money..."

"Got a match?" asked Jason. He lit another cigarette, inhaled deeply like a spent runner, the bones on the upper part of his face drawing through the flesh, and seemed to revive a bit. His legs, slack upon the cot, lay dead as sticks. The soles of his shoes faced the windows. The bottoms had holes in them.

"I don't suppose you heard from her?" said Leon, his hand on the knob.

Jason blew out smoke and frowned toward the ceiling. "She must be in another city, she was speaking about getting transferred."

They were speaking about a young lady whom Jason had lived with some time ago. She had a good job with a large manufacturing company which had sales offices in various cities.

After Leon left, Jason got up from the cot and came over to the letter. The letter was from the young lady; he recognized the handwriting immediately. He tore it open. A five-dollar bill dropped to the floor.

After he read the short note, he shined his glasses slowly and lay down quietly upon the cot again. She wrote that she hoped he was well and would not think about her any more. She made no mention of the money enclosed. She had tried to reform him, had tried to get him straightened out, and had tried to cure his love for gin, but she made no mention of this in her note. No, she said nothing about it. She wrote that she hoped he was well and would not think about her any more.

Fifteen minutes later Jason went downstairs and paid the five dollars against rent due.

The kids from the Catholic school across the street were being dismissed; they came across the street in a noisy flood, swinging their schoolbooks, shouting, their voices dying in the gray, damp air....

ALL DAY LONG, all night long the phonograph-radio feud went on, the music from the horns over the doorways blaring out upon the street. Folk stood before the loudspeakers, the lamps were lit, signs blazed and in the square Comrade Irving Rosenblum (Rosie to his pals) gave the citizenry the lowdown on the graft of Wall Street, telling how every governmental order came from a well-known house of bankers. Rosie stood upon a soap-box, swung his arms (the night was cold), and those who stood directly in front of him, received a spray of spittle now and then.

Rosie was a little feller — black hair, a big, militant nose, a screaming mouth, and a four-dollar overcoat bought at a second-hand joint over on Third Avenue. He called for action, Rosie did. His jaw wobbled, rattling like a small machine-gun, his throat wriggled as if a live fish were flopping inside near the throttle. He had the goods, that orator had, the citizenry stood around and listened.

Officer Terence McGuffy swung his nightstick, just for the exercise of it, and caught a phrase or two. Then he sauntered on, one of the city's finest, a lad who knew the Russian situation from A to Z. The low, thick wall running around the square bulked dim in the dark, sixteen or eighteen inches thick (the square was elevated a bit too, you had to walk up a small flight of steps to tread the historic earth there), and as Rosie's arms shook and waved, the big electric signs blinked back: "SAVE NOW," GUARDIAN LIFE," "WRIGLEY'S CHEWING GUM," "UNION SQUARE SAVINGS BANK,' "CENTRAL SAVINGS," "THE AMALGAMATED," and other staunch and reliable banks. The square was fairly sprinkled with places to dump your money, there were plenty of takers for the cash, earn while you sleep, the pile grows with us.

In the brief pauses, when station announcers stopped to get their wind, you could hear the taxi-dancing jazzbands in the middle of the block blaring strong, urging the couples on. Ten cents a dance... pick your hostesses, boys, here they are, lined up and waiting for your manly arms. The girls, mere kids with painted faces, stood around in long, three-dollar, sweat-shop dresses, giving the lads a dreamy, Greta Garbo glance, looking the boys over, trying to find out who had the most tickets (the girls went fifty-fifty with the house). Some of the men gripped the girls too tightly, pawing a bit, but that was to be expected; the men were mostly foreigners, dark fellows with little, dancing flames in their eyes, and the blond hostesses were grabbed up the fastest. On the dinky platform the jazzband blared — hot, slow music, the wailing, sobbing blues. The numbers were short, a couple of squeezes, a whirl, and another ticket please. The saxophone player, a fellow with a glass eye, squinted every time he was due for a solo number, for if he didn't, he'd stand a chance of having his artificial optic pop out upon the floor. As it was, his eye popped from the socket two or three times a week.

Side streets cut across the town. Rows and rows of rooming houses, tenements, basement speakeasies, small Jewish and Hungarian restaurants, candy stores which did no business dotted the section, with here and there an Italian grocery, bologna hanging in the front windows. The smell was fierce in summer, in the fall the air was cold.

At eight o'clock Rex Bingo came on the air, king of the crooners, singing his sad, sad love songs. His fluted wails floated over the East Side rooftops, into the autumn night.

"This comes to you through the courtesy of Mowitz Brothers, makers of custom-built furniture designed in the famous Mowitz manner, station W K P, please stand by for a few seconds, folks." ...

JASON sent off letters: one, two, three of them. He wrote them in his own hand and did not type as usual. For so many weeks, months, and now years he had thought, worked, and written upon keys that the pen between his fingers felt strange to the touch; he was accustomed only to signing his name: Jason Wheeler, after yours truly, or sincerely yours.

The letters were sent off to Philadelphia.

Replies came, worded exactly the same as the first letter she had sent him. She hoped that he was feeling well and told him not to think about her any more. Jason laid her letters aside. He strolled over to his "source of supplies" and sat at the counter while Pete poured him a cup of coffee.

Darkness had fallen. Turning, he stared toward the street, where the squat supports of the Third Avenue elevated threw shadows into the front of the store. A slow wind stirred the arc lamp outside and the zone of light swayed gently from side to side. Jason sat. When he moved, he heard the faint crackle of her letters in an inner pocket. He stared back toward the swaying zone of light again. Already the jetsam was beginning to float by, wreckage from down the way, fellows in rags, fat women with baggy eyes, drunks who staggered up to you and pawed your coat lapel whining for "a dime f'r cuppa o' coffee G'blessya." There were also a few men who walked stiffly like wound-up toy sentries, their eyes bright and popping, the corners of their mouths jerking; these were the "hoppy" boys, lads who went in for "Chinese stuff," but it cost something to get coked up and most of the drunks had no urge to try and change their luck.

Two old bums mooched along outside, staring inside the store. Both stopped, dug into their pants, and, looking down, counted carefully a few sweaty coins upon their palms. They held a conference and wagged their shaggy heads. One of them pointed to a sign Pete had stuck against the glass and argued hotly with his pal. His pal swore and held out, then gave in. They came inside.

Pete eased up, six years of Third Avenue experience in that cagy dome of his.

"How much you got?" he asked right away.

They slapped the damp coins upon the cracked marble of the counter.

"All right," he said, "I fix you up, I give you both the corned beef hash with mashed on side, also peas."

They said it was all right, then Pete went back and told the cook to warm up that small batch of hash left over from the special he had run noontime.

The two old bums at the counter were talking: "So he comes up to me . . ." "Who?" "Why, the guvner, of course, the old gent whose son sends him ten bucks a week, and he comes up to me and he says, 'Lay off the hookers, take a shot of daisy.' So I plays dumb and I says, 'Daisy? I ain't never tried a shot of dope yet.' And he says, 'My boy sent me the allowance today, come with me, I'll blow you to your first Daisy.' So nacherly I goes along. Well, we goes up two doors south of Uncle Beagle's Pawn Shop and he knocked four times, three fast and one slow, and a fat guy leaves us in. 'Try the pipe first,' says the guvner to me, but I'm an old hand, so I asks for the needle. Better than a hooker of smoke any day, say I. Just knock four times."

The hash arrived. Both sniffed at it, then tore in, shoving the food down. After the repast one of them asked Jason for a cigarette. The ex-poet handed them his pack. They took two apiece and lit up, got off their stools, and left like Park Avenue gentry, blowing cigarette smoke over their shoulders, chatting socially, their bellies warm with food.

The wind died down, the zone of light outside lay like a hoop of silver flat against the pavement. Jason stirred.

"Say," he said to Pete, "I hate to ask you, but can you let me have two bucks until Friday, I've got a check coming."

The Serbian coughed, thought in a flash, then pinged the cash drawer open. Jason took the two damp bills, Pete marked it down upon the slip of paper.

"Thanks," and Jason was off the stool and went outside, walking south toward Uncle Beagle's.

In the store Pete stood staring at the NO SALE sign just registered. A few plates dropped in the rear, he whirled about, heard no accompanying crash. Through the wicket shot out the aged, steamy face of the dish-washer, a crushed and sorry gent, his bald, bluish skull shining in the light.

"No breakerage, boss," he reported and bent to pick the broken crockery from the floor. They had cracked neatly, silently.

Jason, his chin down, his eyes swinging from left to right as he walked, was going south on Third Avenue, wondering how a shot of dope could stack up to a pint of fair-grade gin.

In Cooper Union the lights were lit, the porters were busy mopping there.

Three golden balls swung and swayed, informing the world that Uncle Beagle was here to help in times of stress. In the window (ironwork screening placed before the plateglass for protection after hours) were old guns, fishing tackle, accordions, monkey wrenches, an ivory-handled fancy doorknob, camping knives, a book whose title page read *How to Cure Warts,* nickel-plated wristwatches, fountain pens, and a second-hand fur coat with its good side turned toward the street.

The building two doors south had a brown door. . . .

THE CAPTAIN of police, a big man with a powerful jaw, swung round in his swivel chair and told his male secretary to call in Smith, Bowen, and Oldenheimer, three lieutenants. The secretary, laying his pen down, got up and walked around the captain's desk, shoved the door back, and went out into the outer office. He wore rubber heels and made no sound. When he returned, the three lieutenants were talking at his back; two of them cleared their throats before they reached the door, the third stopped to put his hat on straighter; all came in frowning, in a stern and business-like manner, the city's finest, we are here to serve you.

"Lieutenants, the Reds are due to march today, this afternoon," the captain said, his cold blue eyes flashing in their cold blue flashing manner. "Smith, you're to take charge of the rifle squad; Bowen, you handle the machinegun squadron; have your boys lined up at University Place and Fourteenth Street, a machine-gun in every sidecar, but don't bother about ammunition, we won't use any. Oldenheimer," (and Oldie, a heavy-faced man with sagging cheeks, stiffened), "Oldenheimer, you direct the mounted division. Have the boys swing from the west end to the square, from the northwest maybe, one half up the block on Sixteenth Street, the other half up Fifteenth, or maybe Seventeenth, use your own judgment. Tell them they're not to shoot, no man is to fire a bullet, they can use their riot-clubs. Now, umph, lieutenants, this'll be a big day, the parade has been ballyhooed all over town, the press has got wind of it. The press'll have their camera boys and reporters on the job, you know, umph, what to do. The public will be there. So will the fire department. And, umph, thassall."

The secretary, writing out the previous day's report, was bent over busily as the captain finished, but he had an ear cocked for any forthcoming command. And the command came. Clearing his throat like a commissioner, the captain told his secretary to show Welch and his five patrolmen in. The secretary, laying down his pen, walked around the captain's desk (his rubber heels making no sound), shoved the door back, and went into the outer office; and when he returned, Sergeant Welch with five patrolmen at his heels came filing into the private office, the patrolmen very serious about the ears and eyes, the sergeant coughing gently as he stood stiffly before his chief.

"Have you got some old clothes ready, sergeant?"

"I have, sir," answered Welch, making his report.

"Fine," said the captain and swung round to speak to the five patrolmen who still stood looking serious about the ears and eyes. "Boys, you know what to do, you did a pretty good job in October under the same, umph, circumstances. Any questions you care to ask will be answered by Sergeant Welch. Thassall."

The five patrolmen followed their sergeant out, keeping their serious looks until they hit the outer office, then their faces melted and all felt relief. They went down into a room in the basement and put on old clothes. Two of them pulled on floppy caps, the other three put on shapeless hats which had been stamped upon to make them appear more authentic and shapeless.

In the captain's office upstairs the three lieutenants, after receiving final instructions, were dismissed. As soon as they were gone, the captain phoned his wife to find out if her headache was any better, if the pain over her eyes had gone away yet. He spoke very soothingly over the wire, sitting firm and solid in the wide chair.

The secretary, glancing up from his work, noticed that as the three lieutenants had gone out the last one had left the door slightly ajar, so, laying his pen down, he walked around the captain's chair, came up to the door, and closed it quietly. Then he returned to his desk where he resumed his writing.

The captain, his face close to the mouthpiece of the telephone as if kissing quietly a woman's cheek, was still talking soothingly to his wife. Otherwise the office was very silent.

Meyer Levin

From CITIZENS

The fact that naturalism was a method of writing — that naturalists were not merely unimaginative scribes who could not control their tendency to going on and on, but that they often had purposes in developing their themes through particular use of detail — this fact has been rendered obscure by literary developments of the past several decades. Meyer Levin was an outstanding proponent of the naturalistic method. As a precocious student at the University of Chicago, he pondered and never ceased pondering the meaning of the atrocity committed by his student contemporaries, Leopold and Loeb. He mixed journalism with novel-writing; The Old Bunch *(1935) was a Jewish equivalent of his fellow-Chicagoan Farrell's* Studs Lonigan, *and merits comparison with it. In* Citizens *(1940), Levin sought to penetrate the meaning of the Memorial Day Massacre of 1937, when police at the Republic Steel Company fired upon strikers; the tragedy received public attention when it was taken up by the La Follette Civil Liberties Committee of the United States Senate.*

As MITCH WILNER watched the parade get going, his apprehension lifted. It was just the Fourth of July, just people walking; there was a huge bearish-looking man, Lithuanian or something, riding his kid on his shoulder; there came a cluster of fellows with signs on sticks, some of them he had seen back there in the yard, one was dragging a baseball bat. And not far behind was a group of older men laughing and talking Polish; and walking along in the procession he spotted two little people, a fellow and a girl, walking hand in hand with their faces serious, exactly like drawings of workers in the *New Masses,* you didn't think they actually existed just like that; then came a cluster of housewives in cotton dresses; and, scattered through, more of the fellows carrying signs. As the column lengthened it fanned out until it had no form at all, and reminded him, incongruously, of the field following golfers.

Fellows with white paper armbands walked alongside the column, trying to keep it in shape. Close in, get in line, they repeated, but folks paid no attention, seemingly undecided whether they were a part of the march, or simply spectators; like himself, Wilner noticed, they walked alongside rather than in the parade. As another group of men, obviously strikers, passed him, he saw one fellow stoop and pick up a stone, and heft it. One of the armbanded boys said, half-grinning: "Now, no rough stuff," and the lad with the stone grinned back, but kept the stone.

The buildings petered off; there was one block of open prairie, ending at tracks. Here the column made a right turn, and Mitch saw the factory layout.

Beyond the tracks, on a lip curving into the lake, was the steel plant. The mass of buildings with long high windowless walls and peaked roofs, the batches of smokestacks, stood cut out against lake and sky. There came to him, momentarily, the same sense of inexcusable ignorance he had often felt on driving past such plants, or past oil refineries: how could a man remain so ignorant of these processes that were fundamental to his civilization? He had passed his life within a few miles of all these things, but did not know what the shapes of the buildings held. Why were those smokestacks ranged in series of seven? There must be a purpose to that. And what were the tall pipe-entangled structures? And what did the men do in these places? Exactly what were their jobs? What was the work of a steelworker? He had only a vague picture-idea, from the word "puddlers," of giant-muscled men half naked in front of fierce open furnaces, maybe sticking rods into those furnaces and stirring the living molten steel.

The road now ran parallel with the railway tracks, and on these tracks, between the marchers and the steel plant, stood long lines of boxcars. Evidently they were marching toward a track-crossing that led to the plant gate.

They got machine guns in those boxcars, a fellow in the crowd said.

They got machine guns on the roofs.

You know that watertank in the yard? Where they put up the big searchlight? They got guns in there.

Mitch Wilner glanced at the solid double line of boxcars, like a Chinese wall protecting the plant. It was not difficult to imagine men and guns materializing in the gaping black doorways of the cars.

From spots in the crowd, Mitch heard attempts at singing; they were singing "Solidarity," but the song stumbled and faded out; they were not marching to rhythm. A few voices carried the words on awhile, as if singing for themselves rather than in a crowd.

Now they saw the police.

Where tracks and the road took a slight curve, the police line cut the road. It was not yet the entrance to the plant, for the main buildings and a huge sign, "Consolidated Steel Corporation," could be made out, at least two blocks behind the police line.

All had known the police were waiting. All had seen, vaguely, blue forms in the distance, motorcycles and police cars buzzing on the roads. But now the moment of encounter brought a sharp focus. The police were stationed like a company of soldiers in pictures of old-time wars, soldiers lined up to charge. And behind them their wheeled paraphernalia stood like cannon backing the line of soldiers.

The marchers slackened, the pace became sluggish, and then the flag-bearers halted. They were perhaps a hundred yards from the police; the white road between them vibrated in the direct rays of the sun.

The halt did not seem one of confusion. There was an odd sense of intention, of design in all that happened. The straggling column consolidated, as those behind pressed forward, then, further compressed, the column distended and overflowed on both sides of the road. On the left, the police line ended at some scattered houses. On the right were the railroad and the plant. The police moved quickly, paralleling the expanding front of the marchers. Pairs of police ran, leaping across railway tracks, until their line reached the boxcars.

The flag-bearers still waited. A discussion seemed to be going on between leaders. Mitch noticed the burnt-faced man shaking his head, while that excited, stubby fellow, Mike Sisto, gesticulated toward the boxcars. A couple of men with white armbands took part in the discussion. But none of the people who had seemed to be in charge, in the headquarters, were up in front; neither Kiley, nor Sobol, nor Carl Gaul.

Now a decision seemed to have been reached. The fellows with white armbands scattered over the field calling people back into line.

All waited. Behind the police line, on the porches of houses, photographers scrambled, climbing on railings to take vantage-point pictures. Next to a patrol wagon the newsreel truck stood, and the photographer on the roof of the truck buzzed his camera.

Look, the bitchn finks!

There, on the low sloping roof of one of the plant buildings, as on sloping bleachers, the scabs were assembled, squatting or standing, perhaps a few hundred men altogether, viewing the scene, just like grandstanders at a Fourth of July parade. Muttering and cursing rose all along the line now; Mitch saw more fellows stoop and pick up rocks. But it was a far throw.

The flag-bearers began to walk again, and the crowd behind them walked, a strange, deliberate, silent walk across the remaining hundred paces of no man's land, a testing walk, as if at each step the ground might give way underneath. The police shifted on their feet, nervously. The white strip of road was eaten, step by step. Then police and strikers stood breathing-close, face to face.

And nothing happened. Like throwing a switch when one is fearful of a fuse blowing; but the connection takes place without explosion. They stood, the crowd, the cops, all motionless. Mitch Wilner wove through the crowd, edged up toward the front. The people in the front lines were talking to the cops. "Let us through, why can't we go through, we got a right. Just to the gate, to picket there." The cops were shaking their heads, some grinning, some bored. There was a burnt-faced fellow, and a woman with him, evidently his wife, quite a good-looking young woman, gesticulating, pointing toward the gate. And in the crowd Mitch saw a fellow whom he had known in the old days, one of the old West Side bunch, Sam Eisen. What was he doing here? Sam was a lawyer now, supposed to be a radical or something. The burnt-faced fellow turned around toward the crowd now, with his arm raised, as though counseling patience.

Whole minutes passed. Nothing would happen. The crowd would turn back. Having demonstrated its will, and its control, it would turn back.

Mitch edged still further toward the houses, and there where the column thinned he came into the very front line. He was within arm's length — clubbing length, he realized — of the facing policemen. At that moment an officer of some sort, captain he guessed, came up behind the police. He was old, with a large seamed face, protruding half-closed eyelids, and an almost catatonic rigidity of expression.

In an automatic voice such as bailiffs use in administering courtroom oaths, he reeled off: "... order you in the name of the State of Illinois to disperse and go home..." a formula. His voice was low, careless. Directly behind Mitch people were asking: "What did he say?" Others called: "Let us through; come on, give us a break. The mayor said — "

The officer turned and walked back behind his police.

Mitch Wilner was seized with apprehension. Why had the officer recited that rigmarole? Without even raising his voice. Simply as though he were complying to a formula before —

Yes, something would come, now. They had better turn back. He felt an urge to shout: Back, back, better go back before they... To jump up on something and shout: Go back.

Then he turned, retreating into the crowd, not only to feel people between himself and the police, but with the thought that those immediately around him might turn as he had turned, and that there might be a turning movement in the crowd.

And at the same time he told himself he was being foolish, panicky; here strikers and police had stood face to face for longer than five minutes; all were controlled. He was well among the people now, in the thick. He heard a firecracker pop; and an instant later, a series of firecrackers, like the string of fireworks Mort had let off on the beach. Mitch looked up into the air and saw a missile, a rock perhaps, flying over the police line. Now it will start, he reflected, with fearing, sinking heart; and only then realized that everyone was running, he too was running back down the road. He halted and looked around.

A cloud of smoke rose lazily like a great cigar-puff, lifting upward in the clear still air. That must be tear gas. There was another rattle of explosions. Maybe shooting blanks into the air.

"They're shooting real bullets!" a woman cried, running; and all around him the same words echoed, uttered with surprise, as if for corroboration. "They're shooting real bullets!" Mitch remained standing, as if his standing still there would prove that the police were not actually firing bullets into the crowd; that could not be. Then he saw a man in a blue workshirt, running toward him, cast himself on the ground, exactly like some soldier in a war movie. Or had the man fallen? Wilner realized he had started to run again, and halted now to go back and look at that man, but the crowd swirled him, and a heavy, bareheaded man with his arm across his eyes blocked his way. This man was staggering. "Don't worry, just tear gas, no permanent effect," Mitch said, turning the blinded man and heading him down the road. "You'll be okay in a couple of hours."

"Shooting," the man mumbled, stumbling on his way.

He ought not to stand here. They'd need him at headquarters. Mitch turned once more for a last look, to convince himself that what was happening was happening. The gas cloud had stretched out sausage-shape and was lifting, thinning like torn gauze; through this, he could see the blue line of police approaching. Again, he was possessed by a sense of unreality. This was all like a scene for a movie, yes, or some act in an arena; all staged like a football game, a mimic war; there sat the bleachers crowd; and there movie cameras turned.

He ran from the advancing police. Alongside him as he ran, Mitch saw that huge Lithuanian, with the kid holding his hand, running; and he reassured himself that Syl and the kids must have stayed in the car, or certainly could not have come out very far toward the police, and must have run back when the trouble started. The Lithuanian's kid halted, lifting one foot as though he had stepped on a thistle. "Pa, I'm shot," the kid said. The Lithuanian swooped and picked up the child, running on, as the blood from the boy's foot trickled down his shirt.

Now a car came toward them, cutting through the crowd. Mitch noticed the Red Cross sign stuck under the windshield wiper. He jumped on the running-board. Carl Gaul was driving, accompanied by some fellow he didn't know. "Shooting," Mitch cried. "Must be some fallen up there."

Carl nodded. "We heard it."

The gas cloud had practically disintegrated, the air clearing as the mind clears after a wild, confusing deed. They saw the police come to a halt, drawing together in a sort of line, except for a cop here and there chasing a last fleeing striker. One they saw hurl his club after a man who escaped him, and stand laughing as the club conked;

the fugitive jerked, stumbled a few steps, then, regaining his balance, ran on, his hand awkwardly feeling for the back of his skull.

But mostly the cops were standing still now, looking around them in half-dazed victory, approaching each other with words. Mitch saw forms flat or huddled on the street and on the prairie. Police bent over the forms, prodded, clubbed. Further back, where the line of encounter had been, there was still a pile-up of people, and cops were pulling at arms and legs, whacking at figures that disentangled themselves and scrambled on all fours, skitterwise, to escape. They seized many. Always two cops working together, never a cop alone, pulling a man to his feet and shoving him to and into the patrol wagon. At last the piled group was dissolved, and only the collapsed wounded lay on that spot, like an evaporation residue.

As Carl brought the car to a stop, four policemen hustled toward it.

"Get the hell — " one of the cops began.

Another scratched his ear. "Sonsabitches. All set with their own ambulance!"

Carl jumped out. "Let us pick up these wounded, officer," he said. "We've got a first-aid station back there. These people need immediate attention. This man is a doctor."

As Mitch wore coat and tie, the cops, momentarily, seemed impressed by his appearance. He hurried to the nearest fallen figure. It was a young, husky fellow, who was just trying to turn himself over as Mitch reached him.

"Get hit?" Mitch asked.

"They shot me," the fellow said, wonderingly. His hand moved toward his middle. Mitch opened the shirt and saw a dark hole, like a cigar burn, directly over the navel. It looked so simple and clean. The full danger formed in his mind: abdominal, probably die. He turned the fellow on his side; there was blood enough where he had lain, on his back. The bullet had entered just above the rump, to the right; probably torn kidney and intestinal punctures. "Help me get this fellow into the car," he called. And as people will when directly ordered, two of the police came over and stooped to lift the wounded man. But seeing police, the striker pushed himself to his feet and, leaning on Mitch and Carl, stumbled toward the car, half falling across the back seat. The police watched, their expressions startingly contrasted: the one deepening with shame, the other swelling to rage.

Another car had come up, driven by the dude Art. And immediately afterward there came a big maroon sedan, driven by Jock Kiley. Many of the wounded were hoisting themselves, stumbling to the rescue cars. Mitch hurried toward another sprawled figure, but already with the feeling that it was hopeless; what could he possibly do for all these gunshot-wounded, and after them the broken heads, fractures, concussions! Confronted with so much, he could touch nothing, nothing at all. Instead of being here on the field, shouldn't he be back there in headquarters where he had a few bandages? But no; his first job was to sort, to find the worst bleeders, and the abdominals; to check the true emergencies. This one on the ground was unconscious, with blood welling from under his scalp and matting his hair. But no gun wound. Calling to Carl and the others to take the man, Mitch hurried on, examining the fallen. A few yards away he saw Kiley and a white-haired but spry-looking man working over a bleeder. They had a man whose femoral artery was evidently severed, for blood was geysering through a rent in his trouser-leg. The white-haired fellow had pulled off the wounded man's belt and was strapping it around the leg, above the wound, to make a tourniquet. Mitch went to help them. "That's right," he approved the man's nice, quick movements. "But wait a second." He picked up a small flat stone and wedged it under the belt, so as to press against the artery. The bleeding was shut off.

"Cradle," he said clasping the wrist of the white-haired man; he felt a powerful counter-clasp on his own wrists, and then the heavy drop of the wounded man's arm on his shoulder. They lifted, attempting to cradle-carry him to the car. He was not tall, but hugely thick in the shoulders, and great-chested, a man of about two hundred pounds. Mitch staggered. "Lemme have him, Doc." Kiley slipped his hands under theirs, and the three of them carried the wounded man.

"Know him?" the white-haired helper asked.

Kiley shook his head. The man was muttering his name over for them: "Dombrowsky, Stanley Dombrowsky, me."

They got him into Kiley's car. Dazed, the wounded man felt for the back of his head; he had been clubbed, too. Mitch glanced at the tourniquet. "Ought to hold till you get him there," he surmised, and hurried out onto the field again.

But a pair of cops came charging toward him; the shorter of them, a bull-like man with a blazing red face, cursing in a kind of apoplectic frenzy, and brandishing a long stick, longer than a police club. The end of the stick was bloody. "Get the hell off this field before I run you in!"

"These people need emergency care," Mitch said. "I'm a doctor."

"They'll get all the goddam care they need. They're all under arrest. Now you get the hell off this field — "

Mitch backed away, as from a crazed beast. The man seemed out of his senses, possessed by an elation of violence.

Carl Gaul had filled his car with wounded, and turned it around. "Coming, Doc?" he called; and Mitch hopped on the running-board. The maddened policeman stared at the car, rushed it as it drove off. Mitch saw him halt, frustrated, mouth open, exactly like a bull who has run through a cape. "Get those sons of bitches," the cop screamed hoarsely, "they're our prisoners!" Then he wheeled and charged toward Kiley's sedan.

Edward Dahlberg

From THOSE WHO PERISH

Edward Dahlberg lived a hectic youth which took him through Catholic and Jewish orphanages and a wide succession of common jobs in Cleveland, Kansas City, Portland, Oregon, San Francisco, and elsewhere. He matriculated at the University of California in 1922 and took a degree in the Department of Philosophy at Columbia University in 1925. D. H. Lawrence introduced his first novel, Bottom Dogs *(1930) on an odd note of repugnance; he found its raw, cold prose offensive. Dahlberg was an idealist who had begun by spewing out his bad experiences. He continued this effort in* From Flushing to Calvary *(1932), which, at points, complements the work of Daniel Fuchs. By then, Dahlberg had seen the revolutionary light;* Those Who Perish *was a bitter view of American society. His contribution was a striking, impressionistic prose which put it much beyond a great deal of similarly motivated work.*

ELI MELAMED had made his third round of Woodrow Wilson Park. His face, wind-burnt and hollowed out with tiredness, he decided that he would go to see the Briarcliffs for an hour's rest. Noticing the few finger-like trees, their embryonic buds of leaves — spring buds in reverse gear, for they had been wrinkled and corrugated by the death-fumes of automobile gasoline — he felt the need to get near to something human and warmly domesticated. Already eager to be inside the Briarcliffs' apartment and to shake hands with Edgar, he thought, with renewed courage: "We Jews do not know who we are, or from whence we come. The blood of all nations and races flows through out veins — from feudal times onward, our women have been defiled by Christians, and the offspring of these acts of rapine have passed as 'pure Jews.' " He repeated this, saying to himself: "Perhaps there is the blood of French or Italians, of the Romance Language peoples in my veins; after all, I'm a Sephardic type, and my Palestinian forebears must have been in Spain during the Inquisition." All this he said with the same kind of racial reasoning and inferiority complex that prompts Jews to call a Hitler or an Ivy Lee a Jew.

As Melamed stepped under the pseudo-beachish canopy outside the apartment house entrance, a thin rain began to canter lightly against the sidewalk. Suddenly he turned back, took off his hat and stood under it for a moment, lifting up his chin and face as though he were taking a shower. Melamed wanted to get wet so that it would appear that he had run in on the Briarcliffs for refuge. The rain grew swifter, galloping against the curbs, and Melamed ducked under the canopy again. The elevator took him up to the eighth floor.

Standing in front of the Briarcliffs' door, he turned up his coat collar, unthinkingly shivered for a second, his arms and legs rippling against his suit, as though he were at large and not inside of it, and touched the bell, sotto voce. When Mrs. Briarcliff came to the door, he was wiping the back of his neck and swobbing his face with gymnastic phews and clucks. As he took hold of Mrs. Briarcliff's hand, he shut his eyes, vigorously shook it up and down, piston-like, as if he had to reach up to seize it, and greeted her in a high, off-pitch voice: "So awfully glad to see you, Jenny!" He had never called her Jenny before, and he was appalled by his over-familiarity. "Just ran in out of the rain . . . hope I'm not . . ." He stopped short here, for he heard voices inside, felt that he was intruding, and was afraid that she would give him one of those straight looks that would indicate that he was.

There was something thin-lipped about Mrs. Briarcliff's body. She was one of those women, with long sharp noses and paper-thin throats that readily crease, whom handsome men so often marry. Frequently taken for a Jewess, or suspected of being one because of her nose, she was, as a matter of fact, of old New England stock. Melamed had always been a little afraid of her, because he thought she was Jewish and was hiding it, and because he believed she knew that he thought so. In one of his nasty moments he had had fleeting pictures of her as the wooden American Indian in front of the cigar store, but as he disliked harboring any sort of unkind thoughts about other human beings, he had summarily exorcised this mental photograph of Jenny Briarcliff.

The Briarcliffs' apartment, whose fake medieval wooden panels and electric candle-bulbs made it resemble the interior of Schrafft's restaurant, was filled with people standing around a ping-pong table. Three or four people were seated in chairs behind them drinking cocktails; some were sipping from their glasses and standing. Edgar Briarcliff, who had a clean-cut Arrow collar physiognomy and the Gentile retroussé nose, which American Jews admire, was serving. His opponent was a somewhat hefty woman whose green silk dress noisily rustled against her bust. She had a squat Slavonic nose, and her name was Evelyn Syracuse Beach.

Edgar Briarcliff was cutting the ball low over the net, and Miss Evelyn Syracuse Beach was having considerable difficulty in gauging and returning the serve. While the ping-pong balls sped back and forth across the green table with the clicking precision of typewriter keys, jibes and japes constantly came from the spectators. "Say, Edgar," said a heavily begoggled, gawky Freudian, "a little less sadism in those returns — save that for the wife!" "Oh, Evelyn, put a postage stamp on that last one, and no return address," said another.

When the game was over, Edgar Briarcliff approached Eli Melamed and introduced him, and Melamed shook hands with each one. After a colored maid had brought him a cocktail, Edgar left him.

The spectators were now watching the new game. The man who was serving held the paddle upright against his stomach. His opponent was his wife, and this set in motion the stenciled marital remarks. As the server sprung the paddle so as to release the ball, the psychoanalyst called: "Say, Burt, where did you get that umbilical serve, or what have you?" Melamed also let out a small, guttural he-heh-huh, which sounded like a slender stick being lightly run across a wooden picket fence. He had been admiring the faces around him, and listening with esthetic attentiveness and pleasure to their Aryan, fiscal names. Finally, he had gotten up enough courage to make a complete semicircular smile, showing all his white teeth, for Miss Evelyn Syracuse Beach, but she did not notice him.

The Negro maid came around again with a tray of ice-clinking glasses. Mrs. Briarcliff moved from one couple to the other, and Edgar was seated on a cushion on the floor in the next room, holding a serious theosophical discussion with Mrs. Van Cortland Dinwiddie. Shortly afterwards, Edgar came over and said, "How about a set, Mel-ah-mede?" and Melamed emotionally bubbled over this intimacy.

Melamed went toward one end of the table and picked up his paddle, and Edgar moved toward the other. Eli Melamed, who had played a good deal of ping-pong at the Phoenix Physical Culture Club of New Jersey, now for the first time felt sure of himself.

He had a short, inching, sniping serve, which Edgar was unable to pick up. Melamed won the first five points. The people standing around the table stopped talking and began to watch. Edgar corkscrewed his serve which twisted and landed in an askew cut. But Melamed coolly waited for it to hit the table and then slammed it back across the net with the speed of a football player. Melamed, whenever Edgar returned the ball, ran from one part of the rim of the table to the other, picking up the ball, and lunging in after it with quarterback alacrity and the confidence of good fleshly poundage across his shoulders. As his bow-wing collar touched his neck, he felt as if it were a strong leathern headgear. Melamed took the next three points, and pausing for a second, examined his small feet with glowing sartorial satisfaction.

"Really, you're not the man you were," said Melamed, in a friendly non-competitive spirit, but without looking at Edgar. As he took the ninth point Melamed accidentally caught a vague crosssection of Edgar Briarcliff's countenance, which seemed to have become plaque-like. Looking again to make certain, Melamed missed the next one. The two men changed sides. Melamed laid his paddle down to adjust his suspenders and to catch Edgar's eye, and to soften him with a warm glance. But Briarcliff did not see and was impatient to continue the game.

Melamed then turned to the guests, and parting his lips he imagined that he had smiled at them. No one returned his greetings. However, this slight movement of the lips was more of an unprinted negative in Melamed's mind than an objective salutation. Melamed sent the next three balls wildly off the table, and did not see the following one which Briarcliff lightly popped over the net. His trousers hanging in a wretched defeatist sag, his suspenders loosening again and sprawling over his suspiciously gray shirt, Melamed fumbled another shot. Troubled and unhinged by the silent, tense faces around the table, Melamed felt like an oppressed minority people engulfed by a hostile imperialistic power.

By now Melamed had entirely lost his intuitive and photographic sense of time and place, which had made him so uncannily precise in his serves and returns at the beginning of the game. When Melamed hit the ball off the table again, and both men stooped over to pick it up off the floor, Edgar said: "Too bad, old man, I know how it feels." These words of non-competitive sympathy filled Melamed with gratitude. And when they both stepped forward and bent over to get another ball, Briarcliff patted Melamed's shoulder. Melamed closed his eyes, which simmered with quiescent emotions. His face was covered with the light pink marks of happiness that a lover might have playfully put there with his teeth. He was enormously thankful that it was Edgar Briarcliff and not he who was winning. Melamed gazed at Briarcliff's aristocratic Nordic eyes, mouth, teeth, and cravat, which were of one piece, and felt this was as it should be.

After the game was ended, Briarcliff having won, Melamed thought he had better leave. He had the same unmistakable sense of time now, the precise time for leaving, that he had had at the beginning of the game when he had served and returned each separate, atomic ping-pong ball with an historic intuition of time and place. But he wanted to slip out of the room without leaving, so that there should be no interruption, no gap, no empty and fatuous space between him and the onlooking guests.

But someone began to discuss the German situation. Everyone trailed into the next room, taking chairs or sitting on cushions on the carpeted floor. "Do you think Hitler will last?" someone asked. "I feel that the whole Nazi Youth Movement has a homosexual basis," said the bespectacled Freudian, whose snub Tyrolese nose looked as though it were pressed up against a windowpane. "The only way to approach the whole situation is psychoanalytically," he continued.

"I must tell you of a little experience I had," said Mrs. Van Cortlandt Dinwiddie, who was related to the Astors and Bismarck, and who, genealogically speaking, had a Wotan-like bust. Otherwise, she had Samoan brown eyes and resembled the Phoenician Jack of Spades. "I had dinner with Charmian London, the wife of Jack London, at the Bohemian Club in San Francisco. She told me — and incidentally, I am using this in my memoirs — that she believed that certain meteorological changes which had taken place in 1914 had so unhinged people's nerves that they brought on the World War. I have since developed this thesis as a kind of undertone in my autobiography, which I was going to call *I Have Only Myself to Blame* until I discovered that the title had already been copyrighted and used for another book. Fancy my disappointment.... Anyway, it is my opinion that we are compelled to interpret Fascism in terms of neurones and meteorology. I think that the Versailles Treaty had such a devastating effect upon the nervous system of the German people."

"Don't you think," interrupted Mr. Monte Lorrimer, who had stout Arabic thighs, "that it was the stomach rather than the nerves?"

"I think that the Versailles Treaty," pursued Mrs. Van Cortlandt

Dinwiddie with more resolution than before, "had such an exhausting effect upon the nervous system of the German nation that it turned them into lunatics; so what we have in Germany today is an insane asylum, with the only difference that the few sane people left are straitjacketed and kept in the protective custody of the crazy who are the wardens."

"I think that's a brilliant analysis, Mrs. Dinwiddie," exclaimed the young Freudopath. "Just think what superb endocrine portraits Modigliani could do of Hitler and Rosenberg if he were alive today. Why, the League of Nations would actually sanction intervention so that they could be committed."

"I don't think we'll ever solve the European situation until Germany is wiped off the map. They're always getting us into trouble," stated an intellectual Anglo-American in a dreary adenoidal tone.

"Now take Goering," went on the Psychoanalyst.

"No, *you* take him," popped up Melamed who had been waiting for such an opportunity. Everyone laughed and Melamed's eyes glistened. He had been anxious to be included in the conversation, not because he had anything specific to say, but because he felt unhappily isolated. A Dakota Western-pulp type, with a Semitic Tom Mix proboscis, was so tickled over this bit of repartee that he pulled out his handkerchief and began to loudly boo-hoo into it. He was as shaken up as a large fleshy woman, and Melamed fetched a glass of water from a tray, brought it to him, and sort of held his arm as he drank it down.

"Well, Goering's a drug-addict and a dangerous paranoiac," continued the psychoanalytic student. "He was in an asylum in Stockholm in 1925."

"I don't think it's paranoia, but race," uttered Edgar Briarcliff.

"You're absolutely right," supported Mrs. Briarcliff. "Edgar, it is race."

"You-you — will p-pardon me," stuttered Monmouth Hightower, turning to Melamed. "I didn't get your name."

"Oh, this is Mr. Mel-ah-mede," spoke up Edgar Briarcliff. "Terribly sorry."

"We—ell," continued Monmouth Hightower, who had a dark smutty Mediterranean complexion and was the son of a D.A.R., "I — I have the — the great — greatest fancy for pe — people — of your race. You are Hebrew, aren't you?" Melamed nodded. He was beginning to feel deeply united with these persons and to derive a jubilant aesthetic experience from their Anglican names and countenances.

Seeing Monmouth Hightower in a happily weepy haze he thought his soiled maple hair was the mane of Siegfried.

"But — but I — I be — believe," said Monmouth Hightower, "that the an — antagonism between different nationalities, as — as well as the — the attraction, is chemical. Take — take intermarriage." By this time his mouth had become a nervous hoop out of which the words rolled askew. "And — and just go back to Goethe's *Elective Affinities,* and — and —— "

"Well — ah, per — perhaps there's something in what you say," interrupted Melamed, also stammering, because he felt very sensitive and highkeyed at that moment, and because he believed there was a certain wonderful non-Jewish quality about Monmouth Hightower's Aryan stuttering.

"I — I don't wan — want you to mis — misunderstand me, Mr. Mel — mel — ah — ah — mede. I think your people have gifts of genius, and — and —that accounts for—for my opinion, no doubt, but don't — don't you think the Hebrew people — are a little difficult?"

"Well — ah, per — perhaps there's a certain amount of truth in what you say," answered Melamed. "Of course, if you — you mean some of the pushing aggressive type," added Melamed, feeling that it would be in good taste to be a little anti-Semitic in order to show them how objective and impartial a Jew could be, "I must admit, I find that kind just as objectionable as you do."

"And — and don't you think — think the — the Hebrew people are a little too sensi — sensitive?" pursued Monmouth Hightower.

To prove how outside of it he was, Melamed replied: "Maybe Jews are — to borrow the information Mr. Burt Webb has been so good as to give us — as paranoiac as Goering."

"I think," stated a tallish woman, with a Hittite beak and charcoal Armenian hair, who came from the Arran Islands and who spoke as though it were high time for a little political housecleaning, "that the German-Jews are getting what's coming to them. They not only lorded it over," she sped on in a shrill and impassioned prose, "the poor Russian and Lithuanian Jews who migrated into Eastern Germany, but it was actually German-Jewish money that supported and kept in power the Czar so that he was able to carry on his pogroms. Don't you think that's right, Mr. Mel-ah-mede?" Melamed, who was still occupied tying emotional bonds with these new acquaintances, and who had not been listening attentively, attempted to shuttle back to the conversation.

"Of course, eh, but you know my mother and father were born in Palestine. But then, what you say is . . . Well, I guess it is true the German-Jews were a little impatient about becoming Germans, and no doubt they did lose their heads in the excitement."

"What's your opinion on Russia?" asked Mr. Monte Lorrimer, whose nose, which looked like the toe of Italy, seemed racially at loggerheads with his Ottoman thighs. By now everybody was directing questions at Melamed, presupposing that he as a Jew naturally knew all about Germany, Communism, and the Soviet Union.

"We — well," interrupted the Son of the D.A.R., "I'm in fa — favor of the R — Russian Bol — Bolsheviks, but I don't like — like the Com — com — communists."

"Is — is it true," went on Monmouth Hightower, "that — that Jewish bankers financed Lenin?"

Melamed looked blank, and, weighing his words, he answered: "I — I'd be willing to look that up for you."

"What is the Communist situation in this country?" asked Mr. Lorrimer. He looked with kind eyes at Melamed as he added: "I'm really very interested and would be grateful if you'd tell me."

"Well, I can't say off-hand," asseverated Melamed, "but I'd be willing to look that up too."

"What do you think of the German Terror?" asked Miss Evelyn Syracuse Beach.

"I think it ought to stop," replied Melamed snappily and getting his bearings for a moment.

Three people simultaneously shot questions at him, after which Monmouth Hightower asked: "Mr. Me-mel-ah-ah-mede, what is your opinion of the Com-Com-Communist International?"

"Well, I don't know whether they do or don't," replied Melamed, who now was so harassed that he had become psychologically stone-deaf. And like a deaf person, who pretends he is hearing every word spoken, Melamed replied.

"I believe we should have nothing to do with the boycott," blurted forth Mrs. Briarcliff. "I think it's positively wrong and immoral for one country to attempt to interfere in the affairs of another." Melamed's voice twittered, then died. He said nothing.

There was a pause, and then Melamed said: "I guess I must be going," but as no one noticed him, he remained. Finally, he said goodbye, and sort of waved at every one as though he were running for a street-car, but the others were talking. He got his hat and coat, and as he started to move toward the door, Edgar Briarcliff ran up to him: "Must you be going, old man?" Whereupon those present stopped talking and looked up at him. Mr. Monte Lorrimer smiled at him, and Melamed, beaming, took a tiny step forward and then hurried back to shake hands with Mr. Lorrimer. Looking at the others, whom he did not wish to offend, he shook hands with each one, repeating each time, "So awfully glad to have met you" — falling into that Nordic Bostonese vocabulary. By the time he reached Mrs. Jenny Briarcliff, he was bubbling again with emotion. His eyes half-shut, he grasped Mrs. Briarcliff's wrist, and pressing his fingers hard against it, broke the crystal of her watch. She screamed, and Melamed was so alarmed that he bent down, picked up the pieces of glass, and handed them back to her. Looking at him in amazement, she said, with fingernails in her voice, "Thank you."

After Edgar Briarcliff had shut the door, Melamed stood outside, wondering whether to ring the bell, go in, and apologize all over again to make amends for his clumsiness. He put his finger out, pressed the elevator bell, and then went down the steps, emptily sliding from one side of his suit to the other.

Outside the rain was still thinly scribbling against the curbs. Gazing at the trees, which looked like skeletal umbrella frames without covers, he turned up his coat collar, and, reminding himself that he was without employment and alone, he no longer wondered whether the blood of the Romance Language peoples flowed through his veins.

John Wexley

From THEY SHALL NOT DIE

Radicals in the North gave ringing currency to the slogan: "The Scottsboro Boys Shall Not Die!" The case involved the alleged rape of two white girls who had been "hoboing" out of Alabama into Tennessee, by nine Negro youths and children, and the determined effort of Alabama officials to railroad the Negroes to their death. The National Association for the Advancement of Colored People and the American Civil Liberties Union interested themselves in the case, but the communist-led International Labor Defense captured its direction and profited from the publicity which it received. Samuel Leibowitz, then famous as a criminal lawyer, fought for his clients as best he could under the circumstances. The subsequent history of the case is a tangle of legal and social negotiations, the final result of which was nothing less than an off-the-record compromise between the defense and the determined leaders of the prosecution. John Wexley's They Shall Not Die *(1934) was not only a high point of drama of the period, but an example of theater which was intended to affect events.*

* * * *

JUDGE: Let us now proceed with the trial befo' the jury but befo' doing so, I wish to make a few points clear to the co't. Gentlemen of the jury, it would be a blot on our fair state if you would allow anything to stand in the way of justice. We in the South have always tried to be fair and just. Let us continue that noble record. So far as the law is concerned, it knows neither Jew nor Gentile, black nor white. We must do our duty and if we are true to ourselves then we cannot, no we cannot be false to any man. [*Turns to* DADE.] Will the state kin'ly continue to call its witnesses.

DADE: If it please your Honor, I call Mrs. Virginia Ross.

[*Voices in court.*]

GUARD: Mrs. Virginia Ross.

She enters, crosses to stand and sits. MASON *crosses to her.* DADE *has returned to his seat. She smoothes out her dress, crosses her knees prettily and looks about the court-room with a winsome expression. News photographers take flashlight.*]

MASON: What is your name, please?

VIRGINIA: Mrs. Virginia Ross.

MASON: What is your business?

VIRGINIA: I am a house-wife.

MASON: Were you on that train from Chattanooga . . . ?

VIRGINIA: I absolutely was.

MASON: And were you attacked and ravished by five negroes on that train?

VIRGINIA: They absolutely done that tuh me.

MASON: Can you identify the defendant as one of those who attacked you?

VIRGINIA: I absolutely can.

[*Simultaneous with* MASON'S *question* PARSONS *is made to rise. The court murmurs.*]

MASON: Is this one of the negroes who raped you, Mrs. Ross?

From They Shall Not Die [203

VIRGINIA [*angrily, pointing her finger*]: Yes. He is one of them niggers who done raped me.

MASON: Thank you, Mrs. Ross.

[*As* MASON *seats himself* RUBIN *strides over to her.*]

RUBIN: You have been arrested and convicted and have served sentence for offenses of lewdness and drunkenness. Have you not?

DADE: We object.

RUBIN [*waves a handful of papers*]: I have the proofs and affidavits right here.

JUDGE [*to Clerk*]: Give me the second volume of the State code, please. [*This is done. He refers to it.*]

DADE: We don't care whether this woman has been convicted for forty offenses but she has never been convicted for sleeping with a negro.

RUBIN [*furious*]: She's done that too, and I'll prove it. . . .

JUDGE [*Court in disorder.* JUDGE *raps gavel and leans over.*] Are these violations of city ordinances or state ordinances, Mr. Rubin?

RUBIN: Of course, city ordinances and I beg leave to read them. . . .

JUDGE: I'm sorry, I'm forced to bar them. They are not admissible. Objection is sustained. [*Returns volume to* CLERK.]

RUBIN: I take exception to the court's ruling. It seems to me that if a woman has been convicted of prostitution by a state court or any other court, a jury is entitled to know that. [JUDGE *wags head. Glares at the* JUDGE *for a moment.* DADE *winks to* SLADE.]

RUBIN: What were you doing in Chattanooga?

VIRGINIA: I jest was theah tuh look fo' work.

RUBIN: With whom?

VIRGINIA: With Lucy Wells.

RUBIN: Where did you look?

VIRGINIA: In the cotton mills.

RUBIN: Which ones?

VIRGINIA: Well, yuh wouldn't expect me tuh remember that?

RUBIN: Answer the question.

VIRGINIA [*impudently*]: Well, I jes tol' yuh. How many times do yuh have tuh ask me? I don't remember. . . .

[*Laughter in audience.*]

RUBIN: You testified at the Cookesville trial that you and Lucy Wells slept in the home of a Mrs. Cary Richy on the night before the train ride. Is that right?

VIRGINIA: We did sleep theah.

RUBIN: What street? What number?

VIRGINIA: I don't remember no number. It was the third house from the corner.

RUBIN: What street?

VIRGINIA [*stimulating exasperation*]: I don't exac'ly remember...

RUBIN: As a matter of fact, Mrs. Ross, isn't it true that you got this name Cary Richy from a character in the Saturday Evening Post stories by Octavius Roy Cohen — sis Cary — that you got this name there? [*Offers copy of magazine to Clerk.*]

DADE: Objection. I don't care what she did, the only thing we're interested in is whether she was raped.

RUBIN [*heatedly*]: I'm testing her credibility.

DADE: You know that is no proposition of law.

RUBIN: Address your remarks to the court!

DADE: You make it necessary to address them to you.

RUBIN: I have been a gentleman but I can be otherwise, too.

JUDGE: Wait, gentlemen. Don't either of you say anything. I won't have another word between you. Ask the question and the court will pass on it. General Dade's objection is sustained. Proceed, please.

RUBIN: Didn't you spend that night in a hobo jungle with Lucy Wells, Lewis Collins and Oliver Tulley?

VIRGINIA [*defiantly*]: No, I never done that.

RUBIN: Do you deny you know Lewis Collins?

VIRGINIA: I never heard of him or seen him in my life.

RUBIN: Didn't you make up this whole tissue of lies about these negroes attacking you, and didn't you force Lucy Wells to swear to your lies because you were afraid of being arrested yourself for prostitution?

VIRGINIA [*rising, screams*]: I'll have you know...

DADE [*simultaneously*]: I object.

RUBIN: This is perfectly relevant, your Honor.

JUDGE Well, suppose you revised it, Mr. Rubin.

RUBIN [*after a sigh*]: Did you not make up this story for that reason?

VIRGINIA [*very angrily, in a shrill voice*]: You bet' not talk tuh me in that so't of talk, Mister. I'm a decent lady an' I'll have yuh know...

RUBIN: Answer the question, please.

VIRGINIA: I never done made up no story... you...

VOICE: Let's get that goddam Jew bastard, boys.

[*Terrific noise in court.* SOLDIERS *rush about trying to keep order. The* CAPTAIN *strides here and there pushing people back into their seats and barking at them.*]

RUBIN [*shouting over the tumult*]: I insist on that man's arrest, your Honor.

From They Shall Not Die [205

[*The* REPORTERS *are almost frantic. They also converse excitedly, and rush their messengers out with scribbled telegrams.*]
JUDGE [*rising, shouts to a soldier, while hammering with his gravel*]: Officer, Officer! Have that fellow taken out immediately. [*He sits, still hammering. The feeling in the crowded court-room increases in intensity. All over are mutterings and whisperings. The* CAPTAIN *opens his holster-flap and keeps his hand on his revolver-butt. He strides about giving orders to his men, and keeps a sharp look-out throughout the rest of the scene.*] If anyone in this room cannot behave himself, the place for him is outside!
RUBIN: I have the proof, Virginia Ross . . . that you concocted this whole story to save your own skin. . . .
DADE [*leaping to the front of the jury*]: Go 'haid. Prove it. Why don't you prove it?
RUBIN [*shouting back*]: I'd prove it . . . if I had Lucy Wells on the stand.
DADE [*with a triumphant shout. Jumping up and down in front of jury*]: Yes. Where is Lucy Wells? Where? I would like to know where the state's witness had disappeared to? What has happened to her? Who has done away with her?
RUBIN: I'm not a directory . . . [*slight pause*] and I'd appreciate it if the Attorney General would stop interrupting. [*He speaks quietly with an expression of amusement.*] I'd like to continue my examination.
JUDGE: Proceed.
RUBIN [*to* VIRGINIA *in another tone of voice, almost friendly*]: You say you had to take the freight train home because you had no money?
VIRGINIA: Sho'. I was dead-broke.
RUBIN: And after those negroes had that fight with the white boys and threw them off the train, then they attacked you?
VIRGINIA: Yes, they jumped on me . . .
RUBIN: Was Heywood Parsons one of them?
VIRGINIA: He was the very first. He slammed me down and he ripped off my overalls . . .
RUBIN: Did he hurt you when he slammed you down?
VIRGINIA: Sho'. He hurt my back. . . .
RUBIN: I understand there were stones in the car. Did they make your back bleed?
VIRGINIA: Yes, it absolutely did. And he hit me over the haid with his gun.

RUBIN: And that bled too, didn't it?

VIRGINIA: Yes . . . he hit me right heah. [*Touches the side of her head.*]

RUBIN: I see. [*To the stenographer.*] For the record, the left side of the head. And then he tore your dress off, and attacked you?

VIRGINIA: Yes . . . an' another nigger tore open my legs . . . .

RUBIN: Did he make you bleed there too?

VIRGINIA: Yes, they hurt me terrible down theah. Then he said, 'Listen heah, white gal I'm goin' to . . .'

RUBIN: Well, never mind what he said. Answer only the questions. What happened then?

VIRGINIA: Then he said, after he got through ravashin' me that he was goin' tuh make me have a nigger baby, a black baby . . . an' he was goin' tuh take me up No'th an' make me his woman. . . .

RUBIN: He said that . . . ?

VIRGINIA [*almost screaming*]: Yes an' he said he was goin' tuh cut my neck open if I didn't let him . . .

RUBIN: Wait a minute. Say, you're a little bit of an actress, aren't you?

DADE [*jumping up and shouting*]: Don't answer that!

VIRGINIA [*pleased and rather impudent*]: Well, you're a pretty good actor yo'self.

RUBIN [*back to his usual pounding*]: Tell the jury, Mrs. Ross, why you . . . a complaining witness, were held in jail at Cookesville. What happened in that jail before the grand jury met to indict those nine boys?

VIRGINIA [*in a rage*]: Nuthin'! Nuthin' . . . an' you're a . . .

DADE: I object. This is wholly irrelevant.

RUBIN: It is not irrelevant.

DADE: It has nothing to do with the rape.

JUDGE [*tapping with his gavel*]: What relevancy has this testimony to the case, Mr. Rubin?

RUBIN [*angry*]: I'd like to ask if anyone ever heard in the history of this State of a single white woman being locked up in jail when she is the complaining witness against a negro?

DADE: We object.

JUDGE: Sustained.

RUBIN: Well . . . I'm going to show that the state's chief witness, this woman here, Virginia Ross, is an out-and-out perjurer. That's what I'm going to show before I'm through. This is only the beginning. [*To* VIRGINIA *suddenly.*] That's all.

[*She glares at him, then remembers, rises, looks about the court with pleading eyes and trips off.*]

DADE [*as* RUBIN *crosses to his seat*]: I call Doctor Thomas of Cookesville.

From They Shall Not Die [207

GUARD: Doctor Thomas.
  [*He enters and crosses to the chair.*]
MASON [*having already crossed to him*]: Doctor Thomas, did you examine Virginia Ross and Lucy Wells after they were brought to Cookesville?
DOCTOR: I did, suh.
MASON: What did you find in your examination of the two girls?
[*The court which had been slightly noisy after the exit of* VIRGINIA *suddenly hushes itself and everyone including* JUDGE, JURY, REPORTERS *and* SOLDIERS *lean forward, ears and mouths wide open. Two women rise and leave the room of their own accord.*]
DOCTOR: Well, I examined them one by one and found evidence of spermatozoa in both of them.
MASON: Would this show, Doctor, that these girls had been attacked?
DOCTOR: It certainly showed that they had had commerce with men.
  [*Someone giggles.*]
MASON: Thank you, Doctor.
  [*He seats himself.* RUBIN *crosses to examine him.*]
RUBIN: Doctor Thomas. Wouldn't it be true that if five men had attacked Virginia Ross, there would have been much more evidence of it?
DOCTOR [*cautiously*]: Well, yes . . . there wasn't very much. But there was some.
RUBIN: Was it difficult to find?
DOCTOR: Well, I had to make quite a thorough search . . . into the cervix itself.
RUBIN: As you testified in Cookesville, your examination took place only one to two hours after the alleged attack. Certainly there should have been more evidence found and without any difficulty.
DOCTOR [*warily*]: All things are possible.
RUBIN: When you examined Mrs. Ross, did you find her bleeding from her back or head?
DOCTOR: No, but she did have a couple of small scratches on her arms. . . .
RUBIN [*firmly*]: Kindly answer only my question. Was she bleeding from head or back? Yes or no?
DOCTOR: No suh.
RUBIN: And concerning any small scratches on her arms of hands, couldn't these have happened from the jumping on and off trains and sleeping in the open?
DOCTOR: Yes.
RUBIN: I will now ask you as a physician . . . were there any wounds

or lacerations on her body as there would have been if she had been attacked roughly and in a hurry by five men?
DOCTOR: No.
RUBIN: She didn't bleed anywhere?
DOCTOR: No.
RUBIN: Was Mrs. Ross excited when she came to your office?
DOCTOR: No.
RUBIN: How was her pulse?
DOCTOR: Normal.
JUDGE [*leaning over*]: Was Mrs. Ross nervous or hysterical?
DOCTOR: Both girls were normal, your Honor.
RUBIN: As a medical man, Doctor . . . can you conceive of a woman going through so ghastly an experience as rape by five negroes and yet showing no signs whatsoever of any excitement . . . ?
DADE: We object!
RUBIN [*simulating innocence*]: Do you object to that?
DADE: Yes indeed!
RUBIN: That's all, Doctor. [*Waves magnanimously.*] All right. I'll withdraw it.

[DOCTOR *nods to* JUDGE *and exits.*]

JUDGE: The state will kin'ly proceed.
DADE: The state calls Benson Allen.
GUARD: Mr. Allen.

[*He enters, crosses to seat. Nods to* JUDGE. MASON *has already crossed and proceeds to examine him.*]

MASON: You were at Rocky Point when the train arrived?
ALLEN: Sho'. I was the fust one tuh git the telephone from Stebbinsville 'bout the hull thing.
MASON: And you saw the girls at Rocky Point?
ALLEN: Sho'. I helped tuh place 'em into the automobile.
MASON: Weren't they all hysterical and didn't they accuse the negroes of attacking them?
ALLEN: They were all cryin' an' complainin' of bein' attacked.
MASON: Thank you, Mister Allen. [*He nods to* RUBIN *who rises and crosses to* ALLEN.]
RUBIN: You saw the girls at the station?
ALLEN: I was right theah.
RUBIN: Were they bleeding at all?
ALLEN: Yeah. Mrs. Ross, she was bleedin' turrible-like.

[DADE *makes a gesture of satisfaction and talks excitedly to his colleagues. They laugh and wink to each other.*]

RUBIN: Where did you see any blood?

ALLEN: On her haid.

[DADE *repeats his approval.* RUBIN *glances at him, narrow-eyed.*]

RUBIN: Did you deputies search the defendant, Heywood Parsons?

ALLEN: I searched him, myself.

RUBIN: Did you find a gun on him?

ALLEN: No, but I found a knife.

RUBIN: This knife? [*Indicates a knife lying on a small table near the Clerk.*]

ALLEN: Yes suh, that same knife.

[DADE *suddenly claps his hands and gives a triumphant whoop.*]

RUBIN: Did the defendant say anything when you took it from him?

ALLEN: Yes. He said he stole it from her, from Mrs. Ross.

[DADE *slaps his hand down on the table, with another ejaculation of glee.*]

RUBIN [*heatedly*]: Your Honor, I am amazed at the actions of the chief prosecutor, the Attorney General of this state, who only yesterday said he wanted these negroes to have a fair trial and who is today so shamefully comporting himself before the jury. It is very disheartening and I must move for a mistrial. [*Turns to* ROKOFF.] I never saw anything like this in my life.

JUDGE [*taps gavel to quiet muttering in court*]: Yes, I did heah a little sound. I'm very sorry, Mr. Rubin. I'm sure the General will not repeat it. Motion denied. Proceed please.

RUBIN [*sighs heavily*]: Did you find anything else on the defendant?

ALLEN [*he is very pleased with himself*]: Sho'. I found a half dollar in his pockets. He said he took that from Mrs. Ross too . . .

RUBIN: Oh, he did? Well, what did you do with this fifty-cent piece?

ALLEN: Oh, I don't remember that.

RUBIN: Didn't you show it to anyone?

ALLEN: No.

RUBIN: Didn't you show it to Sheriff Trent at Cookesville?

ALLEN [*irritably*]: But he's dead now.

RUBIN: What difference does that make? Did you show it to him?

ALLEN: No. I didn't.

RUBIN: Whom did you give it to?

ALLEN [*becoming confused and hot under the collar*]: I'm tellin' yuh, I dunno.

RUBIN: Why didn't you bring it up at the Cookesville trial?

ALLEN: I dunno. I don't remember . . .

RUBIN: You swore to tell the truth here, didn't you? Not to lie . . . ?

ALLEN: I swore tuh that an' I am. I jest don't remember . . . I'm tellin' yuh.

RUBIN: Well, I'll tell you something, Mr. Allen. Mrs. Virginia Ross swore here on this chair, not twenty minutes ago that she never had a cent on that trip and that she was *dead-broke*.

ALLEN [*his mouth dropping open*]: Huh?

RUBIN: That's all. [*Turns to Dade.*] Now, General Dade, now you can cheer your head off.

[*Crosses to his seat; noise in court.* ALLEN *leaves.*]

MASON: The state calls Seth Robbins.

GUARD: Mr. Robbins.

[*He enters and seats himself. He is a farmer, dressed in overalls and boots. This is a great experience for him and he revels in it.*]

MASON: Mr. Robbins, what is your business?

ROBBINS: I am a land-holder, suh.

MASON: You testified in Cookesville that you were standing on a hay-wagon in your field and witnessed what happened on the train coming from Chattanooga. Is that correct?

ROBBINS: It sho' is.

MASON: Did you see the negroes throw the white boys off the train?

ROBBINS: I saw that happen.

MASON: What did you see after the boys were thrown off?

ROBBINS: I saw aplenty. One of them white gals was afixin' tuh jump off an' this heah nigger grabbed huld of her an' pulled her back in the train an' slammed her down in the car with a bang.

[*Loud muttering in the court.*]

MASON: Could you see what he did to her there?

ROBBINS: I sho' could, an' I saw aplenty.

MASON: Thank you, Mr. Robbins. [*Nods to* RUBIN *who crosses to table.*]

RUBIN: Where is your hayfield, Mr. Robbins? How far from the railroad tracks?

ROBBINS: Oh, jest a hoop an' a holler away.

RUBIN: How far is that?

ROBBINS: Oh, jest a li'l way.

RUBIN: I offer as evidence, if the court please, this map of Mr. Robbins' farm . . . [*Crosses to* JUDGE *and shows it to him.*] This clearly shows the hayfield to be at least a half-mile distant from the tracks, and therefore the witness could not possibly have seen what occurred on a fast-speeding freight. [*Hands the map to a juror who looks at it and passes it on.*] Perhaps you had a telescope with you, Mr. Robbins?

JUDGE: Mark it in evidence, Clerk. [*Clerk does so.*]

ROBBINS [*not understanding*]: Huh?

RUBIN [*describes with hands and one closed eye*]: A telescope . . .?
ROBBINS: No, I did not. An' don't be so smart with me, suh.
JUDGE: Quiet, please.
RUBIN: When you were standing on that hay-wagon, who was with you?
ROBBINS: A nigger.
RUBIN: You mean a negro. Speak English in this court. [*Muttering in room.*] What is this negro's name?
ROBBINS: I dunno his name. [*He is very angry and scowls at* RUBIN *continually.*]
RUBIN: Why was he never brought to trial at Cookesville to back up your story?
DADE [*leaping up. shouts*]: We don't need a nigger to corroborate a white man's testimony.
[*Muttering in court, sounds of approval. At reporters' table, renewed activity. One of them whistles in amazement.*]
REPORTER: O-oh!
RUBIN: I move for a mistrial.
JUDGE: [*tapping his gavel*]: There will kin'ly be order in the court. Motion is denied. Kin'ly proceed.
RUBIN [*sarcastically*]: I respectfully except. [*To* ROBBINS.] You say you saw a white girl about to jump off the train . . . ?
ROBBINS: I did. She was afixin' tuh jump an' this buck negra, he pulled her back an' slammed her down in the car.
RUBIN: You swear you saw this?
ROBBINS: I do.
RUBIN: How far do you live from Stebbinsville?
ROBBINS: Two and a half mile.
RUBIN: Did you have a car, an auto? In good condition?
ROBBINS: I had a Ford truck an' it was brand new.
RUBIN: Did you have a telephone in your house?
ROBBINS: I did an' I still have.
RUBIN: Well, when you saw this terrible thing, when you saw that a negro was attacking and assaulting a white girl in front of your very eyes, did you go to your telephone and call the sheriff in Stebbinsville?
ROBBINS: No, it jest slipped my mind. But I meant tuh . . .
RUBIN: Didn't you rush to your brand new Ford truck and drive immediately to the authorities to report this horrible crime you witnessed?
ROBBINS: I'm jest tellin' yuh, it slipped by me. An' then I had tuh git the hay in fo' the rain would come.
RUBIN: You, a white Southern gentleman, chivalrous, respecting

white womanhood, saw this terrible attack by a negro on a white woman and you let it slip your mind and worried about your hay and went on with your work as usual? Didn't you ever tell anyone about it?

ROBBINS: No, I ain't tol' nobody.

RUBIN: Nobody in the world?

ROBBINS (*red and perspiring*): No, nobody.

RUBIN (*sharply*): Then how were you called as a witness to the trial at Cookesville? How are you here, now?

ROBBINS (*mopping his face with a bandana*): I dunno.

RUBIN: That's all. (*Crosses back to his table.* DADE *rises and calls.*)

DADE: If it please your Honor, the state rests.

(*Muttering in court.* PEOPLE *stretch and talk.*)

RUBIN: If it please the court, I move for a dismissal of the indictment of the People against Heywood Parsons on the grounds of complete lack of any reasonable evidence.

JUDGE (*perfunctorily*): Overrule the motion.

RUBIN (*almost simultaneously*): Exception.

SOMETIMES THEY SEEMED TO TRY TO SING

> Mary: . . . you have responsibilities?
> Joe: (loudly) *One*, and *thousands*. As a matter of fact, I feel responsible to everybody. . . . I've been trying for three years to find out if it's possible to live what I think is a civilized life. I mean a life that can't hurt any other life.
>
> William Saroyan, *The Time of Your Life* (1939)

> The question is whether they've reached a depth
> Of desperation that would warrant poetry's
> Leaving love's alternations, joy and grief,
> The weather's alternations, summer and winter,
> Our age-long theme, for the uncertainty
> Of judging who is a contemporary liar. . . .
>
> Robert Frost, in *A Further Range* (1936)

Clifford Odets

"I CAN'T SLEEP"

> *Clifford Odets was another of the geniuses of the era, representing, to his admirers, heart, social consciousness, a sense of people, all permeated with salt and humor.* Waiting for Lefty *(1935) brought him fame overnight. Moreover, it seemed calculated to stir the "vacillating" middle class to action with its combination of martial music and agitational phrases and social criticism.* Awake and Sing! *that same year continued Odets's career and maintained his message. Theater-goers watched to see whether his move to Hollywood would affect his work.* Golden Boy *(1937) made contrasting symbols of the boxing game and violin playing, but revealed that Odets's sensibilities were more acute than his grasp of actual social forces. "I Can't Sleep" concentrates the best of Odets in the least compass. It appeared in* New Theater, February 1936.

STANDING on a street corner, a beggar with the face of a dead man. Hungry, miserable, unkempt, an American spectre. He now holds out his hand in an asking gesture as a man walks by. The man stops, looks at the beggar, says:

MAN: (*Angrily*) I don't believe in it, charity! Maybe you think I'm a Rockerfeller! (*He walks away briskly; the beggar lowers his hand and shivers. The man now returns and silently offers him some coins. The beggar refuses by putting his hands in pockets.*)

Take it . . . don't be ashamed. I had a fight in the shop . . . I was feeling sore. Take the money . . . You're afraid? No, I'm giving it to you (*Waits.*) I mean it. Take it. (*Suddenly shouts.*) Say, maybe you think I'll lay down on the ground and die before you'll take it! Look, he's looking at me! All right, I made a mistake, I yelled on you, noo! Don't act like a fool . . . if a person gives you money, take it. I know. I made a mistake in the beginning. Now I'm sorry I yelled on you.

Listen, don't be so smart. When a man offers you money, take it! For two cents I'll call a cop in a minute. You'll get arrested for panhandling on the streets. You know this expression, "panhandling"?

You can't talk? Who says you have to insult me? I got a good mind to walk away. Listen, what do you want from me? Maybe I look to you like a rich man. Poverty is whistling from every corner in the country. So an honest man gets insulted because he offers a plain bum money. Live and learn!

Look, he's looking at me. Maybe you think I'm not honest. Listen, in my shop the only worker the boss gives a little respect is Sam Blitzstein. Who's Blitzstein? Me! Don't think I'm impressed because he's a boss. I just said it to give proof. Everything, "he's tickled to death," a favorite expression by Mr. Kaplan.... Like all bosses: the end of the summer he gives away dead flies! Yes. Yes....

Take the money ... you'll buy yourself a hot meal. I'll take out a nickel from the BMT. I keep for myself five dollars a week and the rest goes in the house. In the old days I used to play a little cards, but in the last few years with such bad conditions I quit playing altogether. You can't talk? (*Laughs bitterly and shakes his head.*) Even my wife don't talk to me. For seven years she didn't speak to me one word. "Come eat," she says. Did you ever hear such an insult? After supper I go in my room and lock the door. Sometime ago I bought for myself a little radio for seven-fifty. I'm playing it in my little room. She tells the girls not to speak to me ... my three daughters. All my life I was a broken-hearted person, so this had to happen. I shouldn't get a little respect from my own children! Can you beat it?

I'll tell you the truth: I don't sleep. The doctors says to me it's imagination. Three dollars I paid him he should tell me it's imagination! I don't sleep at night and he tells me it's imagination! Can't you die? I eat healthful food. For a while I was eating vegetarian in the Golden Rule Cafeteria. It didn't agree with me. Vegetarian, shmegetarian, they'll have a good time anyway, the worms. Headaches, backaches — these things I don't mention — it ain't important. I like to talk to people, but I don't like political arguments. They think I'm crazy in the shop. I tell them right to their face, "Leave me alone! Talk politics, but let me live!" I don't hide my opinions from nobody. They should know what I know. Believe me, I'm smarter than I look! What I forget about Marx they don't know. (*Changes the subject.*) Friday night regular as clockwork I go on the corner and take a shave for twenty cents. After supper I walk in Prospect Park for two hours. I like trees and then I go home. By this time the youngest girls is sleeping but my oldest girl stays up late to do homework. A very smart girl in school. Every month A-A-A. She leaves the report card on the sideboard and I sign it. This will give you an idea she likes me. Correct! Last week I tried to talk to her, a sensible girl, fourteen years old. She ran in the kitchen to my wife. Believe me, my friend, in a worker's house the children live a brokenhearted life. My wife tells her lies about me.

Look, he's looking. What did I do to my wife? I suddenly got an idea the youngest girl wasn't my girl. Never mind, it happened before in history. A certain man lived in our neighborhood a few months. He boarded downstairs with the Bergers, next to the candy store, a man like a sawed-off shotgun. I seen in my young girl a certain resemblance. Suddenly he moved away. On the same day I caught her crying, my wife. Two and two is four! I remember like yesterday I took a pineapple soda in the store. For three weeks I walked up and down. Could I work? Could I eat? In the middle of the night I asked her. She insulted me! She insulted my whole family! Her brother came from Brighton Beach the next day — a cheap race horse specialist without a nickel. A fourteen carat bum! A person an animal wouldn't talk to him! He opened up his mouth to me . . . I threw him down the stairs!

But one thing — I never laid a finger on the girls in my whole life. My wife — it shows you what a brain she's got — she gives my oldest girl a name: Sydelle! S-Y-D-E-L-L-E! Sarah she can't call her or maybe Shirley. Sydelle! So you can imagine what's happening in our house!

Oh, I don't sleep. At night my heart cries blood. A fish swims all night in the black ocean — and this is how I am — all night with one eye open. A mixed up man like me crawls away to die alone. No woman should hold his head. In the whole city no one speaks to me. A very peculiar proposition. Maybe I would like to say to a man, "Brother." But what happens? They bring in a verdict — crazy! It's a civilized world today in America? Columbus should live so long. Yes, I love people, but nobody speaks to me. When I walk in the street I can't stand I should see on every block some beggars. My heart cries blood for the poor man who didn't eat for a few days. At night I can't sleep. This is an unusual combination of worries. I say to myself, "It's your fault, Blitzstein? Let them die in the street like flies." But I look in the mirror and it don't feel good inside. I spit on myself.

I spoke last week to a red in the shop. Why should I mix in with politics? With all my other troubles I need yet a broken head? I can't make up my mind — what should I do? I spoke to a Socialist on the street. A Communist talked in my ears for two hours. Join up, join up. But for what? For trouble?

Don't look at me. I'll say it straight out — I forgot my mother.

Also a dead brother for thirty years dead. Listen, you think I never read a book? "Critique of the Gotha Programme," Bukharin, Lenin — "Iskra" — this was in our day a Bolshevik paper. I read enough. I'm speaking three languages, Russian, German and English. Also Yiddish. Four. I had killed in the 1905 revolution a brother. You didn't know that. My mother worked like a horse. No, even a horse takes off a day. My mother loved him like a bird, my dead brother. She gave us to drink vinegar we should get sick and not fight in the Czar's army. Maybe you think I didn't understand this.

Yes, my blood is crying out for revenge a whole lifetime! You hear me talking to you these words? Is it plain to you my significance? I don't sleep. Don't look at me. I forgot my working class mother. Like a dog I live. You hear the truth. Don't look at me! You hear me?!

Last week I watched the May Day. Don't look! I hid in the crowd. I watched how the comrades marched with red flags and music. You see where I bit my hand? I went down in the subway I shouldn't hear the music. Listen, I looked in your face before. I saw the truth. I talk to myself. The blood of the mother and brother is breaking open my head. I hear them cry, "You forgot, you forgot!" They don't let me sleep. All night I hear the music of the comrades. Hungry men I hear. All night the broken-hearted children. Look at me — no place to hide, no place to run away. Look in my face, comrade. Look at me, look, look, look!!!

[*I Can't Sleep* was first performed on a program for the benefit of the Marine Workers Industrial Union at Mecca Temple, New York, Morris Carnovsky as Blitzstein and Art Smith as the beggar.]

Stephen Vincent Benet

NIGHTMARE NUMBER THREE

Poetry of the Thirties was more varied than most partisans realized. Even the Poetry Society of America continued to hold its meetings and give forums to persons who wished to compare their loves to winds or beech trees, or other natural objects. Stephen Vin-

cent Benét was one of the few poets and story-tellers who could give lyric meaning to American history. For those who used the Saturday Evening Post *as a measure of American Philistinism, it should be mentioned that his classic short story "The Devil and Daniel Webster" first appeared in that publication, in 1936. That year he also published* Burning City, *which included the following poem.*

We had expected everything but revolt
And I kind of wonder myself when they started thinking —
But there's no dice in that now.
                        I've heard fellows say
They must have planned it for years and maybe they did.
Looking back, you can find little incidents here and there,
Like the concrete-mixer in Jersey eating the wop
Or the roto press that printed "Fiddle-dee-dee!"
In a three-color process all over Senator Sloop,
Just as he was making a speech. The thing about that
Was, how could it walk upstairs? But it was upstairs,
Clicking and mumbling in the Senate Chamber.
They had to knock out the wall to take it away
And the wrecking-crew said it grinned.
                                  It was only the best
Machines, of course, the superhuman machines,
The ones we'd built to be better than flesh and bone,
But the cars were in it, of course . . .
                                  and they hunted us
Like rabbits through the cramped streets on that Bloody
   Monday,
The Madison Avenue busses leading the charge.
The busses were pretty bad — but I'll not forget
The smash of glass when the Duesenberg left the show-room
And pinned three brokers to the Racquet Club steps
Or the long howl of the horns when they saw men run,
When they saw them looking for holes in the solid
     ground . . .

I guess they were tired of being ridden in
And stopped and started by pygmies for silly ends,
Of wrapping cheap cigarettes and bad chocolate bars
Collecting nickels and waving platinum hair
And letting six million people live in town.
I guess it was that. I guess they got tired of us

Nightmare Number Three

And the whole smell of human hands.
                                            But it was a shock
To climb sixteen flights of stairs to Art Zuckow's office
(Nobody took the elevators twice)
And find him strangled to death in a nest of telephones,
The octopus-tendrils waving over his head,
And a sort of quiet humming filling the air. . . .
Do they eat? . . . There was red . . . But I did not stop
    to look.
I don't know yet how I got to the roof in time
And it's lonely, here on the roof.
                                      For a while, I thought
That window-cleaner would make it, and keep me company.
But they got him with his own hoist at the sixteenth floor
And dragged him in, with a squeal.
You see, they coöperate. Well, we taught them that
And it's fair enough, I suppose. You see, we built them.
We taught them to think for themselves.
It was bound to come. You see it was bound to come.
And it won't be so bad, in the country. I hate to think
Of the reapers, running wild in the Kansas fields,
And the transport planes like hawks on a chickenyard,
But the horses might help. We might make a deal with the
    horses.
At least, you've more chance, out there.
                                              And they need us, too.
They're bound to realize that when they once calm down.
They'll need oil and spare parts and adjustments and tuning
    up.
Slaves? Well, in a way, you know, we were slaves before.
There won't be so much real difference — honest, there won't.
(I wish I hadn't looked into that beauty-parlor
And seen what was happening there.
But those are female machines and a big high-strung.)
Oh, we'll settle down. We'll arrange it. We'll compromise.
It wouldn't make sense to wipe out the whole human race.
Why, I bet if I went to my old Plymouth now
(Of course you'd have to do it the tactful way)
And said, "Look here! Who got you the swell French
    horn?"
He wouldn't turn me over to those police cars;
At least I don't think he would.

Oh, it's going to be jake.
There won't be so much real difference — honest, there
   won't —
And I'd go down in a minute and take my chance —
I'm a good American and I always liked them —
Except for one small detail that bothers me
And that's the food proposition. Because, you see,
The concrete-mixer may have made a mistake,
And it looks like just high spirits.
But, if it's got so they like the flavor . . . well . . .

Kenneth Fearing

NO CREDIT, DIRGE, LULLABY

>Kenneth Fearing was to Thirties poetry what Odets was to drama: its hope for fresh and revolutionary expression. The poet of Angel Arms *(1929)* — harsh songs conventionally metered — moved through personal chaos and despair to create the vibrant original verse forms and formulations of Poems *(1935)* and Dead Reckoning *(1938).* His poetic impulse did not substantially survive the collapse of radical perspectives in the war and post-war periods.

NO CREDIT
Whether dinner was pleasant, with the windows lit by gunfire, and
   no one disagreed; or whether, later, we argued in the
   park, and there was a touch of vomit-gas in the evening
   air;
   whether we found a greater, deeper, more perfect love, by
      courtesy of Camels, over NBC; whether the comic amused
      us, or the newspapers carried a hunger death, and pub-
      lished a whitehouse prayer for mother's day;
   whether the bills were paid or not, whether or not we had our
      doubts, whether we spoke our minds at Joe's, and the
      receipt said "Not Redeemable," and the cash-register rang
      up "No Sale,"

whether the truth was then, or later, or whether the best had
    already gone —
Nevertheless, we know; as every turn is measured; as every unavoidable risk is known;
    as nevertheless, the flesh grows old, dies, dies in its only life,
        is gone;
        the reflection goes from the mirror; as the shadow, of even a
            communist, is gone from the wall;
        as nevertheless, the current is thrown and the wheels revolve;
            and nevertheless, as the word is spoken and the wheat
            grows tall and the ships sail on —
None but the fool is paid in full; none but the broker, none but the
    scab is certain of profit;
    the sheriff alone may attend a third degree in formal attire; alone,
        the academy artists multiply in dignity as a trooper's bayonet guards the door;
    only Steve, the side-show robot, knows content; only Steve,
        the mechanical man in love with a photo-electric beam,
        remains aloof; only Steve, who sits and smokes or stands
        in salute, is secure;
    Steve, whose shoebutton eyes are blind to terror, whose painted ears are deaf to appeal, whose welded breast will never
        be slashed by bullets, whose armature soul can hold no
        fear.

DIRGE
1-2-3 was the number he played but today the number came 3-2-1;
    bought his Carbide at 30 and it went to 29; had the favorite at
    Bowie but the track was slow —
O, executive type, would you like to drive a floating-power, kneeaction, silkupholstered six? Wed a Hollywood star? Shoot
    the course in 58? Draw to the ace, king, jack?
    O, fellow with a will who won't take no, watch out for three
        cigarettes on the same, single match; O, democratic voter
        born in August under Mars, beware of liquidated rails —
Denouement to denouement, he took a personal pride in the certain,
    certain way he lived his own, private life,
    but nevertheless, they shut off his gas; nevertheless, the bank
        foreclosed; nevertheless, the landlord called; nevertheless,
        the radio broke;
And twelve o'clock arrived just once too often,
    just the same he wore one grey tweed suit, bought one straw hat,

  drank one straight Scotch, walked one short step, took one long look, drew one deep breath,
 just one too many,
And wow he died as wow he lived,
  going whop to the office, and blooie home to sleep, and biff got married, and bam had children, and oof got fired,
  zowie did he live and zowie did he die,
With who the hell are you at the corner of his casket, and where the hell we going on the right-hand silver knob, and who the hell cares walking second from the end with an American beauty wreath from why the hell not,
  very much missed by the circulation staff of the New York Evening Post; deeply, deeply mourned by the B.M.T.,
Wham, Mr. Roosevelt; pow, Sears Roebuck; awk, big dipper; bop, summer rain;
  bong, Mr., bong, Mr., bong, Mr., bong.

LULLABY

Wide as this night, old as this night is old and young as it is young, still as this, strange as this,
  filled as this night is filled with the light of a moon as grey,
  dark as these trees, heavy as this scented air from the fields, warm as this hand,
  as warm, as strong,

In the night that wraps all the huts of the south and folds the empty barns of the west;
  is the wind that fans the roadside fire;
  are the trees that line the country estates, tall as the lynch trees, as straight, as black;
  is the moon that lights the mining towns, dim as the light upon tenement roofs, grey upon the hands at the bars of Moabit, cold as the bars of the Tombs.

Howard Nutt

THE INTELLECTUALS

I think we were followed here.
Perhaps we should change our whiskers
Let's take a table near the door
And speak in whispers.

This is the sort of a place
Where you don't go wising off;
You give the man your order
With a wink and a cough.
You know what's what, and that's enough.
You disagree, but don't get tough.

Suppose you should let slip,
You simply say, "Unquote"
(That woman with her back to us
Is taking notes).
Somebody softsays something;
Somebody overhears;
We tip our glasses in a toast,
Somebody — disappears.

Observe above the hat rack:
The management regrets
It cannot be responsible
For loss of life, or wits.

It's almost tickety-tock.
Beware the cough of the clock.
You're on the spot and you'll get got;
You'd better be ready to duck!
Nobody's going to shout
Look out —   *Look out!*   LOOK OUT!

Archibald MacLeish

AMERICA WAS PROMISES

Archibald MacLeish proved one of the best balanced and adaptable of literary men of his time. He served the magazine For-tune, *was, during the late 1930's and after, Librarian of Congress, and went on to become an Assistant Secretary of State in the Federal government. As a poet he moved from individualistic verses in the 1920's (as, notably, in* The Hamlet of A. MacLeish) *to poems of social significance in the 1930's; outstanding was his* Frescoes for Mr. Rockefeller's City. *MacLeish denounced intellectuals in his* The Irresponsibles *(1940), temporarily giving the country a phrase. Later, he defended Ezra Pound as a true intellectual.* America Was Promises *is MacLeish's most deeply-felt testament of his love for America.*

WHO is the voyager in these leaves?
Who is the traveler in this journey
Deciphers the revolving night: receives
The signal from the light returning?

America was promises to whom?

                                        East were the
Dead kings and the remembered sepulchres:
West was the grass.
                        The groves of the oaks were at evening.

Eastward are the nights where we have slept.

And we move on: we move down:
With the first light we push forward:
We descend from the past as a wandering people from
          mountains.
We cross into the day to be discovered.

America Was Promises

The dead are left where they fall — at dark
At night late under the coverlets.
We mark the place with the shape of our teeth on our fingers.
The room is left as it was: the love

Who is the traveler in these leaves these
Annual waters and beside the doors
Jonquils: then the rose: the eaves
Heaping the thunder up: the mornings
Opening on like great valleys
Never till now approached: the familiar trees
Far off: distant with the future:
The hollyhocks beyond the afternoons:
The butterflies over the ripening fruit on the balconies:
And all beautiful
All before us

America was always promises.
From the first voyage and the first ship there were promises—
'the tropic bird which does not sleep at sea'
'the great mass of dark heavy clouds which is a sign'
'the drizzle of rain without wind which is a sure sign'
'the whale which is an indication'
'the stick appearing to be carved with iron'
'the stalk loaded with roseberries'
'and all these signs were from the west'
'and all night heard birds passing.'

Who is the voyager on these coasts?
Who is the traveler in these waters
Expects the future as a shore: foresees
Like Indies to the west the ending — he
The rumor of the surf intends?

America was promises — to whom?

Jefferson knew:
Declared it before God and before history:
Declares it still in the remembering tomb.
The promises were Man's: the land was his —
Man endowed by his Creator:
Earnest in love: perfectible by reason:

Just and perceiving justice: his natural nature
Clear and sweet at the source as springs in trees are.
It was Man the promise contemplated.
The times had chosen Man: no other: —
Bloom on his face of every future:
Brother of stars and of all travelers:
Brother of time and of all mysteries:
Brother of grass also: of fruit trees.
It was Man who had been promised: who should have.
Man was to ride from the Tidewater: over the Gap:
West and South with the water: taking the book with him:
Taking the wheat seed: corn seed: pip of apple:
Building liberty a farmyard wide:
Breeding for useful labor: for good looks:
For husbandry: humanity: for pride —
Practising self-respect and common decency.

And Man turned into men in Philadelphia
Practising prudence on a long-term lease:
Building liberty to fit the parlor:
Bred for crystal on the frontroom shelves:
Just and perceiving justice by the dollar:
Patriotic with the bonds at par
(And their children's children brag of their deeds for the
       Colonies).
Man rode up from the Tidewater: over the Gap:
Turned into men: turned into two-day settlers:
Lawyers with the land-grants in their caps:
Coon-skin voters wanting theirs and getting it.

Turned the promises to capital: invested it.

America was always promises:
'the wheel like a sun as big as a cart wheel
    with many sorts of pictures on it
    the whole of fine gold'
'twenty golden ducks
    beautifully worked and very natural looking
    and some like dogs of the kind they keep'
And they waved us west from the dunes: they cried out
Colua! Colua!
Mexico! Mexico! . . . Colua!

America Was Promises

America was promises to whom?

Old Man Adams knew. He told us —
An aristocracy of compound interest
Hereditary through the common stock!
We'd have one sure before the mare was older.
'The first want of every man was his dinner:
The second his girl.' Kings were by the pocket.
Wealth made blood made wealth made blood made wealthy.
Enlightened selfishness gave lasting light.
Winners bred grandsons: losers only bred!

And the Aristocracy of politic selfishness
Bought the land up: bought the towns: the sites:
The goods: the government: the people. Bled them.
Sold them. Kept the profit. Lost itself.

The Aristocracy of Wealth and Talents
Turned its talents into wealth and lost them.
Turned enlightened selfishness to wealth.
Turned self-interest into bankbooks: balanced them.
Bred out: bred to fools: to hostlers:

Card sharps: well dressed women: dancefloor doublers.
The Aristocracy of Wealth and Talents
Sold its talents: bought the public notice:
Drank in public: went to bed in public:
Patronized the arts in public: pall'd with
Public authors public beauties: posed in
Public postures for the public page.
The Aristocracy of Wealth and Talents
Withered of talent and ashamed of wealth
Bred to sonsinlaw: insane relations:
Girls with open secrets: sailors' Galahads:
Prurient virgins with the tales to tell:
Women with dead wombs and living wishes.
The Aristocracy of Wealth and Talents
Moved out: settled on the Continent:
Sat beside the water at Rapallo:
Died in a rented house: unwept: unhonored.

And the child says I see the lightning on you.

The weed between the railroad tracks
Tasting of sweat: tasting of poverty:
The bitter and pure taste where the hawk hovers:
Native as the deer bone in the sand

O my America for whom?

For whom the promises? For whom the river
"It flows west! Look at the ripple of it!"
The grass "So that it was wonderful to see
And endless without end with wind wonderful!"
The Great Lakes: landless as oceans: their beaches
Coarse sand: clean gravel: pebbles:
Their bluffs smelling of sunflowers: smelling of surf:
Of fresh water: of wild sunflowers . . . wilderness.
For whom the evening mountains on the sky:
The night wind from the west: the moon descending?

Tom Paine knew.
Tom Paine knew the People.
The promises were spoken to the People.
History was voyages toward the People.
Americas were landfalls of the People.
Stars and expectations were the signals of the People.

Whatever was truly built the People had built it.
Whatever was taken down they had taken down.
Whatever was worn they had worn — ax-handles: fiddle-bows:
Sills of doorways: names for children: for mountains.
Whatever was long forgotten they had forgotten —
Fame of the great: names of the rich and their mottos.
The People had the promises: they'd keep them.
They waited their time in the world: they had wise sayings.
They counted out their time by day to day.
They counted it out day after day into history.
They had time and to spare in the spill of their big fists.
They had all the time there was like a handful of wheat seed.
When the time came they would speak and the rest would
    listen.

And the time came and the People did not speak.

America Was Promises

The time came: the time comes: the speakers
Come and these who speak are not the People.

These who speak with gunstocks at the doors:
These the coarse ambitious priest
Leads by the bloody fingers forward:
These who reach with stiffened arm to touch
What none who took dared touch before:
These who touch the truth are not the People.

These the savage fables of the time
Lick at the fingers as a bitch will waked at morning:
These who teach the lie are not the People.

The time came: the time comes

Comes and to whom? To these? Was it for these
The surf was secret on the new-found shore?
Was it for these the branch was on the water? —
These whom all the years were toward
The golden images the clouds the mountains?

Never before: never in any summer:
Never were days so generous: stars so mild:
Even in old men's talk or in books or remembering
Far back in a gone childhood
Or farther still to the light where Homer wanders —
The air all lucid with the solemn blue
That hills take at the distance beyond change. . . .
That time takes also at the distances.

Never were there promises as now:
Never was green deeper: earth warmer:
Light more beautiful to see: the sound of
Water lovelier: the many forms of
Leaves: stones: clouds: beasts: shadows
Clearer more admirable or the faces
More like answering faces or the hands
Quicker: more brotherly:
                        the aching taste of
Time more salt upon the tongue: more human

Never in any summer: and to whom?

At dusk: by street lights: in the rooms we ask this.

We do not ask for Truth now from John Adams.
We do not ask for Tongues from Thomas Jefferson.
We do not ask for Justice from Tom Paine.
We ask for answers.

And there is an answer.

There is Spain Austria Poland China Bohemia.
There are dead men in the pits in all those countries.
Their mouths are silent but they speak. They say
"The promises are theirs who take them."

Listen! Brothers! Generation!
Listen! You have heard these words. Believe it!
Believe the promises are theirs who take them!

Believe unless we take them for ourselves
Others will take them for the use of others!
Believe unless we take them for ourselves
All of us: one here: another there:
Men not Man: people not the People:
Hands: mouths: arms: eyes: not syllables —
Believe unless we take them for ourselves
Others will take them: not for us: for others!

Believe unless we take them for ourselves
Now: soon: by the clock: before tomorrow:
Others will take them: not for now: for longer!

Listen! Brothers! Generation!
Companions of leaves: of the sun: of the slow evenings:
Companions of the many days: of all of them:
Listen! Believe the speaking dead! Believe
The journey is our journey. O believe
The signals were to us: the signs: the birds by
Night: the breaking surf.

     Believe

America is promises to
Take!

America is promises to
Us
To take them
Brutally
With love but
Take them.

O believe this!

Muriel Rukeyser

POWER

> U. S. 1 *(1938) was Muriel Rukeyser's second book of verse, and was hailed for its "working-class" sympathies, as well as for its effort to integrate the symbols of an industrial society with poetry. She later diverted her intense emotionalism into verse exploring personal symbols, on the one hand, and into prose which curiously absorbed itself in such a subject as Willard Gibbs, the scientist of thermodynamics.* Power *was specifically evoked by the growth of public government power projects, like* TVA.

The quick sun brings, exciting mountains warm,
gay on the landscapers and green designs,
miracle, yielding the sex up under all the skin,
until the entire body watches the scene with love,
sees perfect cliffs ranging until the river
cuts sheer, mapped far below in delicate track,
surprise of grace, the water running in the sun,
magnificent flower on the mouth, surprise
as lovers who look too long on the desired face
startle to find the remote flesh so warm.
A day of heat shed on the gorge, a brilliant

day when love sees the sun behind its man
and the disguised marvel under familiar skin.

Steel-bright, light-pointed, the narrow-waisted towers
lift their protective network, the straight, the accurate
flex of distinction, economy of gift,
gymnast, they poise their freight; god's generosity! give
their voltage low enough for towns to handle.
The power-house stands skin-white at the transmitters' side
over the rapids   the brilliance   the blind foam.

This is the midway between water and flame,
this is the road to take when you think of your country,
between the dam and the furnace, terminal.
The clean park, fan of wires, landscapers,
the stone approach. And seen beyond the door,
the man with the flashlight in his metal hall.
Here, the effective green, grey-toned and shining,
tall immense chamber of cylinders. Green,
the rich paint catches light from three-story windows,
arches of light vibrate erratic panels on
sides of curved steel. Man pockets flashlight,
useless, the brilliant floor casts tiled reflection up,
bland walls return it, circles pass it round.
Wheels, control panels, dials, the vassal instruments.
This is the engineer Jones, the blueprint man,
loving the place he designed, visiting it alone.
Another blood, no cousin to the town;
rings his heels on stone, pride follows his eyes,
"This is the place."

Four generators, smooth green, and squares of black,
floored-over space for a fifth.
                              The stairs. Descend.
"They said I built the floor like the tiles of a bank,
I wanted the men who work here to be happy."
Light laughing on steel, the gay, the tall sun
given away; mottled; snow comes in clouds;
the iron steps go down as roads go down.

This is the second circle, world of inner shade,
hidden bulk of generators, governor shaft,

round gap of turbine pit. Flashlight, tool-panels,
heels beating on iron, cold of underground,
stairs, wire flooring, the voice's hollow cry.
This is the scroll, the volute case of night,
quick shadow and the empty galleries.

Go down; here are the outlets, butterfly valves
open from here, the tail-race, vault of steel,
the spiral staircase ending, last light in shaft.
"Gone," says the thin straight man.
" 'Hail, holy light, offspring of Heav'n first-born,
'Or of th' Eternal Coeternal beam
'May I express thee unblamed?' "
                                                          And still go down.
Now ladder-mouth; and the precipitous fear,
uncertain rungs down into after-night.
"This is the place. Away from this my life
I am indeed Adam unparadiz'd.
Some fools call this the Black Hole of Calcutta,
I don't know how they ever get to Congress."

Gulfs, spirals, that the drunken ladder swings,
its rungs give, pliant, beneath the leaping heart.
Leaps twice at midnight. But a naked bulb
makes glare, turns paler, burns to dark again.
Brilliance begins, stutters. And comes upon
after the tall abstract, the ill, the unmasked men,
the independent figure of the welder
masked for his work; acts with unbearable flame.
His face is a cage of steel, the hands are covered,
points dazzle hot, fly from his writing torch,
brighten the face and hands and marrying steel.
Says little, works: only: "A little down,
five men were killed in the widening of the tunnel."

Shell of bent metal; walking along an arc
the tube rounds up about your shoulders, black
circle, great circle, down infinite mountains rides,
echoes words, footsteps, testimonies.
"One said the air was thin, Fifth-Avenue clean."
The iron pillars mark a valve division,
four tunnels merging.   Iron on iron resounds,

echoes along created gorges. "Sing,
test echoes, sing: Pilgrim," he cries,
singing *Once More, Dear Home,*
as all the light burns out.
Down the reverberate channels of the hills
the suns declare midnight, go down, cannot ascend,
no ladder back: see this, your eyes can ride through steel,
this is the river Death, diversion of power,
the root of the tower and the tunnel's core,
this is the end.

Ezra Pound

CANTO XXXVII, CANTO XXXVIII

In the 1930's, Ezra Pound held the position of a poet and critic whose concern for "social significance" gave him somewhat more title to regard than such of his friends and followers as T. S. Eliot. Although Pound was a patent Fascist sympathizer and anti-semite, these views seemed peccadilloes which time and persuasion might modify. Such an event as the signing of the Nazi-Soviet Pact (1939) helped to compound his and every one's confusion and to dull the force of his malignant outlook and eccentric reading.

THOU SHALT NOT," said Martin Van Buren, "jail 'em
for debt."
"that an immigrant shd. set out with good banknotes
and find 'em at the end of his voyage
but waste paper . . . . if a man have in primeval forest
set up his cabin, shall rich patroon take it from him?
High judges? Are, I suppose, subject to passions
as have affected other great and good men, also
subject to esprit de corps.
The Calhouns" remarked Mr Adams
"Have flocked to the standard of feminine virtue"
"Peggy Eaton's own story" (Headline 1932)

Shall we call in the world to conduct our
municipal government?
Ambrose (Mr.) Spencer, Mr Van Rensselaer
were against extension of franchise.
"Who work in factories and are employed by the wealthy
(State Convention 1821) dixit Spencer:
"Man who feeds, clothes, lodges another
has absolute control over his will."
Kent said they wd. "deplore in sackcloth and ashes
if they preserved not a senate
to represent landed interest, and did they
jeopard property rights?" To whom Mr Somebody Tompkins:
"Filled your armies
"while the priests were preaching sedition
"and men of wealth decrying government credit."
". . . in order to feed on the spoils."
Two words, said Mr Van Buren, came in with our revolution
and, as a matter of fact, why are we sent here?
"as for you Mr Chief Justice Spencer
"if they vote as they are bid by their employers
"they will vote for the property which you so wish to protect."
. . . when a turnpike depends upon congress
        local supervision is lost . . .
not surrender our conduct to foreign associations . . .
working classes
        who mostly
have no control over paper, and
derive no profit from bank stock . . . .
merchants will not confess over trading
        nor speculators the disposition to speculate . . .
revenue for wants of the government
        to be kept under public control . . . do they pour
national revenue
        into banks of deposit
in seasons of speculation?
. . diminish government patronage . . . sailor
not to be lashed save by court . .   . . . . land
to actual settler (as against Mr Clay)
And when her father went broke, Mr Eaton . . gave rise to
Washington gossip . . . . loose morals of Mr Jefferson,
Servility of Martin Van Buren, said Adams (J. Quincy)
when everyone else is uncivil.

"No where so well deposited as in the pants of the people,
Wealth ain't," said President Jackson.
They give the union five years . . .
Bank did not produce uniform currency . .
they wd. import grain rather than grow it . . .
Bank of England failed to prevent uses of credit . . .

"In Banking corporations" said Mr Webster "the
"interests of the rich and the poor are happily blended."
Said Van Buren to Mr Clay: "If you will give me
"A pinch of your excellent Maccoboy snuff . . ."

In Europe often by private houses, without assistance of banks
Relief is got not by increase
    but by diminution of debt.
. . . . . . as Justice Marshall, has gone out of his case . . .

Tip an' Tyler
We'll bust Van's biler . . . . . .
brought in the vice of luxuria sed aureis furculis,
which forks were
bought back in the time of President Monroe
by Mr Lee our consul in Bordeaux.
"The man is a dough-face, a profligate,"
won't say he agrees with his party.

Authorized its (the bank's) president to use funds at
discretion (its funds, his discretion) to
influence press . . .
veto power, with marked discretion, used no further than
in objecting to bank under charter existing.
"Friendly feeling toward our bank in
"the mind of the President (Jackson
whose autograph was sent to the Princess Victoria)
    wrote Biddle to Lennox Dec. 1829
"Counter rumours without foundation, I had
"a full and frank talk with the President who was
"most kind about it (the bank's) services to the country"
    Biddle to Hamilton in November.

"To which end, largely increased line of discounts
1830, October, 40 million

May, 1837 seventy millions and then some.
Remembered this in Sorrento" in the vicinage of Vesuvius
near exhumed Herculaneum . . .
"30 million" said Mr Dan Webster "in states on the Mississippi
"will all have to be called in, in three
"years and nine months, if the charter be not extended . .
"I hesertate nawt tew say et will dee-precierate
"everyman's prorperty from the etcetera
"to the kepertal ov Missouri, affect the price of
"crawps, leynd en the prordewce ov labour, to the
embararsement . . . ."
de mortuis wrote Mr Van Buren
don't quite apply in a case of this character.

4 to 5 million balance in the national treasury
Receipts 31 to 32 million
Revenue 32 to 33 million
The Bank 341 million, and in deposits
6 millions of government money
(and a majority in the Senate)
Public Money is control of the President
from 15 to 20 thousand (id est, a fund for the secret service)

"employing means at the bank's disposal
in deranging the country's credits, obtaining by panic
control over public mind" said Van Buren
"from the real committee of Bank's directors
the government's directors have been excluded.
Bank president controlling government's funds
to the betrayal of the nation . . . .
government funds obstructing the government . . .
and has sequestered the said funds of the government . . .
(with chapter, date, verse and citation)
acting in illegal secret
pouring oil on the press
giving nominal loans on inexistent security"
          in the eighteen hundred and thirties
"on precedent that Mr Hamilton has
never hesitated to jeopard the general
for advance of particular interests."

"Bank curtailed

7 million on a line of
64 million credits.

"Had not Mr Taney (of the treasury) prevented
that branch (in New York) from then collecting
8 million 700 thousand and armed our city with
9 million to defend us (the whole country)
in this war on its trade and commerce,
             Cambreling, Globe Extra 1834
Peggy Eaton's Own Story. And if Marietta
Had not put on her grandmother's dress
She might have lasted, a mystery. If Dolores
Had not put on a hat shaped like a wig
She might have remained an exotic.
Placuit oculis, and did not mind strong cigars.

Irritable and unstable,
Is formed, is destroyed,
Recomposes to be once more decomposed
             (thus, descending to plant life)

Sorrento, June 21st. Villa Falangola
In the vicinage of Vesuvius, in the mirror of memory
Mr Van Buren:
             Judge Yeats, whom I remember etc . . .
Warded off scrutiny of his mental capacities
By a dignified and prudent reserve which
. . long practice had made second nature . . .
Alex Hamilton had been blackmailed but
preferred, in the end, private scandal to shade on his
public career.
Marshall, said Roane, undermined the U.S. Constitution.
No man before Tom Jefferson in my house

Said one of the wool-buyers:
             "Able speech by Van Buren
"Yes, very able."
"Ye-es, Mr Knower, an' on wich side ov the tariff was it?"
"Point I was in the act of considering"
             replied Mr Knower
In the mirror of memory: have been told I rendered
the truth a great service by that speech on the tariff

but directness on all points wd. seem not
to have been its conspicuous feature.
            I thanked him
(James Jones, brother in law of Mr Clinton)
for his kind offer but
said my fortunes were too low in ebb
for me at that moment to compromise.
Lacked not who said that John Adams
disliked not so much the idea of a monarch
as preferred Braintree House over Hanover . . .
and his son, seeking light from the stars
deplored that representatives be paralyzed
by the will of constituents.
"I publicly answered more questions
than all other presidents put together"
    signed Martin Van Buren.
"Mr Webster in debt to the bank"
    Damned yellow rascal, said Clay
"Unnecessary, therefore injurious . . .
interference on the part of the government.
And they and their gang in congress
    debated three months without introducing
one solitary proposition to reverse Taney's decision
or in any way to relieve any distress.
           HIC
           JACET
          FISCI LIBERATOR

CANTO XXXVIII

        il duol che sopra Senna
       Induce, falseggiando la moneta.
           Paradiso XIX, 118.

    AN' THAT year Metevsky went over to America del Sud
(and the Pope's manners were so like Mr Joyce's,
got that way in the Vatican, weren't like that before)
Marconi knelt in the ancient manner
    like Jimmy Walker sayin' his prayers.
His Holiness expressed a polite curiosity
    as to how His Excellency had chased those

electric shakes through the a'mosphere.
   Lucrezia
Wanted a rabbit's foot,
   and he, Metevsky said to the one side
(three children, five abortions and died of the last)
   he said: the other boys got more munitions
(thus cigar-makers whose work is highly repetitive
can perform the necessary operations almost automatically
and at the same time listen to readers who are hired
for the purpose of providing mental entertainment while they
work; Dexter Kimball 1929.)

Don't buy until you can get ours.
And he went over the border
   and he said to the other side:
The *other* side has more munitions. Don't buy
   until you can get ours.
And Akers made a large profit and imported gold into England
Thus increasing gold imports.
   The gentle reader has heard this before.
And that year Mr Whitney
Said how useful short sellin' was,
   We suppose he meant to the brokers
And no one called him a liar.
And two Afghans came to Geneva
To see if they cd. get some guns cheap,
As they had heard about someone's disarming.
And the secretary of the something
Made some money from oil wells
   (in the name of God the Most Glorious Mr D'Arcy
is empowered to scratch through the sub-soil of Persia
until fifty years from this date . . .)
Mr Mellon went over to England
and that year Mr Wilson had prostatitis
and there was talk of a new Messiah
(that must have been a bit sooner)
And Her Ladyship cut down Jenny's allowance
Because of that bitch Agot Ipswich
And that year (that wd. be 20 or 18 years sooner)
They began to kill 'em by millions
Because of a louse in Berlin
   and a greasy basturd in Ausstria

By name François Giuseppe.

"Will there be war?" "No, Miss Wi'let,
"On account of bizschniz relations."
    Said the soap and bones dealer in May 1914
And Mr Gandhi thought:
    if we don't buy any cotton
And at the same time don't buy any guns . . . . . .
Monsieur Untel was not found at the Jockey Club
. . . but was, later, found in Japan
And So-and-So had shares in Mitsui . .
"The wood (walnut) will always be wanted for gunstocks"
And they put up a watch factory outside Muscou
And the watches kept time . . . . Italian marshes
been waiting since Tiberius' time . . .
"Marry" said Beebe, "how do the fish live in the sea."
Rivera, the Spanish dictator, dictated that the
Infante was physically unfit to inherit . . .
   gothic type still used in Vienna
because the old folks are used to that type.
          And Schlossmann
suggested that I stay there in Vienna
As stool-pigeon against the Anschluss
   Because the Ausstrians needed a Buddha
(Seay, brother, I leev et tuh yew!)
The white man who made the tempest in Baluba
Der im Baluba das Gewitter gemacht hat . . .
   they spell words with a drum beat,
"The country is overbrained" said the hungarian nobleman
in 1923 Kosouth (Ku' shoot) sued, I understand
To sit in a café — all done by conversation —
It was all done by conversation,
  possibly because one repeats the point when conversing:
"Vienna contains a mixture of races."
   wd. I stay and be Bhudd-ha?
"They are accustomed to having an Emperor. They must have
Something to worship. (1927)"
But their humour about losing the Tyrol?
Their humour is not quite so broad.
The ragged arab spoke with Frobenius and told him
The names of 3000 plants.
   Bruhl found some languages full of detail

Words that half mimic action; but
generalization is beyond them, a white dog is
not, let us say, a dog like a black dog.
Do not happen, Romeo and Juliet . . . unhappily
I have lost the cutting but apparently
such things do still happen, he
suicided outside her door while
the family was preparing her body for burial,
and she knew that this was the case.

Green, black, December. Said Mr Blodgett:
"Sewing machines will never come into general use.

"I have of course never said that the cash is constant
(Douglas) and in fact the population (Britain 1914)
was left with 800 millions of *"deposits"*
after all the cash had been drawn, and
these deposits were satisfied by the
    printing of treasury notes.
A factory
has also another aspect, which we call the financial aspect
It gives people the power to buy (wages, dividends
which are power to buy) but it is also the cause of prices
or values, financial, I mean financial values
It pays workers, and pays *for* material.
What it pays in wages and dividends
stays fluid, as power to buy, and this power is less,
per forza, damn blast your intellex, is less
than the total payments made by the factory
(as wages, dividends AND payments for raw material
bank charges etcetera
and all, that is the whole, that is the total
of these is added into the total of prices
caused by that factory, any damn factory
and there is and must be therefore a clog
and the power to purchase can never
(under the present system) catch up with
prices at large,

    and the light became so bright and so blindin'
in this layer of paradise
    that the mind of man was bewildered.

Said Herr Krupp (1842): guns are a merchandise
I approach them from the industrial end,
I approach them from the technical side,
1847 orders from Paris and Egypt . . . .
            orders from the Crimea,
Order of Pietro il Grande,
            and a Command in the Legion of Honour . . .
500 to St. Petersburg and 30 to Napoleon Barbiche
from Creusot. At Sadowa
            Austria had some Krupp cannon;
            Prussia had some Krupp cannon.
"The Emperor ('68) is deeply in'erested in yr. catalogue
and in yr. services to humanity"
                                (signed) Leboeuf
who was a relative of Monsieur Schneider
1900 fifty thousand operai,
            53 thousand cannon, about half for his country,
Bohlen und Halbach,
            Herr Schneider of Creusot
Twin arse with one belly.
Eugene, Adolf and Alfred "more money from guns than from
    tractiles"
Eugene was sent to the deputies;
            (Saone et Loire) to the Deputies, minister;
Later rose to be minister,
            "guns coming from anywhere,
but appropriations from the Chambers of Parliaments"
In 1874 rcd. license for free exportation
Adopted by 22 nations
1885/1900 produced ten thousand cannon
to 1914, 34 thousand
one half of them sent out of the country
always in the chamber of deputies, always a conservative,
Schools, churches, orspitals fer the workin' man
Sand piles fer the children.
Opposite the Palace of the Schneiders
            Arose the monument to Herr Henri
Chantiers de la Gironde, Bank of the Paris Union,
The franco-japanese bank
            François de Wendel, Robert Protot
To friends and enemies of tomorrow
"the most powerful union is doubtless

            that of the Comité des Forges,"
"And God take your living" said Hawkwood
15 million: Journal des Débats
30 million paid to Le Temps
Eleven for the Echo de Paris
Polloks on Schneider patents
Our bank has bought us
            a lot of shares in Mitsui
Who arm 50 divisions, who keep up the Japanese army
and they are destined to have a large future
"faire passer ces affairs
            avant ceux de la nation."

e. e. cummings

From eimi

> cummings was one of the Twenties figures who refused to knuckle down to Thirties premises. He had defied the intellectuals who had rationalized American participation in World War I, in his novel The Enormous Room *(1922)*, and written tender, inimitable verses, collected in such books as & *(1925)* and is 5 *(1926)*. eimi *(1933) was a critical account of his visit to Russia. It had all but no influence on the period, though it was one of its distinguished writings.*

(O what a comrade stomachache)
   the was of canned fish which vaguely recall sampling, among other à la russe hors d'oeuvres?
   or that glass of waterless? or
   (heat —
"well it's hot in this room" towerful Chinesey (the gradual knock proved his) opines gradually, gradually disappearing)
   — or 1 bath . . . heavenpointing (language having failed) ogress recently compelled this O how helplessness to agonies of steam . . . scarcely could who locate tubplug . . . scarcely could, fainting, yank same from its suctionloved socket

From eimi [245

(hey nonny no; & today absolutely must follow up twain long since mailed without result letters of introduction from Americans-living-in-Paris to a brace of socialist families
 —probably "just nervousness". Cause: not being seduced by 1 very husbandful gentlemenprefer at 1 very polyglot soirèe intimest —
 "a submarine?" respond I dimly, re Harem's O distant cry
 "lost in the gulf of Finland. Cable just arrived."
 "Tell me" severely asks K "have you—"
 "almost dead" cheerfully she agrees. "But I shall eat breakfast if it's the last thing—"

"comrade" assailing lathered Turk "as one tovarich hangover to another, what should not be undone about this comrade's exit visa and god knows how many—"
 "there's" lathered faintly recommends "no sense in worrying, especially in Russia. Just you make a little list for Nat—write down quite illegibly everything which you don't want not to know—and then very carefully put that list where the ogress will be perfectly sure to throw it away. The rest" he added, sopping blood "is silence, unless—but please don't let me go against your better nature—unless you should presently feel like perhaps dropping any soiled object into yonder socalled laundrybag"
 "I cannot" almost tearfully "impose . . ."
 "you" busily "New Englanders are a very curious" sopping "folk. Folk you" he, beaming, said.

Irremediably bent upon delivering gifts, young Joseph left the Hotel Metropole; more or less mistaking himself for comrade Santa Claus. Now, for a change, I bear no burden beyond knapsack containing 1 immense coffeecan (its lid, battered by customs-comrades at N, is secured with a precious substance called "string" which I've permittedly stolen from 1 of the lathered's "ten thousand gifts") plus 2 books
 goal, those socialist families, fortunately lies in general direction of Western Art
 mail nyet — what care I?
 battle into number 34 tram.
 Un (having allowed others to cut the forward swath) torn, descend (smothered in dismay — for we found no kopeks; then the **outraged tickettakeress bawled Comrades, pass your change: a Rouble has arrived!**) near oasis, trudge dimly to Kropotkin perio-

olok; dimly left, along shady little streetless, past 3 smirking striplings; and without care enter a positively black courtyard.

Now of these portals which might harbour a certain socialist family? — Not here! (this unold nonman washing these 9/8faded thinglesses recoils: terrified, when I pronounce dimly the name) — Not here! (that's all she can say)

& carelessly beat retreat; overturning almost that "cultivated" looking (that not young) nonman — who points, wordless, across the yard to a cleaner than others (newer) portal

knock.

A child opens

"yah americanitz"

— he semisomersaults with joy! rushes (ecstatically crying Come in!) down a short (The American is here!) hall.   Returns, joyous; beckons

2 nonmen adorn a sunful porchless.   1 (Hausfrauish, ample) = larger version of Jill — 1 (tranquil, grandmothery)=something from my past? White ample sit-bulges in a spicandspan frock. Neatandclean grandmother smile-rocks in a black shawl. Both greet myself cordially

I'm sorry not (white sputters French) to have answered the kind note which you wrote us but you know we really couldn't tell where you were because three times a comrade friend came to your hotel with his new film which he greatly wished you to see and three times your hotel didn't know your address or who you were or anything about you . . .

How interesting (marvel) — I certainly remember giving the Metropole my address, although you probably don't believe that

O (she assured) yes I do indeed.   It's not your fault; not anybody's fault: just a Russian habit. Well, you came here anyway! Sadly enough — (cheerfully naming her husband) isn't returning until tomorrow or the day after. He's been for several weeks away on business.   It's the cultural park, you know.   That's one reason I couldn't come out myself to your hotel: now let me (exiting produce another reason

And how do you find yourself liking our country? (genially asks in French French grandmother)

I am (K, dimly) confused

(smiling) Very natural!

(enter white; by child pridefully escorted and proudly bearing reason number 2 — a babyboy bouncing beyond description . . . whom catching) "citoyen russe" (proud grandmother announces) "il est fier" (and he is) dit K

"oui, il est fier!" (black agrees; then, proudestly from fier to me smiling) "le citoyen russe vous salut!"

The American citizen salutes the Russian citizen (to fier I bow. He burps) and proudly delivers to the Russian citizen a slight but sincere token of esteem from certain of his American friends

—O! (everybody, including the baby, shouts. And gloating, and sniffing) "café!" (And white and black and child and citizen exclaim transportedly) "merveilleux!"

My husband can speak (white, coming to her senses sighs) only Russian, with German — see; here's a translation on which we're working together (K's foot in time spears flying page) thanks... but I'd like you to meet my husband. Well, how about dinner tomorrow, provided he's here? So: you're stopping with friends — well, give me your present telephone number and I'll call up later and we'll arrange things: O, and will you please take the telephone number of our friend whose wonderful film you (carefully white does not mention said friend's address: uncarefully I wonder if said friend ever came to the Metropole) absolutely must see. You yourself are living where? "Merci. C'est entendu"

What! (black grandmother) you haven't yet visited the cultural park? (I promise to see it, provided there's time between now and my next socialist family) — why, that's a very important thing (she solemnly said).

There's one mighty handsome church not far — (before I thought) what's its name, please? (Look of pitying scorn from black to ample. Of altruegoism... then, calmly, black names the golddomed; adding calmly

You've witnessed Bread?)

What bread?

Bread the play (severely)

O; yes (dimly) indeed

Such a crisis exists in America (white announces, quite as though myself were 1 Tibetan)

(ignorantly) "oui?"

(black, rock-) O yes! (ing grandmother, serenely, nods) all our friends are coming back to Russia. Of course it's expensive —

He (meaning bouncingest) eats two potatoes (white cries joyfully) he's a three rouble boy!

—I say it's very expensive (grandmother resumes) here in Russia. But (grimly: And How) here only there is HOPE

Yes? (gentlyest; K)

(heartily at whom) "BZFGL" (leering the citizen observes)

no more 4 P.M. . . . no cultural park today. Find the named domes; at carrefour turn left.   Enter, through a sticky gate, grey courtyard: grown little nonmen sit in pale sunlight (& in a sort of garden wanders a little ungrown nonman) — bow; present my 2nd envelope of introduction; the grown chatter, point: left, straight ahead — bowing, K enters a portal.   Climbs, dark: darker . . . in darkest of halls looms another, a huge, nonman further who directs me

Come in! (perfectly as my Russian teacher had pronounced it; almost that might be her voice

but a depthful darkness dogless) spy (at lower end of highceilinged which) 3 mediumsize (1 seemingly young, outslouching lazily and whose undress reminds of uncouth rougeetnoir backlesses sported at The Last Decisive) non-s.   A tall a forbidding a nonfemale nonfigure advancing toward myself

I, American (state; hastily adding the living-in-Paris names which mean apparently nothing to advancing. Who courteously invites me to sit down)

"do you speak English" (timidly inquire)

"ay-yuh leet-el"

"books—cadeau: please!"

"she-yuh ah-oot, wark" (feel from depth negatively hostile stares)

"I" (sitting) "write: name — mine, address — mine"

& the room entirely bulges . . . tall pulls curtain

"telephone" (writing; noting that outslouching is not so old)" — mine"

"gallantly I give you" Turks uplifts gallantly his tiny brimming "the Soviet flies!"

"where?" confrère

"in my vodka, not to mention yours.   —Drink them lady. They are socialist."

"They taste socialist" she scowled

"impossible" Assyrian contradicts "all -ists are tasteless."

"Do you know Bread?" I beg, toasting

"Bread the play? — da"

"having said I did, I feel I ought to"

"briefly" he proclaims "Bread is this. The man loses the girl and wins the day."

"No more flies" (she refuses).   "Which day?"

"my dear — you ask that? why, the socialist day, of course."

"And who wins the girl" K queries

"Oh, the lover wins the girl; but the lover loses the peasants. Therefore the husband, who's also the man, bawls the lover who wins the girl out.   So the girl, who's also the husband's wife, accuses the husband who loses the girl of personal antagonism; whereat the husband is" Assyrian said "aghast."

(Capitalistically) "there seems" (comrade K mutters) "to be a good deal of aghastness kicking around here"

"but, comrade, what can you expect" he asks "when everybody mistrusts everybody because every- . . . — have a bite to eat with us, Nat?"

"no" (entering ½) "thank you" (English haughtily) "very much." But, relenting, does not refuse 1 coffee, 1 cakelet. And she's on her way to her family.   Mellowing, presents Assyrian with a "story, I got it all by myself" about particularly cheap store recently opened for noble comrades who've done their 5 years in a year (whereupon he "good girl" congratulates and Turkess "what would you do without Nat?") then, admitting hunger, rises: bows, goes . . .

"voilà" he said gently.   "The very thing we were discussing. Nat's just as nice as she can be (whenever I lose my temper with Nat I'm genuinely ashamed of myself — though she can be enormously stupid!) and my confère gives Nat clothes and I try and everyone tries to help the poor girl . . . but — do you know something? I can't trust her."

Face of comrade peesahtel expresses wonder

"not that she's dishonest" Turkess said.

"Quite the contrary" agrees Turk "Nat's as honest as the day. Which makes everything much, much worse for everybody, especially for Nat" pause.   "I simply can't trust her with messages to embassies, for instance — it's not that she wants to spy; she's compelled to answer the comrades' questions. So I have to go myself, or send my socalled literary secretary who's an American girl." Pause.   "Never" spilling wearily himself over couch "trust a Russian . . ."

and enters dreamland.

Dreamily "I hate war" the Turkess said

"as a woman, you should" peesahtel affirms

"you mean, war destroys what women create?"

"war is your only rival, I mean.   Or isn't it? — both woman and war being essentially . . .shall we say Sexual Phenomena?"

she thought.   And asked "what's sexual about war?"

"everything is. Not that I've gone over the top with a dreamgirl clenched in a heart of gold and a kind of a knife on the end of a gun, or anything like that . . . little me has only fallen into the merciful mud by day. And by night I've only seen such flowers cruelly opening . . . if there's anything more sexual, probably it's — "

"you mean something by Sexual that I don't" she said.

"I mean intense. Magic, I mean. Among those flowers, nothing is real merely. Everything strictly which they touch or which I feel somehow is transformed; is dreamlike, amazing, actual. Every actually amazing universe — really which has been asleep in (say) a piece of steel or a mountain or an eyelid or particular kind of darkness or hunger or the rain or this or that word or any silence or some gesture — wakes: lives"

"I know a" she muses "girl whose son had to have his toe amputated. And she was ecstatic — No army for him! she cried"

"I want" comrade poietes said "all my toes and I'm sorry for the son; but let him join an ambulance corps when the time — "

". . . well, I'll finish typing Charlie's stuff . . ."

that (awakening who observes) man with the goatee and the mysterious smile equals "a glimpse of old Russia." Had the misfortune, the tragedy, to be born "a gentleman" — son and grandson of landowners; fled from the bolsheviki: returned during nep. "The type of fellow they don't want" in communist Moscow; but goatee "has languages; so he probably earns two hundred and fifty roubles monthly . . . it occurs to me, by the way, that you might get a thousand roubles if you wanted to sell your typewriter"

"how much?" I gasp

"a thousand roubles. Don't stare. In purchasing power, a thousand roubles is not five hundred dollars. It's about one hundred"

"my portable cost only forty dollars new; maybe it was thirty-five"

"yes. But do you remember those Russian boys with that American nailpuller? — let's try it, anyway: I'll have-in a buyingandselling tovarich to look at your wondrous wordmaker, and then we'll see." (P.S. he didn't get the job.) "O — here's" departing "an article which might possibly"

(called Pioneer Americans in Russia. "The American engineer is the 20th century's man in the covered wagon" and "master of the machine, Soviet Russia's god." "Feed an American and you have a civilized being. Half starve him or ration him and you have a savage" — luxury and efficiency being (Marx save the mark!) inextricably intertwined. Capitalist U.S.A. is the model of Soviet

From eimi [251

Russia's 5 year plan, but "the Russian's idea of the shortest distance between two points is a circle" (... isn't it?)) ... Voiceless of a nonman whom I've somewhere met. Probably in this very house. She's by French-English bargaining with Turkess in the hall, re trinkets. Enter(yes; I saw her upstairs, with Chinesey: & she might have been handsome once?) training a powerful pair of eyes upon meless ... enter now a plumper harder nonman ... Now 4 comrades stroll to Turk's "office" where the Turk's tovariching with 2 tovariches — the cheery youth of the rainy day, he with the Oxford accent, and another ... 7 comrades now are mounting this by heat murdered perioolok

"excuse me" (Oxford quoth) "but — are you a ... what is that —. Poyayta?"

(accept the compliment)

"I've heard of you" (he said cheerfully. Pause). "That" whispering, pointing to Harem "is the first time I've seen a woman wearing evening-dress in Moscow" (and right merrily chuckles)

at Tverskaya cheerioing, with his Englishless friend.

"Her husband" to me confrère whispers, indicating bargaining eyes "who's now in exile for ten years — perhaps his sentence will be commuted — has translated some of your poems"

Kem-min-kz stared.

"That's a fact" the Turk whispering nods

"and she speaks French" the confrère said

halt 5 comrades; gallantly while Assyrian coaxes wilted muguet from that shrugging curbstoneghost: beflowered, we wiltingly proceed

(O Paris! I dream) — noone speaks freely here (I try eyes)

"personne!" eyes replies: and burst into Russian

"but certain" to Turk "artists have their own revolution" K insists "compared with which, the socalled social revolution isn't worth ... I won't say"

"yes" shyly "don't tell her" (winking toward eyes) "that"

& at god's — it seems we've been on our way to god — door, Assyrian holds me; whispering "the flesh is weak. The comrades ask questions. Careful"

god introduces nobody (everyone — including Chinesey, more than ever submarine, and the gentlemanly more than ever censors of censors and not exmentor and not comrade Gorky — seems to be chez god ce soir). God says that if his guests can't get acquainted without being introduced they're a lot of somethings (& quite tight he is; & very genial). I'm through a welter of 30 or perhaps it was 40 very singularly untovarich really males and females espying somebody ... who's all dressed up fit to kill, why it's Nat! when

"how long have you been here?" asks casually briskly total (short of stature and mighty of eyeglasses) stranger

"not long"

"how long are you staying?"

"not long"

"did you come with anybody?"

name names

"I'm from the embassy" he said jauntily, looking a little like a goldfish (and, drawing me cornerward, fully describes during several brief businesslike minutes each and every person of personality chez god) "how do you like it here?"

"I feel" truthfully I assert "as if I were standing on my own head"

The total hms, smiles. "Well" he cried crisply "it's like this" — then (slowly and very (very very) softly) "people here are DOING something ... but whether it succeeds or not is quite UNimportant ... and nobody GIVES a damn!"

vanishes

Are you married? (eyes)

"oui" (K)

Do you love your wife? (Chinesey is watching; submarine)

"oui"

(sighing) I was with my husband and now I am alone

— whereupon (Marx bless her!) Nat suggests dancing ... Nat dances as Nat exists, in ½s (eyes watches)

"Maintenant!" (eyes shining)

&, all her selves skilfully to mine gluing, copiously eyes-&-K Inc. meander among watching abundantly And How watchers ... "vous êtes un merveilleux dancer" ... "et vous, madame" ... until

"AGH — mon coeur!" (it clutching; which was knocking to be let out? She sat down

)look around meless

everywhere a terrific (modelled and remodelled and unmodelled by always drinkbringing Mammy Sunshine) putty of nonproletarian of badly thirsting of nobodies — deeplycynically on whom beams the more and more distingué censor of censors; communists don't drink. Whereas the a little drinking Doctor Chinesey more avoids and more these brightly dressed these screaming flatly these lurching dolls ("and nobody GIVES a damn")

Are you acquainted with Dos Passos?

"oui"

From eimi [253

A very great friend. Every evening in Moscow we went to low dumps. I can see him now, dancing, with his —
"first" Nat's ½ and ½ voice shrills above tumult "we shall have" (god pounds for hush) "gypsy songs. Then" (her shrill drowns — "SHUT UP" god yells: unnoise) "we shall have the gypsy dances. I take very greatest pleasure to introduce the very greatest singer in the world" (Turk, almost hidden behind 1 female back of beef, grins) "which will sing now for us the first song." Murmurs . . . as putty pushed by amok god and frantic Mammy forms horseshoelike hole —
occurs, mothered and smothered by hairy vagabondloverish impressario (almost who might be a burlesk edition of comrade Something) unremarkable singing. Then, dancing dishonours having been equally shared by a fatarmed partially dusky hoor and a tiny earnest negroid tart (both immeasurably under wraps) emerges now 1 song, beginning and rebeginning with a moist dark tone; cringily climbing (tumbling; crazily, upyearning) collapsing: smoothly, and languidly, building . . .
"d'amour?" consult now the now ringside Assyrian
"redhot" who nods
— suddenly enter 1 lusciously young female. Timidly who embarks upon the very most completely censored shimmy imaginable . . . uproar: the (hole-in-head having tactfully departed) male population squirms with untrammelled ecstasy. And squirms. But sans remuneration: even god can only make a tree, shyly female (and hurriedly) disappears . . . A motley flock of dittyless ditties "in the" (comrade Nat announcing) "gypsy language" tramples hopeless hope beyond repair.
Hopeless hope thereat invades boisterous banquethall (or god's study, to whose minor side is tacked a porchless) and promptly is greeted with caviarful closeup of our genial host in the actless of presenting the if possible more genial guest-of-honour: Wood was unfortunately that man's name. "Unfortunately" because Wood scarcely is known unto all men when 1 of these twain Quiets (whom our heroless had erstwhile encountered chez Chinesey) uprears his much applauded head and — "spEEsh!" wails god: Dum bows. An hush is with difficulty propagated. Mammy instantly falls through the doorway; while a dinnercoat from which most carelessly she'd not detached herself curls most carefully over backwards even without spilling his Tom Collins. Reigns havoc. And unreigns. Eventualy Dum speaks
— in numbers! (for the numbers came. Sometimes with diffi-

culty, sometimes perhaps a thoughtless thought too easily; but by and large and considering Dum's an engineer — or perhaps that's why — uniformly). On, on, on they march, Dum's uniformly verses properly preceded by the cross of capitalism, during all of 3 whole agonizing minutes and once only are (per somebody's godgiven how prodigious hiccough) punctuated . . . each and every (need we say it?) verse comprises, willy-nilly, nolens volens, a freakish, an even treacherous, ambiguity (or socalled wordplay) re Mr. guestless-of-dishonour i.e. Wood's helpless nomenclature.

& I here solemnly pray, devoutly I here beseech, that — whatsoever may or may not happen — this here comrade will neither do a Daphne nor be a Dum (which of which horrifying alternatives were the more perfectly degrading, your correspondent knows not. He knows only that Wood endured to the endless end; arose — by any other name — ducked twice Wood's head toward everybody: grinned, and said

"thangs"

. . .)

shortly after, this here contrives the pretty acquaintance of a Miss Spenceish (previously cornered by Turk) young lady whose papa follows Dum's calling. Lady whose whole family — including grandma — inhabits Russia (it we're more than less successfully attempting to cause to disappear when porchfinding Queen Mab, née eyes, appears: vigilantly to demand

you have eaten?)

"oui"

"which" the also appearing Turkess unvigilantly asks "of that" pointing "pink lady's legs do you think's the cork one?"

"the left" I guess. "Which?"

"I don't know" she admitted. "Have you met Duranty?"

"where is he?"

"sh. Right opposite us" (an earnest if a jovial poise between tovarich and human being. Seatedly who argues, cheerfully, with a standing heatedly how protesting tuxedo) — "good law! Here's a 'meric'n chile who aint got no gin fizz!" cries Sunshine, handing me same — "do you want to meet him?" the Harem asked

"nn-nn. He's busy. —Any more one-legged people at this party?"

"at this party" she mused "there are many, many threelegged people — O: see that gal? Look out" wandering "she's a reporter"

. . . too late. "Are you Mr —"

"he is my halfbrother — "

"well, I'm connected with" and a very huge connection indeed;

From eimi [255

my halfbrother's favorite yellow journal, in fact. "Would you mind saying something —"
"never speak"
"—anything you like."
"Merde" I said
"I mean, about Russia."
"Russia? is that a disease?"
"is it?"
"I wouldn't know. I haven't got it"
"don't be silly: you're in it."
"I may be in it" grimly K states "but it isn't in me."
Wearily she smiled; sighing "then you won't tell me what you think of — "
K (staring) "for god's sake: do I look like that?"
pause. "No" she said "you don't. All right . . . sorry"
"EYE play TENNIS" cried suddenly entering god's study American "do YOU play TENNIS?"
probably my face expressed doubt; at any rate,
"—DO you?" he cried
and vanished.
"You are from New England, aren't you?" (hysterical, whisperless)
"I was born in Cambridge Massachusetts" our heroless admits
"tell me" this not-quite-woman with dishevelled locks not quite gasps "isn't it wonderful"
"isn't what wonderful" heroless counters cautiously, cautiously edging over into a porchcorner
"everything" ecstatically. And How
"that it isn't" I cheerfully contradict (and wondering if porchless will endure her enthusiasm)
"You're joking!"
"look" said K "there's a street. With houses on both sides of it. And look — there are windows in the houses. —Miraculous!"
a blank stare of complete incredulity "but Don't you See?"
"were you also born in Cambridge Maasachusetts?" comrade K suggests
"yes" dishevelled nods "I was."
"Listen" I said. And she listened. For 5 or 6 or even 7 minutes. But no puns. And her faceless turned the hue of drunkard's puke; her arms tried to make gestures: and (desperate, quivering, amazed) she
b-b-b-b-B-BU-BUT!"
"take off those machineguns" we command "I know you"

"— but . . . you — " upwrithingly "you're just like A Little Boy!" sheless sobbed.

"Not just like" K begged.

"Yes!" sheless howled. "Just like!"

"no. Not just like. I Am a little boy" pause

"are you?" (wonderingly)

"and I like little boys. I like children. Perhaps —" turning through doorway suddenly perceive titanic squabble between god and Wood " — it's just possible"

— "you got My rushn Hat" god shrieked "haven't Either" Wood yelled "You got Mine" —

"that, being a child (and not ashamed) I actually feel these people (actually who are children) directly, entirely; and not as per theories"

her face stopped. Vaguely "you . . . you're not horrible, are you . . ."

"horrible?" politely we recoil

herselfless recoiling — "don't! don't, please don't! — You mustn't!" screams she faintly "you have No Right to put such ideas into my head!"

"if there's any right, you mustn't, you have no right to have been born in Cambridge"

"no but don't you really think — "

"down with thinking. Vive feeling!"

bitterly "the world needs thinking!" her unself insists

"are you the world?"

defiantly "I'm a part of it!" and contemptuous " — but you're really not!"

"quite so. Actually, the world is a part of me. And — I'll egocentrically tell the world — a very small part"

Robinson Jeffers

BATTLE (MAY-JUNE, 1940)

Jeffers, like cummings, had put the individual above society, and, in such books of verse as Roan Stallion *(1925) and* Dear Judas *(1929), emphasized man's primal urges and dark odysseys. The coming of World War II shocked Jeffers into the somber and touching*

Battle (May-June, 1940)

reflections which follow. Although they just miss the Thirties period proper, they help demonstrate that as gray and desperate as the pre-World War II era seemed, it still assumed humanistic principles which mass bombings and other phenomena of all-out war soon brought into question.

Foreseen for so many years: these evils, this monstrous violence,
    these massive agonies: no easier to bear.
We saw them with slow stone strides approach, everyone saw them;
    we closed our eyes against them, we looked
And they had come nearer. We ate and drank and slept, they came
    nearer. Sometimes we laughed, they were nearer. Now
They are here. And now a blind man foresees what follows them:
    degradation, famine, recovery and so forth, and the
Epidemic manias: but not enough death to serve us, not enough
    death. It would be better for men
To be few and live far apart, where none could infect another; then
    slowly the sanity of field and mountain
And the cold ocean and glittering stars might enter their minds.
                                            Another
    dream, another dream.
We shall have to accept certain limitations
In future, and abandon some humane dreams; only hard-minded,
    sleepless and realist, can ride this rock-slide
To new fields down the dark mountain; and we shall have to per-
    ceive that these insanities are normal;
We shall have to perceive that battle is a burning flower or like a
    huge music, and the dive-bomber's screaming orgasm
As beautiful as other passions; and that death and life are not
    serious alternatives. One has known all these things
For many years: there is greater and darker to know
In the next hundred.
                      And why do you cry, my dear, why do you cry?
It is all in the whirling circles of time.
If millions are born millions must die,
If England goes down and Germany up
The stronger dog will still be on top,
All in the turning of time.
If civilization goes down, that
Would be an event to contemplate.
It will not be in our time, alas, my dear,
It will not be in our time.

'TIS THE FINAL CONFLICT

Communism is Twentieth Century Americanism.

Earl Browder, in 1937

They say the red arm of the Proletariat swings
Hammer and Sickle, a quarter moon in the sky,
The dogstar comets leap . . .

Horace Gregory, in *Poems 1930-1940* (1941)

Heywood Broun

FOUR TOPICAL PIECES

REDDER THAN THE ROOSEVELTS

A KIND client has sent to me my dossier from Mrs. Albert Dilling's *The Red Network,* which unfortunately I had not read at all. This single all-too-slender biography has sold the book to still another customer. I am fascinated not only by the subject matter but caught up with the manner of the telling. The style is terse and also free. Mrs. Dilling is, I suspect, own cousin to the Garble sisters whose dialogues are featured by Hi Phillips in his Sun Dial column.

But let me quote and try to show how completely an endearing revolutionary can be limned within the span of a couple of sticks. Had they been chafed together, think of the fire which might have been engendered. That is not the Dilling method. Dispassionately the author states her case and lets the reader soak it in. Here goes:

Broun, Heywood: New York *World-Telegram* newspaperman; resigned from Socialist Party recently, saying, it was reported, that it was not radical enough for him; Rand School; wife, Ruth Hale of Lucy Stone Lg., went to Boston to help stage last-minute Sacco-V. protest meeting (N. Y. *Post,* Aug. 10, 1927); ousted as columnist for N. Y. *World* because of friction over his abuse of the authorities in the Sacco-V. matter; at once engaged by radical *Nation*; principal speaker at Level Club, N. Y. C., blacklist party of speakers barred by D.A.R. as subversives, May 9, 1928. James Weldon Johnson, colored radical, was master of ceremonies and mock trial for revocation of D.A.R. charter was held, Norman Thomas being the judge and Arthur Garfield Hays one of the attorneys; nat. com. W.I.R., 1929; nat. com. W.R. Lg., 1930-1; L.I.D. (bd. dir.,) April, 1931); Recep. Com. Soviet Fliers; Fed. Unemp. Wkrs. Lgs. N. Y., 1933; contrib. *New Masses,* 1933; Nat. Scottsboro Com. of Action, 1933; Emer. Com., Strike Rel., 1933; Il Nuovo Mondo Nat. Com.; sup-

Four Topical Pieces [261

porter Rand Sch., 1933; nat. coun. Berger Nat. Found.; Nat. Com. to Aid Vic. G. Fascism; pres. and org. Am. Newspaper Guild, 1933; Conf. Prog. Pol. Act., 1933-4; Roosevelt appointee, Theatrical Code Authority, 1933.

It is true that I am the pres. but I am not the org. of the Am. Newspaper Guild and most bitterly do I wish to enter a denial of the last accusation hurled by Mrs. Dilling. President Roosevelt did not appoint me to the Theatrical Code Authority. In all fairness to Mrs. Dilling it must be admitted that she did not weave this serious charge out of whole cloth. I must admit that I sat at one hearing before the theatrical code administrator and that Mrs. Rumsey had informed me that I was there to represent the consuming public. But I was not alone in this reckless deed. Side by side with me sat Joseph Wood Krutch, who, as I later learned, is bd. of eds. and drm. etc., and lit. etc. of the *Nat.* At the end of the session, in which William A. Brady, thr. pd., made a long and eloquent speech, a Mr. Rosenblatt asked me if I wanted to say anything. I told him no. He then asked Joseph Wood Krutch, ed. radical *Nat.*, who was almost as eloquent. I was informed that I could get my expenses by turning in an account at the proper office but it happened to be at the far end of the Commerce Building on one of the uncharted corridors and so I said, "Oh, what the hl. I'll stake my country to the $6.15." And that, as Jvh. (Bibl. dty.) is my witness, is the only warrant for the charge that I was appointed to the Thl. Cd. Athy.

That was all the consuming or the theatrical public ever heard from me. And in justice to Mr. Rosenblatt it should be added that undoubtedly when he asked me if I had anything to say he was not cognizant of the fact that I was nat. com. W.I.R. In bringing this matter to light I'll freely confess that Mrs. Dilling has me worried. Indeed, this one revelation in *The Red Network* keeps me tossing and turning at night. Like the young lady in the song, I couldn't say yes and I couldn't say no. Nor is it sufficient to ask indulgence on account of the fact that this was way back in 1929 when I was a young man only nineteen years out of college. How on earth can I explain or justify my being nat. com. W.I.R. when I have not the slightest recollection of what the W.I.R. may be?

Of course, it could be World Institute Reds or Wabbling Into Republicanism. Or for that matter the When in Rome Society. The best I can do is to say that, whether I was a W.I.R. or not in the past, its purposes and its practices elude me now. I can truthfully say that I haven't been to any W.I.R. dance, banquet, or business meeting in the last five years. It must be that I was trying to forget and in this I have succeeded admirably. But there is just one tragic possibility. Perhaps Mrs. Dilling has also forgotten. Come on, Mrs. D., be a good scout and tell me what the W.I.R. is or was so that I can make amends and once more sleep peacefully at night.

Mrs. Dilling has fallen into an inaccuracy in stating that Broun, Heywood (with a little better detective work she might have dug out the "Campbell" for the middle) was "ousted as columnist for N. Y. *World* because of friction over his abuse of authorities in the Sacco-V. matter." My abuse of the authorities did lead to a situation during which I absented myself from the columns of the *World* for several months. That was of my own volition. I got fired by Ralph Pulitzer, almost a year later, after I had returned to the job. The offense was an article in the "radical *Nation*" attacking the editorial policy of the N. Y. *World* as administered largely by Walter Lippmann, p.s.b. Lest there be confusion I may state that p.s.b. is in no sense a radical organization. Some of the most respectable people in the American community belong to it. I appointed them myself. Nicholas Murray Butler is a member and William Randolph Hearst might very appropriately be the org. of this large and inclusive fraternal organization. Madison Square Garden being solidly booked for the season, the members of the p.s.b. have no clubhouse at the moment, although I believe guest privileges have been offered them by the S.N.S.S. — Society of Native Stuffed Shirts.

But to get back to Mrs. Dilling and her all-too-brief biography of Broun, Heywood. Much as I regret to say it, I feel that we have both failed. She has not made out her case and I do not deserve the accolade she has offered. As I read the account of the activities of this *"World-Telegram* newspaperman" I find, not the solid outlines of a red, but merely the portrait of a joiner. Better luck next time, Mrs. D.

> *After a lifetime of battling Big Business, Al Smith became violently pro-management after what he considered to be a betrayal by Roosevelt in 1932, when Roosevelt ran for President instead of supporting him, the Happy Warrior. Al saddened his old friends by speaking at Liberty League affairs, and becoming president of the corporation that bought the Empire State Building, and associating with Du Ponts.*

AMONG THOSE PRESENT

WASHINGTON, Jan. 27 [1936]. — Clara was crying. The rest of the Liberty Leaguers were either laughing or applauding. Al was discussing the issues of the day and he had just said, "I have five children and I have ten grandchildren." Or possibly it was at a later point where he attacked demagogues and cried out in a stirring voice, "There can be only one Capital – Washington or Moscow." At any rate, Clara was crying all over what Jouett Shouse described as "our simple, modest $5 dinner."

"What's the matter, Clara?" asked the gentleman who brought her, "aren't you having a good time?" She lifted her tear-stained face and said, "He's saving the republic."

If I had not been at the party and had merely read the oration it might have been enough to say, "An old man from a tall tower vented an ancient grudge." But, strangely enough, Al Smith did not dominate the evening. At times he seemed no more than some lightning-change artist who had come out from behind the potted palms to amuse the guests.

The whole thing seemed unreal. Certainly it was surprising to hear Al Smith begin a speech with a reference to his wife and end it with the Bible and the American flag. Almost any moment you expected to hear somebody interrupt to say, "This program comes to you through the courtesy of –." Yes, that was the mood, and the announcement might have run, "This program comes through the courtesy of the shade of Mark Hanna and the ghost of Thomas Platt."

As I looked about I almost expected to see Boies Penrose with a crowd at a table just below the speaker's spot on the dais. Of course, I didn't. John W. Davis had that table. And even so one did not feel that we were dining in the land of the living. Practically all the guests seemed to have stepped from a page of Art Young caricatures done during the gay '90s.

It is true Al Smith stopped just this side of attacking the popular election of Senators, but here seemed to be men who saved us from Populism in 1896. This was the guard which dies but never surrenders, the legion dedicated to the theory that the status quo shall not perish from this earth. And they laughed so long and so loud and clapped their hands so heartily that the sound of masses marching was scarcely audible.

"I talked to my workers, 900 of them," said the gray-haired man behind me, "and I told them just what Al is saying tonight. I told them that they'd have to work their fingers off for every last nickel they ever earned, that it always had been so and it always would be so and, by gad, sir, I made them like it."

But now Al was swinging into the question of taxation, and you could have heard a diamond bar pin drop.

"There are three classes of people in this country," said Al, "there are the poor and the rich and in between the two is what has often been referred to as the great backbone of America — that is, the plain fellow. That is the fellow that makes from $100 a month up to the man that draws down $5,000 or $6,000 a year. Now, there is a great big army. Forget the rich; they can't pay this debt. If you took everything they have away from them they couldn't pay it; they ain't got enough."

And the big ballroom of the Mayflower rang with the happy applause of the diners who sat there trying to hide their proud poverty behind brave laughter.

The speaker spoke of those who believe in a liberal interpretation of the Constitution and said, "What I have held all during my public life is that Almighty God is with this country and He didn't give us that kind of Supreme Court."

The Liberty League paid a generous tribute of applause to the Almighty in recognition of His sound principles.

The man introduced as Al Smith hurried on to compare the Constitution with the Bible and finished with a tribute to our National Anthem and our National Emblem. Everybody jumped up and cheered except Clara and myself. I had joined her in weeping. I wept because the Happy Warrior was dead.

Among those present were Felix A. du Pont, Jr.; A. V. du Pont, Mrs. A. V. du Pont, Emile F. du Pont, Eugene E. du Pont, Henry B. du Pont, Mrs. H. B. du Pont, Irenee du Pont, Mrs. Irenee du Pont, Miss Octavia du Pont, Pierre S. du Pont and Mrs. Pierre S. du Pont.

HOOVER SPEAKING

CLEVELAND, June 12 [1936]. — As one who does not like Herbert Hoover I must admit that at least he went down swinging. Indeed, he hit a couple over the fence which were not foul by more than a couple of hundred feet. But I do not wish to be too fulsome in my flattery. I think that the address which Herbert Hoover made to the Republican convention was one of the most dangerous and vicious utterances ever made by a public man in this country before an open assembly. Under the thin disguise of defending "Liberty" Herbert Clark Hoover gave aid and encouragement to every Kluxer, every Black Legionary and every Vigilante in America.

Mr. Hoover is a gentleman who pretends to be able to see around corners. Once, through his extraordinary gift of oblique vision, he professed to see prosperity lurking just behind the bend of the street line. And now he says that he sees red revolution.

The evening did not belong wholly to Hoover. He must share the credit for his gospel with William Randolph Hearst. Like the Lord of San Simeon, the Sage of Palo Alto cries "Communism" whenever three or four liberals are gathered together.

Early in his speech he accused the New Deal of having loosed "the propaganda of hate." He then proceeded for more than forty minutes to heap invectives on all who will not agree to let the issue of patriotism and liberty be decided by a vote of five to four. Under the stipulations laid down by Herbert Hoover, Chief Justice Hughes becomes a soapbox agitator.

"The American people should thank Almighty God for the Consitution and the Supreme Court." Working women in the State of New York who have added hours piled upon their backs for smaller pay should get down on their knees and give thanks to those surrogates of Hoover's heaven who have assured them of their right of contract.

"Lead the attack, retake, recapture and reman the citadels of liberty."

Herbert Hoover would bring comfort to those who are crippled and maimed by a reckless economic system. To such he would say, "Take up your bed and run," for even those who are without arms or legs are not denied a right to the pursuit of happiness in Hoover's generous dispensation. The small children in the mills and factories are to be guaranteed their liberty. Freedom to starve quietly and without any outside interference whatsoever will be assured all under the clarion call of Herbert Hoover.

The voice of Butler, Van Devanter, Roberts, McReynolds and Sutherland is the voice of God. When those five have spoken you know precisely what crumbs you will be permitted to scramble for. These are your liberties. Take them and cherish them, for if you have any idea that there may be a better way you have been poisoned by the ideas of Europe.

By a curious coincidence I followed Mr. Hoover's speech through a proof furnished by the Cleveland *Plain Dealer,* which carries at its masthead the name "Paul Bellamy — Editor." I rather hoped that Bellamy might rise in defense of his New England father and say, "The gospel of brotherhood is rooted in our native soil, and Edward Bellamy, who first gave to America a vision of a co-operative state, was neither muddled nor murderous. When you seek to identify the merchants of venom look to your own lips."

Paul Bellamy, as it turned out, did not get up to say anything during the tirade, but, at least, his conservative paper made the comment the next day: — "If some world power were ready within a few hours to bombard half a dozen American cities, if Communists in arms were encircling Washington and proposing on the morrow to sack and destroy the capital, if the British army were on the point of crossing the lake to thrust a spearhead into the heart of the republic — such a speech as Herbert Hoover delivered to the convention would be completely justified. By no less absurd hypothesis can some parts of it be excused."

The glorification of war was decidedly such a part. In speaking of American ideals of liberty Herbert Hoover said, "Less than twenty years ago we accepted those ideals as the air we breathe. We fought a great war for their protection."

And has the mind of America become poisoned, Mr. Hoover, if many of us are opposed to sending once again our boys and men to make the world safe for your conception of democracy? Your kindly suggestion that another little conflict might be a tonic for national ideals comes strangely from the mouth of the Great Humanitarian. Nor does it fit altogether with your attack upon the gospel of hate.

When Hoover raised the fiery cross and leaped into the saddle, logic did not ride beside him. He canonized five members of the Supreme Court, and the convention sang "As we go marching on." The delegates had forgotten, perhaps, that this song was not dedicated to Chief Justice Taney but to an American radical named John Brown.

GENERAL MOSELEY

I HAVE never met Major General George Van Horn Moseley. In fact, as far as I can remember, it has not even been my privilege to gaze upon his picture. Sight unseen, I conjure him up as an old gentleman with a long, white mustache who fairly bristles with military pomp, patriotism and excellent intentions. Certainly no charge hurled at any man by the Dies Committee should be accepted in whole or substantial part without check and double-check. The General has a right to his day in court, and he has already announced that, far from being a Fascist, he merely seeks to lead true Americans in defense of traditional democratic principles.

And so it is in a friendly spirit that I would like to offer a word of caution and advice to the retired soldier. General, in spite of the intensity of your devotion to the American way, your place is in the ranks and not in the pivotal position of staff officer behind the lines.

Time is a great leveler, and age lays its finger upon the brass hats as well as the corporals and sergeants. You and I, and two or three others, are not as young as we used to be. It is well to face the fact frankly. Our mental and nervous reactions are less rapid than in those fine old days when we were fifty.

You say that it should be the privilege of a patriot to discuss national problems openly and frankly. What rogue will dare deny that? But I think, if you will pardon my glove, General, that you bite off more territory than you can chew at present when you declare that it's your intention to save America from itself. It seems to me that now, and at all times, the United States is rather larger than any single major general. You ask too much in suggesting that the millions should stand stiffly at attention and wait until you have made up your mind just what our marching orders are to be. Has it slipped your mind, Major General Moseley, that you are not in the army now?

If the news-gathering organizations are correct, you announced in El Centro, Cal., "My attention has just been called to press reports to the effect that I am a Fascist." No man may reach the higher brackets in the military service of the United States until he has demonstrated his ability to both read and write the short and simple words of our mother tongue. And when your name was flung into the news the story was not printed obscurely in some remote quarter of the real estate section. No, indeed, General, you had your day on the front page.

The story, on the average, rated a two-column head, and in some journals it commanded an eight-column streamer. And yet you noticed none of this until some old friend or orderly nudged you with the news, "George, did you see the piece in the paper in which your name is mentioned?" With what pursuit were you occupied to the extent of needing an attention-caller to rub your nose in the obvious and make you acquainted with the palpable? The man who undertakes to save America from itself, preserve our democratic institutions from all attacks, cannot afford to be a cloistered recluse to whom the noises of the street come feebly, like bees in swarm around the turning of the road. The man who sees himself as another Washington or Lincoln must sound a trumpet call.

Blow, bugles, blow! No matter how pure his patriotism, it will not suffice if he waves aloft an ear-trumpet and shrills out, "Follow me!" The age of retirement is clearly indicated when the services of an attention-caller become imperative. And so, General, I think you should lean back and take it easy. Avoid starchy foods and too much excitement. A little chess and some debate about Grant's strategy in the

Wilderness are indicated. Can you hear me, General? I was trying to say that this is 1939, and that your mustache is on fire. I hope you won't mind if I call your attention to it. Sooner or later you've just got to learn.

Milton Hindus

POLITICS

The role of communist thinking in American education has yet to be assessed. Evaluation has largely been in the hands of irate partisans of both the right and the left; liberals have tended to avoid the difficult problem. Progressive education has been a stormy petrel in its own right, and has sometimes been dragged into the controversy; those in education who despise progressive education are likely to despise all aspects of communism, and to relate the two. Hindus eventually became emotionally involved in the outlook of Louis-Ferdinand Céline, author of Journey to the End of the Night, *and later Nazi fellow-traveller; still later he became a professor of comparative literature.*

IN HIGH SCHOOL, as anyone will say who knew me at that time, I kept very quiet. Persons who met me later in my revolutionary days and remembered me as a shy boy could not reconcile the two. But there was a simple explanation. I didn't change. These people should have seen me during my elementary school days when I was called "the question box" by some of my teachers who could not keep up with my insatiable curiosity. In high school I was under wraps, so to speak, because of an incident in the last year of elementary school which shattered my confidence for a long time to come.

It happened in this way. History had always been my best subject. That was so because from the moment I began to read, I continually kept reading books of history. We had only a few books in the house, because we were not an intellectual family. We did have two books, however, which I was always reading. One was Montgomery's *American History* — an advanced textbook and certainly difficult reading for a boy of eight. The other book was *A Nemesis of Misgovernment* —

a heavy book which dealt with Russia under the Czars. It had a dull green cover which I clearly remember, though it was by an author whose name I don't remember.

What I got out of these books was not what the authors intended me to get out of them. To me both books were filled with adventure and romance. Simply to look at them was enough to start me dreaming. I was buried in them at every spare moment, and I read them over and over again. If I didn't understand the intricacies of a legislative argument as it was explained by Montgomery, the face of conflict I certainly did apprehend, and I absorbed enough technical information with my enjoyment to last me well into my college years. Most of my knowledge proved beyond the range of my first teachers, and this was taken as a sign to hurry up my studies so that I completed elementary school almost three years ahead of time.

In *A Nemesis of Misgovernment* what impressed me most were the pictures of The Night Patrol of St. Petersburg, the bomb-torn body of Alexander II being taken back to his palace in a sleigh, a string of heads on the belt of a Siberian head-hunter, various marvels of the Czar's palaces, and a succulent verbal description (meant to horrify) of the rape of Jewesses during the Kishinev massacres. My sympathy was on the side of the injured, not only because they were of my own race (of which I was very early conscious, poetically at first and painfully later) but because I was inclined to sympathize with the underdog. Yet my indignation was swallowed up in the sheer thrill of the details, which the author with scrupulousness and the complete lack of humor characteristic of a scholar supplied fully.

The incident occurred in my last year of elementary school in a history class. Because of my superior knowledge I shone especially brightly in this class, and since I felt more and more frustrated as I grew older by my discovering every day that I was not the center of the world, as my mother had done her best to impress upon me, I needed the compensation which my excellence in history supplied to me. The teacher didn't know this, of course. She was a young woman and to her I was simply the nuisance who always threw her class off balance. If she had been better balanced herself, she might have been able to handle me less drastically than she did. But she was not sure of herself, and I was the most serious challenge she had met to her experience. She had a large and unwieldly class of thirty-five or forty students, and that didn't help matters either. I didn't know how much she hated me until that day.

Every time she asked a question to which I knew the answer, I couldn't contain myself. I rose in my seat (we had folding chairs in school in which I could remain half-standing half-sitting) and waved my hand under her nose. One day she couldn't stand it any longer and told me what was on her mind. She asked a question of one of the students to which he didn't know the answer. I was on my feet immediately. She turned on me coldly and said, "Sit down. You're a pest!" That was all she said. I crumpled up, entirely deflated. My overthrow was complete. A few minutes later, she asked me a question to which I did not know the answer. I saw myself as the object of everybody's derision, and the battle for confidence which I was fighting was entirely lost.

Politics possesses two irresistible attractions for the immature mind. It enables that mind, bewildered by its first contact with a reality of infinite complications, to understand the world and to master it.

To enter politics (although the basic motive may lie in fear) requires not a little nerve too, for its object is to direct other men's lives for one's own purposes. But nerve was precisely what had been shattered in my own case by my teacher's crushing epithet. I went through high school stunned. I was still very much interested in history, but I did not sense the practical use to which my knowledge could be put. It was not yet a political tool for me. There were some socialists in high school, but I didn't take much notice of them beyond watching them gather in conspiratorial circles after school was over.

Once I did become interested in politics, I quickly went to extremes. Beginning with a mild shade of liberalism, I went in the space of a year through socialism into communism. My home was a good training ground for politics. Every evening my uncles and their friends gathered round the dining room table and discussed the events of the day. Their opinions differed, so that these discussions became very heated. Sometimes I was allowed to put my own word in. But when they saw the extremes to which my views were tending, I quickly became an outcast. They stopped talking to me.

A newspaper had played an important part in the development of my thought, a liberal paper of which I read the editorials and columnists devotedly every day. I found myself so much in agreement with them that sometimes my enthusiasm spilled over into letters which I wrote to the editor. These were printed in their columns. Later, when I thought that I really had something to say and I wrote to this same paper, my letters were no longer printed.

Political clubs such as I belonged to, whether socialist, communist, or liberal, possessed an inestimable advantage for the growing mind. I regained all my lost confidence. I learned that I could handle myself adequately. My powers were recognized by others, and I recognized myself as an individual. I learned that I had abilities to persuade and to think logically. These were not extraordinary, but they were enough to enable me to hold my own in conflict. I was not feared but I was respected, and this respect pleased me much more than fear would have done. The truth was that I was conscious most of the time of holding myself back, of not driving as far ahead as my strength could have taken me. This was because I shrank from committing myself irrevocably to the cause I espoused. I took refuge in my small role in the organization, because it absolved me from responsibility. I wanted to observe and to criticize, and for both of these occupations I judged the obscurity of the sidelines to be best.

I learned more in the political organizations to which I belonged than I ever did in college. In fact, the chief value of my undergraduate years was that they brought me into conact with such organizations. What was it that influenced me to join them? And after joining, what was it that determined the direction that my views took?

I remember that the novels of Upton Sinclair were the first important influence upon me toward radicalism. And I was not the only one to be influenced by him in that way. Later, when I met S. who was destined to be my political comrade for a time and my personal friend for an even longer time, the first topic of our first conversation was Upton Sinclair. When we had both confessed a taste for his work, we knew that everything else would be settled in its proper time.

Sinclair disposed our emotions favorably toward those who were trying to change society and very unfavorably toward those who were trying to keep it as it was. Since we youngsters were dissatisfied for one reason or another with things as they were, there was no great difficulty in persuading us that the men who were trying to change them were heroes. Imaginative books were the best possible propaganda for the socialist cause, because they disposed us emotionally toward the acceptance of intellectual theories which by themselves were academic and dry as dust.

Afterwards, in due course, there followed the more difficult books of Marx, the economic treatises and the political boxing matches. It was these latter that attracted me most personally. I loved to watch the spectacle of conflict. Still later, it was the romance of the revolution which enticed me, the history of the Paris Commune and the Russian Revolution, Lenin's ride through Germany in a sealed train, the Kornilov rebellion against the Soviets and its suppression, the thousand and one other historical details which the past had enveloped in a thick atmosphere of nostalgia. Motion pictures helped too. Particularly the blood-tingling films of the Russian director Eisenstein —

Potemkin and *Ten Days That Shook The World*. So did music. I never heard *The Internationale, The Red Flag,* and other working class songs without "a quicker blood". I remember a May Day celebration when I came out of the subway station into Union Square just as a band was passing playing the strains of *The Internationale*. I felt completely torn out of myself with excitement.

But in addition to books and the other arts which combined to confirm me in the leftward course I had taken, personal contacts were also important. The chief of these influences was a red-haired college teacher, who was later imprisoned by the State of New York for perjury. A young man in those days, he found it expedient to grow a beard to set him apart from the student body. Perhaps the beard was also a tribute to his admiration for his Russian friends. He wasn't the only communist on the faculty at that time who had a beard.

He astonished us freshman and gained our admiration by his powers of logic. His demonstrations convinced us that he must be cleverer than we were, and since he was a communist, communism must be the correct solution to our troubles. I was a socialist when I entered the class, and I suspect that my marks which were just a shade below superlative were due to that unfortunate choice. But as I succeeded in straightening myself out during the remainder of the term and came around gradually to the teacher's point of view, my marks showed a corresponding increase until, at the end, I stood at the head of the class.

He spoke with a slight stutter unless he spoke very slowly. I recall how he entered the room and began the lesson with a provocative question such as "How many in the class are in principle opposed to the killing of men?" If that formulation were not clear enough, he explained it further until at the end all of us humanitarians raised our hands to indicate our positive answer to his question. Then he began to ask innocent questions of us. We suspected no trap as yet. He asked whether we knew how many men had been killed in the construction of the Empire State Building. Or how many men had been killed at grade crossings in the United States the year before. Or whether we knew that insurance companies were able to predict almost exactly how many lives it would cost to build a structure of a certain size and how many people were going to be killed in the present year and the year following in accidents at grade crossings. We, of course, had not heard of any of these things. They took us by surprise and they shocked our sensibilities. We felt somehow as if our own hands were stained with blood, for weren't we constantly using bridges and buildings and all sorts of modern conveniences that had taken so many lives to build? There followed a question as to whether we were willing to give up these conveniences for the sake of our humanitarian principles. This time we weren't so quick to answer as we had been before. He had us in the grip of his pincers of logic. By the end of the period, few were left who were any longer against the taking of life on principle. The teacher had the same effect on us that Socrates must have had on his opponents. He mystified us and he thrilled us because he showed us the use to which the gray matter in our heads could be put. Before that, it had just lain there.

But there was always another motive in his mind when he did this. If he proved to us that, logically speaking, the end justified the means, he also made sure to tie this up with what was happening in Soviet Russia, which was violating every law of humanity for the sake of the great aim which absorbed her. Those simple exercises in logic cost more than one boy in the class his life. I knew a few myself who would never have been communists but for him. They went to Spain to fight for the Loyalists against Franco and, in the flush of their political enthusiasm, they were killed. He himself didn't go to Spain. His job was to send others. Later, he went to jail for a while when the authorities got wind of what was going on in his classes.

As for myself, the most important thing I got out of his class was the habit of looking up in the dictionary every word I didn't know. No other teacher had succeeded in making me do this. But he was such a stickler for exactness that it was the only way to get by in his class. I thanked him for it later on, not because I looked upon his fanatical pursuit of detail as any more admirably than I had felt it before (it was, I thought and still think, the mark of a petty mind) but because I found that there were a great many other people in the world like him, only some of whom were professional pedants. The only way of holding the attention and respect of such people was to be able to become immersed in the trivia of life.

Once I had become converted to communism, I began to act in what in everyone else's eyes was a very brave way. There was nothing self-conscious about this action. All that I had to do was to open my mouth and say what was bothering me. I was innocent of the world as yet and did not know exactly how dangerous this might be. It was not hard for me to become the student spokesman for communism, because, though there there were many who secretly shared my views and not a few who could have expounded them better than I could, there was nobody who cared to become identified in the eyes of the administration as a revolutionary. I saw then that in order to represent a political viewpoint, it is not necessary to be the wisest or best person in the party; it is simply necessary to say fearlessly what is on people's minds but what they dare not say for themselves.

Professor O. was the Chairman of the Department of Philosophy at that time, and he had a beautiful Oxford accent as well as a melodious, deep voice. Knowing my views, which I frankly expressed, he chose me to address a lecture hall of several hundred students on the subject of Communism. I went to work promptly and prepared a speech of eighteen pages.

The seats of the hall were arranged in semicircular tiers and I stood on the lecture platform with the pages of my speech before me on a lectern. At first, I had to steady myself by holding on to it. I was frightened by the faces in front of me. If I had thought of the fact that behind some of those faces were minds that were better than my own, I would have been even more frightened. Professor O. himself took a place in the audience.

I attempted not only to explain the intellectual content of communism as clearly as I could, but I wanted to gain adherents for the party itself, and so I conducted my speech with a stirring exhortation in my best imitation of the *Daily Worker's* political style, calling upon "the workers, farmers, soldiers, and students of America to rise and to throw off the yoke of imperialist capitalism and to establish a Soviet America."

I'd say that it took courage to do this, if I could also say that I realized the implications of what I was doing — the difficulties that such a speech was bound to get me in with the faculty throughout my college career and perhaps throughout my life in a society against which I was declaring war. Or if I could say that I really grasped the meaning of the words I was saying — what they were bound to mean in actual terms of life and death if they were taken seriously.

I can say none of these things. I neither knew nor understood anything vital about a world in which I thought that I understood everything. I was merely uttering words which had no real meaning to me and which I unconsciously assumed must be just as meaningless to everyone else. My attitude toward the most important concepts was not unlike that of a child toward building blocks which he can knock down at any time without really destroying anything. It would not be important to admit this now if it were not for the fact that there are more people than one cares to admit, and some of them in high positions, for whom it is also true that they are incapable of taking the words they say seriously or of apprehending their full meanings imaginatively. Surely I wasn't so stupid, and I did understand something, but what I understood in relation to the whole truth was like a surface in relation to a deep and solid object, or like the face of a coin, which is divorced from the thickness of its metal and the inscription on its reverse side.

All this was not known to my hearers, who either took me seriously and therefore could not imagine that I did not take myself seriously, or did not take me seriously and therefore did not bother thinking about the matter one way or another. To both of these types, the thoughtful and the thoughtless, I became a hero. The first attributed to me a bravery I did not have, the second a bravado I did not want. And each of them was wrong. I was neither hero nor bravo. I was merely a man in the dark struggling, and it was no enemy I was struggling with, as I imagined at the time. It was myself.

I became a public figure to my fellow students. I emerged from obscurity. But it was a false image of myself which achieved recognition. It was an image propelled by an energy directed towards an entirely different end and it happened to fit in for a moment with the preconceptions and prejudices of those who surrounded me. How many have mounted to the highest summit of fame through just such false recognitions? And, in a sense, it is not almost always destined to be so? Our real self is either buried so deep that it cannot be dug out or else it doesn't exist at all. It is something entirely apart from the material of which we are composed or entirely identical with it. The first is the view of religion, the other of science. There is no middle ground between these conceptions.

On the strength of my appearance in Professor O.'s class, I was invited to join a secret communist literary society, melodramatically named *Pen And Hammer,* of which the red-haired teacher who had initiated me into the mysteries of bolshevism was the president.

But my reputation was not based upon that exploit alone. Another took place on the day when a demonstration of students was being held in the center of the campus over a cause which escapes me now. My college years were all in the heart of the Great American Depression of the 1930's and there were constant demonstrations of students and clashes between students and the authorities. On this particular day the whole class and the teacher were watching what went on outside the windows of our chemistry laboratory. It was in the afternoon, and we were supposed to be conducting an experiment. We heard the crowds of students shouting slogans and watched the speakers waving their hands, and the excitement in ourselves mounted proportionately. Finally I could not stand it any more, and I called out "Come on! What are we doing in here? Let's go!" The whole class turned to me, and the teacher turned too. I realized what I had done. I wanted to pull back my words from the air.

The teacher apparently was himself in secret sympathy with the revolutionary students, and though he hated me for exposing him to a difficult choice before the class where he was the visible representative of authority, he let me go with a mild warning. But word of what I had done got around the school and it increased my reputation for audacity.

I was extremely active politically during those undergraduate years. I went to meetings, distributed leaflets and pamphlets, and spoke on street corners from soap boxes, beer boxes, milk cans, platforms, or anything else I could get my feet on. I developed my voice, learned to silence hecklers, to render them impotent and ridiculous before the eyes of a crowd. I had a ready wit and I learned to handle myself in the midst of any rough-and-tumble that might develop. And always, quite aside from public activities, I talked to anyone and everyone I met. Politics, I discovered, is talk. I learned to distinguish between different types of opponents and to judge the value of allies. I learned how to take advantage of weaknesses, and when it was advisable to withdraw my forces. I never grew tired of talking, of arguing and convincing. I found emotion to be my own strongest weapon. My logic was passable, and I could hold my own with it, but if things went badly for any reason, I could always call up the reserves of passion and a certain knack of stringing together words that had emotional punch in them.

I believed with a terrible earnestness in the truth of what I was saying, and while I held a person in my grip, he could not doubt it either. I put thoughts into the mouths of my opponents, and then I shattered their position. I had never before felt so fully alive. Muscles of my mind come into play which had long been idle.

I even tried making a communist out of my grandfather. He hated the Bolsheviks from his experiences with them in Russia where he had learned that Bolshevism was the enemy of the Jewish religion as it was of all religion, and I think that it broke his heart to see me become a communist. I tried to convince him that communism was the logical conclusion of the teachings of the Prophets, but he didn't listen to me. Like Mark Twain, I found the old man so obtuse I could hardly stand having him around the house, and it took me a long time to become as obtuse as he was.

My ignorance and pretensions in those days appear to me unbelievable. On July 30, 1934, when Hitler purged Roehm and other opponents within the Nationalist Socialist Party, I was on a farm with my mother. I wrote frantically back to my political friends in the city. I was terribly excited. I thought that the proletarian revolution which we had all been waiting for was beginning in Germany. I had not the faintest notion of what was going on. I was like the man in the game of pinning the tail on the donkey who gropes about blindly and finally succeeds in putting it right between the donkey's eyes! In my letters, I made very profound analogies between the situation in Germany (about which I was entirely ignorant) and events during the Russian Revolution of 1917 (about which I was almost entirely ignorant). My analysis was ridiculous, but it sounded good. With a little more training, I could have become a newspaper columnist, who generally makes an even smaller insight based upon fewer facts go a much longer way. For in politics it is impolite to remember what a man or a party said the day before. If that were not the case, most parties would have vanished long ago in the realm of sheer astonishment and disbelief. There are only two things which count in the matter — conviction on the part of the writer and a gift for camouflage.

I read the situation in Germany not for what it was but in terms of my hopes at the time. I knew nothing about Hitler or National Socialism except what the *Daily Worker* told me. Nor would the situation have been improved if I had actually read *Mein Kampf*. I wouldn't have understood it at all. For I would have started with an emotional bias against it, and nothing (at least not in politics) can be understood with the intellect alone. All I was aware of inside Germany in July 1934 was a commotion which I hoped was a revolution against the existing regime. Everything that was favorable to this interpretation I seized and dwelt upon. Everything else I rejected and did not see.

My communist friends in the city knew no more about it than I did. If anything, they knew less, and they were not as ingenious as I was in improvising rationalizations of our mutual desires. They looked upon me as a shrewd analyst and afterwards, when my ideas were exposed as the fantasies they really were, my friends hardly remembered and didn't hold them against me at all, for they still liked me and had faith in my ability and honesty.

The organizer of our local branch of the Young Communist League was an interesting person. He inspired confidence in everyone around him, and I should like to know just how he did it. It's quite easy to say that he had the gift of leadership. He did have it indeed. But what does that mean? What does it consist of? He did not have an extraordinary amount of personal magnetism. I do not believe that he could have convinced anyone of the correctness of communism who was not more than half convinced already. But he bolstered the confidence of those who already belonged to the fold and that was a function hardly less important. It was somehow quite evident the first time you looked at him or spoke to him that he was "a good guy". It inspired us to know that a character of that sort believed as we did.

Partly, of course, he owned his charm to our own enthusiastic eyes, which were only too willing to endow him with the best qualities. We assured each other often what a fine fellow B. was. But it never occurred to us to analyze just what we meant by that.

He was short, and though you could not call him stocky, he was solidly built. He stood upon the floor like a well-made piece of furniture. He stood squarely, and it wasn't easy to budge him. If he stood behind us, it added to our feelings of safety. He seemed to have strong nerves, and that is very important in a political leader when you are in agreement with his views. I have noticed that those individuals who exercise the greatest attractive power initially are not always men with strong nerves. They retain in their characters an element of instability, like unstable chemicals, which affect most strongly those around them because they themselves are wandering and incomplete. If they have any solidity, it is of an acquired sort, the sort that is gained only after an intense struggle for self-mastery. They strive to extract some sort of organization out of chaos. Their confidence is built over a hollow base, and the vacuum and incompleteness felt inside exercise the attractive power over the potential convert. Men who are complete in themselves rarely affect others sympathetically. They may excite envy but nothing else. When people are already in the movement, however, characters like B. play an essential role for them. The B.'s tide the rest over their inevitable, human periods of doubt. They confirm them in the correctness of the course on which they have embarked.

In college, I took part in every rebellion against authority, in every demonstration, every meeting, every outbreak. I learned to distinguish between the types of opposition that we had to face. There was the blunt and brutal type represented by the President of the college, who, when a military review which he was heading was disrupted by rioting students (among whom I was in the forefront), swung his cane against the head of the nearest student, who turned out to be standing next to me. The President then issued a statement to the newspapers in which he called us all "guttersnipes". That became a term of honor for us. We had buttons struck off bearing the legend "I am a guttersnipe" and we sold a few hundred of them on the campus where it became a kind of fad to wear them. The atmosphere of that time is called up with perfect clarity when I think of those buttons.

A conciliatory opponent was G., the dean of the college who was so frail that anyone could have broken him in half, and yet he was frightening because of the authority he represented. He was the kind of man who, instead of quarreling, put his hand on your shoulders and said: "Now, now, boys! Why don't we talk it over first?" He had a fabulous memory for names and faces — something on the order of those who can add up columns of six figures more quickly than a machine, or memorize whole pages of the telephone book. He made personal friends of most of the communist leaders; he used to help them out sometimes. He even lent them money. But in his defense of the social order, he was more reliable and important than the blustering president of the college. That unhappy individual, who died a few years later (I think that it must have been of sheer humiliation) was infallible at being able to excite the worst antipathies of the students whose guide he was supposed to be.

His greatest inspiration was to invite as guests to a student assembly, in a college where 85% of the students were Jewish, an Italian delegation of twenty-one fascist students who happened to be visiting America. It was on that day that I was arrested by college police for distributing leaflets urging the students to demonstrate against this gratuitous insult. The arrest probably saved my career at the college, for it kept me from participation in the riot which followed. This was so violent that a great number of the rioters were expelled from the college.

My passage from liberalism to socialism and finally to communism was hardly significant, organizationally speaking, because the societies to which I belonged were loosely knit and one was able to drop out of them without any noise. But to break with the communists was altogether different. Here, the organization was very tightly knit. It was like joining a gang from which you could only emerge feet first. There was no such thing as resigning from the party. If the going became rough and anyone objected to the way things were being run, he was expelled with all the formality and ritual disgrace with which a man was read out of the bosom of his people. In Russia, the excommunicated one was shot or sent off to some remote corner of Siberia. The reasons for my break with my comrades are a little difficult to assign. Fundamentally, as is the case always in politics, it was a matter of differing temperaments. There were communists whom I liked, but these didn't count for much in the organization. The leaders were all gray, humorless men whose primary qualification for their positions was the ability to take and to carry out orders from Moscow.

Some of my reasons for leaving were, of course, not at all creditable to myself, but they were nevertheless inevitable. With the kind of upbringing I had had, discipline of any sort was irksome, and communist discipline which resembled a strait-jacket was intolerable. Another factor was that a childhood friend of mine, whom I no longer saw frequently but who was fairly close to me in spite of that, belonged to the dissident organization of Leon Trotsky. At first, I hated Trotsky with all the bitterness with which the orthodox hate the heretic. I was ashamed of the fact that like myself he was a Jew and that he had, as I was taught by the party proved a traitor to the cause of the working class. But there were other things working deep within my mind of which I was only dimly aware, and as the revolution did not come as quickly as I had thought it would, my dissatisfactions and impatience rose to the surface. The quarrels between the party and me began about small things. I disagreed at first on matters just to see what would happen. The rudeness with which they slapped down these tentative efforts enraged me, and I complained more loudly. I began to read the opposition press, which no member of the faithful dares to do any more than good Catholics read the books on the Index.

They tried to silence me — first by persuasion and later by threats. But I am by nature very stubborn and opposition only serves to make me more so. I had opened my mouth to say what I thought inside the party as I had previously opened my mouth to say what I thought outside of it, and I wasn't going to close it until either my opponents were beaten down or I was. My weapons were all intellectual, but those who opposed me were not so scrupulous. A trade union organizer came down to our unit and threatened to beat me. I had made some progress with my view among friends who knew me, but this threat did more than anything else to gain sympathy for me. It was the human element in Upton Sinclair's novels that had attracted me to the revolutionary movement, and now I watched the human element in action within the movement itself. People who liked me as a person gradually brought themselves, under the pressure which outraged their individualities as my own had been outraged, to the point of believing that they agreed with my political point of view.

I found how difficult it is in politics not to lose track of the main issues and to fight out the principal battles along secondary lines. For example, my struggle began with such a basic question as the proper policy for trade unions and it ended with the comparatively minor issue of party democracy and the right of members to express their opinions freely. It is a fact well known in military science that battles are rarely fought just where one side or the other had intended that they should be fought. Most of the famous battlefields of the world, like Gettysburg, achieved their distinction in history through a purely fortuitous coincidence of accidental circumstances which forced one side to give battle and the other to accept it on grounds other than those on which they had originally counted.

The battle between myself and the party machine mounted in fury until it seemed as if I would take with me more than half the membership of my unit. But I discovered that nothing is certain in politics — least of all party members. At the last minute many of them drew back. They gave no reason for their defection. They didn't need any reason. I understood what it was that moved them back into the line from which my blows had shaken them loose. It was their fear of solitariness. They were spiritually comfortable in the communist life which they had chosen, and they were afraid of the outer darkness of conventionality into which we were going to be cast.

The climax was reached in my trial before my unit prior to my expulsion from the movement. It took place in the living room of my friend S.'s house (that same S. who had become my friend originally because of our common admiration for the work of Upton Sinclair). He was still my friend, but in political matters he found himself lined up on the opposite side from myself. In fact, he was my chief accuser. It was interesting to observe the relation between personal friendship and politics. The personal relationship was the more important thing, and yet in a crisis, friend could kill friend. He might regret it afterwards, but on the spur of the moment there was nothing more important than ideas.

In a time like ours, when the world seems to be weighted down by too many ideas, when the whole world threatens to go up one of these days in the smoke of an idea, it is hard not to wish sometimes that man could govern himself not by the gray and the abstract but by the palpable and the concrete.

In Céline's *Journey to the End of the Night*, the young soldier Ferdinand wishes that his mother were like a bitch with her instinct to protect her young. Then she would not have consented to send him off in order to defend something so largely unreal as The Fatherland. Who has ever seen, heard, smelled, or touched The Fatherland? But it is just such fictions that end by swallowing up mankind in order that they themselves might live.

So here was my friend S. prosecuting me. And here I was, defending myself against someone for whom, outside of his immediate role as my attacker, I had affection. It was all very dramatic, objective, and intellectual. No one threatened to beat me up. We came to do battle on the field of the intellect and our only weapons were the weapons of ideas. The District of the Communist Party to which we belonged sent down one of its most subtle representatives to combat me. For it was evident that without help, the local group of the faithful would not be able to put me down. He spoke with a slight foreign accent, because he had apparently come from Russia not too long ago, and he spoke calmly, with the kind of patronizing patience that grown-ups often show towards children. His attitude was that his hearers were in danger of being led astray by someone incurably vicious. He had no hope of regenerating me. But he did want to save the rest.

I came to the meeting with a number of heavy volumes of the collected works of Lenin under my arm. With my heavy glasses, bent spine, thinness, and general air of unkeptness, I was a picture of a Radical Intellectual coming to defend himself. I had been studying all night long what it was that I would say. I had read over and over again the relevant passages in the works of the international founder of our party in order to present them to the other members. I put myself in the position of Lenin. What would he have done in a situation similar to mine, I asked myself, and I came to the conclusion naturally that he would have done the same thing that I was doing.

I was the first Trotskyite on the campus, and my historical and documentary interest by themselves were sufficient to make me attract attention. It was just around the time of the first Moscow trials, and this too shed an attractive romantic aura around my dissidence. I was hated by my former comrades, ostracized, and pointed out to the passerby as a curiosity. Years later, I was told by someone who eventually became a friend of mine that the first time he saw me at college, he had felt frightened — such were the lurid tales that had been spread about me. I didn't suspect that I had inspired any such feelings. I just went about my ordinary business and, as the only representative of my point of view among the student body, I was invited to contribute articles to magazines defending it, to participate in forums, to speak to possible new converts. I handed out leaflets, mimeographed a student bulletin, and spoke on street corners again. There grew up around me a circle of people who responded to my type of rhetoric and understood intuitively the emotional logic with which I defended my beliefs.

It was during this period especially that the philosophy of Marxism exercised its greatest influence over me in all realms of life. When I responded to literature or art or music, it was in terms of Marxist categories and explanations that I saw them. It was not only my views of society and government that were affected. It was every realm of human interest and discourse. I wrote essays on Marxian criticism; I delivered lectures on the Marxist interpretation of literature. In this I was helped by the fact that Leon Trotsky, whom I now accepted as my leader, was not only a great politician but a great writer as well. His style was of incomparable brilliance and his sympathies in the field of literature were as wide as they were discerning. It was he who directed my attention first to the work of Céline. Trotsky's *Literature and Revolution* was a kind of bible to me in those days. It is a remarkable book in every sense of the word; it is remarkably well-written and it is remarkably perceptive — not to speak of the fact that much of the material which went into its making was prepared by Trotsky while he was directing the armies of the Revolution. He still found time in those days to read the latest and most advanced novels from Moscow and Paris.

But at the same time as I thought myself a thoroughgoing Marxist and tried with all my might to integrate my world-view with Trotsky's ideas, other parts of my experience clamored for expression, and I was not fanatical enough to deny their rightful claims. I had always had a weakness for the philosophy of Schopenhauer — not only because his pessimism suited my usual mood but because he knew how to express himself as a poet. I even tried to make a difficult reconciliation between the ideas of Marx and Schopenhauer. This I did by saying that Marx was merely for the present hour, to ameliorate existing conditions, but Schopenhauer was for all time, the discoverer of those black truths about life that could not be denied. And as my witness, I took Marx himself who had said somewhere in his works that under communism man would suffer not as an animal but as a human being. That convinced me that Marx, at least, did not dose himself, as some of his followers had done, with over-optimism. Marx did not deny that suffering is the ultimate truth in life, but what he wanted to do was to grant man the leisure for education with which he might dignify his sufferings and raise them above the level of material necessity. Thus I put the aim of the Marxists graphically from an aesthetic point of view, when I said that it was to allow Proust to become a popular author. Today he was a luxury for the few, but tomorrow he would be given to the masses of people. That was all, I thought, that would be necessary; it was as simple as that. The mention of Proust here is significant, for it was Proust who dominated the part of my mental life at that time which was not given over to the revolution. His careful, aesthetic reaction to life was pleasing to my sensibility.

I did not stay much longer in the Trotsky movement than I had in the communist one or in the Socialist one before that. Divorce gets to be a habit — no less in politics than in matrimony. I was in love with an ideal, and that ideal in its completeness could not be found outside of myself. I proved to myself how true is the observation of Hitler that to an imperious temperament like his own, it was out of the question to join an organization which was large and stiff and not subject to much change. He had either to begin one of his own or to join one that was small enough to be stamped with the imprint of his own personality.

By far the most interesting of my experiences were in the smallest splinter groups. There, I got a kind of microscopic view of what went on in larger groups where the individual member does not grasp the pattern to which he belongs, because it is too large for him to grasp. Only the leaders of such groups ever see the whole thing in perspective. I belonged to groups which were small enough, so that every member could properly have been called a leader of them. We gathered in small rooms and parceled out the world among ourselves.

Local politics were too small for our consideration. If anyone had suggested that we interest ourselves in a New York City or state election, he would have been despised. Even national American politics barely entered the range of our vision, which could hardly encompass anything smaller than global thoughts. The hugeness of our conceptions was directly proportional to the weakness of our powers. We were like a paralytic, who has to compensate for the enforced idleness of his physical limbs by a corresponding development of his mental interests. Anyone listening to our discussions might have been terrified by the scale of our visions, and by the callousness and brutality with which we proposed to transform them into realities — until it was realized that we were actually powerless. Between some of our meetings, at least, there might have been a parallel with such as might have taken place in a lunatic asylum. Endless discussion took place on whether the next war between Britain and the United States would begin in South America or in Asia. If it were objected that Britain and the United States were friends, and there seemed to be no actual prospect of war between them at all, the objection would have been met with our contempt. It would have been quite obvious to us that such a person was naive and knew nothing beyond what he read in the papers. We, of course, knew much more. We "knew" that the purpose of the papers was to screen the truth from us, and we also knew that it was an axiom of our particular kind of Marxism that Britain and the United States were rival imperialistic states whose clash was already overdue by a matter of twenty years. We could have brought a sceptic to a confused standstill by quoting to him certain little known facts about cartel arrangements, oil monopolies, and kindred subjects. Precisely because the ordinary person did not know anything about such things, he was likely to be impressed by them — at least momentarily. That is the advantage gained by surprise and novelty and explains much about the use of esoteric political doctrines even by the largest and most successful parties.

Another favorite subject for discussion was exactly where the revolution was likely to start in the United States. It was the opinion of the most erudite of our leaders that the midwest was the likeliest place because of its future industrial dominance of the country. And one bespectacled member whose wife was a school teacher and who had risen to the heights of revolutionary leadership from a more humble position as an instructor of ping-pong left for Chicago in accordance with the implications of this idea — thereby breaking up his home and causing his wife to divorce him. I saw him a year later back in New York a beaten man, but I did not have the heart to inquire about what had happened out in the midwest.

There was a certain grandeur about these theorists, and I am glad of my association with them. There was a headiness in the atmosphere of those small smoke-filled rooms in which we dreamed and laid our plans. Anyone who hasn't felt the excitement of carving up the world just hasn't lived.

There was a letdown when our dreams came to nothing. But the letdown was gradual, while the illusion was sudden and overwhelming. It is surprisingly easy when you sit in a small room with men who believe as you do to forget that there are other men in the world, too many of them, who do not. For this human mind of ours with its limitless reach was especially made to contain illusions. Not all are as ambitious and grandiose as ours were, but almost all are detached at one point or another from the reality that exists. It is just a question of choosing the point of departure and trying to stick as closely to facts as our romantic natures will permit.

I had entered the radical movement alone and I left it again alone. It was like entering and leaving the world. The net result was that I was less lonely for a while. I went into and out of so many parties and organizations that I was bound eventually to end alone. Boredom plays a much larger role in human life and history than is commonly realized. Oswald Spengler was one of the few who realized the role which it plays. He predicted that Marxism would die not of refutation but of boredom.

For a long time, I held to the outward symbols of my revolutionary beliefs. If I were asked, I still said that I was a Marxist. But if further pressed, I had also to admit that I was a non-conformist. If I had had enough confidence in my point of view, I would have started a group of my own. But there was little use in that. I sensed that my beliefs were not strong enough to carry through for more than another six months or a year. I was in the stage of a love affair when the lover himself realizes that he will be healed by time.

My old enthusiasm flared up briefly once more. My old friend S., who had gone into the movement together with me and had been responsible for expelling me from the Communist Party, eventually joined me in my heresy and became a leader of the Trotskyite group. And while in this position, he became involved in a strike and was arrested. A civil liberties issue was involved, and I joined a defense group that was organized around him. It was purely a sentimental gesture on my part. I became very active again, but what I defended was not the politics of my friend, because I no longer agreed with him, but his right to free speech. Thus, the pattern that my rebellion followed against Communist Party discipline was now repeated with regard to the revolutionary movement as a whole. In both cases, I ended with a defense of abstract democratic rights.

That this was an empty, useless, and futile gesture did not occur to me till much later. It was like defending a man's right to sexual intercourse without any consideration of such an institution as marriage or such a feeling as love. In this respect, my position did not differ very much from that of certain psychoanalysts, who play with regard to sex the same role that civil libertarians do with regard to government.

Echoes from my earlier life were heard long after it had ceased to exist for me. When Trotsky was assassinated in Mexico City — though I no longer belonged to his organization — the fact struck me as if it were a personal blow. I felt approximately the way the more sensitive conventional people in this country felt when Roosevelt died. I understood then the meaning of the events in Rome the night before Caesar's death described by Shakespeare, and the happenings in Jerusalem on the night of Jesus' death as the New Testament relates them. I was troubled all night by spectres and the most horrible dreams. The graves opened and gave up their dead, and the ghosts squeaked and gibbered in the cold air of Maine where I happened to be at the time. My whole world was shaken, and, in addition to dreams of terror, I had some wild dreams of sexual orgies too. I seemed to have lost control completely. I woke up feeling entirely exhausted. So I experienced during my lifetime the empty space which a great man leaves behind him and the terror which is caused by his sudden removal from life.

Politics [287

The feelings and visions which we experience in such a circumstance are the greatest possible tribute to the importance of politics among men. Politics is the art (some insist that it is a science, but since it works, as art does, more by an appeal to the heart than to the intellect of man, I prefer to call it an art) of instituting order in the affairs of mankind. Without it no other activity couald be carried on with any security or steadfastness of purpose.

There was an echo of my political interests again when Russia attacked Finland. Ail Marxists, even the Trotskyites, united in defending the indefensible action of Russia. They were forced to do so by their theory, and that showed me how ridiculous the theory itself was. According to the theory, Russia was a worker's state and, therefore, in any clash with a non-worker's state like Finland, we were not supposed to ask questions but to turn out on the side of Russia. But I did ask question of myself. I asked how I could ever be on the side of a bully, theory or no theory. I perceived what many people in my position had lost sight of — that feelings come first and theories afterwards, and if my theories did not fit in with my feelings there was something wrong with my theories and they would have to be revised. I lived through again the drama of ideas which Pierre Bezuhov and Prince Andrey and other advanced young Russian intellectuals are shown by Tolstoy to have lived through in the year 1812. Theoretically, they were on the side of Napoleon — they liked his progressive ideas and they admired his personality — but when he attacked their own country and people, they took up arms against him and helped to kill him. There had been something wrong with their abstract theories, too, which life had corrected.

It was my first vital experience of the importance of nationalism in the modern world. Previously, I had thought myself a complete internationalist. I was a world citizen and I recognized only the world as my fatherland. I had forgotten that I was a Jew, or at least I had done my best to forget it. Now I saw what a hold local attachments and limited loyalties had upon me. These were the kind of loyalties that my grandmother had for her family, which I had once despised but which I now increasingly respected. For what does it profit a man, I said to myself, to believe that he loves the whole world when he is disloyal to his own kin. In the communist movement, I had come across more selfishness and more callousness to the most ordinary and decent human feelings than I had ever come across anywhere else. What sort of saviors were these, I thought, who lied and cheated and deceived. They were quick to see the most minute faults in their opponents; they were entirely blind to their own, but these were nevertheless gross as earth. I had ignored the faults as long as I believed that the communists were essentially noble characters who hoped to do nothing but good. I saw, however, that this was not so. Their high-flown idealisms were used to conceal the baseness of their natures. This was especially evident to me in their attitude toward sex where I saw comrade steal from comrade as soon as his back was turned. The absence of scruples which they decried in the bourgeois world was ten times as bad in their own case.

Finland brought all these thoughts to a head. The unprovoked aggression against a small and peaceful state by the large and heavy Russian bear, covered up as this treachery was by hypocrisy and rationalization, was merely symbolic to my mind of the entire evolutionary fraud of Marxism of which I had been the willing dupe for so long.

The great strength of the communists was that they had fulfilled a spiritual purpose within me and within many of their sincere adherents. Or, at least, we thought that they had fulfilled that purpose until their falseness had become plain. But the spiritual place within, which they had filled so unsatisfactorily and temporarily, needed to be filled whether they did so or not. I became conscious of that in the empty years that followed my break with Marxism both in theory and practice (years that were empty, of course, of nothing save significant experiences). I became conscious that something else would have to take its place — something that would be along the lines of more limited loyalties which, being within ordinary human reach, would end by being more effective and generous than the louder and more pretentious loyalties had been.

John Dos Passos

From ADVENTURES OF A YOUNG MAN

> Adventures of a Young Man *marked John Dos Passos's literary and philosophical dividing-line. Although he had sustained a naturalistic and aloof treatment of the radical Left in* The Big Money *(1936), his prose had held touches of sympathy for its old ideals, its old anticipations. He had continued to avoid public repudiation*

of communism, though he was increasingly in protest against Stalinist tactics. By 1939, however, he was ready to brand Stalinists as enemies of society. Adventures of a Young Man *abandoned such frills as "Newsreels" and "Camera Eyes" to tell the straight story of a young idealist whose standards of human decency were flouted by alleged comrades in the communist movement. Dos Passos offered no alternative hopes to his few readers. His next work was a book of essays, entiled* The Ground We Stand On *(1941). The ground he chose was that of Thomas Jefferson, Alexander Hamilton, Joel Barlow, and other non-contemporaneous sources.*

WHEN THE TRAIN STOPPED Glenn stuck his head out of the window of the thirdclass compartment he had been sitting alone in all the trip to see if the others were getting out. It was raining hard on the glass roof of the railroad station. The gray platforms were empty except for two elderly redfaced porters in the blue tunics who were slowly pushing along a handtruck with a battered muchcorded trunk on it. Down the train a couple of doors opened. Among the few countrypeople in dark clothes who were lowering themselves backwards down the steep steps of the oldfashioned cars, Glenn saw the little man with a rumpled yellow face whose language nobody understood who had been introduced to him in Paris as Peter, and Monty's tall overbelted figure with its ham actor look, and Saul Chemnitz's curly head without any hat on it bobbing from side to side. Glenn hoisted down the heavy box he'd been asked to carry across the border which they had told him was full of X-ray equipment, put his paper parcel of clothes under his arm and followed the straggle of people with bundles that crossed the empty tracks and platforms towards an iron gate with a blue enamelled sign over it saying: SORTIE.

When Glenn stopped to hand his ticket to a greenishgray bleareyed old official at the gate, Saul bumped into him from behind and said "Excuse me" in English. Glenn let his lips form the words "Shut up" and walked on down the scaling stucco passage that led out. At the exit he found himself looking through a curtain of rain at a stonepaved street bordered by a row of stone houses streaming with rain, and wondering what to do next. People brushed past him and hurried out under umbrellas to get into a small wet yellow streetcar. After the streetcar had gone jangling off Glenn set down his box and looked around him. Saul, tall and loosejointed with a jewishlooking nose and pink cheeks, was standing beside him making I'm sorry motions with his lips. Monty was staring out into the rain without moving a muscle of his face like a picture of a highlife movie star; Peter was lost in contemplation of the worn pointed shoes he wore on his feet. Everybody else had gone except a young fellow in mustardcolored corduroys with a dusty blue beret on the side of his head who was leaning against the yellowed printed notices on the wall, reading a paper and rubbing one sockless foot in a grimy canvas sandal against the other. As Glenn glanced in his direction he folded up his paper, and Glen found himself looking into a pair of eyes green as olives set in an oval brown face that had a little light down around the chin and on the cheeks. The boy smiled and came forward showing very white teeth. "Abraham Leencoln," he said very low. His breath smelled strong of garlic. They all four had their mouths open ready to speak. He shook his finger across his mouth and pointed to a big square black limousine that had just driven up in front of them. Monty nodded and opened the door and they all piled in.

As soon as they had gotten themselves and their boxes wedged in the back seats the driver, who was a sandymustached Frenchman with a halfsmoked cigarette in the corner of his mouth, leaned back and shook each of their hands in turn with a "Salut, camarades." The boy with the beret, who had climbed into the front seat, thrust his narrow brown hand back to them and said, "Salud, camaradas."

Everybody pulled a deep breath. "Greetings, comrades," shouted Saul, bubbling over like an opened bottle of pop. Monty took out a package of Luckies and offered them all around. Everybody started puffing out smoke.

Comrades, Saul was declaiming in his stuttering voice, he'd been getting the heebyjeebies. Monty tapped the driver on the shoulder and asked, "Espagna, Wee Wee?" The Frenchman shook his head. The boy in the beret turned around and tapped himself importantly on the chest and said, "Yo Antonio," and made two fingers of one hand ride horseback on the other. Meanwhile Saul babbled on, stuttering through his cigarette, asking everybody if they had ever done any mountainclimbing, saying he sure guessed they were going to get some mountainclimbing experience now and that he wished his stomach didn't feel all knotted up like it did.

Monty said that that was how a yellow streak felt but added solemnly that he mustn't worry, everybody had a yellow streak. Saul interrupted spluttering that he wouldn't miss the experience for a million, the comrades mustn't get him wrong.

After they got clear of the town, the road ran straight through the bottom of a green valley among treecovered mountains, hidden above the first slopes by lowhanging rainclouds. The Frenchman drove very fast. At the end of the valley they jolted over the cobbles of a stone village, shot through a rainwashed square with striped awnings over the storewindows and feathery trees and a babyblue bandstand and on up through small fields of vines and brightgreen patches of early crops. At the turn in the road they got a backward glimpse of the village hemmed in by stone castle walls piling up to a peak in a hunched stone church with a rustcolored roof that moss and shrubs grew on; beyond was the valleyfloor pale bluegreen and steaming with rain.

They had all settled down to enjoying the scenery when there was a whistle from the side of the road and the car stopped with a lurch. They were in front of a new unpainted sentry box that looked like a farmhouse privy from which a wooden bar stuck out across the road. A man with a broad black beard tucked into a rubber hood and cloak, under which was a blue uniform, came out and peered into the car. "Nonintervention," growled the driver in his throat and poked a folder of papers in the officer's face.

He looked at them, frowning and shaking his head, and beckoned the driver to go inside the sentrybox. As he left the car the driver made a downward gesture to the Americans, meaning keep your shirt on, with the palm of his hand. Monty cleared his throat elaborately. Not even Saul said anything. Glenn could imagine he could hear all their hearts thumping.

After what seemed hours, during which loud voices raised in French altercation came from the sentrybox, the driver came back grinning. After he'd climbed in he made them understand that the gendarme had telephoned the frontier and then shrugged his shoulders laughing as if to say what the hell did that matter. Monty passed around his cigarettes again and they all drew in deep sucking breaths.

The driver stepped on the gas and kept on zigzagging up the mountainroad skidding the car around the sharp curves. Then he jammed on the brakes suddenly in front of a field full of sheep all headed one way with their tails to the driving rain and turned under an arch through a mossy stone wall into the courtyard of a farm.

A lanky man in corduroys with a beret on the side of his head and thick black stubble on his lanternchin opened the door of the car with a brokentooth grin and a cheery. "Salud, camaradas americanos," and started hauling out the boxes. They all piled out, and stood around in the downpour watching the lanky man and Antonio fit the boxes into the big saddlebags of four wet mules that were stamping and fretting on the small slippery stone cobbles. Then the Frenchman shook hands all around, said goodby sharply in English to the Americans and drove off down the road.

"Well, Tony," said Monty, "where do we go from here?"

Tony grinned and stuck out his forefinger like a kid playing gunmen at home and said, "España, boom, boom." Then he pointed to the lanky man and said, "Paco."

There seemed to be considerable hurry, Paco explained with elaborate dumbshow that they must climb on the mules on top of the packsaddles and set off leading the first mule. Tony followed after the rear mule yelling Arrhé. They started off along a trail that skirted the old stone walls of the squat farm buildings and cut across a squudgy pasture and then climbed over loose stones through a grove of firtrees. Once in among the firs they left the trail and started straight up the steep slope, Paco and Tony yelling and cursing at the mules in Spanish all the time.

The rain kept on falling and soon worked its way through Glenn's cheap raincoat. The low ragged sky was beginning to go indigo with dark. Glenn was shivering and slid off his mule to walk. It was tough going, slogging up the steep mountainside, where only an occasional rocky glen full of ferns with a brook in the bottom of it broke the monotony of regularly spaced firtrees, through the firneedles soggy underfoot.

It was dark before they came out on another trail that led them round the edges of a narrow valley filled with the roar of a watercourse somewhere below. Glenn found he was stumbling so on the sharp pointed rocks, and stubbing his toes and getting his legs soaked in the muddy pools between, that he climbed up on the mule again; not without Tony's help, who ran forward to grab the saddlebag from the other side. Tony and Paco were soaked to the skin, because their only protection was a narrow blanket pulled over their shoulders, but they were scampering back and forth, shouting merrily at the mules and singing. The Americans were all dead tired by the time they lurched around a spur of rock that jutted suddenly out into the path, and found themselves trotting over a rolling meadow towards the faint light of a doorway. The mules seemed to know where they were going. "Espagna, Wee Wee?" shouted Monty at the guides. They laughed and yelled back, "Dormir Francia, dormir, compañeros."

Two big woolly white dogs came out to bark at them until a woman's shrill voice from inside the house called them off. The Americans slid off their mules and crowded into a small smoky stone room dimly lit by a lantern where a skimpy fire smouldered in a huge stone fireplace. An old man with straggling white whiskers and a bigbreasted blond woman got up from two canebottom chairs as they came in and stood silent, leaning against the wall, looking cannily at them out of sour gray eyes.

Paco made them a speech while Tony scuttled around gathering up sticks to liven up the fire. The old man went out and came back with an armful of bottles of wine that he set out on the oilclothcovered table in front of the fire. Paco had to bring a hundred franc note out of his fat wallet and spread it out in front of her before the woman would start sluggishly laying the table and stirring up supper. Meanwhile the Americans were huddled round the fire drying their shoes and everything they dared take off in the chilly room.

The woman ladled hot soup with bread in it out of a black iron kettle and set a loaf of bread and a stony looking cheese on the table and they ate and drank the sour puckery white wine and began to feel a little better. The old man seemed to be kidding them for drinking so little wine. He made them understand that he was eightytwo years old and drank a bottle with each meal and one for breakfast, three bottles a day, that was why he was so healthy. Glenn had a French phrasebook out on his knee and was getting along famously with the old man, who was telling him he ought to get himself a wife and settle down here, they needed men up here in the Pyrenees, husky young men ought to be in bed with the girls getting children instead of going and getting themselves killed, when Paco tapped him on the shoulder and made the dumbshow of putting his two hands together against his cheek and closing his eyes with a seraphic expression on his face, and whispered *dormir*.

The woman took a candle and groaning at every step led them up a flight of steep tiled stairs to a chilly room with two beds in it. They turned in two in a bed on hard straw mattresses. It was tough getting to sleep because they were still cold and wet and the covers were too short for them. Glenn slept with Saul who kept going into nightmares and waking up screeching. When they finally did warm up and drift off to sleep, bedbugs came out and bit them. It didn't seem as if they'd been asleep a minute before Paco was standing in the center of the room waving a lantern and yelling *arrhé* at them they way he did to the mules.

Downstairs Tony was blowing up the embers of the fire to heat up a saucepan of coffee. They each drank a cup of the sweet watery stuff that tasted of woodsmoke and ashes, and started out into the raw mist already silvery with morning. When they asked where the mules were Paco laughed and said *feeneesh* which was the only English word he knew. The rest of the way was on foot. The six of them took turns carrying the heavy boxes of X-ray equipment.

They warmed up after a while. They were climbing a rocky trail. Soon sweat was pouring off them and they were breathing heavily.

Paco and Tony didn't seem to feel the climb at all and kept disappearing in the mist ahead. The boxes became a torture. The periods he wasn't carrying one Glenn was dreading the next time it would come around to him. His feet got to feel leaden in his stiff boots.

They came out on a rocky ledge with patches of snow on it. A stiff sharp wind blew right through their soaked clothes and sent the mist scurrying past them. Now and then through a tear in the clouds a rolling silvery landscape opened up under their feet. At the top of the ledge they tried to rest in a little gully that was sheltered from the wind, but Paco kept yelling at them to hurry.

They were climbing up a narrow snowy gorge that ended in a sharp lip of freshfallen snow at the top. This must be the border, they were telling each other as they fought, wheezing, for breath. The guides dashed up through the soft snow, sinking in above their knees. Glenn was after them with the box gouging into his shoulder. At the top he paused. This couldn't be right. It seemed a sheer drop into a swirling crater of fog.

But the snow round him was already giving way. He was sliding down a steep soft slope holding onto his box for all he was worth. He stopped with a bang with his legs jammed in a rocky crevasse. Paco and Tony were crowded beside him laughing.

They waited until the others slid down to them and started off at a jogtrot zigzagging down the slope through a downpour of rain. The snow stopped and the hillside became slippery mud among big shaggy evergreens. Glenn was so tired he hardly felt the icy glassclear water of a torrent at the bottom when he plunged into it up to his waist. He struggled across, lunging and slipping on the rolling stones underfoot. The guides were leading them a crazy chase up the other side of the valley again. At last it was time to turn over the box to Monty.

This time climbing was easier because there was a well-made zigzag trail, but Glenn found himself falling flat on his face several times before he got to the top. When he fell he lay still, holding onto the rocks until his strength came back a little. He didn't dare look at the others. The last steep lap up to the pass Paco and Tony had to make several trips to carry up the boxes; over the last rocky stretch the Americans were barely able to inch themselves up hand over hand.

Glenn felt sun warm in his face as he dragged himself up through a shaly runnel, he shook the sweat out of his eyes and lay there looking out at a clear blue sky and a row of snowy rockbuttressed peaks stretching away on either hand. Ahead, looking past a few cottony speeding clouds, he could see, beyond green hillsides cut by deep blueshadowed canyons, a great expanse of country yellow and ruddy in the sun. Just below him on a little grassy ledge Paco and Tony were stretched out on their backs with the boxes in a neat row behind them.

Suddenly he felt very happy. When he started to move again his knees shook so he could hardly keep his balance, his whole body felt light and dizzy. He stretched out on the grass beside Paco. The grass was warm and dry from the sun. He closed his eyes and fell asleep.

When he woke up they'd all taken their pants and shoes and shirts off to dry them. Paco was handing around a small skin of wine he'd taken out of an embroidered bag he wore over his shoulder. Then he made gestures of putting food into his mouth and they all cried sí sí and started reaching for their phrase books. "Well, we're over the border, boys," yelled Saul, and gave out a whoop.

They had to drink the wine out of the little resinous skin; it took considerable aim to get the thin stream into their mouths. Their hands were so shaky they spilled it over their faces and down their necks. That seemed a great joke to Paco and Tony. Only Peter seemed still to have a steady hand.

Then Paco rummaged in his bag some more and brought out a big round loaf of dense white bread and some sausages and cheese. Tony pulled an oblong of chocolate out of his bag and frowning with care laid it on a rock to divide up with his knife into six pieces. While they ate he stood on the edge of the ledge, his cheeks bulging with bread and chocolate and, with the air of a professor in front of a blackboard, pointed out villages and rivers and mountains in the sunburned distance. Then smiling he made a big sweep with his left arm and said, "Nosotros," and a big sweep with his right arm, frowning, and said, "Enemigos." Next he made a pistol out of his hand and pointed down the middle and said, "Boom boom . . . frente de guerra."

"Gosh," Monty said, "it looks like fine country . . . it's almost as good as the view from Mount Frazier." "Where's that?" asked Glenn and Saul. "California . . . of course, that's higher . . . and you can see the sea."

They laughed and Monty drew himself up with a sulky look.

"I tell you, comrades," stuttered Saul, "this walk is some experience."

"Augenblick . . . wunderschön," sighed Peter, opening his mouth for the first time.

"Gosh," said Saul, "the world would be a fine place if it didn't have war and fascism in it."

"Well, it won't have when we get through with it," said Monty.

They rested an hour in the sun and then put their clothes, that were stiff with caked mud, on again and dragged themselves to their feet.

They were all limping as they started out. Glenn felt a sharp stabbing pain in the back of his ankle at every step.

For the first hour they crawled along a barely visible path on the shaly shoulder of the big snowmountain to the left. Now and then one of them slipped and started a little shower of shale off into the treepacked valley a thousand feet below. They were jittery with relief when they came out on a grassy upland pasture with stone huts where Paco made them understand shepherds came in summer. They trotted along, laughing and kidding at a great rate, over the springy gently sloping turf.

At the edge of a grassy knoll full of flowers that overlooked a deep valley ranked with chestnuttrees, Tony suddenly stopped frowning and looked up into the sky. He pointed with his whole arm. "Aviación," he said. Paco stood beside him looking up and frowning at a little V of silver specks crossing the sky far off to the southward. Monty tried to ask if they were ours or theirs, but the guides just shrugged their shoulders and walked on frowning. "Well, comrades," stuttered Saul, "that reminds us of what we are here for . . . no summer vacation . . . but it sure is an experience to see this beautiful country. We were letting ourselves forget our political position." "Don't worry," said Monty. "The Henkels won't let us forget it."

It was late that night before they saw the first houses of Spain. They were walking along a broad smoothpaved muletrail. Below them lights came in sight, flickering in the cool still air. Then they smelt the smoke of fires that had some aromatic herb burning in them. Then, in no time, they were sitting at a long table in a lamplit whitewashed room in a square stone house in front of a roaring fire while a handsome girl with an oval brown face and white teeth like Tony's and a purple and black silk handkerchief on her head, was pouring out thick red wine for them and setting out a big meal of eggs puffy and crisp brown from being fried in olive oil, and pork stewed in tomatoes, and beans and bread. At the end of the table sat a bland little roundfaced man in khaki who said in somewhat slippery English that he was the governmental delegate and had come to greet the brave American fighters for democracy in the name of the Spanish Republic and the workers of hand and brain of the Spanish masses who were fighting for their lives against a double fascist invasion and the perfidy of the other socalled democratic states of Europe.

The Americans were so tired they could scarcely eat, much less listen to the rounded and oddly accented remarks of the governmental delegate. After they had staggered around shaking hands with everybody in the room, the governmental delegate told off a brighteyed young militiaman with a springy step to show them up the stairs to a row of cots that had plenty of blankets, and even clean sheets on them. Glenn never remembered how he got his clothes off.

Next morning when he woke up and sat on the edge of his cot he was so stiff he could barely put his feet to the ground. He was in a clean whitewashed room with a vaulted ceiling. Sunlight was pouring in the windows, that opened clear down to the redtiled floor and had iron railings across them. He cleaned the mud off his pants as well as he could and pulled them on and hobbled to a window and stood in the sun with the tiles warm under his bare feet, looking down into a courtyard. A few chickens were pecking among the cleanswept stones. In a dark arched doorway a girl was kneeling fanning at a charcoal brazier with a little wooden fan. On the warm air Glenn could smell the charcoal and frying olive oil and the heliotrope that grew in a big pot in the corner of the courtyard. Glenn felt like whistling but he didn't because the others were still asleep. He shaved and cleaned himself up at a basin with a towel beside it at the end of the hall, and hobbled painfully down the stairs.

Several militiamen in various uniforms with big pistol holsters on their hips were drinking coffee at the long table. They all raised their clenched right fists in a salute as Glenn came in. Their rifles were stacked in the corners of the room. On of the faces was familiar; rather bulging bright eyes and curly hair cut close on an elongated skull; it was Frankie Perez whom Glenn had known back in Horton. He'd thickened up with the years and his skin was blackish bronze from the sun. He wore a red silk handkerchief round his throat. He stared at Glenn for a minute and then he jumped to his feet and came forward with his hand out. "Sonofabeetch, it's Meester Spotswood."

"Frankie Perez . . . Jesus, I haven't been mister for many a year."

"Compañero is better."

"Isn't it camarada?"

Frankie frowned. "Maybe . . . you join Brigada International?" Glenn nodded. "Communist Party?" Glenn shook his head. Frankie smiled and slapped him on the shoulder. "Drink coffee? Please seet down . . . Hola, Teresa, café," he called over his shoulder. While Glenn sipped his coffee Frankie talked. For many years now he'd been working as a barber in Barcelona, lovely city; at the time of the movement he had fought three days in the streets, then, boom, wounded, get better and again fight; then again wounded.

Glenn suddenly became conscious that the sleeve of Frankie's

298] JOHN DOS PASSOS

khaki tunic was empty: "Explosive bullet . . . and now I am delegate for barbers' cooperatives. . . . Did you hear how the barbers marched to the front when the soldiers had fled from Madrid?"

Frankie was watching his face narrowly. "Friend," he went on. "Here several different kinds of war. We fight Franco but also we fight Moscow . . . if you go to the Brigada you must not let them fight us. They want to destroy our collectives. They want to institute dic-, tatorship of secret police just like Franco. We have to fight both sides to protect our revolution."

Saul had come limping down the stairs looking tousled and unwashed. After lifting his fist and yelling, "Salute, comrades," he had sat down at the table and was listening to what Frankie Perez was saying. Frankie gave him a sharp suspicious look and got to his feet. "I must go for business at frontera." He seized Glenn's hand and held it. "You Americans must not forget you come to help our fight for liberty, not for party business." He turned, saluted with his clenched fist and walked out of the door, swanking a big silver embossed holster on either side of his slim hips.

Saul wrinkled up his nose and started to splutter excitedly in Glenn's ear that this was just the type of provocation by uncontrollable elements they had been warned against; Comrade Silverstone in New York had told them many of the socalled anarchists were fascist spies. "Keep your shirt on, Saul, they can't all be spies," Glenn said with a forced kind of laugh.

He felt suddenly a chill inside him. A lot of things he'd forgotten in the excitement of the trip from New York and dodging across the border came up in his mind like bile from a sick stomach.

His hand shook so he could hardly get his match to his face to light his cigarette. He got up and went outside and walked up and down in the courtyard looking at the flowers and the chickens and the pigeons with rainbow breasts that were strutting and cooing on the stone balconies above his head.

As soon as he got hold of the governmental delegate to see about transportation to training quarters he asked him if he knew where Jed Farrington was. The little Texan? Of course, Farrington was a great man, he commanded a battalion. He would see him. Was he a friend of Farrington? Bueno, bueno. In the afternoon the governmental delegate saw them off in a truck with some more American recruits, fellows they had known on the boat, who had crossed the border at another place. That evening they saw their first bombed villages.

That night they slept in a barracks full of young Spanish peasant boys getting their first training who yelled greetings at the Americans whenever they saw them and crowded round them to give them chunky loosely wrapped Spanish cigarettes. Glenn felt the way he had felt when he had first gone over the gap into Slade County.

First thing next morning they were off again driving across a long red rolling plain misted with the emerald green of new wheat. The soil was red and the villages were red and the longfaced peasants and their mules were covered with red dust that blew in little whirlwinds on the sharp north wind. All day Glenn halfsat halfstood with the other guys holding on to the side of the jolting truck, looking at the dry country and smelling the dry smells of straw and the herb they burned in the fires in the low earthcolored houses, and the smell of mules and dry turds that came from the village streets, feeling strange and lost, wishing he'd stayed home where he understood the language, where he had some way of doping out what things were about. He wondered if the other guys felt the way he did; some of them looked as if they did. He'd feel better when he saw Jed; it was years since he'd seen old Jed; old Jed would help him get his bearings.

Late that afternoon a blankfaced German orderly led him out of the village full of international troops where the truck had unloaded them, along a foot path through an olive orchard, to see Jed, who they said was at the brigade headquarters in the villa of a departed Spanish grandee. At first Glenn didn't recognize the bald brown stout little man, belted into a well-tailored whipcord uniform, who was seated at the end of a long wooden table in a long room hung with portraits of longfaced darkeyed men in tarnished gold frames; but his dark Mexicanlooking eyes and his voice were the same. "Why, Glenn Spotswood, I declare you haven't changed a bit," he drawled.

"Great grief, Jed," said Glenn, laughing happily. "Who would 'a' thought you'd turn out a military man?"

"Sit down, Glenn old man," said Jed, pulling out one of the carved Gothic chairs. "I don't mind tellin' you that I'm happier than I've ever been in my life.... Haven't had a drink since Christ was a corporal ... soldierin' sure does beat wranglin' in front of a Texas jury.... Every played chess? Well, war's the greatest chess game in the world. At least it suits me down to the ground."

"I hadn't thought of it that way," said Glenn.

Jed didn't answer. Suddenly they didn't have any more to say to each other. Glenn found himself fidgeting in his chair. "Say, Jed," he said, clearing his throat, "who else do you think I've run into from Horton?"

"Some of those Mexicans I bet ... we got some good Mexican fliers."

"Frankie Perez."

The smiling hospitable look faded off Jed's face. Glen felt his black eyes boring into him. "Oh, I know all about him." Jed pushed back the big armchair he was sitting in and got to his feet. "What outfit are they puttin' you in?"

"I dunno," said Glenn. "I asked for truck or ambulance driving or repair work . . . I haven't got the taste for killing people you seem to have . . . at least not yet."

Jed shook his small outspread brown hand that had a silver bracelet watch at the wrist. "You make yourself think they're pawns, that's the trick . . . all a chessgame, see? But about this Perez or any of his kind . . . uncontrollables . . . for chrissake, don't monkey around with 'em. . . . The minute the fascists are cleaned out we'll have to clean out those boys."

"But don't they represent a good part of the workingclass?"

"Our business is to win the war . . . they are interfering with our winning the war, see? My only hope is we won't be forced to clean 'em out before we win the war. We've cleaned out some of the worst of 'em already."

Glenn felt again the cold, sick feeling he'd felt when he'd talked to Frankie Perez. He and Jed stood looking at each other. From an adjoining room came Spanish voices and the sound of a typewriter. "Come outside . . . I want to talk to you," Jed said suddenly. He let him out through an iron-studded door into a small stone courtyard with arches and columns. The sharp heels of Jed's wellpolished boots rang on the marble flags. As they went out the gate the sentry clicked to attention. Jed gave him a half salute, half wave of the hand.

They came out on a big terrace with huge old formally arranged box bushes. Below it the garden of elaborately scrolled beds of roses fell away to a row of poplars and a green swirling river. Beyond, across a wide valley cut into green rectangles by the irrigation ditches, rose jagged desert mountains crimson in the sunset. "My, this is the beautifullest damn country," said Jed. "And the greatest people in the world. . . . By God, we can't turn this place over to the wops and the squareheads . . . that's why we got to win this war."

"The Spanish workers have got to win it," said Glenn, his voice faltering in spite of him.

Jed turned on him savagely and stamped his foot on the gravel. "We got to win this war . . . us," he said. "Why did they throw you out of the Party?"

Glenn took a deep breath and squared his shoulders. "That's ancient history," he answered quietly. "I came here to try to help . . .

I'll do any kind of work you people say, except tell other guys to go get their blocks knocked off. I'm fed up with that."

Jed looked down the valley. On the riverbank under the poplars there were clothes spread out. In the green water a couple of black heads bobbed. "I bet that water's cold," he said. He paused and took a deep breath. "If you went home now, what would you tell the folks back home?"

"The truth . . . that's what I've always tried to tell."

"You wouldn't try to make out these damn uncontrollables were martyrs of the workingclass?"

Glenn stood beside him with pursed lips without answering.

"I don't see why the hell they let you come," Jed burst out peevishly. "Haven't we got enough trouble with the fifth column?"

"Jed," said Glenn, "you've known me for years."

"Men change."

"Sure, but not like that."

"We happen to know they do . . . this is not time for the old friend stuff."

"But how can you tell except by how a guy's acted before. . . . How do I know you're all right?"

Jed turned and looked directly in his face with beady, narrowed eyes. "You haven't come all this way to tell me I'm a crook, have you?"

"Have it your own way," said Glenn, and turned and walked off. It was almost dark. He walked back under the olivetrees towards the house at the edge of the village where he was billeted. Overhead every leaf stood out sharp, cut out in tin against the flaming ochre afterglow.

Next morning he was up before daybreak with the casual detachment, waiting in line in a dusty yard hemmed in by adobe walls. The end of the yard was cut off to form a corral for sheep. As soon as the sun was well up the shepherds came, and old men in rusty black cloaks and big flat hats, and opened the tall gates, letting a cut of brightness in across the steaming blue shadow and the crowded backs of the flock. Two little darkfaced boys and some wooly black and tan dogs helped drive the sheep out into the village street and off to pasture somewhere. Then the village bakery, in the basement of the building opposite, opened and women in dark shawls began to cluster round the door waiting for bread. As the shadows narrowed along the walls and the sunlight grew hot, there began way off a low hollow drumming hardly audible in the quiet morning. It was noon before Glenn's name was called. In the stuffy room that had been fixed up as an office, a

Spaniard who spoke English and an American with one leg in a cast, who sat sweating in their shirtsleeves behind piles of typewritten papers, seemed puzzled about what to do with him. Finally they said they'd send him up the line to Jack Stern, and wrote him out a transport order.

Jack Stern was a thinfaced little man with a long nose and a greenish complexion who ran a repairshop and a gas station, in a stone village with a great ruined church with two towers that perched on a bare hogback where the main road climbed up the divide between two eroded rivervalleys. He spent his time worrying about the lack of spareparts and the ignorance of the local mechanics and the bad quality of the gas and his own stomachulcers. At first he was delighted to see Glenn, who at least knew one end of a screwdriver from another, but gradually, as he heard whispering about him from guys coming through, got so that he only talked to him about the work and then only in the short peevish phrases he used to the Spanish helpers. One day Glenn heard him talking to a truckdriver who'd stopped to try to pick up some sparkplugs. "And aint it just my luck," he was saying. "First time I get a guy who's a mechanic and not a muledriver, the bastard turns out to be a Trotzkyist."

Their mess, in the fat widow's house across the street, was a glum business, once they'd run out of the few phrases they could exchange with the Spaniards, because Jack Stern had an idea that every mouthful of food cooked in oliveoil he ate was killing him. Glenn passed the time putting down Spanish phrases in his notebook and keeping a diary, or when he was through work, he climbed to the top of the hill and sat there on a stone looking at the great sweep of country beyond the town, made up of closepacked walls of convents and stone mansions of hidalgos and adobe houses of peasants that seemed to have grown together into a great compact ruin. He could hardly tell which ruins dated from this war and which from old wars centuries ago. Up the road towards the front moved muletrains or great jungling twowheeled carts with canvas covers shaped like snailshells over the driver's seat, pulled by teams of three or four caparisoned mules tandem, often led by a little donkey with a string of blue beads round his neck. Then, as there got to be talk of an offensive, staffcars appeared, weaving in and out of the traffic, and newpainted French trucks packed with brown young men in fresh uniforms who looked at him with brown friendly eyes and clenched their fists in salute as they passed. One day for hours the road roared and clanked with a string of new tanks.

The tanks brought airraids and machinegun strafing and dogfights at the edge of the sky. Nobody had much confidence in the shelter so Glenn and Jack Stern would go on grimly working while the rafters of the repairshop shook with the rending crack of the bombs and the tiles clattered down off the eaves. Every day the guns from the front sounded nearer.

There began to be traffic on the road from that direction, trucks full of civilians, busses jammed with women and children, and then countrypeople driving loaded mules and donkeys, little handcarts stacked with crates of chickens, and household furniture, droves of steers, flocks of sheep and goats, old people painfully dragging bundles, staggering under heavy sacks, lost children. The guns sounded nearer. For a whole day something burned, sending up heavy volutes of smoke beyond the horizon to the westward. The ambulance drivers who stopped for gas said the front had caved in.

One night at midnight a brigade passed on foot going into the lines. The moonlight was bright as day and everybody was jumpy for fear of bombers. For hours Glenn stood by the gasoline pump watching the dustwhite hollowcheeked faces of the young men passing in the moonlight. They were not noisy and singing like most of the outfits that had gone up. Many of them limped. There were no lights, no glint of metal, only here and there the rosy tip of a cigarette passed from hand to hand.

Next day the ambulance drivers said the advance had been stopped. About noon a staffcar of the internationals stopped for gas. In it Glenn recognized a Polish staffofficer and Irving Silverstone in civilian clothes. As he pumped in the gas he watched them eating sandwiches out of a picnic basket and washing them down with wine they drank out of little silver cups, and heard them talking about the campaign to lift the embargo in the United States. As they drove off Irving waved his hand at Glenn and said, "Thanks, comrade," without recognizing him.

When two bespectacled Germans who spoke English followed him out into the repairshop one morning when he was going to work, and whispered in his ear that he was wanted for questioning at the special brigade, he was hardly surprised. He'd been expecting something like that. He couldn't shake off a funny feeling that he was going through a play that he had rehearsed many times.

The German comrades marched him into a room back of headquarters, and then back through a stonepaved courtyard where stood a newlypainted gray truck that had been crumpled up by a bomb like a tin toy somebody had stepped on, in through a little door into a large square building with barred windows. In the passage, where some explosion had knocked off all the skyblue stucco from the walls, stood a sentry with his bayonet set in his gun. One of the Germans took a big key out of his pocket and unlocked an ironstudded door. "You will take the place of a monk," he said with a low laugh.

As soon as Glenn had stepped into the bluepainted cell with only one small heavily barred window high up the wall, the door was slammed after him and he was alone. In the middle of the dirty tiled floor was a wooden pallet with a blanket on it, on which was set a greasy tin cup and plate. There was no other furniture. When the sentry came, keeping him covered with a revolver held in one hand, to feed him out of a bucket of steaming rice at noon, Glenn roared and shouted at him in English and what little Spanish he knew, but the sentry only shook his head with a stupid smile. He was a blueeyed, lighthaired, thicknecked young man with high cheekbones. Glenn gave up trying to talk to him.

Before he'd let Glenn eat, prodding him from behind with the revolver like a farmer driving an ox, the sentry pushed him out into the main passage and down it to a latrine where there was also a bucket for washing, stood patiently until he was through, keeping him covered all the time, and then marched him back to his cell.

The night there was another bombing, far enough away so that Glenn could distinguish the bumble of each circling plane, and the shriek of the bombs hurtling down and the deep rumbling snarl of the explosions. After the bombing this time there was the rattatat of machineguns, strafing the road probably; where the hell was our pursuit, or the antiaircraft battery back of the church, Glenn caught himself asking aloud.

Next day he tried to make the sentry understand that he wanted a shave and writingpaper and something to read, but the man shook his head with narrowed eyes and said mañana knowingly in Spanish. The next night was quiet. Glenn was asleep when the door, rattling open and banging against the wall, woke him with a start.

"Heraus," said a mild voice. Glenn staggered up off the pallet blinking. A small figure in a neat uniform was pointing a rifle at him in the position of a man at bayonet practice. A smoky lantern at the man's feet threw both their shadows enormous and gesticulating on the walls of the cell above them. The man picked up the lantern with one hand and awkwardly shouldered the rifle and marched Glenn down the black passage outside his cell into a room several doors down.

The room was tall and white and brilliantly lit by an acetylene lamp that hung from the ceiling. Glenn found himself standing under the lamp in the middle of a floor littered with papers and cigarettebutts staring into three faces behind a board table that was piled with red cardboard folders. Their eyes were redrimmed and bloodshot and their cheeks were drawn in under their cheekbones. They looked as if they hadn't slept for nights. It was an instant before Glenn recognized the middle face as that of the man who didn't seem to understand any known language coming across the border, whom they'd introduced to him as Peter. The man to the left was one of the bespectacled Germans who had made the arrest, the man to the right, he couldn't be mistaken, he'd known in New York. "Say, aren't you Bernard Morton?" he said in a low, puzzled tone.

"Sure . . . we know each other," said Morton slowly, without changing the expression of his face. As he spoke he reached for a cigarette out of a pack on the table in front of him and lit it from the butt he took out from between his heavy lips without taking his yellowishgray eyes off Glenn's face. It seemed to Glenn that his cropped hair was whiter than when he'd last seen him. His broad face had a ruddy outofdoor look that was faintly reassuring.

Peter shook his finger impatiently in front of Morton and began to speak in slow precise British English; all the taut lines on his yellow face moved as he pronounced the words, shadowed by the glary lamp overhead like the lines on a reliefmap: "We are informed that you represent the Trotzky counterrevolutionary organization in America and were one of the channels of communication engaged in actively preparing the Barcelona uprising."

"Better make a clean breast of it, Spotswood," Morton interrupted in a not unfriendly tone. "The less you waste our time the easier you'll get off."

"Don't vorry, he vill not get off . . . " said the German, relighting a stump of a cigar that had gone out. "Ve have evidence enough to shoot him tonight." The German's bloodshot eyes rolled as his mouth made an Oh to let out a big blob of cigarsmoke.

"How have you communicated with Francisco Perez?" asked Peter, trying to stare down Glenn as he shook a stubby forefinger at him across the desk.

Glenn rubbed the stubble on his chin with the fingers of one hand. It shot through his head that they were all staring mad. "I have only seen him once, at that village we spent the night after getting across the border . . . you were there."

"I am in many places," said Peter, without smiling. "Naturally there you established contact with this movement of counterrevolutionary wreckers and spies?"

"It was a coincidence," said Glenn. "I hadn't seen him since years ago in Texas. I helped him with a pecanshellers' strike."

They all threw back their heads and laughed drily, drowning out his words.

"Skip it . . . coincidences don't happen," said Morton, writing something down on the pad he had in front of him.

"And your notebook," asked the Berman, "is that a coincidence too?"

"Very interesting," said Peter. "A literary gentleman."

Glenn felt himself coloring up. "There's nothing in that of military significance. I just wanted a record . . . Jesus Christ, all the guys keep diaries."

Morton lit himself another cigarette. "Not to use as a basis of an attack upon the party leadership," said Morton.

Glenn recognized the little black shiny oilcloth book he'd bought in Paris. They were passing it from hand to hand, pointing places out to each other with their pencils, rolling bloodshot eyes, with dry cackling chuckles, taking notes on the pads in front of them. Glenn tried to remember what he'd written, but his head was empty.

Morton leaned back, yawning and stretching. "They threw you out of the Party, didn't they? They had good reason. . . . I came here to try to get you off . . . but if you won't talk, what the hell?"

"There's nothing to talk about . . . I've done absolutely nothing outside of my work. There are plenty of people who know all about me. . . . Ask any oldtimers. Ask Jed Farrington, or Irv Silverstone if he hasn't gone home yet."

"Hum," said Morton, "so you know Comrade Silverstone was here? That little visit was supposed to be private."

Peter nodded his head gravely. "We have the reports of the comrades."

"It's no use trying to shield anybody," said Morton. "I don't suppose you know that Perez was shot for armed resistance in Barcelona the third of May."

"But I don't know anything. You people have kept me rotting in this damn repairshop," said Glenn.

"Put him back on ice for a couple of weeks," said Morton, yawning again. "Maybe he'll remember something." He lit himself the last cigarette in the pack and crumpled the paper up and tossed it into the corner of the room.

"Look here, comrades," said Glenn, "how about dropping all this nonsense and letting me go to the front? I applied to go to the tank school two months ago."

Peter got to his feet. "We are not the comrades of Trotzkyist-Bukharinist wreckers.... We are a court of inquiry."

"Unless we're damn lucky we won't need to go to the front. The front'll be right here looking for us," said Morton and shoved back his chair and started striding heavily up and down the room, puffing smoke as he went. Peter walked up to Glenn and put his pale face close to his. The pupils of his eyes were dilated and had a little jerky motion from side to side, Glenn felt the sour smell of his breath through his yellow teeth. "When did you last communicate with the opposition?"

"What's the use of my talking if you won't believe what I say?" yelled Glenn. Up to then he'd managed to keep his voice steady, but now his nerves were beginning to go. In spite of him his hands were clasping and unclasping.

"Snap it up, comrades," said Morton, "we got to go to bed sometime ... we won't do anything till we get orders in answer to our report, anyway. Take him away, Fritz...."

Back in his cell Glenn was taken with a fit of shaking. He rolled himself up in his blanket and lay face downward on his board pallet and tried to think. Up to then he'd thought he didn't give a damn, but now he knew he wanted to live, he wanted to be free, he wanted to go home. Crazy plans for escaping began to race through his head.

The barred window was silvery with a new day. Through it on the fresh morning air came a smell of charcoal, then a smell of coffee, then a smell of frying oliveoil. Outside, Spanish soldiers were cooking breakfast. The early morning smell was cosy and foreign; he couldn't share their breakfast. Why the hell had he come over anyway. He remembered the dry unfamiliar smell of the country, the strange voices, the odd taste of the smoke, the dusty villages, the smell of men's dung behind walls.

Suddenly he heard a boom, followed by a distant loudening shriek like a piece of goods being torn and then a shattering crash. This wasn't aviation. This was shelling. They must have the bead on the place from a battery somewhere. The front most be a whole lot nearer.

Suppose they captured the village, would they shoot him? Maybe not as an American. Hell, they shot first and asked questions afterwards, when they didn't rip you open and wind your guts round your neck. Another came in, another, another. Shaking and sobbing he lay flat on his face on the boards. After a while the shelling eased off.

He didn't hear any sounds of commotion outside; they couldn't have hit anything of importance. He began to get control of himself, to tell himself stories about when he'd been a kid, to recite scraps of verse. He turned over on his back; everything was quiet. He fell asleep.

He woke up with a start. Blue sky showed bright through the barred square of window. He was trying to tell himself the whole thing had been a nightare, the questioning, the shelling, the thoughts, when the door opened and the same sentry came in with his streaming bucket and ladled him out what passed for coffee into his cup. The sentry was real enough.

Gradually from day to day his life lapsed into a routine of hunger and meals, and trips down the corridor to the latrine. All that varied was the sound of the guns. He started making marks on the plaster walls to keep track of the days. At the end of the seventh day he could hear machineguns distinctly. The next day there were men firing rifles from the roof above him. If couldn't be long now.

He started working on a mock heroic testament, writing with his finger on the soft blue wash that still covered parts of the walls. *I, Glenn Spotswood, being of sound mind and emprisoned body, do bequeath to the international workingclass my hope of a better world,* but he suddenly felt ashamed and rubbed it all out with the palm of his hand.

That evening the sentry didn't bring him any supper. The night was quiet and he slept well except for one bombing that set off a series of explosions that sounded like an ammunition dump, and brought down a lot of plaster from the ceiling.

When he woke up at daybreak he found that some pieces of tile roof had come hurtling through the bars of his window and had landed at the foot of his bed. He got up and yelled for the sentry and beat on the door of his cell, but nobody came. Finally he had to make water in the corner of his cell.

The racket started up again with a bang sometime during the morning. At the height of it the door opened and Morton stuck his head in. He needed a shave. He was wearing a helmet off which the khaki paint had scaled. "You still here?" He had to yell to be heard. "Well, I'm goin' to let you out. I'll probably catch hell for it, if I live long enough." He gave a dry snicker. "There's hell to pay, Spotswood." They stood there looking at each other and half laughing. Morton's eyes looked yellow in his face that was black with oil and dust. He was out of breath. "You said you wanted to go to the front?"

Glenn nodded.

"Well, there are some of our boys with two machineguns in a pill-box to the left of hill 14. They got to have water. You got to take it to 'em. They are the only thing that's keeping the wops out of this dump. Tell 'em to stick for another half hour, see, they got to cover us while we get some junk out of here." Glenn was following him down the tall corridor. Blue daylight shone through several jagged holes in the wall that had appeared in the night. At the end there was a cobbled court with a pump in the middle of it where a man with his scalp all clotted with blood was pumping water. The man was Peter.

Glenn, Peter, and Morton stood on the cobbles in the bright noon sunlight looking at each other. The sun beat down hot. Their shadows were small blobs underfoot on the bright cobbles.

Glenn took a deep breath of the dusty air. The artillery had stopped. Only occasional machineguns and rifles kept up a distant ratatat and a zing, plunk and a whining overhead. Above them in the very blue sky swallows circled squeaking.

"All right," Glenn said. "Where do I go?"

He lifted one of the buckets to his lips and took a deep swig of the clean cold water. Then he stuck his head under the pump and said to Peter: "Pump me a little, will you, I haven't washed for days." Peter seemed so astonished by the request he just stood there, but Morton stepped over and gave the pumphandle a couple of swings. Peter looked in Glenn's face with his narrowed, bloodshot eyes. "You vill go?" he asked.

Glenn looked straight at him. "What do you think I came here for?" he asked. Then he saw Peter's strained eyes move sidelong towards Morton. Morton's eyes dropped and he scruffed at the cobbles with the muddy toe of one boot. He kept from looking at Glenn. "Somebody's got to go. We can't," he said. Glenn understood.

His throat got stiff but he didn't let his mouth tremble. They had two new corrugated iron buckets. He picked one up in each hand. Morton motioned with his head and led the way to a door that opened under the arches of the cobbled court. He pulled it open and stepped back in a hurry.

Through the door they could see the crumbling walls of what had been a street of adobe houses. Under the brilliant sun every cobble of the street stood out clear. Beyond the houses a wagonroad curved up a bare yellow hill. At the top, in the ruins of a chapel, lighter shadows moved in the blackness behind some sandbags.

Morton pointed with a crooked forefinger that was black with powder and oil. He was careful to keep his eyes from meeting Glenn's. "That's where our boys are. You see way across the river; that's the enemy." Behind some walls in the distant purple shadow Glenn could see spots moving. Everything swam from the brightness of the sunlight after so many days of dark. "Now, when we get our gun in place we can shell this hill for a few minutes. Give you fellers a chance to run for it, see? No use trying to carry anything away. You'll have to be careful because they can enfilade that road."

Glenn had been telling himself the thing was just to put one foot in front of the other. He was busy keeping his knees from doubling up under him. When they hit him, they'd hit him. Maybe he wouldn't be killed.

Morton was still talking but Glenn couldn't hear his voice any more. He was walking, lifting first one foot then the over over the uneven cobbles between the yellow adobe walls. Sunlight danced in bright sharp rays in the water in the new buckets. Something that grew among the cobbles smelt like thyme when he stepped on it. He felt the deep regular breathing of his lungs, the one two, one two of his steps, the hot sweetness of the air.

As he stepped out from behind the last wall one of the buckets was suddenly empty. He must walk as carefully as he could so as not to spill the other. Something that must be bullets teased past him. On the slope ahead of him things were playfully kicking up little puffs of dust. The racket was beginning again. He was halfway up the hill before they brought him down. For a second he had no pain. He thought he'd stubbed his toe on a stone. Too bad the water was all spilled in so much blood. Must get out of this, he said to himself, and started to drag himself along the ground. Then suddenly something split and he went spinning into blackness. He was dead.

AN OPEN LETTER TO AMERICAN INTELLECTUALS

The Modern Monthly (originally The Modern Quarterly) was almost entirely the brainchild of Victor Francis Calverton (born George Goetz), who, in the 1920's, established it as a vehicle for freethinking, socialistic, and otherwise non-conformist individuals. Calverton was eclectic in his thought, utilizing sociology, Marxism, literary values, and other means for a critical view of American life. In the 1930's, he attracted numerous intellectuals dissatisfied with official communist dogma. They tended to be sympathetic to Trot-

skyite internationalism, though not relinquishing their independence. The communist assault on the memorial meeting held by the socialists in Madison Square Garden for the Austrian Social Democratic workers shot down by the Clerical-Fascist Dollfuss regime shocked them into drawing up the following protest. Among the signers were A. J. Muste, long associated with Christian Socialist ideals and labor organization; Louis F. Budenz, a communist wheelhorse, who joined the Catholic Church and later became famous for his sensational testimony against his former comrades; James Rorty, poet and critic of advertising and other American institutions; and James Burnham, who moved from Trotskyite communism to anti-communism, during which he achieved a best-seller, The Managerial Revolution *(1941).*

THE FASCIST BULLETS which killed trade union and Socialist working men in Austria also dealt the final blow to the social-democratic theory of "gradualism." The blood and terror of that planned and premeditated coup showed that, in the post-war world, the policy of gradually building socialism alongside of capitalism brings only shameful defeat. It proved with utter finality that the social-democratic reliance upon parliamentary democracy leads straight to Fascism: to the crushing of the labor movement; to the degradation of the professional workers, the intellectuals; to the destruction of civil liberties; to the brutal persecution of racial and religious minorities; in sum, it is a surrender to medievalism and barbarism.

That was the clear lesson roared by the cannons that shattered the cooperative homes of the Austrian workers, burying men, women and children in their ruins.

What did the Communist Party of the U.S.A. do to enforce this lesson and mobilize the masses of the American working class? It committed an act of insane hooliganism. When the Socialist Party and a number of trade unions assembled 20,000 workers in Madison Square Garden to protest against the killing of the Austrian workers by Fascists and against Fascist tendencies in the U.S., the Communist Party deliberately broke up that meeting, and by that act of monstrous and irresponsible treachery proved its utter unfitness to lead and direct an effective revolutionary movement.

Thousands of workers, their hearts filled with bitterness by the news out of Austria, sat in their homes listening to the radio, waiting for the voice of militant American labor to hurl the challenge back into the throats of Fascism here and abroad. What they heard was chaos, and the smash of the auctioneer's hammer signalizing the bankruptcy of both parliamentary Socialism and of the American Communist Party.

312] AN OPEN LETTER TO AMERICAN INTELLECTUALS

Unless, then, you are willing to be active or passive participants in the triumph of reaction, whether it bears the name of Fascism or some other, you must immediately join in the movement to build a new, effective, intelligent and responsible revolutionary party in the U.S. The supreme crisis in the history of this country is approaching. The future hangs upon what you and other groups in the nation do in the weeks and months just ahead.

A brief analysis of the situation will show that this is a sober truth.

Consider, first, the events in Austria and their implications. Austrian workers had built a powerful and progressive trade union movement. They had developed also a powerful Social-Democratic party. The intellectual level of the Austrian party movement was high and it was among the most vigorous and aggressive in the world Social-Democratic movements. It was the strongest single party in Austria. Forty percent of the voters in the entire nation supported it in elections. It had an overwhelming majority of the vote in the capital city of Vienna. For a number of years the control of Vienna was in its hands. The Austrian social-democracy had built up a remarkable series of cooperative, cultural and recreational enterprises. The houses for workers built by the Socialist municipality of Vienna gained world-wide admiration.

As has been made clear again in recent days by statements of the exiled leaders of the Austrian social-democracy, Dr. Bauer and Dr. Deutsch, the movement clung to parliamentary methods, defended the bourgeois Austrian Republic, asked only to be permitted to go ahead with its social reforms and peaceful propaganda for further Socialist measures. It persisted in this course though it was well aware of the existence in Europe and increasingly in Austria itself, of black, reactionary forces which wanted to smash the unions, wreck the cooperatives, destroy all civil liberties, and enslave the workers under a "totalitarian" state. It persisted in this course, even when it saw Fascists violating all democratic procedures and destroying all democratic institutions whenever they had a chance. Only a few months ago it offered an alliance to Chancellor Dollfuss, an avowed and bitter foe of Socialism, for the defense of the Republic. In the face of developments in Austria, the statement that a revolutionary labor movement gives rise to Fascism and the suggestion that if only labor will remain strictly legal and parliamentary, then reaction and Fascism will not make headway, becomes ridiculous. It was precisely because the Austrian labor movement was *not* revolutionary, because it stuck to legal and parliamentary methods, that Fascism has triumphed in Austria.

The failure to establish a new Socialist economy in Austria when

An Open Letter to American Intellectuals

bold measures might have made this possible (at least if support had been given in time by Social-Democratic parties in such countries as Germany) left the field to the parties representing the decaying capitalist system. There, as elsewhere, capitalism tried to save itself at the expense of the wages and standards of living of the workers. There, as elsewhere, Fascism sprang up to force reductions upon the workers and violently to suppress discontent in whatever sections of the population it might arise.

Because the Austrian social-democracy failed to take adequate measures against Fascism in its beginnings, Fascism was free to choose its own time to launch its decisive attack upon the workers and the workers' movement. The workers' press was stopped, and their homes and labor headquarters invaded. The Austrian workers refused to submit like cowards. They called a general strike. The police and troops then began to shoot them down. They fought back as best they could. Heroically, the men and women together defended their homes. It was then too late. They were brutally murdered. Their unions, their cooperatives, their political party, their rights along with the lives of the finest among them, are all being destroyed.

For the militancy and courage of the Socialist workers in Austria in their last stand against Fascism, we can have only the highest admiration, especially when we recall the astounding failure of either the great Social-Democratic or the great Communist party of Germany to offer one gesture of resistance to Hitler when he rode into power, and the submissiveness which the workers in many lands have often displayed in the face of poverty, injustice and brutality.

This cannot blind us, however, to the futility and danger of social-democratic policies which had misled these heroic workers and placed them in an impossible and tragic position. Intelligent men and women in the U.S. who are not indulging in fantasies and wishful thinking but who are really determined to achieve a new social order in which there shall be plenty and security for all and in which, therefore, the life of freedom and cultural development for all will be possible, must decisively repudiate social-democracy and withdraw support from the Socialist party. The Socialist party in the U.S. is no more to be trusted than was the Social-Democratic party of Austria; it is indeed far from possessing the numbers, the intellectual weight and clarity, the determination of the Austrian party before the recent débâcle. The notion that a party as unquestionably wedded to social-democratic policies and as heterogeneous in its composition as the Socialist party of the U.S. can be made over into an instrument for effective revolutionary action is preposterous.

The Communist Party is equally hopeless. An exhaustive outline of the reasons for the collapse of the Communist party of the U.S. and of the Third International cannot be set forth in this brief statement. (Note: Such an analysis is being prepared by the American Workers Party and will shortly be available.) A crisis, however, often gives to those who have eyes to see, a vivid, dramatic and conclusive revelation of the weakness and rottenness of a movement or party which has made great and apparently justifiable pretensions. Thus were the pretensions of the Social-Democracy and the Second International exposed at the outbreak of the Great War in 1914. Lenin and many others saw then that a new movement would have to be built. An epoch had passed, and with it the instrument forged in that epoch had also to be discarded.

Thus the incident in Madison Square Garden on February 16, 1934, and the recent course of the Communist Party which led to this incident gives a lurid and unforgettable picture of the degeneration which has taken place in the Communist movement and its inability to cope with the problems raised by the world threat of Fascism.

All the workers in the U.S. including the politically backward, *i.e.* the majority among them, as well as practically all other elements in the country, had been stirred to resentment by the unprovoked attack by Austrian Fascists upon the trade unions and the civil rights of the people and by the wanton destruction of workers' homes and the brutal massacre of men, women and children, when in the face of terrible odds these workers sought to defend themselves, their homes, their children. Everywhere admiration had been aroused for Austrian workers who chose to die fighting rather than in the concentration camps of an Austrian Hitler. No such general and unmixed resentment against an outbreak of Fascism had been aroused in the U.S. when Mussolini came to power in Italy or on the advent of Hitler in Germany a year ago. At that time there were anti-Semitic elements in the U.S. who were not outraged by the Hitler attack on the Jews and other more numerous elements who were anti-Communist and inclined to condone Hitlerism as the only way Germany had to avert "Bolshevism." No such factors appeared in the foreground, to limit or modify the resentment against Austrian Fascism or the sympathy for Austrian trade union and Socialist workers.

Here was an opportunity, then, such as has never before occurred in the U.S. to picture to the workers of the U.S. what Fascism really means, to arouse hatred for it in their breasts, to show them how certain it is that reaction and Fascism will some day attack their homes and seek to abolish their liberties, to arouse a sense of solidarity with the workers of other lands, suffering under the Fascist terror — above

An Open Letter to American Intellectuals [315

all, to unite the workers both radical and conservative, regardless of political affiliations, in a common protest and so to lay the foundations for a genuine united front against Fascism and the war danger. Here, furthermore, was a golden and unprecedented opportunity to present the necessity of revolutionary action to American workers, the refusal to use which had so obviously failed to save the Austrian workers from brutal attacks by reactionaries, and so to attach the growing militancy of the American workers to a revolutionary objective.

The common sense, not to speak of the revolutionary statesmanship, to take advantage of so tremendous an opportunity proved to be utterly lacking in the Communist Party of the U.S. The C.P., by booing, cat-calls, attempts to "capture" the meeting and the platform, and all sorts of hooliganism, broke up the gathering of 20,000 workers in Madison Square Garden. The word that went, therefore, to the workers and to the ruling class in the U.S. was that in the presence of the menace of Fascism, of the working-class dead of Vienna, Communists and Socialists of the U.S. were beating each other up and that their meeting ended in a riot, the capitalist police having finally to step in lest actual loss of human life occur. So far as the Madison Square Garden meeting is concerned, the word that goes out is one of despair to the workers and of hope to Fascists in the U.S. and throughout the world, the word that radical workers cannot unite among themselves, that in the face of the greatest challenge they can fight only each other instead of the enemy.

Can it be that the Communists, irritated by the fact that Socialists in Austria had put up a courageous even though hopeless battle at the last moment, and had demonstrated "that they could and would fight" — while the Communists in Germany had for one reason or another failed to put up any fight when Hitler came to power in that country — felt that they had to demonstrate that they too were fighters and could think of no better way to do so than to engage in the insane and sadistic adventure of breaking up a trade union and Socialist demonstration?

This action of the Communists was a climax to the policy of sectarianism, disruption and hooliganism which has marked the course of the C.P. in recent years. It was a deliberate action. The foremost figures in the C.P. including Clarence Hathaway, editor of the *Daily Worker*, and Robert Minor, led the insane movement to break up the Socialist meeting.

That the statesmanship of the Communist Party, the representatives of the Third International in the U.S., which lays claim to being the vanguard of the workers' revolutionary movement of the world, could rise no higher in this crisis than a gangster attack on trade union and Socialist fellow-workers is a tragedy for the working class. It is the final proof that so far from being the leader of the revolutionary movement of the workers, the C.P. has become a major barrier to the revolution.

No self-respecting intellectual can support a policy of disruption, infantile adventurism, breaking up workers' meetings, hooliganism, a policy of aping Fascist tactics. The Communist Party no longer has any other policy. It has demonstrated that in the presence of the deepest tragedies for the workers and of the greatest opportunity to advance labor solidarity, it can only disrupt and destroy. Relentless opposition must be offered to the desperate and criminal adventures in which it engages in the hopeless attempt to give an impression of life and vigor as it loses the support of the masses, undermines the morale of its own membership, and becomes organizationally and intellectually bankrupt.

We call, therefore, upon all intellectuals who are sympathetic to the revolutionary movement to repudiate the action of the Communists at Madison Square Garden, to leave the Communist Party if they are party members, and to repudiate also any of the Communist auxiliary organizations, well described as "innocents' clubs" in most instances, except in such cases, if there be any, where those organizations can be readily taken out of mechanical domination by the C.P. and given a genuine united front character.

Such primarily negative action is, however, not enough. The temptation, which will probably arise for some, to stand on the sidelines, to turn in disgust from the revolutionary task because the revolutionary movement seems unable to get rid of confusion and discord and infantilism, must at all costs, and now more than ever, be fought down. Yielding to that temptation on the part of the intellectuals will mean betrayal of the working class, of science, of culture, of liberty, of themselves.

Capitalism will resort to reaction, under the name and form of Fascism, or some other, in the U.S. as elsewhere. This country has its own history, tradition and conditions of which due account must be taken, but we cannot by some clever Rooseveltian trick evade the unfolding of basic economic and political developments under capitalism. We did not have, as many also of the intellectuals believed, a "new capitalism" in 1928, which had banished poverty and unemployment forever and under which stocks increased in value by geometric progression, world without end. Let us not deceive ourselves that we shall not have to face here also the choice between reaction,

An Open Letter to American Intellectuals [317

on the one hand, and a truly scientific economy under a genuine workers' democracy on the other.

Destruction will overtake us if we ignore the danger and fail to prepare. A few years ago men laughed at Mussolini. A year ago they laughed at Hitler. A few months ago they laughed at the idea that Fascism could come to gentle, "democratic" Austria!

When war broke out in Europe, we were eventually dragged into it. This war between Fascism and the workers is also world-wide. We cannot keep out of it. We must organize to fight and defend our unions, our homes, our liberties, our right to live in security and plenty on this continent.

Those forces which during the post-war orgy speculated in human lives, debauched the government, plunged us into the depression and brought starvation in the midst of plenty to the American masses, which today admit that every inhabitant of the country could have an income of $5000 per year at present prices and still try to make them contented with a pittance in wages or with "subsistence farms" while they destroy food and other goods, which club and shoot workers even in ordinary peaceful strikes for better conditions or union recognition — surely it is plain that they will stop at nothing.

Capitalism will try to save itself at the expense of the standards of living and the liberties of the masses.

Nowhere have reaction and Fascism been seriously challenged except by a militant labor movement. Hence the determination of capitalism everywhere to limit the growth of that movement and to crush it when it becomes powerful.

Reaction and Fascism can be prevented or crushed and a scientific economy achieved in the U.S. only by a revolutionary movement of the masses, inspired and guided by a revolutionary party which faces in a realistic fashion the economic, political, and cultural factors in the American scene, which orients itself first of all upon the industrial working class but rallies all potentially revolutionary elements in the population, which springs out of the American soil yet is part of and helps to build an international revolutionary movement to destroy capitalism, Fascism and war, and within whose ranks policy is determined by party democracy and carried out by an iron discipline, and which is determined to take power and to become the nation.

Such a part is the American Workers Party which is now being built under a Provisional Organizing Committee. The decision to begin building the A.W.P. came out of the experiences of the Conference for Progressive Labor Action in unions and unemployed leagues, organization campaigns and strikes over a number of years. It was a response to the demands of workers in these mass organizations who believed that an effective revolutionary party was imperatively needed in the U.S. and that neither the Communist nor the Socialist party could supply the need. We have seen how recent events have furnished startling confirmation of that judgment.

Now the Party must be built. There can be no delay. The obvious collapse of the old radical parties, both on the national and the international field, demands the immediate building of the new Party. The swift pace of economic and political developments in the U.S. and elsewhere, the possibility that Fascism or war may, almost in a moment, engulf us in horror and destruction, likewise forbids delay.

The American Workers Party claims to understand the nature of the revolutionary change that alone can save our society from continuing and increasing disintegration. It claims further that with the support of the workers of this country it will be able to lead correctly in the movement to bring about this change, and to establish a free workers' democracy guaranteeing peace, security and the opportunity of individual development for all.

The justification of the claim of the American Workers Party to lead the revolutionary movement to victory must, of course, be proved in action. The only assurance that it will lead, and will lead correctly to the final goal, will be the determined union of the advanced workers and producers of the United States in its ranks.

Especially do we call in this statement upon the professional workers in this country — doctors, architects, engineers, scientists, teachers, lawyers, artists, writers — to help build the American Workers Party. Your condition is becoming steadily and rapidly worse. There is no chance under the present order for its betterment. Unemployment among you is extraordinarily high and the chances for new recruits from graduate and technical schools even for finding any sort of job are fast disappearing. You have been watching with growing alarm the fate of the professionals under Fascism. The traditional hesitancy of American professional workers to take part in social and political activity must now be overcome. We call upon you, as well as all other workers who are no longer willing to suffer needless injustice, who have decided not merely to complain at but to change society, we call upon all the forces determined to bring a new social order out of the ruins of the old, to unite.

A. J. Muste - Louis F. Budenz - Sidney Hook - James Rorty - V. F. Calverton - George Schuyler - James Burnham - J. B. S. Hardman - Gerry Allard - Elmer Cope - Larry Heimbach - Harry A. Howe - Larry Hogan - Arnold Johnson - Ludwig Lore - Ernest Rice McKinney - Anthony Ramuglia - William R. Truax.

Sidney Hook

THE FALLACY OF THE THEORY OF SOCIAL FASCISM

> *Sidney Hook once seemed destined to be one of the philosophers of American Marxism. A brilliant young instructor, a Guggenheim Fellow in 1928-29 (he was born in 1902), he produced* The Metaphysics of Pragmatism *(1927),* Towards the Understanding of Karl Marx *(1933),* American Philosophy — Today and Tomorrow *(1935),* From Hegel to Marx *(1936), and* John Dewey — An Intellectual Portrait *(1939), and contributed to* Planned Society — Yesterday, Today, Tomorrow *(1937), and similar collections.*
>
> *With some others, however, he soon became disgusted with Stalinist deeds and attitudes of the period. In 1933 he began a systematic examination of Stalinism, and before long he reached a position where he was prepared to regard even the non-Stalinist communists as "midget totalitarians." Such works as* Reason, Social Myths and Democracy *(1940) and* The Hero in History *(1943) contain a critique of the philosophical and political grounds of Bolshevik-Leninism in all its varieties.*
>
> *His subsequent intellectual development found expression in such volumes as* Education for Modern Man *(1947),* Heresy, Yes — Conspiracy, No *(1953), and* Political Power and Personal Freedom *(1959).*

EVERY sincere opponent of fascism must have been mortified by the catastrophic disruption of the Madison Square Garden protest meeting against the Vienna massacres last spring, and the disastrous consequences which it has had upon all united front activities of the American working class. Even the report of the Investigation Committee of the American Civil Liberties Union, in placing chief responsibility for the occurrence upon the Communist Party, points out how necessary working class unity against fascism is and why such events make unity impossible. But the American Civil Liberties Union could not, in the nature of the case, examine the relationship between the peculiar united front policies of the Communist Party and the fundamental theory from which such tactics flow and must flow. One does not have to subscribe to the dogma that theory and practice are always organically connected, to realize that no *resolution* to change a set to tactics will have any appreciable effect, if a political theory is still avowed whose logical and psychological corollaries sanction the very conduct which is verbally deplored. The Communist International is wedded to the theory of "social-fascism." Whoever seriously desires to defeat fascism — whether he be liberal, socialist or communist — must come to grips with this theory, must grasp its meaning and trace its practical implications for anti-fascist movements and activities. Such an analysis becomes absolutely imperative in view of the thesis held by a great many unofficial communists as well as by some members of the Communist Party unofficially that the theory of social fascism is not only responsible for such events as Madison Square Garden but was one of the most important causes for the tragic defeat of the German working class and the victory of Hitler.

The classic expression of the theory of social-fascism was given by Stalin:

> "Fascism is a fighting organization of the bourgeoisie, an organization that rests on the active support of social democracy. Social democracy is objectively the moderate wing of fascism. There exists no reason for supposing that the fighting organization of the bourgeoisie can achieve decisive successes in their struggles or in their leadership of the country without the active support of social democracy. And there is just as little reason to suppose that social democracy can achieve decisive successes in its struggles or in its leadership of the country without the active support by the fighting organization of the bourgeoisie. These organizations do not contradict each other, but complete each other. They are not antipodes but twins . . ."

On the face of it to regard the social-democracy as a twin or wing of fascism is to bring these movements into a startling juxtaposition especially from the perspective of a united anti-fascist front. Already in 1875 Marx had bitterly condemned his followers for saying that "in opposition to the working class, all other classes form only a homogeneous reactionary mass." And Engels, seven years later, amplified this criticism in a latter to Bernstein with the following words:

> "The idea that the coming revolution will *begin* on the basis that

The Fallacy of the Theory of Social Fascism

'here is Guelph and there is Ghibelline' is clearly a childish one — the idea that the whole world will be divided into two armies — on one side ourselves, and on the other the whole 'single reactionary mass'. This is as much as to say that the revolution must begin at Act V, and not Act I."

If it is wrong to regard all classes other than the working class as constituting one reactionary mass, it must be positively fantastic, to regard all political *parties* other than the Communist Party as wings of fascism. Expect on one assumption, viz., that there is no other working class party except the Communist — an assumption which confuses the difference between a *revolutionary* working class party and a *non-revolutionary* working class party with the difference between a working class party and a non-workingclass party.

This confusion is topped off by identifying a non-revolutionary working class party with a counter-revolutionary party and serves as the basis for the conclusion expressed by Karl Radek at the last Congress of the Russian Communist Party that "there is no struggle for the cause of the working class apart from the struggle of the Bolshevist Party under the banner of Lenin and the leadership of Stalin. Whoever attempts to oppose the general line of the Party of Lenin automatically places himself on the other side of the barricade." Whoever then opposes the theory of social-fascism is himself a social-fascist, and whatever communist group differs with Stalin, from the right or the left, is counter-revolutionary.

In support of Stalin's thesis it might be urged that the historical situation since 1914 is quite different from that of 1875 and of capitalism. Indeed, the Thirteenth Plenum of the Executive Committee of the Communist International has just declared that "social-democracy continues to play the role of the main social prop of the bourgeoisie also in the countries of open fascist dictatorship." The import of these statements will be considered later in their bearings upon the possibility of united anti-fascist action. Here we must address ourselves to the question of their historic truth.

When capitalism was in its ascendency the rôle of the social-democracy was to organize the working class for independent political and economic action. Even though its practices were more reformist than revolutionary, not even its harshest critics characterized it before 1914 as the third party of the bourgeoisie. It was the collapse of the Second International, revealing as it did the extent to which social patriotism and petty bourgeois ideology had eaten into the core of the largest national parties, that marked the close of the progressive epoch of social-democracy. In the post-war period, wherever a revolutionary situation developed, the Social-Democracy was entrusted with the task of restoring law and order (Germany), or of introducing measures of stabilization at the cost of the working class (England) which the bourgeoisie could not have attempted itself without provoking overt revolution. It cannot be denied by the objective observer that the historic function of Social-Democracy since 1918 has been to suppress or abort all revolutionary movements throughout the world independently of whether it shared power in a coalition government or not.

Now in virtue of what traits was the Social-Democracy able to perform this task of revolutionary frustration? Why could the bourgeoisie rely upon the leadership of the Social-Democracy to do its disagreeable political chores? It is clear that only because the Social-Democracy was a working class organization supported by powerful trade unions and large masses of the population could it head off revolutionary disturbances. If the Social-Democracy had no mass following, or if the leadership of the Social-Democracy could not control or influence its following, it would never have been called in to administer the interests of the state. It is important to remember that the Social-Democracy nowhere was permitted to control the state apparatus, the armed forces, courts, schools, etc., nor did it ever make an attempt to do so. It was used, and it gladly allowed itself to be used, as an *instrument* of the classes which controlled the state. But it could only be an effective instrument — when a social revolution was on the order of the day — because it was a mass organization with mass influence. This mass base was necessary not only for the function it was called upon to play but it is obvious — or should be obvious — that the mass base was even more necessary to the *leaders* of the Social-Democracy. For it served both as a source of income and of prestige to the leadership, and, what it more important, as the only club which the leadership could wield to win political concessions from the bourgeoisie. Although this is obvious or should be obvious, I stress the point because it has an important bearing upon the subsequent argument. Without independent mass organization of the workers, the leadership of the Social-Democracy would never be given an opportunity to execute governmental duties — even if it were nothing else but the opportunity to betray the revolution. The very existence of the leadership is therefore inextricably bound up with the existence of its mass organization.

Where the decline of capitalism enters an acute stage, the dominant industrial and financial classes reach out for a sharper and more efficient instrument to consolidate their rule. Fascism now replaces Social-Democracy as the savior of law and order — rent, interest and profit. Using the disgruntled elements which have been freshly pauperized by economic processes and which are hot with resentment against the paper privileges and rule of the Social-Democracy, Fascism wipes out all vestiges of democratic political rights and directly coordinates the state with the needs of a *Gleichgeschaltet* economy. In order to accomplish this it *necessarily* must destroy all independent mass organizations of the working class — a policy which is everywhere the defining political characteristic of Fascism. I say that it must *necessarily* do this for at least two reasons. (1) The economic program of Fascism, doomed as it is to ultimate failure, would be bankrupted immediately if the workers' organizations actively opposed the scaling down of wages, the retrenchment in the social services and the mobilization of labor battalions for national defense. (2) Since the economic program of Fascism together with its frenzied cult of nationalism accelerates the drift towards war, it becomes imperative to keep the rear free from any political ferment, and the lines always open by which the nation's industry feeds the front. This demands the practical militarization of labor power — and marks the end not merely of other political parties but of all trade-unions, cooperatives, sport and cultural organizations of the working class.

We can now draw our conclusions together and compare them with Stalin's theory of social-fascism. Without mass organizations of the working class, the Social-Democracy — together with its leadership — cannot exist. Without destroying all organizations of the working class, Fascism cannot exist. Therefore, the advent of Fascism to power spells the death of Social-Democracy. Even though both are instruments of the bourgeoisie in bolstering up capitalism, there is an objective antagonism between them which is irreconcilable. Capitalism cannot cashier its old servant (Social-Democracy) without ordering its new servant (Fascism) to destroy it. The working-class slave who has felt the lash of the old servant now faces the drawn knife of the new. Shall he say that both servants "do not contradict each other but complete each other. They are not antipodes but twins?" (Stalin) And if the working-class slave is a Communist who will be the *first* to feel the knife of the Fascist servant, is it not plain insanity at that moment to berate the old servant whose life is at stake, too, for the past lashings? That Fascism must destroy the Social-Democracy there can be no doubt after the Italian, German and Austrian experiences. When Otto Bauer on bended knees petitioned Dollfus to come to an understanding with Austrian Social-Democracy, Dollfuss could no more make concessions to him than a general of an army can make important strategic concessions to the general of an enemy army which he is about to engage in desperate battle. The victory of Fascism demanded the crushing of Austrian Social-Democracy; with his organization crushed, of what use could Bauer be to Dollfuss? When the hour arrives at which the bourgeoisie decides to hand over power to the Fascists nothing can save the Social Democracy — and its leaders — except complete apostasy. And not even the most rabid Communists will claim that most of the Social-Democratic workers and leaders have been guilty of this, and that bag and baggage desertions to Fascism can be found only among Social-Democrats.

The objective logic of the situation and the compulsion of events have so clearly shown the absurdity of the view that fascism and social-democracy are twins, that official communists have surreptitiously sought to revise Stalin's theory of social-fascism and to substitute a weakened form of the doctrine. Social-Democracy is social-fascist, now, not because it is a wing of fascism, but because it paves the way for fascism by weakening the revolutionary struggles of the preletariat. What, does Social-Democracy deliberately — do even its leaders — pave the way for their own certain destruction? No, runs the answer according to the revised theory of social-fascism, the objective effects of their compromise, independently of their own will, prepare the victory of Fascism — their subjective intentions be damned! But the revised theory of social-fascism leads to absurd consequences. If the leaders of Social-Democracy are social-fascists because they pave the way for fascism, then the members of the Social-Democracy are social-fascists because, in spite of the historic record and the exhortations of the Communists, they persist in supporting their leaders. They are misled? So are their leaders who are preparing their own doom when they prepare the way for Fascism. It is either a case of the blind leading the blind or else in the Communists' own words "subjective intentions be damned" — without the support of their members, the leaders of Social-Democracy could not pave the way for fascism. The rank and file of Social-Democracy would, then, have to be regarded as social-fascist. But how can this be squared with the veritable Commandment of the Communist Party, violation of which is punished with immediate expulsion; "Thou shalt not regard thy Social-Democratic brother as a social fascist; only his leaders." Secondly, if any organization which prepares the way for the victory of Fascism is social-fascist, then if it ever be established that the communist theory of social-fascism, by making genuine unity of the German working class impossible, helped Hitler come to power, if ever it be demonstrated that the Communist theory of the "united front-from-below" helped the Social-Democratic leadership which was preparing the way for Fascism to keep its influence on its rank and file, if ever it be that any Communist Party error, in theory or practice, helps the Fascists (subjective intentions be damned!) – why, there is no help for it but to regard the Communist Party, on its own theory, social-fascist, as the twin of Fascism. The only way to escape this conclusion is to deny that the Communist Party can make errors.

I return to Stalin's theory of social-fascism which his own disciples, although true to it in practice, have sought to soften verbally.

Granted that the Social-Democracy will not lead a genuine fight against Fascism, that their generals are old women, blind in both eyes, gifted with gab and talking against time, – what is the function of a Communist Party under those circumstances? The function of the Communist Party is to win over to their own position the mass following of the social-democratic leadership. How can this be done? The answer made by all who subscribe to the theory of social-fascism is *"by a united-front-from-below."* The *united-front-from-below* is declared to be a fighting organization of the rank and file of the Socialist Party (or conservative trade unions) with the members of the Communist Party (or Red trade-unions) for certain specific issues. The invitation to common action is directed by the Communist Party *not* to the Socialist Party as such but by the Communist Party – or a group ostensibly controlled by that Party – to the membership of the rival organization. Since the invitation is not official, the leadership of the Socialist Party invariably construes such a united front offer as an effort to split their organization and turn their membership against them. And since the Communist Party in urging "a united-front-from-below" calls upon its prospective rank and file allies within the Socialist Party to join with it, despite and against the wishes of the Socialist Party leadership, the latter are always able to cite the very pronunciamientos of the Communist Party as evidence for their charge of disruption and insincerity against it.

It is not hard to see why "the united-front-from-below" cannot succeed. After all, the fact that the rank and file of the Socialist Party are still within that organization indicates that they have the same degree of confidence in the principles and leadership of the Socialist Party as the members of the Communist Party have in their own principles and leadership. To expect the Socialist Party rank and file to violate the express injunction of their own leaders to have nothing to do with such manoeuvres (who say, "if the Communist Party sincerely desired a united front they would offer it to the organization") is to expect them to desert their party and to become communists and allies of the Communist Party. Such an expectation reveals that the "united-front-from-below" is not a united front at all but merely another name for agitation and propaganda among the members of the Socialist Party and other organizations to join in a common defensive or offensive action, to surrender their socialist "illusions" and embrace revolutionary communism. Such agitation and propaganda goes on — or should go on — all the time, and whether or not it fails or succeeds usually has nothing to do with what the particular agitational technique is *called*. But where such agitation is carried on under the guise of being something else, it is likely to become a boomerang.

As a matter of historic fact, the united-front-from-below has not only failed to win the membership of the Socialist Party, it has reinforced the influence and hold of the leadership of the Socialist Party upon its members precisely at those moments when the disastrous consequences of the course the Socialist Party was pursuing was itself driving the Socialist Party members to the left. This results from the psychological hostility generated between the Socialist Party and the Communist Party workers when the Socialist Party workers maintain their party discipline and refuse to unite with the Communist Party "despite and against" the will of their leadership. The normal member of the Communist Party — no matter what he is told — cannot help but regard the Socialist Party member who persists in listening to his leaders as objectively supporting them. In the eyes of the rank and file of the Communist Party, the rank and file of the Socialist Party therefore become Social-fascist or worse. This leads not merely to hard feeling but often to actual rioting between them. I myself witnesses many brawls of this character in 1928-9 when both parties were ignoring the young but very active Nazi party. When Zorgiebel, the Social-Democratic police chief of Berlin, was treating demonstrations of workers in the same way as other police officials throughout the world, the Communist Party could not understand why the honest and militant members of the Social Party would not join with it in common protest against Zorgiebel and his rule. Before long they were calling the Social Party rank and file *"kleine Zorgiebels,"*, and *Zwischenfälle* between the *Reichsbanner* and the *Rotfront* multiplied. This "kleine Zorgiebel" period was officially condemned by the Communist Party but although the epithet was dropped the feeling behind it could not so easily disappear.

Indeed, the whole theory of the united-front-from-below received its great historic test in the events leading up to Hitler's accession to

The Fallacy of the Theory of Social Fascism

power. It becomes necessary, therefore, to examine the German situation with some care in order to determine the degree of responsibility which the theory of social-fascism and its consequences bear for the greatest disaster suffered by the international working class since August 4, 1914.

The relevant historical analysis may conveniently focus around the questions: Why did Hitler succeed in coming to power so easily? Why was Fascism able to put through a program which the capitalist state had not dared to propose, even in days when the revolutionary potential of the country was not so high? The obvious answer is that Hitler came to power as easily as he did — without an open struggle — because the German working class did not present a unified front against him. I am not one of those who believe that even if the entire German working-class had actually opposed him, it is a foregone conclusion that he would have been defeated and that the workers would have marched on to a victorious social revolution. But at least there would have been a gigantic struggle with the prospects for ultimate victory favorable. The real question, then, becomes the following: Granted that the role of the Social-Democratic leadership is what the Communist Party declares it to be *why did the Communist Party fail to win over to its position a majority of the German working-class?* This was their self-confessed duty; their failure to perform it demands an explanation. It is *this* question which demands an answer — and not another one which the Communist Party leaders uneasily substitute for it — a substitution which testifies either to their unwillingness to grapple with the central issue or to an amazing political naiveté. The question which they substitute for the essential one is: Why did not the Communist Party give battle to Hitler? Some communists after the heroic resistance of the Austrian Social-Democrats, raised the question whether the practical and moral advantages of some kind of open struggle against Hitler — no matter how unsuccessful — would not have been greater than the inglorious defeat without battle. To this the Communist Party answers that such a struggle, in view of the great disparity of forces, would have been bloody and foolish adventurism. Undoubtedly. The Communist Party could no more have corrected the practical consequences of its three year theory of social-fascism by a twelfth hour stand against Hitler, no matter how desperate, than Austrian Social-Democracy could overcome the consequences of its own policy of revolutionary emasculation by its final gesture of resistance, no matter how heroic. Just as we ask the Social-Democracy; why was it that the resistance of the Austrian workers was doomed to failure? so we must ask the Communist leaders: why was it that the German Communist Party was not in a position to lead an armed defence against Hitler, why did it fail to unify the German working classes behind it?

The answer is clear. The Communist Party of Germany failed to win a majority of the working-class to its banner because its chief instrument for effecting this — "the united-front-from-below" — proved to be disastrously inadequate. And yet if the theory of social fascism were sound, this would have been impossible. For the German Social-Democracy, although it played the game of the bourgeoisie, could not prevent the economic and social conditions going from bad to worse. Despite its own pacifist program, it supported the *Panzerkreutzerbau;* despite its liberal phrases, it concluded a Concordat with the Catholic Church; despite its professed support of the workers, it repudiated the pro-labor findings of its own arbitration commissions when the Ruhr industrialists fumed and threatened; despite its theorists who spoke of the stabilization of capitalism, wages fell; unemployment increased and the cost of living mounted. The objective social conditions for the rise of communism — or at least for winning over the social-democratic workers — were as favorable as if they had been made to order in behalf of revolutionary Marxism. And yet — nothing happened. The relative percentage of the Communist Party vote to the total vote cast in 1932 was not much higher than it was in 1923-4. No appreciable inroads were made into the Socialist Party. The "united-front-from-below" had failed.

It could not help but fail. For the theory of social-fascism prevented the Communist Party from seeing the distinctive feature of fascism and drawing proper political conclusions therefrom. It reasoned that because there was no difference between the *Gummiknuppel* in the hands of a Social-Democratic policeman and the *Gummiknuppel* in the hands of a Nazi Storm trooper, there was no essential political difference between the Social-Democratic government and the Fascist State. And if there were no important difference between the Social-Democracy and Hitler, it followed *a fortiori* that there could be no important differences between Hitler and Schleicher, Schleicher and Papen, Papen and Bruening. That is why everything outside of the Communist Party was thrown into the same pot as constituting one reactionary mass. That is why the Communist Party characterized Bruening's regime as already Fascist, then Papen's regime, then Schleicher's regime, so that when the Fascist Hitler came to power, theoretically it was not prepared for the difference in political *quality* which the

The Fallacy of the Theory of Social Fascism [329

difference in political *degree* had brought about.* It was only on the eve of its destruction that it woke up to the political importance of the differences between a regime which permitted mass organizations of the working-class, *including the Communist Party,* to exist and one which did not. One of the Communist Party leaders went so far as to say "once they (the fascists) are in power, *then* the united front of the proletariat will be established and it will make a clean sweep of everything." Alas! he is now among the swept!

That the Communist Party which had made the theory of social-fascism part of its flesh and blood, actually stood behind these words was revealed in the incredible piece of political insanity of which it guilty in 1931. In order to dissolve the Prussian Diet which was under the control of the Social-Democracy, the Nazis introduced a referendum for a new election. The growth in the Nazi sentiment made it a foregone conclusion that they would be able to capture Prussia — the largest state in Germany — and begin their "national dictatorship." The Communist Party — instead of offering an official united front to the Socialist Party against the Fascists — actually supported the Nazi referendum. And after all, if the Socialist Party and the Fascists are not antipodes but twins" — why not? A year later some of the Communist spokesmen were uncertain of the wisdom of this particular action, which in the eyes of the Social-Democratic workers looked like a "united-front-from-below" with the Fascists, but in expressing their disapproval of it they did not condemn its legitimate parent, the theory of social-fascism, with as much as a single word. When the Communist Party leaders were warned by Trotsky and others to reverse their course and learn from the Italian experience, they responded: "Germany is not Italy." To-day, instead of learning from the German experience, they still insist upon the validity of the theory of social-fascism and the united-front-from-below, deny that the German Communist party suffered a defeat, and repeat that Hitler cannot last as long as Mussolini because "Germany is not Italy." In fact, despite the thousand proofs which establish the theory of social-fascism as a political perspective of defeat and the united-front-from-below as an instrument of workingclass demoralization, the Executive Committee of the Communist International delivers itself of the following (in 1934) "The Plenum fully approves the resolution of the Presidium

*(It is significant that in 1932, O. Piatnitsky, one of the leading figures of the Comintern, in criticizing the German Communist Party for calling the Bruening government openly fascist, characterizes in the very same speech Papen's regime as a fascist dictatorship. *The Work of the Communist Parties of France and Germany,* 12th plenum of the ECCI, Eng. trans., pp. 39, 42.)

of the ECCI of April 1, 1933, on the situation in Germany and the political line pursued by the Central Committee of the Communist Party of Germany, headed by Comrade Thaelmann, before and at the time of the fascist coup." The resolution of April 1, 1933, it is needless to point out, gave a blanket approval on all the main points. But the question which defies answer is: How could events have turned out as they did, if the objective situation was so favorable and the theory, strategy and tactics, sound? No wonder the Communist International denies that the Communist Party suffered a defeat in Germany.

At this point one may legitimately inquire whether any other tactic could have been pursued in Germany or anywhere else. To which one must simply respond that the tactic of the united front in its classic form of organization with organization should have been followed all along the line. The united front is sometimes dubbed by those who espouse the "united-front-from-below" as the "united-front-from-above." But the united-front-from-above is a pleonasm — it simply means a united front, just as the united-front-from-below means no united front at all. The tactic may be briefly described as follows. In the face of a common danger or in the interests of a common action, one organization addresses an *official* communication to the other inviting it to appoint a committee to meet with its own committee to arrange for united front activities. The invitation is published in the official press so that the membership of both organizations is appraised of the fact and kept posted on developments. This is an important feature conveniently forgotten by those who characterize the united front of organizations as a secret pact consummated by leaders behind the backs of the membership. Just as important is it that the offer made be couched not in the abusive language of political controversy but in such a way that the membership of the other organization can be convinced that is a sincere overture and not a mere agitational manoeuver.

Now let us assume an ideal situation in which an organization C addresses a united front offer to organization S. *If* the invitation is accepted, then in the common struggle the workers will have every opportunity to discover which organization is truly militant in defence of their common interests. The consequences of the struggle constitute an excellent objective test of the validity of the general programmatic line of the organizations. For example, if it is a united front against fascism, the logic of event as revealed in the necessities of militant action may more effectively dispose of the illusions of pacifism and parliamentary cretinism than hundreds of dry disquisitions and thousands of impassioned harangues. There is then no good reason why anyone who is sincerely interested in combatting a common danger should oppose a united front especially if it is made clear that the common action does not imply the amalgamation of the organizations and the surrender of their right to criticize each other's general program. As Trotsky has put it: "They march separately but strike together." It is understood that all united front agreements must be scrupulously observed. Those who march in front cannot bear banners denouncing those who march behind (or even their leaders), and vice versa. Let us assume, however, that organization *S*, or its leadership, refuses to accept the open offer of a united front from organization *C*. Now the rank and file of *C* can approach the rank and file of *S* with the simple question: "Why does your organization refuse to fight with us against a common enemy? They cannot say that we are insincere before they actually attempt to work with us." Meanwhile the common danger is growing greater and greater. At first the rank and file of *S* will support the decision of their leaders even if with some misgivings. A short time elapses and again organization *C* openly proposes a united front with *S*. If organization *S* still refuses, the policy must appear peculiar to its rank and file who, although they do not yet believe that their leaders are afraid to fight, wonder whether their caution does not go too far. The offer is renewed again and again until organization *S*. finds itself compelled by the mass pressure of its own rank and file to accept, or else watches large portions of its membership go over to organization *C* confirmed in their suspicion that organization *S* is not interested in a militant defence of workers' interests. The situation has been, of course, ideally drawn: there are always complicating factors present. But every time this tactic has been followed, notably by the Bolshevist Party in 1917, it has succeeded either in effecting a genuine united front or else making it possible for the organization which proposes it to win over to its side a majority of the working-class.

This, then, is the tactic which the Communist party in Germany should have pursued if they were interested in opposing Hitler's rise to power. Had they in 1930 abandoned the theory of social-fascism and taken this course, the Social-Democratic workers would have come over in large numbers by 1933. As a matter of fact, however, anyone who proposed such a program was denounced as a social-fascist, and local organizations which tried to effect a working unity with local organizations of the Socialist Party were threatened with expulsion. The only line of defence which the Communist Party took for its suicidal policy was that until the Socialist Party was hurled out of the government in July 1932, no real united front with it was possible.

"How," they asked, "could a united front be made with a Party which was in a sense a part of the government, whose police representatives in Prussia had been responsible for bloody May 1, 1929 and who were still forbidding out-door Communist demonstrations?" The very question indicated how seriously the Communist Party underestimated the Fascist danger in Germany.

The classic answer to this question was made by Leon Trotsky who pointed out that an essentially similar situation confronted the Bolsheviks in Russia when Kornilov marched against Kerensky. At that time Lenin was in hiding and Trotsky and other leading Bolsheviks were in jail. In Kerensky they saw the representative of the Russian bourgeoisie and landlords but nonetheless they hastened to support him against the Bolshevik-eater, Kornilov. A few months later they settled accounts with Kerensky. But at the time of the Kornilov danger, although they knew that Kerensky had been negotiating with him, and that the ultimate social allegiances of both were the same, the Bolsheviks were wise enough to realize that their own fate depended upon recognizing the differences between Kerensky and Kornilov. In supporting the first against the second, they were not only defending themselves but strengthening their position in relation to Kerensky. The very rifles which were handed out to the workers in July to stop Kornilov's advance were used by them against Kerensky in October.

The orthodox communist response to the argument advanced by Trotsky consists of two mutually incompatible arguments. The validity of the analogy drawn from the Kornilov-Kerensky episode is denied on the ground that Hitler had not yet begun an armed struggle for power; at the same time it is asserted that as a matter of fact on July 20th, 1932, when Papen unceremoniously took over power in Prussia, the Communist Party officially extended a united front offer to the Social Democracy. The first argument simply supports the point made earlier that the Communists expected to make their united front offer *after* Hitler had taken power; the second argument is based upon legend not historic fact.

When the Social-Democrats were kicked out of power in Prussia, the Communist Party issued a call for a general strike. The Socialist Party immediately denounced the slogan as a provocation. A general strike has to be prepared for, they said, it cannot be called at a moment's notice: its success is only possible if the workers are prepared to go over to a general offensive. As a matter of fact the Socialist Party leadership had pinned its faith in Hindenburg and the decision of the German Supreme court and were prepared to go to any lengths to avoid

The Fallacy of the Theory of Social Fascism

a struggle. The call of the Communist Party to the German Social-Democracy was not an official united front offer but a published manifesto in the *Rote Fahne* (which was promptly suppressed) and was dimilar in tone to the pronunciamientos issued with such montonous regularity by the *Anti-Faschistische Aktion* (a communist organization) to the members of the Social-Democracy. Sentiment in the Socialist Party for active opposition to Papen's *coup* was very strong, but the Communist Party call was met with the same distrust as its earlier appeals for a united front. Indeed, even if the Communist Party had made a real offer of a united front to the Socialist Party it is questionable whether *at that time* the refusal of the Socialist Party to accept it, would have provoked a revolt in its own ranks. For after all, the fruits of a vicious and mistaken policy last even after the policy is changed. Early in July the Social-Democratic leadership explaining to its membership why it scorned the Communist party united-front-from-below said: "Every politically enlightened person knows that the only [united front] negotiations which promise success are these initiated and conducted by the organizational centers." To which the *Rote Fahne* (July 5th, 1932) again reiterated: "Between the leadership of the S.P.D. and K.P.D. there exists fundamental and irreconcilable differences. Therefore *our struggle for a red united front is a struggle against the social-democratic politics, against the social-democracy party, and against its representatives.*" In view of this, even if the Communist Party had reversed itself on July 20th and offered a real united front of organizations *and it must be remembered that it did not do this* — progress in winning the social democratic workers would have been extremely slow. Further, I shall argue below that unless the theory of social-fascism had been abandoned, no united front tactic with the Socialist Party would have been successful.

But the sorriest commentary upon the whole united front tactic is to be found in the declaration of the Communist International itself which had ordered and continually sanctioned the united-front-from-below-and-behind policy. *After* Hitler had come to power and outlawed the Communist Party, *after* the German proletariat had been bound hand and foot and prepared for the headsman's axe, the Communist International cabled to *all* the Communist Parties of the world, on March 17, 1933:

"The Executive Committee of the Communist International recommends to the Communist Parties of the various countries to approach the Central Committee of the Social-Democratic Parties belonging to the Labor and Socialist International with proposals regarding joint actions against Fascism and against the capitalist offensive."

The Communist International in its eagerness fell all over itself and even offered to abstain from criticism of the Socialist Party organizations during the period of the united front action. Reconcile these words, if one can, with the united-front-from-below! "The Executive Committee considers it possible to recommend to the Communist Parties during the time of common fight against capital and Fascism to refrain from making attacks on Social-Democratic organizations" (!)

This cable is itself final proof — if any be needed — that a change in policy *was* ordered. Otherwise there would have been no cable. But now, if this new policy was justified *after* Hitler rose to power why was it wrong *before* he reached power; before the Communist Party was cut to pieces? And if the united front was unjustified, say in America, *before* March 1933 why was it justified *after* March 1933?

But developments since the issuance of this historic cable are even more interesting. For more than a year the Communist Parties of the world have been attempting to apply the united front tactic but without abandoning the theory of social-fascism. In no country of the world have they succeeded in making an indentation upon the Socialist Parties. On those rare occasions upon which the Socialist Party and its auxiliary organizations have accepted the Communist Party offer, the behavior of the Communist Party membership towards its "social-fascist" allies disrupted united front action and gave the Socialist Party leadership a welcome opportunity to withdraw with the support of their own membership. And so long as the Communist Party membership believes the Social-Democracy to be a wing of Fascism, it is psychologically impossible for its behavior to be any different. As a rule, however, the Socialist Parties of the world have refused to have anything to do with the Communist Party united front invitations. Normally this would have given the Communist Party a remarkable opportunity to agitate successfully among the rank and file. But even in this situation the record shows miserable failure. *The Social-Democratic workers themselves* resent the theory of social-fascism and despite the distinction which the Communists make between the Socialist Party leadership and membership, the rank and file socialist, just like the rank and file communist, regards an attack upon *his* organization, as an attack upon himself. When he repudiates the agitation of the Communist Party member, the latter, despite orders from above, cannot but regard him as actively supporting the policy of social-fas-

The Fallacy of the Theory of Social Fascism

cism and falling into the category of "the little twins of fascism." And so the mad circle goes, made more and more vicious by Madison Square Garden incidents. Even the non-radical press jeers that socialists and communists unite to fight each other rather than the common danger. And indeed, unless human beings change their natures overnight or unless Communists become Christians, nothing else is to be expected so long as the essential definition of Social-Democracy, drilled into the heads of Communist rank and file, makes Social-Democracy a species of fascism rather than a working-class organization hostile to fascism and which must be convinced that fascism can only be defeated by the proletarian revolution.

The failure of the policy of the united front tactics of the Communist Party in the last year is documented in the latest instructions of the 13th Plenum of the ECCI which once more calls for "a united-front-from-below," against and despite the wishes of the Social-Democratic leaders. Such sudden turns and zigzags are eloquent testimony, if any more were needed, of political bankruptcy. Judged by its fruits, the theory of social-fascism must be regarded as the political epitaph of the Communist International. The disease which killed it — now it can be told and *proved* — is national bolshevism.

I can find no more fitting close than the parable with which Leon Trotsky closes his criticism of the criminally stupid course of the Communist International:

"A cattle dealer once drove some bulls to the slaughter-house. And the butcher came nigh with his sharp knife.

'Let us close ranks and jack up this executioner on our horns', suggested one of the bulls.

'If you please, in what way is the butcher any worse than the dealer who drove us hither with his cudgel?', replied the bulls, who had received their political education in Manuilsky's institute.

'But we shall be able to attend to the dealer as well afterwards!' 'Nothing doing', replied the bulls, firm in their principles, to the counsellor. 'You are trying to shield our enemies from the left, you are a social-butcher yourself'.

And they refused to close ranks."

SCALES AND MEASURES

The last year (1933-34) has seen a quickening in the growth of revolutionary literature in America. The maturing of labor struggles and the steady increase of Communist influence have given the impetus and created a receptive atmosphere for this literature. . . ."

William Phillips and Philip Rahv, in *Proletarian Literature* (1935)

Dr. Wilcox talked very interestingly about the practitioners who accepted the results of science without any sense of the ability, labour and devotion that went into producing them; he said this failure made the acceptance largely ineffectual in practice. . . . One could write a very good essay on the practical value of reverence.

Albert Jay Nock, in *A Journal of These Days, June 1932-December 1933* (1934)

William Phillips and Philip Rahv

RECENT PROBLEMS OF REVOLUTIONARY LITERATURE

> *Phillips and Rahv were among the founders of* **Partisan Review**, *which, in its inception, was a publication for communist intellectuals. The two worked closely, first in support of the Party's tenets, then, following the Moscow Trials of 1936, in moving away from them into what they called "a kind of independent and critical Marxism." They moved rapidly away from political radicalism of any kind, though they and their associates maintained a kind of critical attitude toward American mores, on a rarified level. Rahv himself emerged as an admirer of Henry James.*

THE last year (1933-34) has seen a quickening in the growth of revolutionary literature in America. The maturing of labor struggles and the steady increase of Communist influence have given the impetus and created a receptive atmosphere for this literature. As was to be expected, the novel — which is the major literary form of today — has taken the lead. Cantwell, Rollins, Conroy, and Armstrong have steered fiction into proletarian patterns of struggle. In the theatre, *Peace on Earth, Stevedore,* and *They Shall Not Die* show a parallel growth. The emergence of a number of little revolutionary magazines, together with the phenomenal success of the weekly *New Masses,* has provided an outlet for the briefer forms of writing. *The Great Tradition,* by Granville Hicks, has launched us on a revaluation of American literary history.

This new literature is unified not only by its themes but also by its perspectives. Even a casual reading of it will impress one with the conviction that here is a new way of looking at life — the bone and flesh of a revolutionary sensibility taking on literary form. The proletarian writer, in sharing the moods and expectations of his audience, gains that creative confidence and harmonious functioning within his class which gives him a sense of responsibility and discipline totally

Recent Problems of Revolutionary Literature [339

unknown in the preceding decade. Lacking this solidarity with his readers, the writer, as has been the case with the aesthetes of the twenties and those who desperately carry on their traditions today, ultimately becomes skeptical of the meaning of literature as a whole, sinking into the Nirvana of peaceful cohabitation with the Universe. Indeed, it is largely this intimate relationship between reader and writer that gives revolutionary literature an activism and purposefulness long since unattainable by the writers of other classes.

However, despite the unity of outlook of revolutionary literature, it contains a number of trends embodying contradictory aims and assumptions. It would be strange indeed, if the class struggle did not operate *within* revolutionary literature, though it is most clearly defined in the fight against bourgeois literature. The varying backgrounds of revolutionary writers and the diverse ways through which they come to Marxism set the frame for this inner struggle. Moreover, since forms and methods of writing do not drop like the gentle rain of heaven, but are slowly evolved in creative practice conditioned by the developing social relations, it is only natural that sharp differences of opinion should arise. To a Marxist such differences are not personal and formal, but actually reflect the stress of class conflict. Thus, the development of revolutionary literature is not unilinear; its progress is a process unfolding through a series of contradictions, through the struggle of opposed tendencies, and it is the business of criticism[1] to help writers resolve these contradictions. Unless criticism fulfils this task, the progress of revolutionary literature is retarded and certain writers may even be shunted off their revolutionary rails.*

Thus far Marxian criticism in this country has not faced the problem squarely, nor has it stated the diverse tendencies. The illusion has been allowed to spread that revolutionary writers constitute one happy family, united in irreconcilable struggle against capitalism. To a considerable extent, therefore, an atmosphere of empiricism has resulted, where writers clutch at the nearest method at hand without conscious selection, unfortified by criticism with the Marxian equipment necessary for coping with the problems of creative method. Some incidental pieces of criticism have helped to guide writers and readers, but on the whole no attempt haas been made to place such theoretical work in the center of our discussions.

---

*By "criticism" we do not mean the body of formal analysis alone. Throughout this editorial most of our references to "critics" and "criticism" are meant to include the whole organizational and editorial leadership of revolutionary literature, the writer's critical attitude to himself and to others, as well as formal analysis.

Neither have critics given writers adequate guidance in their quest of realistic revolutionary themes. Many young writers have declared themselves for Communism, and have joined the John Reed Clubs, but with few exceptions, they have not shown as yet a sufficient understanding of the meaning of such declarations in practice. What does the present paucity of authentic revolutionary short stories prove? Most of our writers have not grasped the fact that workers' struggles cannot be written about on the basis of inventiveness or a tourist's visit. The profile of the Bolshevik is emerging in America, heroic class battles are developing, new human types and relations are budding in and around the Communist Party; obviously, therefore, revolutionary fiction cannot be produced by applying abstract Communist ideology to old familiar surroundings. The assimilation of this new material requires direct participation instead of external observation; and the critic's task is to point out the dangers inherent in the *spectator's* attitude. The critic is the ideologist of the literary movement, and any ideologist, as Lenin pointed out "is worthy of that name only when he marches ahead of the spontaneous movement, points out the real road, and when he is able, ahead of all others, to solve all the theoretical, political, and tactical questions which the 'material elements' of the movement spontaneously encounter. It is necessary to be critical of it [the movement], to point out its dangers and defects and to aspire to *elevate* spontaneity to consciousness." (*A Conversation With Defenders of Economism*).

The most striking tendency, and the most natural one in a young revolutionary literature, is what is commonly called "leftism." Though it has seldom been explicitly stated in literary theory, its prejudices and assumptions are so widespread that at this time its salient features are easily recognized. Its zeal to steep literature overnight in the political program of Communism results in the attempt to force the reader's responses through a barrage of sloganized and inorganic writing. "Leftism," by tacking on political perspectives to awkward literary forms, drains literature of its more specific qualities. Unacquainted with the real experiences of workers, "leftism," in criticism and creation alike, hides behind a smoke-screen of verbal revolutionism. It assumes a direct line between economic base and ideology, and in this way distorts and vulgarizes the complexity of human nature, the motives of action and their expression in thought and feeling. In theory the "leftist" subscribes to the Marxian thesis of the continuity of culture, but in practice he makes a mockery of it by combating all endeavors to use the heritage of the past. In criticism the "leftist" substitutes gush on the one hand, and invective on the other, for analysis; and it is not difficult to see that to some of these critics Marxism is not a science but a *sentiment*. This tendency has been so pervasive that even some of our more important works suffer from elements of "leftism." (It is obviously beyond the scope of this editorial to analyze the subtle way in which "leftism" has affected various revolutionary works.) The long article on *Revolutionary Literature in the United States Today,* published in the *Windsor Quarterly* (Spring 1934) is a critical complement to "leftism" in poetry and fiction. It fails to see literature as a process, so much so that it absurdly identifies the "coming of age" of American literature with the unemployed demonstration of March 6, 1930. Though it shuttles from a purely literary to a purely political point of view, never integrating the two, its emphasis throughout is schematically political.

"Leftism" is not an accidental practice, nor can it be regarded merely as youthful impetuosity. Its literary "line" stems from the understanding of Marxism as mechanical materialism. In philosophy, mechanical materialism assumes a direct determinism of the whole superstructure by the economic foundation, ignoring the dialectical interaction between consciousness and environment, and the reciprocal influence of the parts of the superstructure on each other and on the economic determinants. The literary counterpart of mechanical materialism faithfully reflects this vulgarization of Marxism. But its effects strike even deeper: it paralyzes the writer's capacities by creating a dualism between his artistic consciousness and his beliefs, thus making it impossible for him to achieve anything beyond fragmentary, marginal expression.

At the other extreme we find a right-wing tendency, which is equally unsuccessful in imaginatively recreating the proletarian movement. The right-wing writer is usually very productive, but his work differs but slightly from that of liberal bourgeois writers. His acceptance of the revolutionary philosophy is half-hearted, though he makes sporadic use of it. The source of his attitude and practice is political fence-straddling, disinterest in Marxism, and lack of faith in the proletariat.

We realize, of course, that on their way to the revolution many fellow-travelers must inevitably tread this path. Nor would it be correct for Marxists to taunt and bludgeon them when their pace is slow. But passivity is equally incorrect. It must always be remembered that the fellow-travelers are trailing, not leading the literary movement, and our critics must not only make this clear but must give them concrete direction in order to help them solve their problems as quickly as possible. No doubt many fellow-travelers resent criticism, especially Marxist criticism, and some of our revolutionary editors and critics, unfortunately, in their endeavor to strike the proper note in their relations with fellow-travelers, frequently seem unable to distinguish between diplomacy and analysis, or between those who lead and those who trail behind — not that diplomacy has no place in literary criticism, but, generally speaking, *it should be put in its place.*

It should not be assumed that by elimination those writers who do not swing in either of these two directions have solved the problems of revolutionary writing. There is a large and diverse group who plunge into *easy* forms, drifting on the current of chance, without any sharp consciousness of their problems. The implication of their practice is that for the purposes of revolutionary literature, one form is as good as another, and that in general the old forms can be taken over bodily. For all practical purposes, they, as well as the other groups, have shown little audacity in reaching out for the vast raw material of art that the proletarian struggle is constantly erupting.

In this editorial, some of our problems have been implicitly touched upon. In the main they consist of: 1) The degree of the writer's awareness of *strata* in his audience, 2) The method of imaginatively assimilating political content, 3) The differentiation between class-alien and usable elements in the literature of the past, and 4) the development of Marxist standards in literature.

Not a few proletarian writers have grappled with these problems. In his recent series of articles on *Revolution and the Novel* in the *New Masses,* Granville Hicks has probed these problems in fiction. However, though Hicks has helped to clarify our approach, his method of classifying unimportant details, as well as his choice of critical subjects, is removed from the way the writer faces these problems. The writer does not decide *a priori* whether he will write a dramatic or complex novel; his choice is determined by a number of psychological and thematic factors. In general Hicks has given us a class analysis of the more obvious elements in fiction without first establishing essential Marxian generalizations about the relation of method to theme and form in terms of expanding audiences and new standards.

Obed Brooks is another critic who has concerned himself with some aspects of these problems. Michael Gold and Joseph Freeman are the earliest pioneers of Marxian criticism in America, and their work has been mostly in the nature of direct *general* class warfare against bourgeois literary ideology. They fought valiantly to win a place for proletarian writers in American literature. Joshua Kunitz brought to America some of the experiences of Soviet writers. Some of our poets have been searching for poetic forms and themes that adequately express the emotional equivalents of the social-economic scene.

But only in the novel, the most successful genre of our literature, have any far-reaching attempts been made toward the solution of these problems.

These problems cannot be solved by decree or dogma. Solutions will be made step by step, in the course of the continuous interaction of literary theory and literary practice. In this editorial, however, we wish to indicate several means of approach.

The very existence of two main types of revolutionary writing, the more intellectual and the more popular, shows that there is a division in our audience in terms of background and class composition. Workers who have no literary education prefer the poetry of Don West to that of Kenneth Fearing, whereas intellectuals reverse this choice. The proletarian writer should realize that he is functioning through his medium within the vanguard of the movement as a whole. As such, his task is to work out a sensibility and a set of symbols *unifying* the responses and experiences of his total audience. Insofar as this cannot be done overnight, his innovations must be constantly checked by the responses of his main audience, the working class, even while he strives to raise the cultural level of the masses.

The question of creative method is primarily a question of the imaginative assimilation of political content. We believe that the sensibility is the medium of assimilation: political content should not be isolated from the rest of experience but must be merged into the creation of complete personalities and the perception of human relations in their physical and sensual immediacy. The class struggle must serve as a premise, not as a discovery. This the "leftist" does not do on the grounds that such a method dilutes the political directness that he aims at; actually, however, he defeats his purpose, inasmuch as he dissolves action and being in political abstractions. To a Marxist the bourgeois claims of universality are an empty concept; those elements in art that have been called universal are merely those that have recurred so far. The problem of the revolutionist is not to seek universals but usables, for his task is to create a synthesis and not merely an innovation. Ultimately, of course, the question of usables involves, first, the retaining of the cultural acquisitions of humanity as a *background of values,* and secondly, a selection of specific contributions by individual bourgeois writers.

Unless we are acutely aware of the body of literature as a whole, no standards of merit are possible. The measure of a revolutionary writer's success lies not only in his sensitiveness to proletarian material, but also in his ability to create new landmarks in the perception of reality; that is, his success cannot be gauged by immediate agitational significance, but by his recreation of social forces in their entirety. This becomes specific literary criticism when applied by choice of theme, character, and incident. And here it is necessary to stress what many writers tend to forget: literature is a medium steeped in sensory experience, and does not lend itself to the conceptual forms that the social-political content of the class struggle takes most easily. Hence the translation of this content into images of *physical life* determines — in the aesthetic sense — the extent of the writer's achievement.

Ernest Sutherland Bates

T.S. ELIOT:
LEISURE CLASS LAUREATE

> Ernest Sutherland Bates (1879-1939) was a humanist and former professor of literature and philosophy who interested himself increasingly in libertarian points of view. He was literary editor of the Dictionary of American Biography, and joined V. F. Calverton as an associate editor of the Modern Monthly. In 1930, he issued This Land of Liberty. 1936 was his most remarkable publishing year, giving him a best-seller, The Bible Designed to Be Read as Living Literature, and also The Story of the Supreme Court, The Story of Congress, and (with Oliver Carlson) Hearst, Lord of San Simeon.

THERE SEEMS an almost providential propriety in the appointment for the current year of T. S. Eliot as Professor of Poetry at Harvard on the Charles Eliot Norton Foundation. The Overseers may well have rejoiced at the singular stroke of good fortune which enabled them to secure not merely a distinguished poet but a Harvard graduate, not merely a Harvard graduate but also a man of New England family, not merely a man of New England family but also an Eliot. The far-off relative in whose honor the Foundation was named, Charles Eliot Norton, was, it will be recalled, a notable Boston Brahmin of the late nineteenth century in whom the religio-literary virtues of both the Nortons and Eliots were deemed appropriately to culminate. Translator of Dante, editor of the letters of James Russell Lowell, author of a *List of the Principal Books relating to . . . Michael Angelo,* professor of the history of art at Harvard, he was a perfect representative of the period when the declining genius of New England turned gracefully from the vulgar work of creation to the more elegant accomplishments of translation and scholarship, fondly believing that it was thus transmuting earlier personal values into a higher, more impersonal substance. In reality, of course, this substance was nothing but the leisure class attitude of a privileged group living upon the credit of their ancestors and atoning for their spiritual impotence by rehearsing the glories of the past. To this amiable task, however, they brought a considerable intellectual endowment, sufficient to maintain the tradition of useless learning in the American university for many years. Gradually expelled from all the social sciences as these became more vitalized, the rear-guard of that tradition finally took sanctuary in the literary departments where its representatives still linger, cultivating an uneasy disdain for a world which they have failed to understand or master. It is their great good luck to have now found, in T. S. Eliot, a man of real genius to rationalize their defeat into an appearance of victory.

The leisure class, by which is meant, of course, not the nouveaux riches, but the relatively small group of those in America to the manner born, is no longer the complacent "good society" of Norton's day. "Good society" in the older sense has all but vanished, and those members of it who survive are scattered, uncertain, disquieted, haunted by a nightmare vision of the end. The older aristocratic rationalizations: dignity, the cloak of pride; reticence, the cloak of scorn; chivalry, the cloak of condescension; — where are they now? Chill memories of Riverside Drive are small comfort in the presence of Park Avenue and Broadway, parallel viae sacrae of contemporary vulgarity. Even such harmless classical allusions as "viae sacrae" begin to sound pedantic. As for classical education itself, formerly one of the most obvious badges of "the gentleman," what Thorstein Veblen well called "Conspicuous Waste," it has long since given way to education in the sciences — those base, utilitarian pursuits which were once regarded as but little better than actual labor! Leisure class faith in itself has been sapped by these successive defeats. It is no wonder that leisure class slumbers are haunted by the face of Demos, half mocking, half menacing.

The situation was beginning to be clear so long ago as 1910 when Thomas S. Eliot was a student at Harvard. Revolt against traditionalism had reached even to Boston. Traitors were appearing in the aristocratic and academic ranks themselves: Miss Amy Lowell was smoking cigars and Theodore Roosevelt and Woodrow Wilson were offering pipes and cubebs to the multitude. Poets were about to spring up like dandelions on every hillside. Denunciations of the older aesthetics and morality were soon to din the air. And beneath the rising noise was a real determination to accept modern life realistically and make the best of it by a creation of new values.

Was the youthful T. S. Eliot in sympathy with this progressive movement? It has often been supposed so on the strength of some of his early poems. He could then, at any rate, laugh in pungent verse at the devotees of the Boston *Evening Transcript,* could paraphrase Gautier with gusto in "The Hippopotamus," that quite definitive satire of the Church with its

> At mating time the hippo's voice
> Betrays inflexions hoarse and odd,
> But every week we hear rejoice
> The Church, at being one with God

and could feel a certain admiration for his "Miss Nancy Ellicott" who

> Strode across the hills and broke them,
> Rode across the hills and broke them —
> The barren New England hills.

Are not these "barren New England hills," the source of the "mountains of rock without water" in "The Waste Land"? It would indeed be pleasant to be able to claim so excellent a poet as a former ally on the basis of these early poems, but the evidence is insufficient. Mr. Eliot hesitated, life beckoned, but in the end even then he turned back to

> Matthew and Waldo, guardians of the faith,
> The army of unalterable law.

His most important poem of the period, 'The Love Song of J. Alfred Prufrock," certainly one of the most remarkable works ever produced by a poet in his early twenties in its successful simulation of the disillusionment of middle age, was a minor classic of frustration written ten years before the mood became popular in America. But if "Prufrock" introduced a style and manner which were new in American literature, it none the less belonged to traditional poetry. Its cultured hero, on the fringe of fashion, who has slain his power of action through rationalizing his fear of life in the perpetual question, "Would it have been worth while?" had behind him a long literary ancestry in other countries. J. Alfred was a late descendant of the world-weary Childe Harold, Rolla, and Oblomov: the romantic ideal now stripped of the last traces of the heroic; the final degradation of a once powerful aristocracy into an impotent leisure class of scholar gentlemen whose pride had degenerated into the pleasure of cleverly analyzing their own impotence in the most telling language. The modernization of the type had already been achieved by the French Symbolists who were the first to recognize the unhappy plight of the purely literary man in our society; the languorous measure of "Prufrock" belonged to Mallarmé, the conversational-ironic style to Laforgue, the general spirit to the whole French group.

The fiction of advanced age maintained in so many of Mr. Eliot's poems is an obviously apt symbolism for one speaking as the representative of a class and culture that have grown old and sterile. (One recalls the splendor of sterility in Mallarmé's "Herodias"). Thus Mr. Eliot's "Gerontion" commences, "Here I am, an old man in a dry month"; in "The Waste Land" the author appears as "I, Tiresias, old man with wrinkled dugs"; in "The Song of Simeon" he assumed the rôle of one who has "eighty years and no tomorrow"; in "Ash Wednesday" he asks himself, "Why should the agèd eagle stretch its wings?" In similar vein is the idealization of the past at the expense of the present, Mr. Eliot's sharp juxtapositions of the two being with him a constant method which in less skillful hands would have degenerated into a mere mannerism but through which in reality he achieves many of his most telling effects. Equally poignant and in keeping with this poetry of decadence is the recognition of inner aridity and the recurrent cry for water, water in Mr. Eliot's poetry having a double symbolism, sometimes representing a longed-for Nirvana sea of forgetfulness and peace capable of probably correct explanation in Freudian terms as a yearning for the lost peace of the womb.

Consonant with both Freudian and Marxian explanations is Mr. Eliot's pervasive dread of sex. Neglecting the Freudian approach, which is likely to seem a little impertinent with living writers, it is sufficient here to point out the other interpretation, which applies, of course, not only to Mr. Eliot but to the whole New England tradition of hostility to sex. Women, however good custodians of property they may be when left to themselves, as a lure to men are the only successful rivals of wealth. Sex is a rebellious force which refuses to recognize social stratifications. A sufficiently powerful and self-confident aristocracy may tolerate it, but either a rising bourgeoisie or an uncertain leisure class will recognize it as the great enemy that removes the landmarks.

Sex attraction is summarized by Mr. Eliot in Grishkin's "subtle effluence of cat" unequalled even by the "sleek Brazilian jaguar" which does not "distill so rank a feline smell." This effective reduction of the naughty Grishkin to the animal level would have been approved of by Charles Eliot Norton, although he would doubtless have been a little shocked by the boldness of the language. "Subtle" and "rank" are, however, contradictory, an instance of intuitive confusion extremely rare in Mr. Eliot's poetry and so all the more significant of emotional disturbance. Sex may be regarded as physically disgusting (the attitude of the American school-boy of whatever age) but it nevertheless possesses an undoubted potency which is resented by Mr. Eliot. It is a part of that vulgar actuality of life the impact of which on a sensitive personality supplies the starting point for so much of his poetry.

Vulgarity is for Mr. Eliot as it was for Henry James the one unforgivable sin. Whereas a true humanist like Mr. Santayana can relish vulgarity in its place, witness his essay on Dickens, the more feminine apostles of culture in America have small stomach for it. Mr. Eliot, however, is a far more virile writer than Henry James, and he does not turn his eyes away from the large portion of the world which he dislikes. In unforgettably incisive verse he has depicted, or suggested, the sordid, shabby aspects of the contemporary city, its noisome smells, its dirt, its squalor. These qualities have, for him, even infected the countryside, where he continues to brood upon them without relief. But never by any chance does he show the slightest suspicion that these unpleasant factors of modern life have any removable social causes. Rather, they seem to be the malign creations of an incorrigibly perverse human nature, and he certainly so regards them. He is not a New Englander for nothing. In his eulogistic essay on Machiavelli, he defends the Italian author from the charge of cynicism; Machiavelli's indictment of human nature, he avers, is not a matter of distortion nor is it merely a partial truth; it is the whole truth in regard to human beings in so far as they are unillumined by divine grace. So the hideousness of modern civilization is for Mr. Eliot not a product of machinery or industrialism; it is a product of man's evil will.

It will now, perhaps, be sufficiently evident why Mr. Eliot did not choose, and could not choose, to devote to the service of American letters a poetic talent greater than that of any other American of his generation, including a versatile command of rhythm and diction, a striking imagination, and a brilliant wit, Gallic rather than Anglo-

Saxon. Some congenital defect of generous human sympathy blinded him to the emergent values in our raw and struggling life; he could perceive merit only where it had always been perceived. During the decade from 1910 to 1920 American writers remade American literature, but T. S. Eliot was not one of them. Like Henry James before him, clinging to the old New England of the leisure class which was passing away, he sought and found that old New England in old England. Despite his limitations of outlook, the loss to American letters was very great; possibly, the loss was also, in part, Mr. Eliot's.

Identifying himself as closely as possible with his adopted country — where the word "we" appears in his essays it means always "we English," and "our tendencies," "our appreciations," mean British tendencies and appreciations — he attempted to supply the loss of living values by a knowledge of dead ones. Gallantly he sailed into that wide sea of erudition where Ezra Pound's ill-ballasted bark was just then foundering, and he returned with numerous treasures reclaimed from the deep, but with the essential man within unchanged. The evil sense of futility that had entered into this latest representative of the leisure class was not to be assuaged by mere learning, however great.

So came *The Waste Land,* generally interpreted as an expression of "post-war disillusionment" — what would the critics have done during the last decade without that convenient phrase? Actually, the poem was concerned with the same theme as Mr. Eliot's others, the breakdown of society and the impotence of those who once were rulers but are rulers no more. Both the manner and the matter were familiar in his writings — the swift transitions, the invidious idealizations of the past, the mingled rejection and pricking of sex, the oft-repeated cries for water, the vivid pictures of vulgarity (Madame Sosostris, the snuffling fortune-teller; Mr. Eugenides; the slangy friend of Lil; the modern analogue of Dante's Pia, born at Siena-Highbury, undone at Maremma-Richmond). All these factors functioned, however, on a new and larger scale; the broken, fragmentary form corresponded more fully with the vision of chaos come again; and the blatant rhythm of modern life, HURRY UP PLEASE ITS TIME, was rendered with more exacerbating insistence. But while in these ways the attack on modernism took on a broader meaning, the leisure-class element of Conspicuous Waste was also emphasized in the foreign tags and recondite allusions which might have been aesthetically justified on several grounds had not the explanatory notes which were never meant to explain made so arrogantly clear an underlying purpose to astound the public by all this display of jewelled erudition.

Then followed "The Hollow Men" (1925), a further celebration of futility. "We are the hollow men," sang Mr. Eliot, "we are the stuffed men." And he sang so movingly that many a young poet in England and America began to make it a point of honor to become hollow and stuffed even if he had not been so before. If, however, once freed from the verbal magic, one asks prosaically just who "we" are, the answer, "everybody today," will not quite do. No one, whatever the opprobrious epithets he may be in the habit of applying to the creators of the new Russia, the Lenins, Trotskys, Gorkys, and Stalins, would ever think of calling them hollow or stuffed. Nor do the terms seem at all applicable to the workers in modern science, the Einsteins, Plancks, Hunt Morgans, and hundreds of others engaged in reshaping physics, biology, and the social sciences. Mr. Eliot's hollow man is obviously the homeless "humanist" vainly seeking in the waste land of modernity the comfortable leisure class hospices of old. This hollow man is indeed lost, as every individual in any age is lost who cannot find living values beyond his own personality. Meanwhile, however, the social-revolutionary and the social-scientific movements, working on parallel lines, both contain quite evidently just such living values. But since both movements are destructive of the old leisure class tradition, Mr. Eliot will have no traffic with them. He would rather die of thirst than drink of any cup but his own.

That cup, is, of course, the cup of literature. It really contains, Mr. Eliot believes, or at least it should contain, all values. In a rather naive passage in *The Sacred Wood* he quotes, "Some one said: 'The dead writers are remote from us because we *know* so much more than they did.' " "Precisely," Mr. Eliot adds, "and they are that which we know." His quick retort has a characteristic verbal brilliance but entirely misses the point. To Mr. Eliot "knowledge" means, as he says, knowledge of dead writers; to "Some One" it presumably meant, as to most people, primarily scientific knowledge of the world about us and of ourselves. In so far as it is true, Mr. Eliot elsewhere in the passage asserts, that we know dead writers better than they knew themselves, it is because modern anthropology and psychology have given us new insights into human motivations and relationships, not because we are acquainted with the dead writers more intimately than they themselves were, which we most certainly are not.

But even with his cup filled with dead writers in "The Waste Land" and "The Hollow Men," Mr. Eliot declared the brew unfit to drink. He peevishly poured the stuff all over the lot and then declared that his cup, and every other cup, was empty. It was a broad confession of bankruptcy made in the name of the whole human race. And although the whole human race had not commissioned Mr. Eliot to make any such confession, the gesture, considered simply as a gesture, did not lack magnificence.

Confessions of bankruptcy are usually, however, made with secret reservations. There are certain fragments stored against the ruins. One washes his hands of liabilities, and then, presto, the bankrupt is back at the old stand again, as prosperous as ever. It is a sleight of hand performance that has been particularly perfected in America, and is the envy and despair of Europeans. Mr. Eliot is American in this, at least, that he has been able to perform the trick with the necessary solemnity of countenance and with every appearance of believing in the righteousness of the enterprise. Unfortunately, it is only too certain that he does believe in it. There is no corruption of the heart involved, Mr. Eliot's personal integrity is stainless, but there is an unconscious corruption of the intellect which is fully as melancholy.

The method of the literary escape from insolvency, which Mr. Eliot is not the first to use, is really simplicity itself. It consists in the transference of the threatened assets to certain long established corporate interests — in Mr. Eliot's case, "classicism in literature, royalism in politics, and anglo-catholicism in religion." He has recently stated, in an interview with Mr. Karl Schriftgiesser of the Boston *Evening Transcript,* that his royalism is not designed "to overthrow the Constitution of the United States" — a comforting assurance that ought to keep him out of the clutches of Mrs. Frothingham — and that what he has said about the Church is "only directly applicable to England," and that, in short, his essays "require a good deal of interpretation for American readers." Apparently they require reinterpretation for some English readers, also, judging from Miss Rebecca West's characterization of most of them as a "flustered search for coherence disingenuously disguised by a style that suggests he has found it."

Mr. Eliot seems, superficially at least, to have been guided in his transfer of stocks by personal predilections instead of asking first whether the corporations were themselves really solvent, just as an otherwise shrewd business man will sometimes entrust his holdings to the hands of his friends without perceiving that these friends are quite unfit for the trust. So Mr. Eliot seems to have taken the vestigial remnant of royalty in England with more seriousness than any Englishman would do. So though he sees that London Bridge is falling down he will not admit that St. Paul's is crumbling. So he can delude himself into fancying that his literary masters, the French Symbolists and late Elizabethans, are in some way connected with classicism, instead of their being, as they clearly are, along with Mr. Eliot himself, the supreme instances of decadent romanticism. So, at least, on the surface. Underneath, as we shall see later, the earthly insolvency of his chosen institutions constitutes a heavenly merit.

The well justified recognition of Mr. Eliot's ability as a traditional poet and as a purely technical critic of literature has been carried over by his injudicious followers, and even by some who are not followers, into an entirely unjustified acclamation of him as a thinker. In reality, like many a greater poet than himself, so soon as Mr. Eliot forsakes direct intuition for generalization or logical coherence he trips and stumbles in amazing fashion. The distintegrating effect of his example upon the intelligence of those who admire him not wisely but too well is clearly illustrated in an article by Edmund Wilson in *The New Republic* on "T. S. Eliot and the Church of England" which is particularly significant because Mr. Wilson is normally so excellent a writer. In this truly remarkable article Mr. Wilson characterizes Mr. Eliot as "perhaps the most important literary critic in the English speaking world," a "subtle and original" thinker, whose faith in the supernatural is something that can no longer be shared by any "first class mind" and is "sadly symptomatic of the feeble condition" of contemporary thought. Mr. Eliot is in a feeble condition and hasn't a first class mind but he is, nevertheless, "perhaps the most important literary critic in the English speaking world." Such confusion of thought is so unusual with Mr. Wilson that it can only be attributed to the hypnotic influence upon him of Mr. Eliot's own habitual confusion.

Three quite typical instances of this confusion will suffice, I hope, as I have no wish to urge to the point of churlishness the intellectual limitations of a writer who in all matters purely aesthetic is so highly gifted.

On page 140 of "The Sacred Wood" we read, concerning Blake:

> It is important that the artist should be highly educated in his own art; but his education is one that is hindered rather than helped by the ordinary processes of society which constitute education for the ordinary man. For these processes consist largely in the acquisition of impersonal ideas which obscure what we really are and feel. ... Blake ... knew what interested him, and he therefore presents only the essential ... And because he was not distracted, or frightened, or occupied in anything but exact statement, he understood.

Three pages farther on, we find:
> Blake was endowed with a capacity for considerable understand-

ing of human nature, with a remarkable and original sense of language and the music of language, and a gift of hallucinated vision. Had these been controlled by a respect for impersonal reason, for common sense, for the objectivity of science, it would have been better for him. What his genius required, and what is sadly lacked, was a framework of accepted and traditional ideas. . . .

Each passage, it will be observed, makes sense, if taken by itself, but when juxtaposed they cancel. Blake's genius was assisted by his unfamiliarity with impersonal ideas, but what it needed and sadly lacked was a familiarity with impersonal ideas. It is an impasse. One can only stop reading and rub his eyes.

But Mr. Eliot is also able to refute himself in a single sentence. In the essay on "Imperfect Critics" he writes:

> And whatever our opinion of Swinburne's verse, the notes upon poets by a poet of Swinburne's dimensions must be read with attention and respect.

If the vague word "dimensions" refers to bulk, the sentence means that however little we may esteem Swinburne's verse we must give heed to his opinions because he wrote so much verse — in which case even Eddie Guest would qualify as a literary critic. On the other hand, if "dimensions" refers to quality the sentence becomes even worse, meaning that however little we may esteem Swinburne's poetry we must give heed to his opinions because of the excellence of his poetry. One is tempted to quote Mr. Eliot's own words regarding a sentence of Professor Whitehead: "I believe that the passage . . . is nonsense."

Whenever the issue regards ideas in which Mr. Eliot has a vested interest he drops all pretense of logic and even forgets his learning. Thus, concerning Shelley in the article on "Poetry and Propaganda" in *The Bookman,* he writes:

> Shelley must have had an aesthetic intuition that there is no God and that the Christian religion is an odious lie; for he could hardly have reached such passionate conviction on the subject from mere reasoning. (Of course, it is possible that he read Rousseau and Voltaire, or even Godwin).

Here the confusion seems deliberate: obviously, one may reach convictions concerning the reality of God and the truth of Christianity through reasoning (the added word "mere" merely expresses Mr. Eliot's underlying contempt for reasoning); and by simply turning to the Necessity of Atheism note in *Queen Mab* Mr. Eliot may learn exactly how Shelley's reasoning led to his conclusions. Equally obviously, the degree of passion added to intellectual conviction will be derived from other elements of experience, in the instance cited, from moral, not aesthetic considerations, as Mr. Eliot may also learn by turning to *Queen Mab*. Mr. Eliot has indulged his desire to sneer at Shelley's "atheism" by coining a question-begging phrase. To add, in the face of Shelley's constant references to them, that "it is possible that he read Rousseau and Voltaire, or even Godwin" is like saying that it is possible that Mr. Eliot has read Donne and Dante, or even Shakespeare. But just how Shelley — even with this dark possibility of his reading what all his generation read fully admitted — managed to extract atheism from the deistic Rousseau and Voltaire, this, Mr. Eliot does not explain.

In fact, where ideas, as contrasted with images or intuitions, are concerned, Mr. Eliot never explains. Of the three articles of his credo, classicism, royalism, and anglo-catholicism, he says:

"I am quite aware that the first term is completely vague" [to which the rational answer is, why then use it?];

"I am aware that the second term is at present without definition" [thus suggesting all sorts of portentous meanings hidden in the simple word "royalism"but wisely leaving them undeveloped];

"The third term does not rest with me to define" [Anglo-Catholicism too holy to be defined by anyone but a bishop! Will someone kindly page the Hippopotamus? Hip! Hip! Hip! The Hippopotamus! HURRY UP PLEASE ITS TIME for Mr. Eliot has lost his sense of humor].

The explanation of all this avoidance of definition is not difficult. Mr. Eliot has evidently not reached *his* passionate convictions through reasoning, mere or otherwise. The terms in his credo do not stand for definite ideas. They are what Professor Dewey would call "honorific words" given a Platonic status by an ardent devotee of words. The King, Church, and Classicism of which Mr. Eliot speaks are not factors in this mundane world; as such, they would be subject to defeat and have in fact already been defeated. It is the very completeness of this defeat, their very irrelevance to the actual world, that renders them so satisfying to Mr. Eliot's subconscious yearning for Nirvana. They are thus preserved inviolate forever from any taint of that vulgarity which infects all living things. Mr. Eliot has ended by rationalizing his leisure class clean off the face of the earth into the Platonic heaven.

Whether this result will be permanently gratifying to the more prosaic of Mr. Eliot's followers may be doubted, but there is no question that it is gratifying to Mr. Eliot himself. He has reached his destined goal. The cry for water — for security — for peace — which has echoed through his poetry from the beginning has been answered. That the answer has been accompanied by an evident decline in the quality of his poetry, a decline noted by even his friendliest critics and strikingly apparent in the trite rhythms and imagery of *Ash Wednesday* as compared with the originality of *The Waste Land* — this was the necessary price to pay. Poetry is born of the earth and senses; it is no creature of the stratosphere. Poets cannot surrender, on pain of ceasing to be poets. Mr. Eliot has indeed found the longed-for supernal water. But the last word remains with the fortune-teller, Madame Sosostris:

Fear death by water.

I'LL TAKE MY STAND

I'll Take My Stand, issued by a group of self-styled southern agrarians in 1930, boasted a remarkable set of contributors. These included the novelist and critic Stark Young, the poet and prize-winning novelist Robert Penn Warren, influential poets and critics John Crowe Ransom and Allen Tate, the historian Frank L. Owsley, the story-teller Andrew Lytle, among others. They defied the North, the radicals, and existing conditions at home and abroad to develop their theme in excellent if somewhat parochial prose. Though apparently Quixotic in their effort, as in the following tenets of their creed, they won impressive victories, capturing outposts in the North which no northerner could possibly have hoped to gain in the South without surrendering his point of view, his information, and his accent. Ransom became a professor at Kenyon College, in Ohio, and editor of the Kenyon Review, *influential in literature departments; Allen Tate served as a distinguished professor in various universities of the North, as did Warren; Stark Young was not only drama critic of the* New Republic, *but author of the best-selling* So Red the Rose *(1934), which, in no Platonic sense, sold the southern attitude to northern fiction readers. And so others of their gallant company.*

A Statement of Principles

THE AUTHORS contributing to this book are Southerners, well acquainted with one another and of similar tastes, though not necessarily living in the same physical community, and perhaps only at this moment aware of themselves as a single group of men. By conversation and exchange of letters over a number of years it had developed that they entertained many convictions in common, and it was decided to make a volume in which each one should furnish his views upon a chosen topic. This was the general background. But background and consultation as to the various topics were enough; there was to be no further collaboration. And so no single author is responsible for any view outside his own article. It was through the good fortune of some deeper agreement that the book was expected to achieve its unity. All the articles bear in the same sense upon the book's title-subject: all tend to support a Southern way of life against what may be called the American or prevailing way; and all as much as agree that the best terms in which to represent the distinction are contained in the phrase, Agrarian *versus* Industrial.

But after the book was under way it seemed a pity if the contributors, limited as they were within their special subjects, should stop short of showing how close their agreements really were. On the contrary, it seemed that they ought to go on and make themselves known as a group already consolidated by a set of principles which could be stated with a good deal of particularity. This might prove useful for the sake of future reference, if they should undertake any further joint publication. It was then decided to prepare a general introduction for the book which would state briefly the common convictions of the group. This is the statement. To it every one of the contributors in this book has subscribed.

Nobody now proposes for the South, or for any other community in this country, an independent political destiny. That idea is thought to have been finished in 1865. But how far shall the South surrender its moral, social, and economic autonomy to the victorious principle of Union? That question remains open. The South is a minority section that has hitherto been jealous of its minority right to live its own kind of life. The South scarcely hopes to determine the other sections, but it does propose to determine itself, within the utmost limits of legal action. Of late, however, there is the melancholy fact that the South itself has wavered a little and shown signs of wanting to join up behind the common or American industrial ideal. It is against that tendency that this book is written. The younger Southerners, who are being converted frequently to the industrial gospel, must come back to the support of the Southern tradition. They must be persuaded to look very critically at the advantages of becoming a "new South" which will be only an undistinguished replica of the usual industrial community.

But there are many other minority communities opposed to industrialism, and wanting a much simpler economy to live by. The communities and private persons sharing the agrarian tastes are to be found widely within the Union. Proper living is a matter of the intelligence and the will, does not depend on the local climate or geography, and is capable of a definition which is general and not Southern at all. Southerners have a filial duty to discharge to their own section. But their cause is precarious and they must seek alliances with sympathetic communities everywhere. The members of the present group would be happy to be counted as members of a national agrarian movement.

Industrialism is the economic organization of the collective American society. It means the decision of society to invest its economic resources in the applied sciences. But the word science has acquired a certain sanctitude. It is out of order to quarrel with science in the abstract, or even with the applied sciences when their applications are made subject to criticism and intelligence. The capitalization of the applied sciences has now become extravagant and uncritical; it has enslaved our human energies to a degree now clearly felt to be burdensome. The apologists of industrialism do not like to meet this charge directly; so they often take refuge in saying that they are devoted simply to science! They are really devoted to the applied sciences and to practical production. Therefore it is necessary to employ a certain skepticism even at the expense of the Cult of Science, and to say, It is an Americanism, which looks innocent and disinterested, but really is not either.

The contribution that science can make to a labor is to render it easier by the help of a tool or a process, and to assure the laborer of his perfect economic security while he is engaged upon it. Then it can be performed with leisure and enjoyment. But the modern laborer has not exactly received this benefit under the industrial regime. His labor is hard, its tempo is fierce, and his employment is insecure.

The first principle is that it must be enjoyed. Labor is one of the largest items in the human career; it is a modest demand to ask that it may partake of happiness.

The regular act of applied science is to introduce into labor a labor-saving device or a machine. Whether this is a benefit depends on how far it is advisable to save the labor. The philosophy of applied science is generally quite sure that the saving of labor is a pure gain, and that the more of it the better. This is to assume that labor is an evil, that only the end of labor or the material product is good. On this assumption labor becomes mercenary and servile, and it is no wonder if many forms of modern labor are accepted without resentment though they are evidently brutalizing. The act of labor as one of the happy functions of human life has been in effect abandoned, and is practiced solely for its rewards.

Even the apologists of industrialism have been obliged to admit that some economic evils follow in the wake of the machines. These are such as overproduction, unemployment, and a growing inequality in the distribution of wealth. But the remedies proposed by the apologists are always homeopathic. They expect the evils to disappear when we have bigger and better machines, and more of them. Their remedial programs, therefore, look forward to more industrialism. Sometimes they see the system righting itself spontaneously and without direction: they are Optimists. Sometimes they rely on the benevolence of capital, or the militancy of labor, to bring about a fairer division of the spoils: they are Coöperationists or Socialists. And sometimes they expect to find super-engineers, in the shape of Boards of Control, who will adapt production to consumption and regulate prices and guarantee business against fluctuations: they are Sovietists. With respect to these last it must be insisted that the true Sovietists or Communists — if the term may be used here in the European sense — are the Industrialists themselves. They would have the government set up an economic super-organization, which in turn would become the government. We therefore look upon the Communist menace as a menace indeed, but not as a Red one; because it is simply according to the blind drift of our industrial development to expect in America at last much the same economic system as they imposed by violence upon Russia in 1917.

Turning to consumption, as the grand end which justifies the evil of modern labor, we find that we have been deceived. We have more time in which to consume, and many more products to be consumed. But the tempo of our labors communicates itself to our satisfactions, and these also become brutal and hurried. The consitution of the natural man probably does not permit him to shorten his labor-time and enlarge his consuming-time indefinitely. He has to pay the penalty in satiety and aimlessness. The modern man has lost his sense of vocation.

Religion can hardly expect to flourish in an industrial society. Religion is our submission to the general intention of a nature that is fairly inscrutable; it is the sense of our role as creatures within it. But nature industrialized, transformed into cities and artificial habitations, manufactured into commodities, is no longer nature but a highly simplified picture of nature. We receive the illusion of having power over nature, and lose the sense of nature as something mysterious and contingent. The God of nature under these conditions is merely an amiable expression, a superfluity, and the philosophical understanding ordinarily carried in the religious experience is not there for us to have.

Nor do the arts have a proper life under industrialism, with the general decay of sensibility which attends it. Art depends, in general, like religion, on a right attitude to nature; and in particular on a free and disinterested observation of nature that occurs only in leisure. Neither the creation nor the understanding of works of art is possible in an industrial age except by some local and unlikely suspension of the industrial drive.

The amenities of life also suffer under the curse of a strictly-business or industrial civilization. They consist in such practices as manners, conversation, hospitality, sympathy, family life, romantic love — in the social exchanges which reveal and develop sensibility in human affairs. If religion and the arts are founded on right relations of man-to-nature, these are founded on right relations of man-to-man.

Apologists of industrialism are even inclined to admit that its actual processes may have upon its victims the spiritual effects just described. But they think that all can be made right by extraordinary educational efforts, by all sorts of cultural institutions and endowments. They would cure the poverty of the contemporary spirit by hiring experts to instruct it in spite of itself in the historic culture. But salvation is hardly to be encountered on that road. The trouble with the life-pattern is to be located at its economic base, and we cannot rebuild it by pouring in soft materials from the top. The young men and women in colleges, for example, if they are already placed in a false way of life, cannot make more than an inconsequential acquaintance with the arts and humanities transmitted to them. Or else the understanding of these arts and humanities will but make them the more wretched in their own destitution.

The "Humanists" are too abstract. Humanism, properly speaking, is not an abstract system, but a culture, the whole way in which we live, act, think, and feel. It is a kind of imaginatively balanced life lived out in a definite social tradition. And, in the concrete, we believe that this, the genuine humanism, was rooted in the agrarian life of the older South and of other parts of the country that shared in such a tradition. It was not an abstract moral "check" derived from the classics — it was not soft material poured in from the top. It was deeply founded in the way of life itself — in its tables, chairs, portraits, festivals, laws, marriage customs. We cannot recover our native humanism by adopting some standard of taste that is critical enough to question the contemporary arts but not critical enough to question the social and economic life which is their ground.

The tempo of the industrial life is fast, but that is not the worst of it; it is accelerating. The ideal is not merely some set form of industrialism, with so many stable industries, but industrial progress, or an incessant extension of industrialization. It never proposes a specific goal; it initiates the infinite series. We have not merely capitalized certain industries; we have capitalized the laboratories and inventors, and undertaken to employ all the labor-saving devices that come out of them. But a fresh labor-saving device introduced into an industry does not emancipate the laborers in that industry so much as it evicts them. Applied at the expense of agriculture, for example, the new processes have reduced the part of the population supporting itself upon the soil to a smaller and smaller fraction. Of course no single labor-saving process is fatal; it brings on a period of unemployed labor and unemployed capital, but soon a new industry is devised which will put them both to work again, and a new commodity is thrown upon the market. The laborers were sufficiently embarrassed in the meantime, but, according to the theory, they will eventually be taken care of. It is now the public which is embarrassed; it feels obligated to purchase a commodity for which it had expressed no desire, but it is invited to make its budget equal to the strain. All might yet be well, and stability and comfort might again obtain, but for this: partly because of industrial ambitions and partly because the repressed creative impulse must break out somewhere, there will be a stream of further labor-saving devices in all industries, and the cycle will have to be repeated over and over. The result is an increasing disadjustment and instability.

It is an inevitable consequence of industrial progress that production greatly outruns the rate of natural consumption. To overcome the disparity, the producers, disguised as the pure idealists of progress, must coerce and wheedle the public into being loyal and steady consumers, in order to keep the machines running. So the rise of modern advertising — along with its twin, personal salesmanship — is the most significant development of our industrialism. Advertising means to persuade the consumers to want exactly what the applied sciences are able to furnish them. It consults the happiness of the consumer no more than it consulted the happiness of the laborer. It is the great effort of a false economy of life to approve itself. But its task grows more difficult every day.

It is strange, of course, that a majority of men anywhere could ever as with one mind become enamored of industrialism: a system that has so little regard for individual wants. There is evidently a kind of thinking that rejoices in setting up a social objective which has no relation to the individual. Men are prepared to sacrifice their private dignity and happiness to an abstract social ideal, and without asking whether the social ideal produces the welfare of any individual man whatsoever. But this is absurd. The responsibility of men is for their own welfare and that of their neighbors; not for the hypothetical welfare of some fabulous creature called society.

Opposed to the industrial society is the agrarian, which does not stand in particular need of definition. An agrarian society is hardly one that has no use at all for industries, for professional vacations, for scholars and artists, and for the life of cities. Technically, perhaps, an agrarian society is one in which agriculture is the leading vocation, whether for wealth, for pleasure, or for prestige — a form of labor that is pursued with intelligence and leisure, and that becomes the model to which the other forms approach as well as they may. But an agrarian regime will be secured readily enough where the superfluous industries are not allowed to rise against it. The theory of agrarianism is that the culture of the soil is the best and most sensitive of vocations, and that therefore it should have the economic preference and enlist the maximum number of workers.

These principles do not intend to be very specific in proposing any practical measures. How may the little agrarian community resist the Chamber of Commerce of its county seat, which is always trying to import some foreign industry that cannot be assimilated to the life-pattern of the community? Just what must the Southern leaders do to defend the traditional Southern life? How may the Southern and the Western agrarians unite for effective action? Should the agrarian forces try to capture the Democratic party, which historically is so closely affiliated with the defense of individualism, the small community, the state, the South? Or must the agrarians — even the Southern ones — abandon the Democratic party to its fate and try a new one? What legislation could most profitably be championed by the powerful agrarians in the Senate of the United States? What anti-industrial measures might promise to stop the advances of industrialism, or even undo some of them, with the least harm to those concerned? What policy should be pursued by the educators who have a tradition at heart? These and many other questions are of the greatest importance, but they cannot be answered here.

For, in conclusion, this much is clear: If a community, or a section, or a race, or an age, is groaning under industrialism, and well aware that it is an evil dispensation, it must find the way to throw it off. To think that this cannot be done is pusillanimous. And if the whole community, section, race, or age thinks it cannot be done, then it has simply lost its political genius and doomed itself to impotence.

[*Contributors*: Donald Davidson, John Gould Fletcher, Henry B. Kline, Lyle Lanier, Andrew Lytle, Clarence Nixon, Frank Lawrence Owsley, John Crowe Ransom, Allen Tate, John Donald Wade, Robert Penn Warren, and Stark Young].

THE BODY OF THE NATION

BUT THE basin of the Mississippi is the Body of The Nation. All the other parts are but members, important in themselves, yet more important in their relations to this. Exclusive of the Lake basin and of 300,000 square miles in Texas and New Mexico, which in many aspects form a part of it, this basin contains about 1,250,000 square miles. In extent it is the second great valley of the world, being exceeded only by that of the Amazon. The valley of the frozen Obi approaches it in extent; that of the La Plata comes next in space, and probably in habitable capacity, having about eight-ninths of its area; then comes that of the Yenisei, with about seven-ninths; then Lena, Amoor, Hoang-ho, Yang-tse-Kiang, and Nile, five-ninths; the Ganges, less than one-half; the Indus, less than one-third; the Euphrates, one-fifth; the Rhine, one-fifteenth. It exceeds in extent the whole of Europe, exclusive of Russia, Norway, and Sweden. It would contain Austria four times, Germany or Spain five times, France six times, the British Islands or Italy ten times. Conceptions formed from the river-basins of Western Europe are rudely shocked when we consider the extent of the valley of the Mississippi; nor are those formed from the sterile basins of the great rivers of Siberia, the lofty plateaus of Central Asia, or the mighty sweep of the swampy Amazon more adequate. Latitude, elevation, and rainfall all combine to render every part of the Mississippi Valley capable of supporting a dense population. As a dwelling-place for civilized man it is by far the first upon our globe.

Mark Twain's *Life on The Mississippi.*

Pare Lorentz

THE RIVER

PREFACE*

THE TEXT *in this book has been taken verbatim from a motion picture, "The River," which I produced for the Farm Security Administration, U.S. Department of Agriculture.*

The photographs either are from the movie itself, or, with a few exceptions, were made by government cameramen working in the same areas in which we made the picture.

The narration for the movie was not written until we had hewed 80,000 feet of film down to 2900 feet. It was intended as a functional text to accompany Mr. Virgil Thomson's score, and to fit the tempo of the sequences in the picture.

I have not changed the words for two reasons: the text now provides a permanent record of the motion picture, and, originally utilitarian writing, I think it explains the pictorial story of the Mississippi River better than it might were it elaborated into a smoother and more conventional form.

I am greatly indebted to scores of hard-working civil servants who furnished me with information during the preparatory stages of "The River"; but the three books which I found essential to any understanding of the old river were Mark Twain's "Life On the Mississippi"; still the most accurate book ever written on the subject; the Mississippi Valley Committee's Report, (1934, Department of Interior), the best-written government report I've ever read, and Lyle Saxon's "Father Mississippi."

I am also greatly indebted to Ed Locke; to Roy Stryker, of the Farm Security Administration; and to Charles Krutch, of the Tennessee Valley Authority, whose enthusiastic help in assembling the photographs made the book possible.

I list elsewhere credits for the pictures we used other than those from the motion picture.

PARE LORENTZ

*Preface and text are from the book, pub. 1938, Stackpole Sons, New York.

From as far West as Idaho,
    Down from the glacier peaks of the Rockies —
From as far East as New York,
    Down from the turkey ridges of the Alleghenies
Down from Minnesota, twenty five hundred miles,
    The Mississippi River runs to the Gulf.
Carrying every drop of water, that flows down
    two-thirds the continent,
Carrying every brook and rill, rivulet and creek,
Carrying all the rivers that run down two thirds
    the continent,
The Mississippi runs to the Gulf of Mexico.

Down the Yellowstone, the Milk, the White and
    Cheyenne;
The Cannonball, the Musselshell, the James and
    the Sioux;
Down the Judith, the Grand, the Osage, and the
    Platte,
The Skunk, the Salt, the Black, and Minnesota;
Down the Rock, the Illinois, and the Kankakee
The Allegeheny, the Monongahela, Kanawha, and
    Muskingum;
Down the Miami, the Wabash, the Licking and
    the Green
The Cumberland, the Kentucky, and the Tennessee;
Down the Ouchita. the Wichita, the Red, and
    Yazoo —

Down the Missouri three thousand miles from the
    Rockies;
Down the Ohio a thousand miles from the Alleghenies;
Down the Arkansas fifteen hundred miles from
    the Great Divide;
Down the Red, a thousand miles from Texas;
Down the great Valley, twenty-five hundred miles
    from Minnesota,
        Carrying every rivulet and brook, creek and rill,
Carrying all the rivers that run down two-thirds
    the continent —
The Mississippi runs to the Gulf.

New Orleans to Baton Rouge,
Baton Rouge to Natchez,
Natchez to Vicksburg,
Vicksburg to Memphis,
Memphis to Cairo —
We built a dyke a thousand miles long.
Men and mules, mules and mud;
Mules and mud a thousand miles up the Mississippi.
A century before we bought the great Western River, the Spanish and the French built dykes to keep the Mississippi out of New Orleans at flood stage.

In forty years we continued the levee the entire length of the great alluvial Delta,
That mud plain that extends from the Gulf of Mexico clear to the mouth of the Ohio.
The ancient valley built up for centuries by the old river spilling her floods across the bottom of the continent —
A mud delta of forty thousand square miles.
Men and mules, mules and mud —
New Orleans to Baton Rouge,
Natchez to Vicksburg,
Memphis to Cairo —
A thousand miles up the river.

And we made cotton king!

We rolled a million bales down the river for Liverpool and Leeds . . .

1860: we rolled four million bales down the river;
Rolled them off Alabama,
Rolled them off Mississippi,
Rolled them off Louisiana,
Rolled them down the river!

We fought a war.
We fought a war and kept the west bank of the river free of slavery forever.

But we left the old South impoverished
 and stricken.
Doubly stricken, because, beyond the tragedy of war, already the frenzied
 cotton cultivation of a quarter of a
 century had taken toll of the land.
We mined the soil for cotton until it would
 yield no more, and then moved west.
We fought a war, but there was a double
 tragedy — the tragedy of land twice
 impoverished.

Black spruce and Norway pine,
Douglas fir and Red cedar,
Scarlet oak and Shagbark hickory,
Hemlock and aspen —
There was lumber in the North.

The war impoverished the old South, the railroads
 killed the steamboats,
But there was lumber in the North.
Heads up!
Lumber on the upper river.

Heads up!
Lumber enough to cover all Europe.
Down from Minnesota and Wsiconsin,
Down to St. Paul;
Down to St. Louis and St. Joe —
Lumber for the new continent of the West.
Lumber for the new mills.
There was lumber in the North
 and coal in the hills.
Iron and coal down the Monon-
 gahela.
Iron and coal down the Alle-
 gheny.
Iron and coal down the Ohio.
Down to Pittsburgh,
Down to Wheeling,
Iron and coal for the steel mills,
 for the railroads driving

West and South, for the new
    cities of the Great Valley —

We built new machinery and
    cleared new land in the
    West.
Ten million bales down to the
    Gulf —
Cotton for the spools of England
    and France.
Fifteen million bales down to the
    Gulf —
Cotton for the spools of Italy and
    Germany.

We build a hundred cities and a thousand towns:
St. Paul and Minneapolis,
Davenport and Keokuk,
Moline and Quincy,
Cincinnati and St Louis,
Omaha and Kansas City . . .
Across to the Rockies and down from Minnesota,
Twenty-five hundred miles to New Orleans,
We built a new continent.

Black spruce and Norway pine,
Douglas fir and Red cedar,
Scarlet oak and Shagbark hickory.

We built a hundred cities and a thousand towns —
But at what a cost!
We cut the top off the Alleghenies and sent it
    down the river.
We cut the top off Minnesota and sent it down
    the river.
We cut the top off Wisconsin and sent it down the
    river.
We left the mountains and the hills slashed and
    burned,
And moved on.

The water comes downhill, spring and fall;

Down from the cut-over mountains,
Down from the plowed-off slopes,
Down every brook and rill, rivulet and creek,
Carrying every drop of water that flows down
    two-thirds the continent
1903 and 1907,
1913 and 1922,
1927,
1936,
1937!

Down from Pennsylvania and Ohio,
Kentucky and West Virginia,
Missouri and Illinois,
Down from North Carolina and Tennessee —
Down the Judith, the Grand, the Osage, and the
    Platte,
The Rock, the Salt, the Black and Minnesota,
Down the Monongahela, the Allegheny, Kanawha and Muskingum,
The Miami, the Wabash, the Licking and the
    Green,
Down the White, the Wolfe, and the Cache,
Down the Kaw and Kaskaskia, the Red and
    Yazoo,
Down the Cumberland, Kentucky and the Tennessee —
Down to the Mississippi.
New Orleans to Baton Rouge —
Baton Rouge to Natchez —
Natchez to Vicksburg —
Vicksburg to Memphis —
Memphis to Cairo —
A thousand miles down the levee the long vigil
    starts.
Thirty-eight feet at
    Baton Rouge
River rising.
Helena: river rising.
Memphis: river rising.
Cairo: river rising.

A thousand miles to
   go,
A thousand miles of
   levee to hold —

Coastguard patrol needed at
   Paducah!
Coastguard patrol needed at
   Paducah!

200 boats — wanted at Hickman!
200 boats wanted at Hickman!

Levee patrol: men to Blytheville!
Levee patrol: men to Blytheville!

2000 men wanted at Cairo!
2000 men wanted at Cairo!

A hundred thousand men to fight
   the old river.

We sent armies down the river to help the engi-
   neers fight a battle on a two thousand mile
   front:
The Army and the Navy,
The Coast Guard and the Marine Corps,
The CCC and the WPA,
The Red Cross and the Health Service.
They fought night and day to hold the old river
   off the valley.
Food and water needed at Louisville: 500 dead,
   5000 ill;
Food and water needed at Cincinnati;
Food and water and shelter and clothing needed
   for 750,000 flood victims;

Food and medicine needed at Lawrenceburg;
35,000 homeless in Evansville;
Food and medicine needed in Aurora;
Food and medicine and shelter and clothing for
   750,000 down in the valley.

Last time we held the levees,
But the old river claimed her valley.
She backed into Tennessee and Arkansas
And Missouri and Illinois.
She left stock drowned, houses torn loose,
Farms ruined.

1903 and 1907.
1913 and 1922.
1927.
1936.
1937!

We built a hundred cities and a thousand towns —
But at what a cost!

Spring and fall the water comes down, and for years the old river has taken a toll from the Valley more terrible than ever she does in flood times.
Year in, year out, the water comes down
From a thousand hillsides, washing the top off the Valley.
For fifty years we dug for cotton and moved West when the land gave out.
Corn and wheat; wheat and cotton — we planted and plowed with no thought for the future —
And four hundred million tons of top soil,
Four hundred million tons of our most valuable natural resource have been washed into the Gulf of Mexico every year.

And poor land makes poor people.
Poor people make poor land.
For a quarter of a century we have been forcing more and more farmers into tenancy.
Today forty percent of all the farmers in the great Valley are tenants.

Ten percent are share croppers,
Down on their knees in the valley,
A share of the crop their only security.
No home, no land of their own,
Aimless, footloose, and impoverished,
Unable to eat even from the land because their
 cash crop is their only livelihood.

Credit at the store is their only
 reserve.
And a generation growing up
 with no new land in the
 West —
No new continent to build.
A generation whose people
 knew King's Mountain, and
 Shiloh;
A generation whose people
 knew Fremont and Custer;
But a generation facing a life
 of dirt and poverty,
Disease and drudgery;
Growing up without proper
 food, medical care, or
 schooling,
 "Ill-clad, ill-housed, and ill-
 fed" —
And in the greatest river valley
 in the world.

There is no such thing as an ideal river in Nature, but the Mississippi is out of joint.
Dust blowing in the West — floods raging in the East —
We have seen these problems growing to horrible extremes.

When first we found the great valley it was forty percent forested.
Today, for every hundred acres of forests we found, we have ten left.
Today five percent of the entire valley is ruined forever for agricultural use!
Twenty-five percent of the topsoil has been shoved by the old river into the Gulf of Mexico.
Today two out of five farmers in the valley are tenant farmers — ten

percent of them share croppers, living in a state of squalor unknown to the poorest peasant in Europe
And we are forcing thirty thousand more into tenancy and cropping every year.
Flood control of the Mississippi means control in the great Delta that must carry all the water brought down from two-thirds the continent
And control of the Delta means control of the little rivers, the great arms running down from the uplands. And the old river can be controlled.
We had the power to take the valley apart — we have the power to put it together again.

In 1933 we started, down on the Tennessee River, when our Congress created the Tennessee Valley Authority, commissioned to develop navigation, flood control, agriculture, and industry in the valley: a valley that carries more rainfall than any other in the country; the valley through which the Tennessee used to roar down to Paducah in flood times with more water than any other tributary of the Ohio.

First came the dams.
Up on the Clinch, at the head of the river, we built Norris Dam, a great barrier to hold water in flood times and to release water down the river for navigation in low water season.

Next came Wheeler, first in a series of great barriers that will transform the old Tennessee into a link of fresh water pools locked and dammed, regulated and controlled, down six hundred fifty miles to Paducah.

But you cannot plan for water unless you plan for land: for the cut-over mountains — the eroded hills — the gullied fields that pour their waters unchecked down to the river.
The CCC, working with the

forest service and agricultural experts, have started to put the worn
fields and hillsides back together;
black walnut and pine for the worn
out fields, and the gullied hillsides;
black walnut and pine for new
forest preserves, roots for the cutover and burned-over hillsides;
roots to hold the water in the
ground.

    Soil conservation men have worked
our crop systems with the farmers of
the Valley — crops to conserve and enrich the topsoil.
    Today a million acres of land in the
Tennessee Valley are being tilled
scientifically.

    But you cannot plan for water and land unless
you plan for people. Down in the Valley, the
Farm Security Administration has built a model
agricultural community. Living in homes they
themselves built, paying for them on long term
rates the homesteaders will have a chance to share
in the wealth of the Valley.
    More important, the Farm Security Administration has lent thousands of dollars to farmers in
the Valley, farmers who were caught by years of
depression and in need of only a stake to be self-sufficient.

    But where there is water there is power.
    Where there's water for flood control and water
for navigation, there's water for power —

    Power for the farmers of the Valley.
    Power for the villages and cities and
factories of the Valley
      West Virginia, North

Carolina, Tennessee,
Mississippi, Georgia
and Alabama.
 Power to give a new
Tennessee Valley to a
new generation.
 Power enough to
make the river work!

EPILOGUE

We got the blacks to plant the cotton and they gouged the top off
 the valley.
We got the Swedes to cut the forests, and they sent them down the
 river.
Then we moved our saws and our plows and started all over again;
And we left a hollow-eyed generation to peck at the worn-out
 valley;
And left the Swedes to shiver in their naked North country.
1903, 1907, 1913, 1922, 1927, 1936, 1937 —
For you can't wall out and dam two-thirds the water in the country.
We built dams but the dams filled in.
We built a thousand mile dyke but it didn't hold;
So we built it higher.
We played with a continent for fifty years.

Flood control? Of the Mississippi?

Control from Denver to Helena;
From Itasca to Paducah:
From Pittsburgh to Cairo —
Control of the wheat, the corn and the cotton land;
Control enough to put back a thousand forests;
Control enough to put the river together again before it is too late
 ... before it has picked up the heart of a continent and shoved
 it into the Gulf of Mexico.

Index

Alroy, John, 172 ff.
Anderson, Sherwood, 17, 19, 32 ff.

Bates, Ernest Sutherland, 344 ff.
Bellamy, Edward, 8
Benet, Stephen Vincent, 217 ff.
Bernays, E. L. 5
blacks, 14, 24, 99, 201 ff.
Brooks, van Wyck, 6
Broun, Heywood, 21, 118 ff., 131-32, 260 ff.

Cabell, James Branch, 7-8, 18
Caldwell, Erskine, 13, 19, 100 ff.
Calverton, V. F., 310 ff.
Cantwell, Robert, 18
Carlson, John Roy, 15
Chamberlain, John, 13
Coffee-Pepper Bill, 25
communists, 1, 13-14, 15 *et seq.*, 53, 59 *et seq.*, 65 ff., 80 ff., 132 ff., 143, 177 ff., 214 ff., 268 ff., 310 ff.
Cummings, E. E., 244 ff.

Dennis, Lawrence, 15
Dahlberg, Edward, 193 ff.
Dewey, John, 80 ff. 123
Dilling, Mrs. Albert, 260 ff.
Dos Passos, John, 8-9, 13, 288 ff.
Dreiser, Theodore, 7

Engle, Paul, 5
EPIC (End Poverty in California), 7
Eliot, T. S., 344 ff.

Fadiman, Clifton, 5
Farrell, James T., 9-10
Fascism, 15, 94 ff., 106, 197-98, 310 ff.
Fearing, Kenneth, 13, 220-22
Federal Arts Projects, 3, 24, *et seq.*, 140 ff.
Flanagan, Hallie, 140 ff.
Ford (Henry, and plants), 3 *et seq.*, 12, 37
Fuchs, Daniel, 22-23, 193

George, Henry, 8, 49
Gilfillan, Lauren, 65 ff.
Gold, Mike, 7, 18

Halper, Albert, 23, 176 ff.
Hazlitt, Henry, 16
Hemingway, Ernest, 5, 7, 86 ff.
Hicks, Granville, 19, 120
Hindus, Milton, 268 ff.
Hitler, Adolf, 50 *et seq.*, 197
Hook, Sidney, 319 ff.
Hoover, Herbert, 1 *et seq.*, 59, 123, 264-66
Hopkins, Harry, 128, 141

I'll Take My Stand, 355 ff.

Jeffers, Robinson, 256-57

Kempton, Murray, 28
Kromer, Tom, 39 ff.

Landon, Alfred M., 4

[377]

Levin, Meyer, 10, 23, 185 ff.
Lewis, Sinclair, 7
Loeb, Harold, 5
Long, Huey, 15
Lorentz, Pare, 12, 364 ff.

MacLeish, Archibald, 13, 101, 224 ff.
Maltz, Albert, 23, 106 ff.
Markham, Edwin, 7
May Day, 3
McKenney, Ruth, 5
Mencken, H. L., 126 ff.
Minor, Robert, 5
Mussolini, Benito, 50

New Deal, 2 ff., 126 ff., 134 *et seq.*
New Masses, 13, 40, 133
New Yorker, 12
Nock, Albert Jay, 49 ff.
NRA (National Recovery Act), 3 *et seq.*
Nutt, Howard, 223

Odets, Cliford, 19, 162 ff., 214 ff.
Oursler, Fulton, 18

Pearson, Drew, 21
Pegler, Westbrook, 21
Perelman, S. J., 162 ff.
Phillips, William, 338 ff.
Pound, Ezra, 234 ff.

Rahv, Philip, 338
Roosevelt, Franklin D., 3 *et seq.*, 33, 49 *et seq.*
Ross, Leonard Q., 57 ff
Roth, Henry, 21-22
Rukeyser, Muriel, 231 ff
Russell, Bertrand, 81

Saroyan, William, 6, 13, 23, 86 ff.
Saturday Evening Post, 4, 23, 27
Section (7A) NRA, 3
Sinclair, Upton, 7, 131-32
Slesinger, Tess, 165 ff.
Soviet Union. See Communism
Stalin, Josef, 27
Steffens, Lincoln, 67, 123
Stein, Gertrude, 32-33
Steinbeck, John, 12, 16-17, 94 ff.

Trotsky, Leon, 80
Trumbo, Dalton, 19-20
Twenties, 25-26, 28

Union Square, 57 ff. 176 ff.
unions, 3 *et seq.*, 65 ff., 124, 186 ff.

Wallace, Henry A., 21, 128, 153-54
Warren, Robert Penn, 13
Wexley, John, 201 ff.
Wilson, Edmund, 13, 120 ff.
Wolfe, Thomas, 10-11
Wright, Richard, 19, 24